UNDUE
INFLUENCE

Undue. More than necessary; not proper; illegal.

Influence. Power exerted over others.

Undue influence. Persuasion, pressure, or influence short of actual force, but stronger than mere advice, that so overpowers the dominated party's free will or judgment that he or she cannot act intelligently and voluntarily, but acts, instead, subject to the will or purposes of the dominating party.

Misuse of position of confidence or taking advantage of a person's weakness, infirmity, or distress to change improperly that person's actions or decisions.

—Black's Law Dictionary, Sixth Edition

Other books by Ron Arnold

James Watt and the Environmentalists
Regnery Gateway

The Grand Prairie Years
Dodd Mead

Ecology Wars: Environmentalism as if People Mattered

EcoTerror: The Violent Agenda to Save Nature

With Alan Gottlieb

Trashing the Economy

Politically Correct Environment

Books Edited by Ron Arnold

Stealing the National Parks
by Don Hummel

Storm Over Rangelands
by Wayne Hage

People of the Tongass
by K. A. Soderberg and Jackie DuRette

It Takes A Hero
by William Perry Pendley

The Asbestos Racket
by Michael Bennett

Eight Steps towards Libertarianism
by Joseph S. Fulda

UNDUE INFLUENCE

WEALTHY FOUNDATIONS, GRANT-DRIVEN ENVIRONMENTAL GROUPS, AND ZEALOUS BUREAUCRATS THAT CONTROL YOUR FUTURE

Ron Arnold

The Free Enterprise Press
BELLEVUE, WASHINGTON
Distributed by Merril Press

First Edition
Published by the Free Enterprise Press

Typeset in Times New Roman by The Free Enterprise Press, a division of the
Center for the Defense of Free Enterprise, 12500 N.E. 10th Place, Bellevue,
Washington 98005. Telephone 425-455-5038. Fax 425-451-3959. E-mail address:
books@cdfe.org. Cover design by Northwoods Studio.

U N D U E   I N F L U E N C E   is distributed by Merril Press, P.O. Box
1682, Bellevue, Washington 98009. Additional copies of this book may be ordered
from Merril Press at $16.95 each. Phone 425-454-7009.

LIBRARY OF CONGRESS CATALOGING-IN-PUBLICATION DATA
Arnold, Ron
      Undue influence : wealthy foundations, grant-driven environmental
groups, and zealous bureaucrats that control your future / Ron Arnold.
— 1st ed.
          p.   cm.
      Includes bibliographical references and index.
      ISBN 0-939571-20-X (pbk.)
      1. Environmental policy —Corrupt practices—United States.
2. Environmental protection—Economic aspects—United States.
I. Title.
GE180.A76 1999
363.7'00973—dc21   99-43093
                                                                  CIP

PRINTED IN THE UNITED STATES OF AMERICA

CONTENTS

To Janet Arnold
non plus ultra

AUTHOR'S PREFACE

This book grew out of a report to Congress. The report was titled "Battered Communities," and was the lead testimony presented at a June 9, 1998 hearing of the House Committee on Resources. As executive vice-president of the Center for the Defense of Free Enterprise, I presented the testimony as part of the Center's program to preserve the resource communities of America.

Battered Communities made the case that supposedly charitable environmental organizations with tax subsidies were exercizing undue influence over the lives of rural Americans with public policy measures which cut off access to vital natural resources that give all of us food, clothing, and shelter.

The report exposed hidden linkages between popular environmental groups and wealthy elites in the foundation community, revealing the astonishing fact that many foundations create public policy programs themselves and then invite specific green groups to take their money and do their bidding with it.

More shocking was the discovery of complicity between the foundation / green group alliance and government employees to enforce their policy preferences. The government influence sources ranged from the highest to lowest ranks, from the White House to the outhouse in a remote national forest, all overseen by zealous bureaucrats intent on shutting out natural resource producers in the name of saving nature.

After the release of *Battered Communities*, the Center was deluged with requests not only for copies of the report, but also for more in-depth information on the true scope of the problem. It became clear that a book-length treatment was essential.

Undue Influence was the result. It took more than a year of research to uncover all the personal linkages between wealthy foundation elites, green groups and the bureaucracy. Many key foundation and green group leaders refused to be interviewed or never returned calls and emails. Government officials stonewalled my requests, with the exception of a few Freedom of Information Act requests that actually got answered in a timely manner.

My research was based on public records to the extent possible. The Foundation Center's grant records and green group Form 990 IRS reports were essential starting points. The staggering amount of information on the World Wide Web yielded a number of postings obviously not meant for public consumption. Disgruntled environmentalists provided internal documents from the Nature Conservancy and the National Audubon Society.

I am indebted to many who helped in assembling the information for this book. Dr. Bonner Cohen gave generously of his time and knowledge of the Environmental Protection Agency and gave permission to quote extensively from his published works. Paul Ehinger of Paul F. Ehinger & Associates provided employment data for timber jobs lost to the spotted owl campaign. Tom McDonnell of American Sheep Industry Association offered valuable insights on agricultural issues. Caren Cowan of New Mexico Cattle Growers Association helped track down data on grazing issues.

Rob Gordon and Jim Streeter of National Wilderness Institute pointed me to information on the U.S. Fish & Wildlife Service and gave permission to quote from their work on Carol Browner and the E.P.A. Eric Williams of Environomics was instrumental in digging out the story of foundation funding relating to ballot issues in Montana. David Ridenour of the National Center for Public Policy Research gave permission to quote from his organization's many reports on a spectrum of issues. R.J. Smith of Competitive Enterprise Institute explained private conservation initiatives.

Prof. Bob Lee of the University of Washington described his experience with the FEMAT team and the Clinton forest plan. Prof. Charles McKetta of the University of Idaho provided economic studies and explanations of his work on the job loss impact of federal actions. Prof. Matt Carroll of the University of Idaho provided materials on the moral exclusion of loggers and miners. Dave Hessel, retired timber manager of the U.S. Forest Service, described the weekly meetings held in 1995-96 by Katie McGinty. David Ford of the Certified Forest Products Council graciously explained the foundation origins of his organization. Frank Gladics of the Independent Forest Products Association provided insight into industry views on forest certification.

Teresa Platt of the American Fur Commission proofed the manuscript and offered helpful suggestions. Numerous sources in government provided information on condition of anonymity. I thank you, and deplore the circumstances that required your anonymity. Many more helped than I can mention. You know who you are, and you have my gratitude.

Any merit this book may have belongs to these fine people. Any errors of fact or judgment are mine alone.

Undue Influence is the third book in the *Environmentalism Exposed* trilogy. You may wish to read *Trashing the Economy* and *EcoTerror,* which set the stage for the events in this final volume.

Ron Arnold
Bellevue, Washington

INTRODUCTION
BY CONGRESSMAN RICHARD POMBO

During the last fifteen years there has been a proliferation of well-funded organizations whose stated goal is to protect the environment. Many of these groups have become increasingly involved in lobbying Congress and taking local, state and Federal agencies to court. Activist environmental groups are part of the Washington, D.C. establishment, now having 3,400 full time employees, including leaders who often make $150,000 or more, as well as a small army of outside contractors such as scientists, lobbyists, lawyers, and public affairs specialists.

To pay for these costly operations, environmental groups are relying more and more on wealthy non-profit foundations to fund their operations. Membership dues and the members themselves play a declining role. According to a recent article in the *Boston Globe,* foundations invest at least $400 million a year in environmental advocacy and research. The largest environmental grant-maker, Pew Charitable Trusts, gives more than $35 million annually to environmental groups.

Advocacy for environmental policy initiatives pertaining to western forests, mining and development of domestic energy resources is largely financed by foundations. Some foundation grants are spent spying on the perceived opponents of environmental groups and on efforts to discredit or smear these opponents. A common target of these efforts are property rights and resource provider groups associated with the Wise Use movement. How can spending tax-exempt funds on this type of activity be defended?

Federal polices implemented as a result of environmental advocacy financed by private foundations are trampling on property rights. They are shutting down the timber industry, the mining industry and the oil and gas industry. These policies are creating misery in rural areas dependent on resource production. Small communities and families in rural areas are reeling, while environmental groups are collecting rewards of six figure grants from rich, private foundations. Why is this sort of activity subsidized by the taxpayer?

Foundations and "public interest" non-profits are a big, influential and expanding industry. During the last 15 years, the number of foundations has nearly doubled from 22,000 to 39,000, while foundation assets now exceed $200 billion. Half of these assets are controlled by fewer than 200 foundations.

Big foundations, which have a distinctly liberal cast, use their tax-exempt dollars to fund everything from the environmental movement to studies supporting the welfare state to population control. When used to finance "public interest" group advocacy, foundation wealth has an enormous influence on which public policy is adopted. In fact, most significant policy initiatives undertaken today by the Federal government have foundation support, and many are implemented as a result of foundation-funded advocacy.

Foundations have no voters, no customers, no investors. The people who run big foundations are part of a small, elite, insulated group most of whom live in the eastern United States, hundreds or even thousands of miles from the areas affected by the environmental policies they support. They have no way of receiving feedback from those affected by their decisions, nor are they accountable to anyone for promoting policies which adversely affect the well-being of people or local economies.

Tax exempt foundation funding of environmental advocacy groups unfairly tilts the playing field against the views and input of those most affected by the policies advocated. The average citizen's voice and input in the government decision-making process is often drowned out by advocacy groups largely funded by foundations, making our government seem even more remote and less responsive to the needs of the average citizen.

Many of you will be surprised to learn about the prominent role of foundations in funding environmental advocacy groups and the extent to which this funding influences government policies. I strongly recommend Ron Arnold's book, *Undue Influence,* which details the foundation funding of many environmental groups and initiatives. This book explains the role that foundation money plays in environmental issues and shows how it determines policies that the Federal government undertakes to implement.

Richard Pombo
Member of Congress

PART ONE:

ENVIROMANIA

▲▲▲▲▲
_____

PORTENTS

Across America, while urban areas enjoy an economic boom, rural communities are suffering unprecedented social and economic losses. Their suffering is directly linked to a bewildering array of government actions allegedly protecting the environment. All segments of natural resource goods-production are being systematically crippled. Government actions are unduly influenced by an interlocking triangle of agenda-driven federal employees, grant-driven environmental organizations, and prescriptive funders in private foundations.

ENVIRONMENTALISM IS NOT WHAT YOU THINK IT IS. It is not about the environment. It is about power.

It is well known that numerous former executives from environmental organizations occupy positions within the federal bureaucracy. It is less well known that thousands of activist members of advocacy groups are employed by federal agencies—in positions that give them opportunity to exercise agenda-driven influence over goods-production decisions. It is even less well known that agency personnel provide inside information to environmental leaders inviting pressure to force federal actions that the agency would not itself initiate.

It is well known that environmental organizations use lawsuits, lobbying, election campaigns, and administrative pressure to block economic activities they dislike. It is less well known that large networks of environmental organizations coordinate to systematically target specific rural communities for economic dismantling. It is even less well known that secretive fiscal agents distribute funding, training and computer equipment to create "grassroots" coalitions of environmental groups for specific programs directed against resource producers.

It is understood that private foundations provide substantial support to environmental organizations. It is less understood that a number of private foundations have become prescriptive rather than responsive. They design the programs, select the funding recipients and direct grant-driven projects for a substantial number of environmental organizations. It is even less well known that foundation board members occupy seats on the board of directors of a large number of environmental organizations.

This interlocking triangle of

- *grant-driven environmental groups,*
- *prescriptive private foundations, and*
- *zealous bureaucrats*

constitutes the real environmental movement.

They act in concert to exert undue influence over public policy that affects the future of every American.

They were not elected.

They are totally unaccountable.

They are engaged upon the largest unacknowledged program of social and economic displacement in American history.

CHAPTER 1

SILENT SCANDAL

A bewildering array of federal actions is crippling rural goods-producing economies in the name of protecting nature. An urban-rural prosperity gap widens because of these actions, which damage county tax bases and vital services such as roads, schools, and law enforcement. The flow of goods being destroyed includes water production, farming, ranching, mining, timber, oil and gas, roads, and manufactured goods—in short, everything physical or material that industrial civilization needs to thrive. An "iron triangle" of coordinated interests provokes the federal actions: environmental groups, wealthy foundations, and zealous bureaucrats. Their campaign of rural cleansing is turning vital resource producers into despised and disposable inferiors.

THE DOW JONES INDUSTRIAL AVERAGE BUZZING around in five digits. Employment at high levels. Gross Domestic Product growing merrily in a troubled world. The Federal Reserve happy enough to keep interest rates low.

With the new millennium looking that good, how could anyone believe that the environmental movement is dismantling industrial civilization piece by piece?

Why don't we hear about it? Or see it on television?

The answer is simple.

It's invisible.

First, the locus of the problem is literally out of sight, beyond the gridlock, past the city limits, after the last suburb. Out in the country. In the forests and grasslands and rivers and mountains. In rural America.

Second, the focus of the problem falls on cultural blind spots. It's the modern rendition of an age-old conflict, the urban sophisticate versus the country bumpkin. So ordinary that nobody sees it.

We categorize each other with stereotypes. City slickers. Boorish hill-billies. The wine and cheese set. Joe Sixpack. Volvos. Gun racks.

Two Americas.

Urban America.

Rural America.

Two Americas with divergent customs, rules, and wisdoms, inextricably wedded in conflicting attitudes, values, and beliefs.

Rural Americans tend to emphasize the basic needs for sustenance and safety, for a stable economy, fighting crime, strong defense forces; despite their hardy religious disposition, they are materialists.[4a]

Urban Americans tend to emphasize the social and self-actualization needs for a sense of belonging, more say in government, "ideas count," beautiful surroundings, and nature; they are post-materialists.

The urban majority has the votes. And the power. And the jobs. And the money. Urban dominance.

The rural minority has the logging shutdowns. And the mining stoppages. And the road moratoriums. And the fishing bans. And the ranching suspensions. And the farming restrictions. Rural cleansing.

While urban areas enjoy an economic boom, rural communities across the nation are suffering terrible social and economic pain. And the mass of Americans don't have a clue.

How do you make the invisible visible?

THE VISIBLE DAMAGE

When the Washington, D.C.-based non-profit Corporation for Enterprise Development (CFED) published its 1998 report, *The Development Report Card for the States*, it focused on the "urban-rural prosperity gap"—the degree to which rural areas trail urban areas in earnings and employment levels.[4b]

While national unemployment rates hover around 5% and urban centers may have only 2.8%, rural counties commonly suffer more than 10% joblessness, the report found. All fifty states were ranked using a list of statistics including employment growth, unemployment rate, average earnings and growth in earnings. The primary author was Daphne Clones, senior policy analyst with CFED, which functions as both think tank and consulting firm.[4c]

The phrase alone—"urban-rural prosperity gap"—is drenched in human drama. Urban mass media can see human drama. Associated Press editors saw. They assigned reporter Mark Jewell to cover the issue. The Los Angeles Times picked up one of his stories on the state with the widest urban-rural economic gap: Washington.

THE URBAN - RURAL PROSPERITY GAP
STATE RANKINGS:
WIDEST GAP (1) TO SMALLEST GAP (50)

1. WASHINGTON
2. MASSACHUSETTS
3. NEW YORK
4. IOWA
5. (TIE) MISSOURI
   SOUTH DAKOTA
7. GEORGIA
8. (TIE) VIRGINIA
   ILLINOIS
10. NEBRASKA
11. DELAWARE
12. MONTANA
13. UTAH
14. WYOMING
15. KANSAS
16. MINNESOTA
17. CONNECTICUT
18. MISSISSIPPI
19. (TIE) FLORIDA
    WISCONSIN
21. CALIFORNIA
22. COLORADO
23. TEXAS
24. IDAHO
25. (TIE) MAINE
    MICHIGAN

27. ARKANSAS
28. ARIZONA
29. (TIE) KENTUCKY
    NEW HAMPSHIRE
31. SOUTH CAROLINA
32. LOUISIANA
33. PENNSYLVANIA
34. (TIE) NEW MEXICO
    NORTH DAKOTA
36. OREGON
37. INDIANA
38. MARYLAND
39. (TIE) RHODE ISLAND
    WEST VIRGINIA
41. VERMONT
42. ALABAMA
43. OHIO
44. TENNESSEE
45. HAWAII
46. OKLAHOMA
47. NORTH CAROLINA
48. NEVADA
49. NEW JERSEY*
50. ALASKA

*New Jersey has no area classified as nonmetropolitan

Source: *The Development Report Card for the States*, Corporation for Enterprise Development, 1998, Washington, D.C.

The commonplace image Washington State evokes is one of Boeing airplanes, Starbuck's latte-land, Microsoft's ultimo-rich chairman Bill Gates, and Seattle's Space Needle with Mount Rainier, sentinel of wildness, hovering over skyscraper-jammed Puget Sound.

Urban Washington.

A.P. reporter Jewell looked for "the other Washington" in a little-known county named Pend Oreille (the locals pronounce it "Ponderay") and a small town there called Newport.

He wrote:

> Separating this northeastern Washington town and Seattle are 300 miles as diverse as any on Earth—stark desert, the majestic Columbia River and the startling beauty of the Cascade Range.
>
> But that expanse is trifling compared with the economic gap between this town and the state's largest city.
>
> The urban-rural economic gap in Washington state is the largest in the country, and for most of the state's rural counties, the software millionaires and aerospace engineers of Puget Sound seem worlds away.[6a]

Pend Oreille County had 15% unemployment when Jewell's story broke. Seattle had 2.8%. Marginal workers in Seattle groused about their lousy $7 or $8-an-hour wages. "A $7- to $8-an-hour job is a good job here," said Jim Jeffers, director of Pend Oreille County's economic-development council.[6b]

The whole four-county northeastern tier of Washington State, butted up against the Canadian border, is the same. Just west of Pend Oreille County lies Stevens County (11.3% unemployment), then Ferry County (12.7% unemployment), then Okanogan County (12.4% unemployment), which runs westward all the way up to the crest of the Cascade Range, looking down on urban Puget Sound. From Pend Oreille's border with Idaho, three heavily forested, mineral-rich mountain ranges link the Rocky Mountains on the east to the Cascades on the west: the Selkirks, the Kettle River Range, and the Okanogan Highlands.

Washington Governor Gary Locke (D-Seattle) was perplexed by the report, urging the 1998 Legislature to lessen the economic chasm between the urban and rural sections of his state. Being home to the worst such split in the nation was a dishonor Locke said was unacceptable.

His proposed solution was the usual blind-sighted let's-send-urban-things-to-rural-areas plan, replacing the resource class with a spectrum of urban gentry, rich retirees, modem gypsies, and welfare families.

Mark Jewell, unlike many journalists, reported the reasons for the gap. "There's little mystery in why there is a gulf," he wrote. His take: Boeing and Microsoft were the high-tech wind beneath Puget's Sound's flourishing wings. Rural Washington, conversely, was being depressed by "new stricter environmental regulations." In a nutshell:

The disparity can be traced in part to a slump in natural resource-based industries like timber and mining—long the lifeblood of the rural West and now stymied by debate over new priorities that value forests over timber, mountains over mines.[7]

He's telling us the slump was policy-induced. *Policy-induced.* Induced by environmentalists. By a debate.

To many of us who don't live in rural America, the idea of a *debate* by environmentalists thwarting the big multinational corporations behind timber and mining seems impossible, even absurd. Industrial fat cats can always finagle their way around government regulations, can't they?

Likewise, city-dwellers just *know* that the slump is the fault of the loggers and miners, not those who value forests over timber, mountains over mines: loggers have cut down all the trees so there are none left, haven't they? And miners have overmined the mountains until there's only pollution left behind, haven't they? And besides, they're crude, destructive, uneducated, bigoted social misfits who deserve to be despised and vilified, aren't they?

No sympathy there.

Rural dwellers who routinely see vast forests and untapped mineral deposits on their three-hour drive to the nearest international airport would chuckle knowingly at their ignorant city-brethren if they weren't suffering so desperately from the effects of such ignorance.

And rural dwellers who have watched timber companies and mining companies depart after years of losing to environmentalist protests and legal challenges know firsthand that the big multinational corporations they used to work for—much less the little local outfits—are not invincible.

Washington State Representative Bob Sump (R-7th District) mourns that twenty years ago his rural locale, Ferry County, was self-sustaining. "Today," he says, "due to environmental over-regulation, it is an economic wasteland."

Just what is the "environmental over-regulation" Rep. Sump is talking about?

If you ask around rural Washington State—or anywhere in rural America, for that matter—you quickly discover an array of federal laws, government land ownerships competing against private property, agency actions, presidential proclamations, administration "initiatives," administrative appeals and a maze of obscure regulations so bewildering it defies description, much less comprehension (see overleaf).

FEDERAL ACTIONS CRIPPLING RURAL GOODS-PRODUCING ECONOMIES

FEDERAL ACTIONS TRIGGERED BY ENVIRONMENTALIST PROTEST

Timber Sale Appeals: delays or kills by attrition any Forest Service timber sale through a complex appeals process and costly lawsuits.

Mining Permit Appeals: delays or kills by attrition any federal mining permit through a complex appeals process and costly lawsuits.

Cattle Grazing Permit Appeals: denies ranchers the use of their private rights in split-estate federal grazing lands.

The Endangered Species Act – lawsuits can stop any economic activity on federal or private property to save any species placed on a government list. Environmentalists can force listings of species to destroy goods producers.

National Environmental Policy Act – lawsuits can delay or kill by attrition any economic activity on federal land through a detailed study of the activity's environmental impact.

Clean Air Act – lawsuits can stop any economic activity that generates dust, smoke or particulates near a national park for visibility reasons.

Spotted Owl Restrictions – lawsuit-induced ruling forbids disturbing habitat in a circle around every known spotted owl nesting site: no roads, no timber harvest, no mining, no homebuilding. Owl not truly in danger, according to skeptics in the scientific community.

AGENCY ACTIONS AND PRESIDENTIAL PROCLAMATIONS

Wetlands Regulations (Clean Water Act of 1972) – can stop any economic activity on federal or private property that may disturb places that an official labels "wetlands." Used to stop farming, ranching, home building, commercial development.

Bureau of Reclamation - attempts to stop farmers from using irrigation water and abrogate water rights.

Riparian Area Regulations – can fence off the water of a farmer or rancher to protect streams so cattle cannot drink.

Restoration Regulations – can eradicate all signs of civilization and prevent any future human use.

Frank Church - River of No Return Wilderness Management Plan (Jan 1998) - Proposal would cut in half the Outfitters and Guides (Idaho Outfitters and Guides Association) river rafting launch dates and party size.

Hells Canyon National Recreation Area; Wallowa Whitman National Forest Record of Decision Feb. 24, 1998, Non-Motorized Period of 21 days duration. No jet boat traffic was allowed on a 71.5 mile stretch of the Snake River in Hells Canyon, preventing private property owners access to their land because the only access is by river. Forest Service law enforcement agents with sidearms enforced the ban.

Grand Staircase-Escalante National Monument (Presidential Proclamation of September 18, 1996) – Planned in secrecy and implemented by surprise. Established a 1.7 million acre protected area in Utah enclosing school lands, along with many private homes, ranches, and businesses. No Utah state, local or congressional officials were consulted.

ADMINISTRATION "INITIATIVES" NOT AUTHORIZED BY CONGRESS

Rural Roads Moratorium (Federal Register January 28, 1998) – Forest Service Chief Mike Dombeck issued an order halting road construction and repair on federal lands under his jurisdiction. On February 11, 1999, the administration extended the road moratorium. Road closures have also been ordered, reducing rural transportation capability for essential travel including fire fighting and emergency medical evacuation.

Clean Water Act; Vice President Initiative (Nov 7, 1997) – new regulations that gradually tighten water use in a large network of watersheds so that homes, farms and towns will no longer remain.

American Heritage Rivers Initiative (Executive Order April 10, 1998) – vast project for increasing federal control over land adjoining selected rivers.

Interior Columbia Basin Ecosystem Management Project (ICBEMP) – a plan to establish federal control over 72 million of the 144 million acres in the basin covering portions of Oregon, Washington, Idaho, Montana, Wyoming, Utah and Nevada.

EPA Regional Ecosystem Demonstration Projects: Region 1: New Hampshire Resource Protection Pilot; Region 2: Long Island Sound; Region 3 Mid-Atlantic Highlands Assessment; Region 4: Mobile Bay; Region 5: Lakewide Management Plans (Lakes Michigan, Erie, Superior) - Glacial Lake Chicago Crescent - Lake Superior Basin - Upper Wolf River Watershed - St. Louis River/Bay, MN/WI - Milwaukee Estuary, WI - Maumee River, OH - Oak Savannas; Region 6: Coastal Wetlands of Louisiana; Barataria Terrebonne National Estuary Ecosystem Initiative; Region 7: Great Plains Initiative; Platte River; Region 8: Colorado Plateau Ecosystem Protection Initiative; Rocky Mountain Headwaters Mining Waste Initiative; Upper Arkansas Watershed Initiative; Missouri River; Clear Creek; Colorado River Basin Salinity Control Program; Region 9: San Francisco Bay/Delta Estuary Initiative; Region 10: Willamette River Basin.

The Interior Department's "Central Texas Rare Species Conservation Plan" — forces land owners in 40 Texas counties covering an area of more than 1 million acres to either "voluntarily" surrender use of their property rights to protect two endangered bird species or risk enforcement actions with severe penalties of fine and imprisonment.

Resource people think they have the law on their side: the Multiple Use - Sustained Yield Act of 1960 is supposed to guarantee access for all users of federal land. It also protects forests by limiting the trees cut to no more cubic volume than grows back every year forever.

But decades of the environmentalist message that "all the trees are gone" has turned public opinion against cutting any trees at all, especially the federal old growth that for a century was planned as the timber basket of America where generation after generation of trees would be grown and harvested and regrown in an endless cycle. Critics sneer at sustained yield as mere "tree farms."

They want "sustainable" forests, not "sustained yield." You can measure sustained yield in cubic feet of wood. Sustainability is an opinion with no measurements. You can define it with values, attitudes, beliefs or anything else you want. You can stop anything with beliefs.

Resource people have found this policy debate hard to win: in courtrooms, the Endangered Species Act trumps all other laws.

Such details don't make national headlines. If you're Duane Vaagen, co-owner of Vaagen Brothers Lumber Company, you've watched helplessly as the four-county area sank into economic distress.

"Our company has two sawmills," says Vaagen, "one in Republic and one in Colville."

Republic, Washington (population 1,030), in Ferry County, is a little mountain town with one traffic light where State Road 20 intersects Main Street (officially, it's Clark Street, but everybody calls it Main Street). Its major watering hole is the Hitchin' Post Cafe, and tourists have two or three motels to choose from.

Colville (population 3,742), about 50 miles east on SR 20, is a big city by comparison, with a real street grid, a hospital, a historical park and even an airfield—but the nearest commercial airline service is 70 miles south in Spokane.

"My dad Burt started the company in 1952 with my uncle Bud," says Duane, "in a little place called Squaw Creek about 15 miles east of Colville. We took over the Republic mill from another company in 1982."

Duane and his mother Roberta are now among the co-owners, and "our 230 employees own a little less than half the company."

Both Colville (established 1855) and Republic (incorporated 1900) began as mining towns, quickly added logging and ranching and, much later, recreation. The stores and cafes in both places still have that plain old "somebody-lives-here" feel that gets polished off the city versions. And there's no such thing as a secret in these parts. Everybody knows everybody else and a stranger might as well be hauling a billboard.

Vaagen's 230 co-owners count on timber sales from the two local national forests, the Okanogan (1,706,00 acres, 44% of Okanogan County) and the Colville (1,096,000 acres, the northern half of Ferry, Stevens and Pend Oreille Counties).

Those timber sales have become tougher to get.

Jon Newman, Vaagen's plant manager in Republic, has worked at this mill for twenty-five years. He goes through a lot of bureaucracy to supply the mill with logs. He can't submit a bid on federal timber for his mill until Forest Service bureaucrats first prepare a Forest Plan to comply with all applicable laws. Newman has seen the Okanogan and Colville National Forests go through several Forest Plan cycles, each one with less timber offered for sale.

The trees are there. The sales are not. Why?

The federal planning process can be influenced by anyone, and environmental groups have become adept at influence. Even if the details are cryptic, just scan the charts on the next two pages. They make a point.

Once this planning stage is complete, the Forest Plan is thrown open to public comment, where Vaagen's co-owners are again at the mercy of any environmental group that wants to further delay or stop their operation. All the group has to do is write negative comments, or file an appeal on the timber sale, which can be as simple as writing a letter. Sometimes the Forest Service just withdraws the sale without explanation.

Duane Vaagen has seen the two national forests hit by more than 110 environmentalist appeals between 1990 and 1998, an average of more than one a month (charts on two following pages).

"It used to be the harder you worked the more money you made," says Vaagen. "No more. I've seen our Northwest timber industry go from around 1,000 sawmills down to about 400. You're lucky to have a two percent return on assets. In the stock market everybody's shooting for 20 percent. We'd be tickled to have 5 percent."

Environmental laws and protests have taken their toll.

Vaagen's is the only sawmill left in Republic. Ten sawmills in the four-county area have shut down since 1990, victims of the usual stresses of business—plus environmentalist administrative appeals that were one straw too many.

The loss of the bigger mills, of course, hurt most. Back in 1991, Spokane Lumber Company shut down its sawmill in Tonasket (population 1,025) in Okanogan County, throwing 170 people out of work, and in 1997 Omak Wood Products declared bankruptcy and shut down its sawmill. The plywood plant reopened, but with a net loss of 160 jobs.[11]

COLUMBIA BASIN TIMBER SALE APPEALS, 1990 - 1998
FILED IN OKANOGAN AND COLVILLE NATIONAL FORESTS

YEAR	TIMBER SALE NAME	APPELANT	DISPOSITION
1990	Mayfly	Sierra Club, Cascade Chapter	Forest Service Withdrew Sale
	Spur	Roger Jackson	Affirmed - No Logging
	Boulder	Pend Oreille Environmental Team	Reversed - Logging Approved
	Deer	Kettle Range Conservation Group / Orient Water Co.	Reversed - Logging Approved
	Gatorson	Kettle Range Conservation Group / Citizens Opposing Gatorson Sale	Upheld - No Logging
	Calispell	Pend Oreille Environmental Team	Litigation
1991	Kelard	Kettle Range Conservation Group	Forest Service Withdrew Sale
	Tom/Roes	Kettle Range Conservation Group	Forest Service Withdrew Sale
	Bea	Inland Empire Public Lands Council	Forest Service Withdrew Sale
	Brown Supplement	Wesleyan University Environmental Interest Group	Dismissed - Logging Approved
	Burgett	Methow Forest Watch	Remand (Delay)
	Chewuch Blowdown	Wesleyan University Environmental Interest Group	Affirmed - No Logging
1992	Coyote	Methow Forest Watch	Affirmed - No Logging
	Douglas Salvage	Sierra Club, Cascade Chapter	Forest Service Withdrew Sale
	Leola	Greater Ecosystem Alliance	Affirmed - No Logging
1993	Little Bonaparte	Tonasket Forest Watch	Affirmed - No Logging
	Muckamuck	Sierra Club, Cascade Chapter	Affirmed - No Logging
	Nicholson Salvage One	Tonasket Forest Watch	Dismissed - Logging Approved
1994	Poverty	Sierra Club, Cascade Chapter	Affirmed - No Logging

	COLUMBIA BASIN TIMBER SALE APPEALS, 1990 - 1998 FILED IN OKANOGAN AND COLVILLE NATIONAL FORESTS		
YEAR	**TIMBER SALE NAME**	**APPELANT**	**DISPOSITION**
	Tonata Range Allotment Plan (Grazing)	Predator Project, Rest the West	Grazing Decision Reversed
	Stony Hudson	Citizens for Responsible Logging	Dismissed - Logging Allowed
1995	Seldom Seen	Inland Empire Public Lands Council	Affirmed - No Logging
	Thomboy	Kettle Range Conservation Group	Affirmed - No Logging
	Pack-to-Go	Inland Empire Public Lands Council	Affirmed - No Logging
1996	Chewelah	Inland Empire Public Lands Council	Affirmed - No Logging
	Wolfman	Inland Empire Public Lands Council	Affirmed - No Logging
	Addy Salvage	Kettle Range Conservation Group	Affirmed - No Logging
	Eagle Rock	Kettle Range Conservation Group	Affirmed - No Logging
	Danny	Northwest Ecosystem Alliance	Dismissed - Logging Allowed
1997	Crown Jewel Mine (Mining Permit)	Okanogan Highlands Alliance	Affirmed - Mine Permit Delayed
	Long Draw Salvage	Northwest Ecosystem Alliance	Forest Service Withdrew Sale
	New Moon	Kettle Range Conservation Group / Inland Empire Public Lands Council	Affirmed - No Logging
	North Sherman and Fritz	Washington Wilderness Coalition	Appeal Resolved

This list of 33 appeals is only a representative sample of the more than 110 actual appeals filed on these forests from 1990 to 1998. Each appeal cost Forest Service budget and reduced economic activity in the county.

The planning process may involve an Environmental Assessment (EA), or, if environmental groups mount a legal challenge, a court could require a costly and time-consuming full-blown Environmental Impact Statement (EIS).

YEAR	COMPANY SHUT DOWN	JOBS
1989	WTD/Orient Lumber	35
1990	Charles E. Dagnon	2
	WTD/Valley Wood Products	40
1991	Spokane Lumber Company	170
1993	Ross Pallet Shop	3
	Zerba Brothers	5
1994	S.I.R. Timber Products	12
1995	John Chopot Lumber Company	30
1998	Omak Wood Products (sawmill)	
	Omak Wood Products (plywood)*	540

*Omak Wood Products filed for Chapter 11 bankruptcy in 1997. Its sawmill is closed. In March 1997 Omak listed 540 employees. The plywood plant closed in 1998. A new owner, Washington Veneer, a subsidiary of Quality Veneer, reopened the plywood plant with 380 employees in 1999. Net loss, 160 jobs.

Most of the smaller mills went out of business for ordinary reasons: poor management, production problems, and the like. But not all.

Duane Vaagen says, "It's so complex an industry and there are so many variables, there's no guarantee. And the sawmill people such as us and the other little independents take all the risks. Anymore it's all risks and no rewards."

He doesn't mind taking risks, not when they do a better environmental job and provide the opportunity of making a reasonable profit.

"Our contract crews have really gone to mechanized logging," says Vaagen. "They use these self-contained trucks that cut small trees to length right on the site, very little impact. They can cut the tree down, then limb it and then have a computer that cuts it to proper diameter. That's good for the environment and good for business. But it costs half a million dollars for one of these machines."[14a]

Vaagen is well aware that the Sierra Club has adopted a resolution calling for "Zero Cut" on federal forests—they want him to get no timber from lands that were originally intended "to furnish a continuous supply of timber for the use and necessities of citizens of the United States."[14b]

Vaagen knows the Kettle Range Conservation Group that has filed so many appeals in the local forests. It's based in Republic in an office just off main street, next to the Hitchin' Post Cafe. It's run by a man named Tim Coleman, with a friend named Mike Peterson. Both had their beginnings in the radical group Earth First! Peterson was arrested in the 1988 Earth First! blockade of the Okanogan National Forest supervisor's office to protest loss of lynx habitat to logging; Coleman can be seen in law enforcement videos of the Earth First!ers, but he was not arrested.[15]

Vaagen says, "Back in 1988, Earth First! held its annual gathering not far from here. We soon found spikes driven into logs that damaged the bandsaw in our mill. We kept that very quiet because the more said about it the more it might happen. We only reported one incident, but it happened several dozen times. We're lucky it never broke the bandsaw, just broke the teeth off and caused downtime and repair cost, over $50,000. But no suspects were ever identified and we just let it go."

Coleman and Peterson were not implicated, but their in-your-face temperament has not diminished, and has even gained a patina of respectability: they now use the government they once blockaded to eliminate the resource class.

Vaagen says, "There isn't that much federal timber available nowadays. It's all tied up. So we buy about two-thirds of our timber from small private owners. We go in and thin the trees out for the owners and we do a good job so we get to go back the second and third time."

There has been other fallout.

"Idaho has passed a law that makes it illegal for Washington companies to cut timber there and bring it into Washington for processing," Vaagen muses. "But it's legal for an Idaho company to come into Washington, cut timber and take it into Idaho and process it there. We have protested, but we can't afford to challenge it."

States fighting over the scraps.

And the appeal-writers have hurt county government badly.

The vast majority of county commissioners in rural America resent these appeals because they not only hurt local businesses and employment, but also take away from the county budget.

The Forest Service does not pay local taxes, but Congress has evolved a system to make up for the lost revenue, including "25 Percent Payments" based on national forest income and earmarked for public schools and county roads, and "Payments In Lieu of Taxes" (PILT), an entitlement program based on a tangled acreage/population formula and not earmarked for public schools or county roads. Congress fully funded the PILT program only once in its 25-year history, and has steadily allocated less and less of the formula's promise, giving out only 53% of the formula amount in 1997. Income from national forests has taken a nosedive with the incremental shutdown of timber harvest nationwide.

Rural County Commissioners all over the Northwest are concerned about the collateral damage from reduced timber harvest.

One single environmentalist lawsuit, the highly publicized Spotted Owl dispute, shut down a substantial part of the federal timber harvest, resulting in the closure of 187 mills in Oregon, Washington and California and the loss of 22,654 jobs—and concentrated the timber industry in the hands of big companies that owned their own private timberlands.[16]

Then the big timberland owners felt environmental laws reaching to their private lands as well. In 1998, giant Louisiana-Pacific—bleeding from product liability lawsuits over defective siding—sold off all its California timberlands when environmental restrictions made logging them too costly, both in lost revenues and in public relations damage control.

MILL CLOSURE DATA - SAWMILLS, PLYWOOD AND VENEER PLANTS, AND PULP MILLS - SPOTTED OWL AREA - 1/1/89 THROUGH 11/30/97

LOCATION	RELATED TO SPOTTED OWL	NOT RELATED TO SPOTTED OWL	TOTAL CLOSURES
Oregon	113	14	128
Washington	49	9	58
California*	25	2	27
Totals	187	25	212

*California mill closures include only facilities in the following counties: Siskiyou, Trinity, Shasta, Mendocino, Butte and Tehama. Closed mills all had a dependence on federal timber. Owl areas of redwood region counties Humboldt and Del Norte were excluded.

JOB LOSS DATA - SPOTTED OWL AREA - 1/1/89 THROUGH 11/30/97

LOCATION	RELATED TO SPOTTED OWL	NOT RELATED TO SPOTTED OWL	TOTAL JOB LOSS
Oregon	15,151	2,550	17,701
Washington	3,970	1,132	5,102
California*	3,533	44	3,577
Totals	22,654	3,726	26,380

*Mill jobs lost: 15,599; logging jobs lost, 7,055; not segregated in chart. Data from mills closed by fire, strikes, and those not dependent on federal timber, including Weyerhaeuser mills, were excluded from this analysis. Woods job losses were calculated on the basis of 1.2 jobs per million board feet of harvest decline. Area studied includes only lands subject to Spotted Owl or President's Forest Plan Option 9 rules. Some excluded mills may have been dependent upon "owl forests."

Source: Paul F. Ehinger & Associates, Eugene, Oregon.

A few years later the Spotted Owl controversy migrated to the Southwest. Arizona's forest products industry was decimated in 1996 by a lawsuit brought by the Southwest Center for Biological Diversity (1997 income: $523,467) that extended a nine-month ban on commercial logging in eleven Southwestern national forests. The environmentalist suit claimed the U.S. Forest Service had failed to take the necessary steps to ensure the survival of Mexican spotted owls. U.S. District Judge Carl Muecke refused to lift the ban, which continued to close down sawmill after sawmill, leaving a few tribal enterprises as the remaining goods producers of timber. The trail of destruction left by Southwest Center for Biological Diversity and allies over the Mexican spotted owl is like the catastrophe left by the Audubon Society over the Northern spotted owl.

On the other hand, destroying rural roads has turned into a goldmine. Tom Hirons used to be a logger in Oregon. He still has his logging equipment, but now, he says, he's working on U.S. Forest Service projects "decommissioning" roads (removing high maintenance culverts from marginal roads that could feasibly be repaired in the future) and "obliterating" roads (restoring roadbed contours to their original slope, thus creating permanent off-limits nature preserves).

"They pay better to tear out roads than I ever made logging," Hirons says ruefully. "Down at the Detroit Ranger Station the guy said the Forest Service had more budget to eradicate roads than to build them last year. That's government programs for you."[17a]

Rural cleansing. Dismantling industrial civilization piece by piece.

Things should be better in the sixteenth state down the urban-rural prosperity gap: Minnesota. But St. Louis County, Minnesota—the largest county in America—feels like it's in a war, according to County Commissioner Dennis Fink. "The economy and the way of life of thousands of St. Louis County families are under attack," said Fink. "Radical environmentalism threatens to shut down logging on all federally owned lands."[17b]

Minnesota State Senator Sam Solon agrees. "The timber and wood products industry is a $7 billion segment of our state economy employing more than 61,000 workers," Sen. Solon said. "The U.S. Forest Service's decision to place a moratorium on construction of new logging roads into Minnesota's national forests has a chilling effect on our state's timber and wood products industries. In addition, the failure to negotiate contracts for the allowable timber harvest in our area is having an immediate impact on the economy of this region and the families who depend on forestry to sustain their livelihoods."[17c]

David Glowaski, Mayor of the little town of Orr, Minnesota, is deeply troubled over the way things are going in his town. "For over 100 years the forest industry has been the heart and soul of our existence," Mayor Glowaski said. "Because urban America is becoming so economically affluent in comparison to rural America, which is declining economically, communities like ours cannot combat the powerful special interest organizations on an equal basis. Their economic power channeled through these environmental organizations in pursuit of their agendas are becoming more of a threat to our very existence in a life we love and want to maintain.

"As the U.S. Forest Service succumbs to 'enviro-pressures,' they strangle our economic base and do not meet their mandated timber harvest levels. Most of our residents are descendants of pioneers who want to carry on their heritage in a sustainable manner and pass this on to our children.

"Our children's fears keep growing. Are we going to have to leave our homes? Is dad going to lose his job? Why can't we hunt and fish where we used to? Everyday questions from the children in our community, including my own."[18]

Glowaski and Fink worry about more than timber shutdowns. Government competition for land is a serious factor.

"Government is aggressively purchasing private lands to be set aside or removed from production," Commissioner Fink said. "A perfect example would be the proposed purchase and designation as 'Prairie Grasslands,' of some 77,000 acres in Western Minnesota."

Fink expresses the concerns of many rural residents about the actual result of all this land disappearing into government hands:

"It seems clear to me that there is the intent to remove our population from rural areas and resettle them in more populated 'core areas' with connecting corridors and buffer zones, leaving the vast amount of our land to nature, with little or no interference by humans," Fink says grimly.

A controversial notion.

"The evidence is in the actions: government agencies buying up private property at excessively high prices. The taking of private property through designations and regulation must stop!"

Once digested into the federal domain, private land never comes back. And the pace of land consumption by the government is accelerating. "In St. Louis County alone," says Fink, "22,000 acres were purchased in 1997 'to be preserved for our children.' Today, 63% of our county is government owned. How much land needs to be set aside 'for our children' so they can't use it either?"

Rural cleansing. Dismantling industrial civilization piece by piece.

But Fink is asking an important question:

WHO OWNS YOUR FUTURE?

The ownership of private property is considered by many to be the cornerstone of America's freedom and success. The Supreme Court of the United States appears to agree. It held in the case of Lynch v. Household Finance Corporation, decided March 23, 1972:

> [T]he dichotomy between personal liberties and property rights is a false one. Property does not have rights. People have rights. The right to enjoy property without unlawful deprivation, no less than the right to speak or the right to travel, is in truth, a 'personal' right, whether the 'property' in question be a welfare check, a home, or a savings account. In fact, a fundamental interdependence exists between the personal right to liberty and the personal right in property. Neither could have meaning without the other. That rights in property are basic civil rights has long been recognized.[19a]

If that is true, it is fair to ask what will become of the personal right to liberty if government becomes the nation's dominant landowner.

And that leads to the question of how much of America's 1,940,011,400 acres government already owns.

Here's the score:

Urbanites are usually stunned to learn that the federal government manages a third—32.6 percent in 1992—of the entire nation, mostly in rural areas, "a huge federal domain of ownership that is hard to reconcile with the reputation this country has as a citadel of reliance on markets and the private sector," as the President's Commission on Privatization reported in 1988.[19b]

To get a grip on the breadth of a federal government that runs almost one out of every three acres in the nation, consider that every one of the fifty states contains land owned by the federal government, not just the eleven Western states we usually think of as being federally dominated.

Delaware is 19% federally owned; New Jersey and New Hampshire are both 13.2% federal; Virginia is 11.8% federal; and the feds own more than 7% each of Arkansas, Florida, Maryland, Michigan, Minnesota, North Carolina, Vermont, West Virginia, and Wisconsin.[19c]

The Western states, as reputed, really are dominated by federal ownership:

Nevada is more than 82% federal land; Alaska is 66%; Utah, 64%; Idaho, 62%; Oregon, 60%; Wyoming, 49%; California nearly 47%; Arizona 44%, and so forth down to Washington, at 26.8% the *least* federally owned Western state besides Hawaii (16.7%), which has other particulars that make comparisons problematic.[20a]

Then you have to figure out which federal agency owns how much. Some round numbers are useful for comparison.

- The U.S. Forest Service (USFS) manages about 192 million acres;
- the Bureau of Land Management (BLM) manages about 270 million acres;
- the National Park Service (NPS) manages about 80.7 million acres;
- and the U.S. Fish and Wildlife Service (USFWS) manages about 91 million acres.

That's just the "biggies" in federal lands. It doesn't count the land owned by the Department of Defense and other federal agencies.

You can see this summary for yourself on the Park Service website at http://www.nps.gov/legacy/acreage.html. The BLM's website says it manages 264 million acres, not 270: close enough for government work.

Do the arithmetic and you get 632,700,000 acres, 32.6 percent, or, in round numbers, one-third of America.

On the other hand, the 1992 National Resource Inventory, carried out by the National Resources Conservation Service (NRCS) of the U.S. Department of Agriculture, said there were 407,988,700 acres of federal land in 1992, 21 percent, a little over a fifth of America.[20b]

Only the federal government could lose track of 224,711,300 acres of land. What became of the difference?

Two things: some land was wrapped in weasel-words, and other land was obfuscated by accounting methods.

Weasel words: Notice that the statements above say the federal agency "manages" so-and-so many acres. It doesn't say they *own* it. *Manages.*

Like that 80.7 million acres managed by the National Park Service: more than 2.8 million acres of it is private property. Says so on their own website.

How can that be?

Here's the brutal truth: If some bureaucrat draws a line on a national park map and your property happens to be inside the line, you become an "inholder," subject to federal authority, and you are about to live in interesting times.

Accounting methods: The National Resources Conservation Service doesn't count lands managed by federal agencies unless they have deed and title. And the NCRS also didn't count the Tennessee Valley Authority lands or a lot of other categories.

So we have a fifth of the nation in actual federal ownership, but a third of it under federal management.

Very clever, these bureaucrats.

There's a lot of non-federal land out there behaving as if it were federal land. Who really owns it then?

You can argue about that in a court of law, but the federal government has two advantages over you: it never dies and it prints the money.

So much for federal land, theirs and yours.

But that doesn't count the land owned by state and local governments.

How much is there?

The truth is, we don't know.

The 1992 National Resource Inventory covered some 800,000 sample sites representing the nation's non-federal land, theoretically including all non-federal government land, with what NCRS claims to be 95 percent reliability. Okay, 800,000 *is* a lot of sample sites.

Its inventory used a "state and local ownership" category that included land owned by states, counties or parishes, and municipalities. It came up with 6 percent of America's 1.9 billion acres owned by state and local governments.

However, that's not very convincing when you consider all the actual governments enumerated in the 1992 Census of Governments, which identified 85,006 government units that existed in the United States as of January 1992.[21]

Yes, there are 85,006 governments in the United States.

In addition to the federal government and the 50 state governments, there are 84,955 units of local government. Of these, 38,978 are general-purpose local governments—3,043 county governments, and 35,935 subcounty general-purpose governments (including 19,279 municipal governments and 16,656 town or township governments). The remainder, more than half the total number, are special-purpose local governments, including 14,422 school district governments and 31,555 special district governments such as port authorities, local improvement districts, conservation districts, and so on.

There's no indication that the NCRS counted the land owned by those 45,977 special-purpose local governments.

It did count certain Native American tribal lands as government lands, including "individual trust lands and land that is administered but not owned by the Bureau of Indian Affairs." That showed 2 percent of America owned by tribal governments.

That's a lot of competition against private property for *land*, the basic resource from which most fundamental production arises.

In actual fact, nobody, not the U.S. Census Bureau, not the National Conservation Resources Service, not the federal agencies, has a clue how much of America all these combined governments really own. Or control.

It could well be more than half.

And it's growing steadily.

What this may portend for the personal right to liberty remains to be seen.

Where is the pressure coming from to eliminate the resource class and diminish private property ownership?

Is it all from little local groups like the ones in rural Washington?

Ferry County Commissioner Jim Hall has often wondered where Tim Coleman and his Kettle Range Conservation Group gets the money to make a cottage industry of fighting goods production in his county. IRS databases show the Kettle Range Conservation Group's 1997 revenues as $81,635 with assets of $49,507. That's not much money, but it seems to be highly leveraged to stop goods production. How can that be?

Hall said, "Tim Coleman came to visit me shortly after I was elected County Commissioner. He brought two friends. They were from the W. Alton Jones Foundation. They tried to convince me to back down on the platform I had run on, which was in favor of natural resource industry jobs in Ferry County. It took me awhile to realize that the W. Alton Jones Foundation was located in Virginia and had been giving a lot of money to environmental groups all over Washington. What were these out-of-state foundation men doing with a local environmentalist on their leash? What were they doing here at all?"[22a]

What indeed?

The W. Alton Jones Foundation was established in 1944 by "Pete" Jones, who had a distinguished career in the oil industry (the CITGO Oil fortune). He had no interest in environmentalism. His wife and daughter and grandchildren did. They outlived him and got his money. The foundation's mission, according its current literature, is "to protect the Earth's life-support systems from environmental harm and to eliminate the possibility of nuclear war." That's the new version. We'll see the original in the next chapter.

Financial data for fiscal year ended December 31, 1997: Assets: $370,538,404. Income (from a managed investment portfolio): $52,450,156. Total grants authorized: $26,983,718. Total grants disbursed: $25,261,551. 1998 grants budgeted: $32,000,000.[22b]

The W. Alton Jones Foundation makes grants in two areas: environmental protection through its Sustainable World Program, and nuclear warfare prevention through its Secure World Program.

But the way it makes grants is of particular interest.

Consider this advice to grant-seekers in its brochure:

> The foundation works principally through foundation-defined initiatives addressing its priority issues. These initiatives usually take the form of coordinated grants to multiple institutions, each of which focuses on one or more components of an overall campaign defined by the foundation's mission. Proposals for participation in these initiatives are invited by the foundation.[23]

Note several key items:

Foundation-defined initiatives. In other words, a few foundation executives and staff members write the social engineering plan.

Coordinated grants. In other words, the social engineers orchestrate numerous agreeable groups to put the foundation's plan in action.

Invited by the foundation. In other words, don't call us, we'll call you if we think you're worthy enough to do our bidding.

The W. Alton Jones Foundation is not responsive.

It is prescriptive.

It writes the social engineering prescription.

If you're Duane Vaagen or his 230 co-owners or Minnesota county commissioners, or anybody else who depends on natural resources in rural America, you take the social engineering medicine.

Okay, who gets invited to take W. Alton Jones Foundation money? Lots of people, evidently. Here's a sample from the $2,511,855 that Jones orchestrated for grassroots projects in 1997, not counting the $11,582,550 they spent on their main environmental initiative, the Sustainable World Program:

Blue Mountains Biodiversity Project May 1997 - $18,000. A Project of the League of Wilderness Defenders. Fossil, OR. For public education and forest monitoring efforts in the Blue Mountains of eastern Oregon.

British Columbia Environmental Network Educational Foundation May 1997 - $40,000. Vancouver, BC. To conduct citizen forest watch and to train and coordinate activists in key regions of the province.

Canadian Rainforest Network Nov. 1997 - $40,000. Vancouver, BC. To coordinate and support grassroots forest protection efforts on BC's mid-coast.

Central Oregon Forest Issues Committee Nov 1997 - $9,000. Bend, OR. To monitor and work to improve forest management practices in the Deschutes and Ochoco National Forests, and one Bureau of Land Management district in central Oregon.

Coast Range Association Nov 1997 - $52,000 over 2 years. Newport, OR. To organize grassroots watershed groups in Oregon and educate the public about forest watershed protection.

Columbia River Bioregional Education Project May 1997 - $10,000. Oroville, WA. To monitor Forest Service timber sales and promote environmental education in the Okanogan Valley of eastern Washington.

Environmental Protection Information Center Nov 1997 - $40,000. Garberville, CA. To protect the privately held Headwaters redwood forest in northern California.

Friends of the Granby May 1997 - $5,000. Grand Forks, CANADA. To promote public education, forestry oversight, and alliance building to protect threatened areas adjacent to the Granby Wilderness.

Gifford Pinchot Task Force Nov. 1997 - $26,000. Vancouver, WA. To improve forest management and public participation on the Gifford Pinchot National Forest in southern Washington state.

Granby Wilderness Society May 1997 - $5,000. Grand Forks, CANADA. To promote public education, forestry oversight, and alliance building to protect threatened areas adjacent to the Granby Wilderness.

Headwaters Nov. 1997 - $80,000 over 2 years. Ashland, OR. To promote the economic and social benefits of environmental protection and build a stronger base for forest conservation in southwestern Oregon.

Kettle Range Conservation Group May 1997 - $15,000. Republic, WA. To protect ancient forests and conduct forest watch activities in the Columbia River highlands of northwest Washington state.

Klamath Forest Alliance Nov 1997 - $80,000 over 2 years. Etna, CA. To build a community-based constituency for forest protection, and to influence Forest Service management in northern California and southwestern Oregon.

Laskeek Bay Conservation Society Nov 1997 - $29,000. Queen Charlotte City, Haida Gwaii. To conduct volunteer field science and education programs designed to promote conservation and protect forests in Haida Gwaii.

Oregon Natural Resources Council Fund Nov 1997 - $40,000. Portland, OR. To protect forest watersheds in Oregon and rally further support for their protection.

Raincoast Conservation Foundation May 1997 - $40,000. Victoria, BC. To develop scientific bases and strengthen First Nations support for protection of the greater Rivers/Smith Inlet ecoregion of the central coast of British Columbia.

Sierra Club of British Columbia Nov 1997 - $50,000. A Chapter of the Sierra Club of Canada Victoria, BC CANADA. To protect and preserve the coastal forests of Vancouver Island, Haida Gwaii, and the central BC coast.

T. Buck Suzuki Environmental Foundation May 1997 - $27,105. Vancouver, CANADA. To protect salmon habitats in British Columbia by monitoring forest management and by pressing for stricter enforcement of British Columbia's Forest Practices Code.

Umpqua Watersheds Nov 1997 - $17,500. Roseburg, OR. To protect forest biodiversity in southern Oregon through forest monitoring and community education in the Umpqua River Watershed.

Valhalla Wilderness Society Nov 1997 - $40,000. New Denver, BC CANADA. To protect community watersheds in southern BC.

Western Canada Wilderness Committee Nov 1997 - $80,000 over 2 years. Vancouver, BC CANADA. To build a greater constituency for the protection of BC's mid-coast Great Bear Rainforest.

It takes a certain talent to read these grants. They're written in *foundationese*, a language of genteel euphemisms and pretentious circumlocutions.

For example, that first grant of $18,000 "For public education and forest monitoring efforts in the Blue Mountains of eastern Oregon."

What does that mean?

The $18,000 went to the Blue Mountains Biodiversity Project, a little group based in Fossil, Oregon, and run by a dreadlock-coifed man named Michael Christensen, who uses the alias Asanté Riverwind.

W. Alton Jones Foundation gave Mr. Riverwind's group $11,410 in 1994, $13,140 in 1995, $18,000 in 1996, and another $18,000 in 1997.

While being supported by W. Alton Jones Foundation grants, Mr. Riverwind had a federal conviction for blocking Forest Service Road 4555 on the Malheur National Forest on March 21, 1996 with an overturned pickup truck and logs, cutting off access to the Reed Fire Salvage Timber Sale, where units were actively being logged. Perhaps that is what foundationese means by "forest monitoring."

After federal law enforcement officer Gale Wall served Riverwind with at least five Notices of Violation, Assistant U.S. Attorney Barry Sheldal filed an Information (prosecutor's indictment) against Riverwind, who entered a guilty plea to one count of blocking a federal government road by leaving a wrecked vehicle and erecting barriers, a misdemeanor. On May 8, 1997, Federal Judge Ancer Hagerty of the United States District Court in Portland, Oregon, ordered Riverwind to pay a $300 fine, $252.52 restitution and a $25 fee assessment, and placed him on probation until restitution was paid. Riverwind paid the next day. Case No. 9757.

Law enforcement documents show the cost of cleaning up Mr. Riverwind's mess was $15,886.60. Minus Riverwind's payment of a total of $577.52, that leaves the taxpayer $15,309.08 short.[25]

Why didn't the W. Alton Jones Foundation step up to the cashier with its deep pockets and pay for their grantee's mischief? It's not clear. If we can believe their brochures, Mr. Riverwind had been invited to take their money and use it for "foundation-defined initiatives." Well, whose work product was the blockade, anyway?

The Jones Foundation wasn't just a trusting donor that offered money to a man who later had an embarrassing run-in with the law. Before they financed Riverwind's group they were well aware that he had a previous arrest record (for disrupting and occupying a National Forest Supervisor's office in Seattle, Washington, on May 30, 1990), as did other grant recipients: Mike Peterson, now of Kettle Range Conservation Group, Mitch Friedman, now of Northwest Ecosystem

Alliance, and Phil Knight, co-founder of the Predator Project, had been arrested in the July 5, 1988 Earth First! occupation of the Okanogan National Forest headquarters. That pattern alone is noteworthy.[26]

Could it be that their indifference to certain legal niceties was the *reason why* the W. Alton Jones Foundation gave them grants?

And another thing: The W. Alton Jones Foundation grant to Tim Coleman's Kettle Range Conservation Group—"To protect ancient forests and conduct forest watch activities in the Columbia River highlands of northwest Washington state"—doesn't mention sending two foundation men from headquarters in Virginia to intimidate Ferry County commissioner Jim Hall out of keeping his campaign promises to support natural resource production. You just have to know what "protecting ancient forests" means in foundationese.

Artful grant descriptions aside, it's fairly clear from these sample grants that W. Alton Jones Foundation doesn't want anybody logging or mining much of anywhere—certainly not in rural Washington state.

But how can Tim Coleman's little group do such economic damage? Even with a big foundation's money behind it?

It can't. Not alone, anyway.

Remember, other groups filed appeals on the Okanogan and Colville National Forests, too. And they had wealthy foundations pulling their strings, too. In a highly organized and coordinated fashion.

It's interesting to see the pattern of funding behind all these groups:

Kettle Range Conservation Group (Republic, Washington); EIN 943175114; Income: $81,635 Assets: $49,507 Last filed: Feb 1997 Exempt since July 1996.

Sample Grants:

1997 $10,000 Bullitt Foundation.

1996 $15,000 Brainerd Foundation. To protect the roadless areas and ancient forests of the Okanogan, Kettle and Columbia Highlands regions of north-central Washington and south-central British Columbia, and to support development and dissemination of restoration guidelines for recovery of bull trout.

1996 $1,500 Brainerd Foundation. Hardware and Technical Assistance grant.

1996 $18,000 W. Alton Jones Foundation, Inc. To protect forests and conduct forest watch activities in Colville and Okanogan National Forests.

1996 $11,500 Bullitt Foundation. To oversee management activities on private, state and federal lands in north central and eastern Washington and south central British Columbia.

1995 $18,450 W. Alton Jones Foundation, Inc. To protect ancient forest and conduct forest watch activities in Colville and Okanogan National Forests.

1994 $18,450 W. Alton Jones Foundation, Inc. To monitor forestry practices in the Colville and Okanogan National Forests.

Northwest Ecosystem Alliance (NWEA) FORMERLY: (1995) Greater Ecosystem Alliance. 1421 Cornwall Ave., Ste. 201, Bellingham, WA 98225-4519 USA. PHONE: (360) 671-9950 FAX: (360) 671-8429 E-MAIL: nwea@ecosystem.org Mitch Friedman, Exec.Dir. FOUNDED: 1989. MEMBERS: 1,900. MEMBERSHIP DUES: individual, $30 annual; family, $40 annual. STAFF: 5. INCOME: $246,632. ASSETS: $12,538. LAST FILED: Feb 1996. EXEMPT SINCE: Apr 1993. EIN 943091547.

DESCRIPTION: Protects and restores wildlands in the Pacific Northwest and supports such efforts in British Columbia. The Alliance bridges science and advocacy, working with activists, policymakers, and the general public to conserve our natural heritage. TELECOMMUNICATION SERVICES: website, http://www.pacificrim.net/~nwea. PUBLICATIONS: Cascadia Wild; Protecting an International Ecosystem. PRICE: $12.95. Northwest Conservation: News and Priorities, quarterly. Newsletter. PRICE: included in membership dues; $30.00/year for nonmembers. CIRCULATION: 3,000. [Encyclopedia of Associations]

Sample grants:

1998 $30,000 Bullitt Foundation

1998 Brainerd Foundation: $20,000 to support monitoring and evaluation of federal, state and private land management plans for the Westside forests of Washington and Oregon.

1997 $41,000 Bullitt Foundation

1997 Brainerd Foundation. $20,000 to protect the integrity of Washington State's territorial ecosystems through litigation, public education and innovative advocacy efforts focused on roadless areas, salmon and wildlife, municipal watersheds, Habitat Conservation Plans and the Loomis State Forest.

1996 $35,000 W. Alton Jones Foundation, Inc.

1996 $35,000 Bullitt Foundation.

1996 $10,000 Bullitt Foundation.

1993 $35,000 Bullitt Foundation. For Northwest Forests program.

1992 $10,000 Foundation for Deep Ecology. For general support.

Okanogan Highlands Alliance; EIN 911571661 Income: $50,783 Assets: $32,461; Last filed: Feb 1996; Exempt since Jan 1993.

Sample grants:

1997 $15,000 Brainerd Foundation. To support continued efforts to challenge the permitting of an open-pit, cyanide-leach gold mine, and to empower its rural community and the state to hold the green line against a large, multinational mining corporation.

1996 $10,000 Brainerd Foundation. For a public education and outreach effort concerning a proposed cyanide leach open-pit gold mine on Buckhorn Mountain.

1996 $30,000 Bullitt Foundation. To challenge Battle Mountain Gold Company's proposal for open-pit, cyanide-leach gold mine in Okanogan Highlands

1994 $35,000 Bullitt Foundation. To challenge proposed development of first large, open-pit cyanide-leach gold mine in Washington.

Inland Empire Public Lands Council; Income: $321,673; Assets: $60,388; Last filed: Feb 1997; Exempt since May 1994.

Sample grants:

1997 $35,000 Bullitt Foundation.

1996 $25,000 W. Alton Jones Foundation, Inc. To raise public awareness about links between destructive logging practices and lead contamination in Coeur d'Alene basin, and to increase citizen participation in restoration efforts for watershed.

1996 $40,000 Bullitt Foundation. For Forest Watch program.

1995 $40,000 W. Alton Jones Foundation, Inc. To monitor U.S. Forest Service activities in inland Columbia River basin.

1995. $20,000 Turner Foundation.

1995 $10,000 Compton Foundation, Inc. For Forest Watch Program.

1994 $10,000 Compton Foundation, Inc.

1994 $40,000 W. Alton Jones Foundation, Inc. For legal advocacy on behalf of national forests east of Cascades in Washington and Idaho.

1994 $50,000 Bullitt Foundation. For Forest Watch program to train citizens to monitor U.S. Forest Service activities in national forests.

1993 $40,000 W. Alton Jones Foundation, Inc. To establish full-time legal services program to serve grassroots forest conservation efforts in four-state inland Pacific Northwest.

The Predator Project, Bozeman, Montana. Income $220,273; Assets 36,675.

Sample grants:

1997 $15,000 Turner Foundation.

1996 $15,000 Henry P. Kendall Foundation. To complete final phase of ecosystem-wide inventory of road densities and decreasing habitat security for wildlife in Greater Yellowstone Ecosystem.

1996 $10,000 Foundation for Deep Ecology. For general support.
1996 $15,000 Turner Foundation.
1995 $6,000 Turner Foundation.
1994 $10,000 Bullitt Foundation. To compile data and lay out procedural groundwork necessary to help activists force closure of inappropriate and illegal roads in selected national forests of Northern Rockies and Greater Northwest.

Washington Wilderness Coalition, Seattle WA. 1997 Income $405,706; Assets $4,011.
Sample grants:
1996 $20,000 Bullitt Foundation. To expand organization's grassroots outreach activities to reach broad cross-section of public.
1993 $27,500 Bullitt Foundation. For Northwest Forests program.

Sierra Club, San Francisco, CA. 1997 Income $56,797,289 Assets $28,787,350. **Sierra Club Foundation**, San Francisco, CA. 1997 Assets $30,087,104 Income $34,113,541. **Earthjustice Legal Defense Fund** (formerly Sierra Club Legal Defense Fund), San Francisco, CA. 1997 Income $14,059,266 Assets $13,457,757.
Sierra Club sample grants cannot be evaluated because Sierra Club chapters such as the Cascades Chapter, which filed the rural Washington appeals, are semi-autonomous and have only limited access to the huge sums in the parent organization and its related groups.[29]

Some interesting patterns appear in the grants that these appeal-writers get. You no doubt noticed that certain names show up more than once. And they're only connected to grants that sound wonderful in foundationese, but have no effect other than rural cleansing, eradication of timber and mining and ranching and other natural resource industries.

Names like W. Alton Jones Foundation, Bullitt Foundation, Turner Foundation. Year after year. Almost like they were deliberately trying to destroy rural goods producing economies.

It's worth a quick look at one of them: the Bullitt Foundation, based in Seattle, Washington. It was established in 1952 by Dorothy S. Bullitt, real-estate mogul, member of so many boards that her resume reads like a Seattle history text, and founder of King Broadcasting Company, the local NBC affiliate. When Bullitt died in 1989, her two daughters, Harriet Stimson Bullitt and Priscilla ("Patsy") Bullitt Collins, privileged children of a Northwest legend, took over the foundation with other family members and turned it to a single-minded purpose:

The foundation has one primary goal: to protect and restore the natural physical environment of the Pacific Northwest. The foundation prefers to fund projects that leverage resources, show possibilities for multiplier effects, address priority needs where government fails, and show discernible impact.[30]

These people who never had to work for their money now have assets in excess of $103,000,000 and income of $9,772,795 (from investments) of which they gave away $5,064,200 in 1998 to the following list:

1000 Friends of Oregon
1000 Friends of Washington
10,000 Years Institute
Adopt-A-Stream
Alaska Center for the Environment
Alaska Clean Water Alliance
Alaska Conservation Alliance
Alaska Conservation Foundation (Alaska Rainforest Campaign)
Alaska Institute for Sustainable Recreation and Tourism
Alliance for Education
Alliance for Justice
Alliance to Save Energy
Alpine Lakes Protection Society
Alternative Energy Resource Organization
American Lands Alliance
American Lung Association of Washington
American Rivers
Bellingham Bay Aquarium
BC Environmental Network Educational Foundation
BC Spaces for Nature
BC Wild
BC Wild (Gowgaia Institute Society)
BC Wild (Nakina Center for Aboriginal Learning and Living)
Better Environmentally Sound Transportation
Bicycle Transportation Alliance
Cabinet Resource Group
Canby High School
CCHW: Center for Health, Environment and Justice
Center for Environmental Citizenship
Center for Environmental Law and Policy
Center for Marine Conservation
Center for Natural Resource Policy
Center for Science in Public Participation
Central Area Development Association
Central Cascades Alliance
Chehalis River Council (Friends of Grays Harbor)
Citizens for a Better Flathead
Citizens for a Healthy Bay
Citizens for Sensible Transportation
Clark County Citizens in Action
Clark Fork-Pend Oreille Coalition
Clayoquot Biosphere Project
Coast Range Association
Colorado Audubon Council
Columbia Basin Institute
Columbia Basin Institute (Cascadia Times)
Columbia-Pacific Resource Conservation
Columbia River United
Communities United for People (Workers Organizing Committee)
Community Coalition for Environmental Justice
Community Networking Technologies
Concilio for the Spanish Speaking
Conservation Biology Institute
Consultative Group on Biological Diversity
Corporation for the Northern Rockies
CUB Educational Fund
David Suzuki Foundation
Desktop Assistance
Down Home Project
Earth Day Network
Earth Island Institute (Whales Alive)
Earthjustice Legal Defense Fund
East Kootenay Environmental Society
Ecology Center
Ecotrust Canada
Environmental Coalition of South Seattle
Environmental Defense Fund
Environmental Fund of BC
Environmental Justice Action Group
Evangelicals for Social Action (Green Cross)
Evergreen Land Trust (River Farm Community Land Trust)
First Nations Development Institute
Flathead Lakers
Food Alliance
Forest Service Employees for Environmental Ethics
Free Ride Zone
Friends of Clark County
Friends of Clayoquot Sound
Friends of Eugene
Friends of Skagit County
Friends of the Bitterroot
Friends of the Cedar River Watershed
Friends of the Columbia Gorge
Friends of the Earth
Friends of the San Juans
Gallatin Institute
Georgetown Crime Prevention and Community Council

Georgia Strait Alliance
Global Rivers Environmental Education
    Network
Government Accountability Project
Great Bear Foundation
Greater Yellowstone Coalition
Green/Duwamish Watershed Alliance
Green Fire Productions
Hanford Education Action League
Headwaters
Heart of America Northwest Research Center
Hells Canyon Preservation Council
Henry's Fork Foundation
Hoh Indian Tribe
Idaho Conservation League
Idaho Rivers United
Idaho Rural Council
Idaho Sporting Congress
Idaho Watersheds Project
Idaho Wildlife Federation
Institute for Fisheries Resources
Institute for New Economics Public Interest
    Research Association
Interrain Pacific
Issaquah Alps Trails Club
KCTS Television
Kentucky Environmental Foundation
    (Chemical Weapons Group)
Kettle Range Conservation Group
Kiket Bay Organization
Kitchen Garden Project
Land and Water Fund of the Rockies
Land Conservancy of Seattle and King County
Land Trust Alliance
Lands Council
League of Conservation Voters Education Fund
Leavenworth Audubon Adopt-a-Forest
Lewis and Clark College
    (Northwest School of Law, Pacific
    Environmental Advocacy Center)
LightHawk
Long Live the Kings
Lower Columbia Basin Audubon Society
    (Save the Reach)
Marine Conservation Biology Institute
Marine Life Sanctuaries Society of British
    Columbia
Mason County Community Development
    Council
Mineral Policy Center
Ministry of Saints Martha and Mary
Montana Environmental Information Center
Montana Environmental Information Center
    (Rock Creek Alliance)
Montana Wilderness Association
Montana Wildlife Federation
Nanakila Institute
National Audubon Society
National Audubon Society (Columbia River
    Bioregion Campaign)

National Audubon Society (Western Mining
    Action Project)
National Wildlife Federation (Alaska Office)
National Wildlife Federation (Pacific
    Northwest Office)
Native Forest Council
Natural Resources Defense Council
Nature Conservancy of Idaho
Nature Conservancy of Oregon
Nature Conservancy of Washington
Next Step Association
Nonprofit Risk Management Center
Northwest Bicycle Federation
Northwest Coalition for Alternatives to
    Pesticides
Northwest Council on Climate Change
Northwest Earth Institute
Northwest EcoBuilding Guild
Northwest Ecosystem Alliance
Northwest Energy Coalition
Northwest Environment Watch
Northwest Environmental Advocates
Northwest Renewable Resources Center
Okanogan Highlands Alliance
Olympic Environmental Council
Olympic Peninsula Foundation
Oregon Environmental Council
Oregon League of Conservation Voters
    Education Fund
Oregon Natural Desert Association
Oregon Natural Resources Council Fund
Oregon Trout
Oregon Water Trust
Orlo Foundation
OSPIRG Foundation
Pacific Environment and Resources Center
Pacific Forest Trust
Pacific Rivers Council
Palouse-Clearwater Environmental Institute
    (Idaho Smart Growth)
People for Puget Sound
Pilchuck Audubon Society
Portland Art Museum (Rainbow Video &
    Film Productions)
Portland Audubon Society
Portland State University Foundation
    (Columbia/Pacific Institute)
Portland State University Foundation
    (Center for Watershed & Community
    Health)
Predator Project
Public Employees for Environmental
    Responsibility
Puget Soundkeeper Alliance
Rails to Trails Conservancy
Raincoast Conservation Foundation
Rainforest Action Network
RE Sources
Regulatory Assistance Project
Renewable Northwest Project

River Network
Rivers Council of Washington
Rocky Mountain Institute
Round River Conservation Studies
Save Our Wild Salmon Coalition
Sawtooth Society
Sea Resources
Seattle Audubon Society
Seattle Tilth Association
Seaview Coastal Conservation Coalition
Sierra Club Foundation
Sierra Club of Western Canada Foundation
Sierra Legal Defence Fund
Silva Forest Foundation
Siskiyou Regional Education Project
Skagitonians to Preserve Farmland
Snake River Alliance Education Fund
Soda Mountain Wilderness Council
Solar Energy Society of Canada
St. Vincent de Paul Society of Lane County
Stillaguamish Citizens' Alliance
Student Conservation Association
Surface Transportation Policy Project
Sustainable Communities Northwest
Sustainable Fisheries Foundation
Tahoma Audubon Society
Technical Assistance for Community Services
Thoreau Institute
Tides Center (Environmental Media Services)
Tides Center (Environmental Working Group)
Tides Center (Honor the Earth Fund)
Tides Center (Northwest Jewish Environmental Project)
Tides Center (ONE/Northwest)
Tides Center (Pacific Biodiversity Institute)
Tongass Conservation Society
TREEmendous Seattle
Trout Unlimited
Trust for Public Land (Cedar River Associates)
Tualatin Riverkeepers
United Vision for Idaho
University of Washington, Center for Urban Horticulture

Urban League of Portland
Valhalla Wilderness Society
Washington Citizen Action Education and Research Fund
Washington Coalition for Transportation Alternatives
Washington Council for Fair Elections
Washington Environmental Alliance for Voter Education
Washington Environmental Council
Washington Native Plant Society
Washington Physicians for Social Responsibility
Washington Public Interest Research Group Foundation
Washington State Catholic Conference
Washington State University at Vancouver
Washington Toxics Coalition
Washington Trout
Washington Wilderness Coalition
Washington Wildlife and Recreation Foundation
Waste Action Project
WaterWatch of Oregon
Wenatchee Valley College
Western Canada Wilderness Committee
Western Environmental Law Center
Western States Center
Wilderness Society
Wilderness Society (ForestWater Alliance)
Wilderness Watch
Wildlands Center for Preventing Roads
Wildlands Project
Wildlands Project (Yellowstone to Yukon Conservation Initiative)
Wildlife Conservation Society
Willamette Riverkeeper
Willamette Valley Law Project
Women's Voices for the Earth
World Media Foundation
World Resources Institute
Zero Population Growth, Seattle Chapter

That's a lot of people wanting to end natural resource extraction in rural America. But that long list explains a good deal of how little outfits like the Kettle Range Conservation Group can have a devastating effect on rural economies. They have friends. Coordinated, orchestrated friends.

Harriet Bullitt and Patsy Bullitt Collins, orchestrators, are classic patricians, world's best directors of everybody else's lives, intolerant of opposing views, determined to retire the resource class.

Patsy tells the story about going as a child during the 1930s to a bee farm in Woodinville, a tiny town near Seattle: "I used to go sit in the woods with a friend and try to go to Nirvana," Patsy says. "We'd close our eyes and say, 'Ommm.' At our 50th reunion, we both remembered that and I asked her, 'Did we really get there, to Nirvana?' And she said, 'Yes, it's just that we never came back.' Now I go to Woodinville and I get lost. It's a suburb. Where's the little bee farm? This is very silly and romantic, I suppose, but it is a part of our life. When you see something and then it's gone, you say, 'Does it all have to go?'"

Harriet is just as determined as she looks out from her houseboat on Seattle's Lake Union (*Sleepless In Seattle* was filmed nearby). She can see across the water to where her grandfather's timber company clearcut a forest to build the Ballard section of town. Her money came from cutting trees before it came from broadcasting.

"We grew up around big cedars and clear water," she says. "When it begins to change it's like a disaster happening to your family."[33a]

Harriet is infuriated at the idea of anybody else cutting trees.

That's the Bullitt sisters. Their philanthropy is pure revenge.

Rural cleansing. Destroy rural America to save it.

Even the Seattle Times, itself owned by Seattle nobility (the Blethen family), had to comment—politely, of course—about how batty, dogmatic and even rabid the Bullitt sisters could be in their environmental crusade:

> They were raised in the sheltered atmosphere of the old Seattle aristocracy, and it's no surprise that their view of the environment is romantic and simplistic. Even they admit it. Eccentric hobbies aside, they've been so elusive publicly that what does come as a surprise is that beneath the well-bred dignity and naivete, they're strong-willed and focused, perhaps even calculating, when it comes to their cause.[33b]

CIRCLING THE WAGONS

Rural families all over the Pacific Northwest say "Amen!" to that.

Traditionally, rural America has fought back with little citizen groups that pop up everywhere a new restriction is proposed. In the early 1990s, in the tiny town of Chesaw, Washington, a group called the Common Sense Resource League formed to counter out-of-town protests against Battle Mountain Gold Company's proposed new Crown Jewel gold mine nearby.

"This country was founded on mining and logging back 100 years ago when my grandfather homesteaded this land," said Bob Hirst, then-president of the League. Hirst, now in his early 70s, was elected an Okanogan County commissioner in 1998.[33c]

The conflict in Chesaw pitted loggers, ranchers and farmers, whose families settled the region, against big-city activists who allied themselves with a handful of back-to-the-land families that moved to Chesaw more than 20 years ago, but are still considered newcomers.

A local environmental group called the Okanogan Highlands Alliance (see chart, page 13) has conducted a campaign against the mine for years. The group's leader, David Kliegman, has in-depth contacts with big money: the Bullitt Foundation gave the group $25,000 in 1998 with the blunt comment, "The grant supports the organization's efforts to halt Battle Mountain Gold's proposed mine and prevent a precedent for chemical-leach mining in Washington State."

You can almost see Patsy crying over the bee farm.

When the Forest Service approved the Crown Jewel mine, Kliegman used the computer network of the environmental movement—funded in part by Seattle-based desktop-publishing millionaire Paul Brainerd (he created PageMaker)—to generate vociferous protests.

Brainerd is another story. We'll unfold that in the next chapter.

The conflict followed a well-worn pattern: environmentalists striving to generate a level of anxiety sufficient to kill the mine and demean Houston-based Battle Mountain; supporters touting the mine's safety features and economic benefits and bragging up Battle Mountain's excellent operating plan.

Ground has yet to be broken for the Crown Jewel mine.

Rural cleansing. Dismantling industrial civilization piece by piece.

Everywhere in rural Washington you'll find grassroots outfits with names such as the Upper Columbia Resource Council, the Ferry County Action League, and the Okanogan County Citizens Coalition (OC3).

Over the years, these local economy support groups have seen their hopes dashed time and again. They witness their communities and way of life being systematically destroyed and they have no power to stop it. The conflicts have gone on for so long and taken such a disastrous toll that rural economy support activists who were once fired up and eager to fight for community survival have given up in depression and despair.

Irene Hilderbrant, a logger's wife in Ferry County, wrote in a 1998 note to a friend, "Unless you're living it, no one realizes the emotional strain on families fighting to make a living from natural resource jobs. With so many rules and regulations to live by, it's very hard to maintain an even keel, emotionally."[34]

Very hard. Especially when the hopes vanish.

In 1994, Phelps Dodge began the process of getting the McDonald Gold Project approved near Lincoln, Montana, but was so daunted by environmentalist protests by 1997 that it sold out to a little company without the resources to complete the permit process. The permit process halted when new owner, Canyon Resources, fell behind on its payments for the required environmental-impact statement. Montanans then passed a ballot initiative in 1998 that prohibited construction of mines using the cyanide process, an initiative orchestrated by out-of-state environmental groups and funded behind the scenes by their foundation supporters.[35a]

Mining heavyweight Noranda "mothballed" the copper-rich Montanore Mine project near Libby, Montana after it was cleared by federal authorities but underwent a debilitating appeal by environmental groups. The proposed mine passed one regulatory hurdle after another, yet faltered because of a concentrated campaign by grant-driven environmental groups such as the Mineral Policy Center, which is supported by prescriptive private foundations, including the Pew Charitable Trusts and the Rockefeller Family Fund.[35b]

Newmont Gold similarly gave up its Grassy Mountain Mine in Oregon after a campaign by Oregon Natural Resources Council, backed with money from the Bullitt Foundation and other wealthy supporters, placed an anti-mining initiative on the 1994 state ballot. Newmont spent $3.5 million fighting the initiative, which was killed by Oregon voters, allowing the company to continue exploring the property. In 1996 Newmont abandoned the project, taking a $33.8 million write-off for the losses it entailed. They said a new survey didn't find as much gold as they originally estimated, but insiders say they simply wanted out of the environmentalists' crosshairs.[35c]

With these rich rural cleansing foundations behind the scenes all over the country to block forestry and mining and farming and ranching, you'd be inclined to think they get together and strategize it.

They do.

STRINGS

It's called the Environmental Grantmakers Association. EGA is an informal unincorporated association of some 200 foundations and donor programs. It is the power elite of environmentalism. Many of the environmental movement's programs are designed by EGA member foundations, not by the organizations we commonly think of as environmental groups. Collectively, EGA members give over half a billion dollars each year to environmental groups.

That's a good start on total enviromania.

Let's see a little of how they do it.

Maine sits squarely in the middle of the nation's urban-rural prosperity gap list, tied for 25th place with Michigan. Maine has very little federal land, and therefore its rural areas should have very little problem with grant-driven environmentalists and the prescriptive foundations behind them, right?

Wrong again.

A consortium of thirty-five environmental groups is trying to nationalize and de-develop huge chunks of Maine—and New Hampshire and Vermont and upstate New York—so there will be 26 million acres of federal land there.

Preposterous? Not a bit.

The Northern Forest Alliance is the name of the consortium, and their stated goal is: "To achieve a sustainable future for the 26-million-acre Northern Forest, in which its Wildlands are permanently protected, its forests are sustainably managed, and its local economies and communities are strong and vibrant."[36a]

If that sounds a lot like foundationese, read on.

A little background helps.

The idea for the Northern Forest Alliance came from a 1982 National Park Service report. It proposed the federalization of twenty-seven huge "landscapes" in "The Northern Forest." The Park Service gave its "landscapes" such names as the "Catskills" in New York, the "Northeast Kingdom" in New Hampshire and Vermont, the "North Woods" and the "Washington County Coast" in Maine. They wanted to do a big federal study.

That was in the Reagan years, and the Park Service realized they would not get money to plan a massive expansion of the same federal domain that the Reagan administration was busy trying to sell off. So they turned their project over to the National Parks and Conservation Association (NPCA), a private environmental group that was created in 1919 by Stephen Mather, the first Park Service director. Mather's purpose for the organization was to do things for the Park Service it could not do for itself, like create plans for a massive expansion of the federal domain.[36b]

In 1988 the NPCA completed its work, unveiling the grand plan for wholesale federalization of the Northern Forest as well as other areas of the country. The plan urged "mega-conservation reserves in the northeast" and proposed eight huge new national parks in the Northern Forest.

Realizing that locals would not likely welcome a federal takeover, the NPCA called New England the "conservation challenge of the 1990's." Environmental groups then used the NPCA plan as a map as they lobbied for a government study. In late 1988 they convinced Congress to authorize a Northern Forest Land Study to be conducted by a Northern Forest Lands Council, largely staffed by Forest Service bureaucrats. Congress also authorized the Forest Legacy Program, which made the affected states eligible for federal acquisition monies to purchase conservation easements, which are agreements not to develop your property.

The Council and the study and the Legacy Program generated explosive controversy. Ask Erich Veyhl of Concord, Massachusetts, who organized homeowners on the Maine coast. Or ask Bob Voight of Lubec, Maine, who co-founded Maine Conservation Rights Institute. They've both been fighting to keep private lands in private hands since these land-taking proposals first surfaced. They had plenty to fight.

In 1990, Michael Kellett, the Wilderness Society's New England director, told a Tufts University audience about the 26-million acre Northern Forest, "I think it's likely this will all end up, most of this will end up being public land, not by taking away, but that will probably be really the only alternative."[37]

Then, Brock Evans, a vice president of the National Audubon Society, told the Tufts audience, "For a century, I think it's safe to say, timber companies up there have owned all 26 million acres. Once it was all public domain, then it went to the private domain where it's been for a very long time. I don't agree that we can't get it all back. You have lots of strong urban centers where support comes from. We should get all of it. Be unreasonable. You can do it."

Two Americas.

Urban America.

Rural America.

Save rural America from the people who live there.

Rural cleansing.

Today more than thirty environmental groups are being unreasonable in the Northern Forest Alliance. They include:

1) The Adirondack Council; 2) Appalachian Mountain Club; 3) Appalachian Trail Conference; 4) Association for the Protection of the Adirondacks; 5) Conservation Law Foundation; 6) Defenders of Wildlife; 7) Garden Club of America; 8) Good Wood Alliance; 9) Green Mountain Club; 10) Green Mountain Forest Watch; 11) Maine Audubon Society; 12) National Audubon Society; 13) National Wildlife Federation; 14) Natural Resources Council of Maine; 15) Natural Resources Defense Council; 16) New England Forestry Foundation; 17) New Hampshire Rivers Council; 18) New Hampshire Wildlife Federation; 19) New York League of Conservation Voters; 20) New York Rivers United; 21) Residents' Committee to Protect the Adirondacks; 22) Sierra Club; 23) Sierra Student Coalition; 24) Student Environmental Action Coalition; 25) Trout Unlimited—Basil Woods Jr. Chapter; 26) Trust for Public Land; 27) Vermont Alliance of Conservation Voters; 28) Vermont Audubon Council; 29) Vermont Land Trust; 30) Vermont Natural Resources Council; 31) The Wilderness Society; 32) World Wildlife Fund.

To the public, it's not at all apparent what role foundations had in making the Northern Forest Alliance happen. On the face of it, the Alliance seems like a spontaneous, if remarkably unusual, gathering of organizations with sometimes competing goals and always competing needs for funding.

If you had been a fly on the wall at the Environmental Grantmakers Association annual retreat in October 1992, you would have heard a foundation man named Chuck Clusen explain the Northern Forest Alliance to other foundation leaders, beginning with his personal background, which is also useful for our own understanding:

"Well, during the 1970s and '80s," said Clusen, "I was involved as an advocate in a great number of forest issues in large part dealing with wilderness. I started at the Sierra Club where I was for eight years. Then I was Vice President for Programs at the Wilderness Society for eight years. I also was greatly involved in the Alaska lands. I led the Alaska Lands Coalition during the lands fight in the late '70s and 1980s. And in the late '80s I spent a period of time in the Adirondacks. I was the Executive Director of the Adirondack Council. So my background is advocacy, it's public lands, it's land use regulations and so forth. Now for three years I've been with the American Conservation Association, which is a foundation. It's Laurance Rockefeller's foundation. He has specialized over the many years in sort of land use kinds of issues.

"In any case, the environmental community across these four states, which really did not have a history of collaboration, has come together in a very large coalition called the Northern Forest Alliance, and now [1992] has I think 28 organizations. It has the major national groups as well as all the principal state groups in these four states.

"And I've been working with them over the last year and a half. One, on their development of political strategies and so on. But also to facilitate their development of a campaign plan very similar to the Alaska situation as to a campaign that will probably go on for at least a decade."[38]

Not so spontaneous.

Although the Northern Forest Alliance has an office in Montpelier, Vermont, The Appalachian Mountain Club has acted as its fiscal agent and has received many foundation grants for the Alliance, hiding a lot of money from public view. The history of these grants is revealing. Study them a little. It's their own words.

1990 **Jessie B. Cox Charitable Trust** gave $60,000 "To develop site-specific strategy for long-term protection of New England's northern forests."

1991   **American Conservation Association, Inc.** gave $35,000 "For pro-
tection of northern forest lands of Maine, New Hampshire, Vermont
and New York."

Jessie B. Cox Charitable Trust gave $50,000 "For second-year
support of Northern Forest Lands Project, effort to develop site-spe-
cific strategy for long-term protection of New England's northern
forests."

1992   **Surdna Foundation, Inc.** gave $100,000 "For continued support
of Northern Forest Alliance, collaboration of leading New England
and national conservation organizations to preserve northern forest
lands."

American Conservation Association, Inc. gave $15,000 "For pro-
tection of northern forest lands of Maine, New Hampshire, Vermont
and New York."

Jessie B. Cox Charitable Trust gave $40,000 "For final grant for
Northern Forest Lands Project, effort to develop site specific strategy for long-term protection of New England's northern forests."

The John Merck Fund gave $65,000 "For Grassroots Action Project
which assists environmental organizations in northern New England
in developing more effective alliances with local communities and
with interest groups outside traditional environmental movement."

1993   **Geraldine Rockefeller Dodge Foundation, Inc.** gave $25,000 "To
help coordinate and provide direction for newly founded Northern
Forest Alliance, coalition of conservation organizations seeking to
create sustainable management plan for Northern Forest."

Richard King Mellon Foundation gave $50,000 "To create system
of protecting wildlands, promoting sustainable forests and supporting local economies while insuring ecological sustainability."

The John Merck Fund gave $135,000 "For continued support of
Grassroots Action Project, which helps environmental organizations
in northern New England develop more effective alliances with local
constituencies."

1994   **The Pew Charitable Trusts** gave $350,000 "For matching grant for
Campaign for the Northern Forests to establish forest reserves in
northern New England and New York."

Compton Foundation, Inc. gave $25,000 for unspecified support.

Moriah Fund gave $70,000 "For data gathering and analyses of
biodiversity and land use in U.S. Northern Forests and for Northern
Forest Alliance to protect natural resources and strengthen community economies."

The John Merck Fund gave $50,000 "For continued support of

Grassroots Action Project, which helps environmental organizations in northern New England develop more effective alliances with other organizations."

1994   **Surdna Foundation, Inc.** gave $100,000 "For coordination of campaign by Northern Forest Alliance to preserve Northern Forest Lands."

Jessie B. Cox Charitable Trust gave $100,000 "For central office operations and for outreach program. Grant made through Appalachian Mountain Club."

1995   **The John Merck Fund** gave $25,000 "To evaluate involvement with communities in Upper Androscoggin River area of Maine and New Hampshire to develop strategies for stabilizing local economy and protecting high-quality forest and water resources."

The John Merck Fund gave $50,000 "Toward launching Androscoggin Valley Project, which is aimed at increasing community involvement in local conservation projects and at assisting communities in developing strategies for sustainable economic diversification and job creation."

Richard King Mellon Foundation gave $50,000 "Toward Northern Forest Land Project to protect ecological resources."

Geraldine Rockefeller Dodge Foundation, Inc. gave $25,000 "To continue grassroots and education efforts to protect natural and human communities of Northern Forest."

Jessie B. Cox Charitable Trust gave $150,000 "For continued support of central office operations and state caucus outreach and organizing activities. Grant made through Appalachian Mountain Club."

1996   **Jessie B. Cox Charitable Trust** gave $125,000 "For final grant for outreach, organizing and communications activities of Alliance state caucuses in Maine, New Hampshire and Vermont and for central office. Grant made through Appalachian Mountain Club."

Moriah Fund gave $65,000 "To promote protection and sustainable use of Northern Forests and for Northern Forest Alliance."

The Pew Charitable Trusts gave $400,000 "For campaign to establish public forest reserves in northern New England and New York."

The John Merck Fund gave $50,000 "For Androscoggin Valley Project, which seeks to increase community involvement in local conservation projects and to assist communities in rural area along Maine-New Hampshire border in developing strategies for sustainable economic diversification and job creation."

Weeden Foundation gave $10,000 "For continued support for protection of Northern Forest of New England."

1997 **Geraldine R. Dodge Foundation, Inc.** gave $15,000 "For general support for Northern Forest Alliance, coalition of conservation organizations creating sustainable management plan for 26-million-acre Northern Forest."

Weeden Foundation gave $10,000 "For continued support for overall coordination and implementation of Campaign for the Northern Forest."[41a]

That's foundationese.

It's also $2.2 million that's almost impossible to trace. And that's only the part that *could* be traced. There's probably twice that much undetected. Some went straight to the Northern Forest Alliance. Most of it went through the Appalachian Mountain Club. From foundations prescribing social change in their glass towers. From foundations with the intent to federalize and de-develop 26 million acres of New England.

Yet you'd never know it reading the grants.

Part of the reason is that a very intelligent man figured out early that the bold "take it all back" arrogance of Brock Evans and his ilk was generating serious community resentment all over New England. His name is Francis W. Hatch, chairman of the John Merck Fund, a private foundation based on the pharmaceutical fortune.

You see his grants up and down the last few pages. You see close coordination between Merck and the Jessie B. Cox Foundation (the Wall Street Journal money). They're both based in Boston, and their leaders talk to each other. You see a whopping $350,000 in 1994 from the Pew Charitable Trusts and another $400,000 Pew grant in 1996. You see certain names such as Surdna several times. They're all members of the Environmental Grantmakers Association. They all agreed with Hatch.

Hatch realized that the wise use movement could stop the "big park" approach dead in its tracks. So he got the local environmental groups together and told them to change course, to dress like lambs, not lions, and use indirect means to get the land out of commodity production and into permanent wilderness preserves. It meant wiping some egg off their faces, but it also meant victory where none could otherwise be had.

Cold, calculated, relentless green greed.

And they're pulling it off.

On March 3, 1999, the New England Forestry Foundation (NEFF, 1997 income, $1,870,237, assets $16,881,228) announced that the wealthy industrialists of the Pingree Family would sell them the development rights to 754,673 acres of northern Maine forestland—approximately 80 percent of their land-for $28 million.[41b]

The conservation easement "prohibits all structural development and promotes sustainable forest management." It is not clear if "sustainable forest management" includes timber harvest at commercial levels.

It was the largest forestry restriction project of its kind ever attempted, an area twenty percent larger than the state of Rhode Island.

It also reflects a Hatch strategy of buy-it-first-then-sell-it-to-the-government perfected during the 1970s by the Nature Conservancy.

Join the American Farm Bureau in thinking about conservation easements for a second: You retain title to the land, but you have sold important rights to use it. You obtain a tax write off immediately and lower taxes thereafter. In the near term, the cash and the tax benefits are good for the land owner. But what happens if you or your heirs cannot afford those lower taxes any more? Or when the time comes to sell your land? Who would buy land that has a hampered use or income stream? The government, of course.[42]

In December of 1998, the Conservation Fund purchased over 300,000 acres from Champion International in New Hampshire, Vermont, and New York and pursued state, federal and private funding to close the deal.

A few weeks later, the Nature Conservancy announced the purchase of 185,000 acres along Maine's St. John River from International Paper, adjacent to the Pingree lands. A high Nature Conservancy official, Daniel R. Efroymson, is also vice-president of the Moriah Fund, whose grants are listed on pages 39 and 40.

The Champion and International Paper lands are outright purchases, one already looking for government owners.

Bob Perschel, chairman of the Northern Forest Alliance and Northeast Regional Director for the Wilderness Society, said of the Pingree purchase, "It's the soul-satisfying sound of another big piece of the Northern Forest puzzle clicking into place."

What satisfies Perschel's Boston-based soul terrifies the rural souls who will feel the impact of "sustainable" forest management.

Mary Adams of Garland, Maine, has become a local legend for taking on the huge apparatus of environmentalism with activism, newsletters and a popular website.

Adams said, "I'm happy for the Pingrees. Still, they remind me of the Boston ladies who told a milliner, 'We don't have to buy hats. We have our hats.' The Pingrees have their fortune.

"But the people who have to go out and buy wood to supply their mills are about frantic. They're already having trouble finding timber that's not locked up. I'm afraid we're going to be faced with what I call 'wine and cheese' logging—what some urbanite thinks logging is when he has a wine glass in his hand and doesn't have a payroll to make."[43a]

Rural cleansing. Dismantling industrial civilization piece by piece.

POWER

While it's true that the power and pressure of grant-driven environmental groups and prescriptive private foundations can begin the dismantling of industrial civilization in rural America, it takes the force of government to finish the job.

The Northern Forest project, for example, would be impossible without the help of activist federal employees: High-ranking administration appointees who made sure the right people got on staff, Forest Service personnel who staffed the Northern Forest Lands Council, Park Service personnel who contributed to the Northern Forests Lands Study, lower-level technical employees who gave special access to their environmental soul-mates and none to natural resource workers and property rights defenders.

Then there are the government grants.

What? Government gives money to private environmental groups?

Yes, by the billions.

For example, several members of the Northern Forest Alliance received grants from the Environmental Protection Agency: Appalachian Mountain Club, $5,000; National Wildlife Federation, $306,237; Natural Resources Defense Council, $749,301; Trout Unlimited, $24,000; Trust for Public Land, $30,000; World Wildlife Fund, $1,220,540.[43b]

Government officials feeding their pigs.

Who are all these government officials?

The average urban dweller runs into government officials mainly in the form of traffic cops. Things are different in rural America.

If your natural resource job lies within the boundaries of one of the 155 National Forests, you fall under the authority of the Forest Service, an agency of the U.S. Department of Agriculture, and a big landowner in rural America, even in the East, where National Forests are far more important to rural economies than urbanites imagine—ask Congressman John Peterson of Pennsylvania, where protesters have blocked hardwood chip mill operations—and even in prairie states such as Kansas, Nebraska, and Oklahoma because the Forest Service administers the 19 National Grasslands, too.

If you're a rancher who owns grazing rights in federal lands, you may fall under the authority of the Bureau of Land Management, an agency of the Department of the Interior—and in some cases, the Forest Service, too, since it manages a patchwork of arid lands in the West.

If you're a farmer and you use irrigation water, you probably fall under the authority of the Bureau of Reclamation, an Interior Department agency that regulates dams and water flows.

If an endangered species shows up where you work or even on your private property, you definitely fall under the authority of the U.S. Fish and Wildlife Service (USFWS), an Interior Department agency. You could also get a call from the National Marine Fisheries Service (NMFS), part of the National Oceanic and Atmospheric Administration, an agency of the Department of Commerce—USFWS and NMFS both have responsibilities in enforcing the Endangered Species Act.

If wetlands come into the picture, count on seeing the Army Corps of Engineers and the Environmental Protection Agency.

If you happen to own land that has become surrounded by one of the national parks created since 1872, you're an "inholder," and will feel the authority of the National Park Service, yet another Interior Department agency.

If you want to build a strip mine, you'll have to go through the Interior Department's Office of Surface Mining for two permits: a mining permit issued under the Surface Mining Act, and a National Pollution Discharge Elimination System permit issued under the federal Clean Water Act, which also has to be approved by the Environmental Protection Agency.

If you already extract and sell minerals from a mine leased on federal lands, you'll pay the Interior Department's Minerals Management Service rent and royalties, as do nearly 70,000 leaseholders who pay about $4 billion a year, down from $10 billion a few years ago.

If you are beset with pests—insects, weeds, animals—and you use any kind of chemical pesticide—insecticides to protect your apple crop, herbicides to save the wheat from being crowded out, fungicides to keep potato crops from molding, whatever—the Environmental Protection Agency's Office of Pesticide Programs will tell you what you can and can't do, along with state agencies. And the EPA will show up on literally hundreds of other issues covering everything from too much dust in your parking lot to too little ozone above the Antarctic.

This is just the beginning of the bureaucracy brigade that rural Americans must deal with daily. There are a lot more agencies that can stop your paycheck with a word.

And some that try to take your property away from you without paying for it.

GOOD NIGHT, COWBOYS

Nevada is practically the bottom—Number 48—of the urban-rural prosperity gap chart, so you wouldn't expect its rural hinterlands to be suffering much, certainly not as much as Maine (#25), New Hampshire (#29), and Vermont (#41).

Wrong again.

Because most of those arid hinterlands are inhabited by self-employed ranchers and farmers who pay their few hired hands decent wages, there's not much unemployment to measure alongside the jobless of Las Vegas and Reno.

The Monitor Valley of central Nevada is a forbidding Great Basin desert to tourists but a lush mountain-held Eden to the folks who live there. And those ranchers and farmers out by Fallon and Tonopah are being hit hard by environmentalists just the same as elsewhere.

Only in this case the environmentalists work for the Forest Service and the Bureau of Land Management and the Bureau of Reclamation.

And they're using every regulation and every technicality they can devise to get rid of those ranchers and farmers.

George Benesch used to be a resource economist for the U.S. Forest Service's Toiyabe National Forest, which covers a good bit of central Nevada. Benesch is now an attorney specializing in water and grazing issues and represents beleaguered ranchers and farmers.[45]

He charges that the Forest Service is regularly deploying legal and administrative attacks for the purpose of getting privately owned resources away from U.S. citizens without paying them fair market prices.

They do it on two levels, Benesch says: Strategically, the federal government is trying to create broad new legal precedents in both state and federal law to nullify the water and range rights of families who have lived here for generations. Agencies want to "unify" the private water and grazing rights with the land, which belongs to the United States, and they don't want to pay for it.

Tactically, Forest Service officials routinely and knowingly subject individual ranchers and farmers to regulatory harassment designed to drive them off the range. Rural cleansing.

Ranchers find their fences cut—after the Forest Service notifies them that their cattle have strayed onto a forbidden area and must be retrieved at the cost of a heavy fine. Who cut the fences at just the wrong place?

Regulatory harassment more often tends toward clever Catch-22 situations. Say you're Duane Page, a fictitious rancher in Monitor Valley. You own Mine Creek Ranch, which is your private property with no federal ownership involved. You also own water rights and grazing rights on federal lands, a property arrangement known as a "split estate," meaning that the property rights are split between two owners, you and the federal government.

But you obey federal laws regulating grazing on split estate federal lands. One fine day in Spring you are told to keep your cattle on Mine Creek Allotment "A" for thirty calendar days, no more, no less. The grass runs out on day 28, as the agency knew it would because you told them so when they ordered your cattle there. A bureaucrat comes out on day 30 and finds you have overgrazed the range, and cuts the allowable size of your herd to "sustainable" levels, and insists you pay a heavy fine.

When you move your cattle to Allotment "B" you discover that the fence around your livestock watering tank has been smashed down because the water was needed for wild horses that are protected by the Wild Horses and Burros Protection Act of 1971. Your water has been consumed down to a level that endangers your cattle and you have to truck emergency water in.

Months later, in mid-January, an agency technician with a master's degree in conservation biology from Yale—but who can't identify milo maize when he sees it—comes to Allotment "C" for a range condition inspection. He finds the meadow—which was a sea of grass horse-belly high in June—is so grassless that you must not use it any more. You have destroyed the range, he says. You point out that the grass always dies in winter and that it will be just fine in another six months. He says that's your opinion. And, no, he won't come back to re-inspect next June. What would be the point? You won't be grazing there anyway.

Few ranchers and farmers in Nevada have the financial resources to defend themselves from unlawful or arbitrary actions by the Forest Service or the Bureau of Land Management, says Benesch. Most are busy simply scrambling to make a living.

"And that's what makes it real tough, because it's all you can do to keep your fences repaired, and maybe to get a couple of new fields re-seeded, and cut your hay, and irrigate the stuff."

Benesch says, "When you get in these situations where you basically have a full-time beef with the Forest Service or with the BLM, or with the Bureau of Reclamation if it's Fallon, over your water rights—and let's say you have a secondary beef over your grazing permits—after a while, there's no time left for you to farm. Or, if you go ahead and farm instead of fight—soon you've been steamrolled."

"I can name twenty ranchers that have gone broke," says Benesch. "The feds just shake the tree," is the way he puts it. "If you do it long enough, pretty soon everything falls off."

Rural cleansing. Dismantling industrial civilization piece by piece.

ENERGY DRAIN

The Multiple Use - Sustained Yield Act of 1960 gives a false sense of security to resource producers. Access to federal lands for legitimate resource extraction is supposed to be guaranteed by that law.

As the resource class has discovered to its dismay, that all depends on who is administering the law.

The environmentalist shock treatment has hit none harder than the oil and gas exploration community. These are the wildcat oilmen of American legend who still walk every basin, examine and re-examine every geological formation, and take every risk to bring in that big one.

George M. Yates is a third generation New Mexico oilman. His grandfather was a pioneer oilman who brought in the first productive oil well in Southeastern New Mexico back in 1924. His father got into the oil business after he graduated from college as a geologist in the 1930s. Yates has been in the oil business since 1969.

"Dad and I were partners for years until he passed away at the age of 88," said Yates. "We're explorationists—we look for oil and gas and develop discoveries."[47]

Yates currently serves as chairman of the Independent Petroleum Association of America, and is a former director of the Denver-based Mountain States Legal Foundation.

"Let me tell you a story," said George Yates.

"In 1997, after exploring several years, I found an oil and gas prospect in a New Mexico basin that had never produced. That was a tremendous achievement that very few explorationists see.

"I had federal leases on a fairly large acreage in an approved Bureau of Land Management oil and gas unit. The location looked great. I had seismic. I had a structure there with enough potential to talk a couple of partners into joining with me and drilling a well.

"My leases were time-limited, and we ran into an unavoidable delay. Getting an extension from the BLM under such circumstances is usually no problem. But the BLM refused to grant my extension.

"It was denied, BLM said, because an unidentified environmental group had claimed that my drilling site was in the habitat of an endangered species.

"So, before my lease ran out, we moved in a rig and drilled and made a discovery. We discovered gas seventy miles from existing production. A new field. The chances of that were probably one in a hundred.

"Now we needed to lease more land in the basin to claim the entire discovery. But BLM refused to do any leasing pending a review of the area.

"That discovery still sits in the ground. The stoppage was instigated by an environmental group that has not come out of the shadows. There has never been a public hearing.

"We applied for approval to drill three additional wells in the unit where we found the gas. It was already an approved federal oil and gas unit and we were the designated operators. It took about twelve months to get the approval—ridiculously long.

"When the BLM finally approved the location, they specifically denied us to lay any gathering systems—pipelines—so we could never market any production.

"That is typical of how resource producers of all kinds are being treated on federal lands—lands that are supposed to be multiple use.

"Oil and gas exploration in the United States is going the way of mining, and outside of Nevada, there hasn't been a new mine approved in America in something like ten years."

In July 1998, the Independent Petroleum Producers of America filed a lawsuit charging that the U.S. Forest Service violated the Constitution and federal law when it refused to allow oil and gas leasing in the Lewis and Clark National Forest west of Great Falls, Montana.

Yates said, "For years the Forest Service has been preparing to engage in environmentally-sensitive oil and gas leasing in the area. Now, with absolutely no factual basis, it has changed its mind. That's illegal."

Rural cleansing. Dismantling industrial civilization piece by piece.

MOTOR TRAIL BLUES

Environmental groups often say their pressure on the resource class is for the benefit of recreation—for Americans outdoors.

That misrepresents the real agenda, says Clark Collins, executive director of the Pocatello, Idaho-based Blue Ribbon Coalition, a grassroots umbrella group supporting motorized recreation, including snowmobiling, trail biking, off-road trekking and many non-motorized recreations such as horse packing and mountain bicycling. More than 300 recreation groups make up the coalition.[48]

Collins, an Idaho native, came to his present position the hard way: he found his own favorite outdoor recreation, trail biking, thrown out of one area after another by environmentalists.

First came presidential executive orders in 1977 that resulted in plans to close numerous trails on federal lands to motorized vehicles. Hikers only. Collins volunteered with several recreation groups to fight the closures, became a group officer, and was invited to testify before congressional hearings. His activism won him wide recognition as a spokesman for motorized recreation.

Then the Sierra Club recommended that a trail system near Pocatello, the West Mink Roadless Area, be designated wilderness under the Wilderness Act of 1964, which forbids any type of motorized vehicle. The environmental group gained endorsements for the idea from Idaho's governor, from a congressional candidate, and a number of state legislators.

"That did it," Collins said. "I got a bunch of my friends and fellow recreationists together and we systematically removed those endorsements. Except for the governor. When I finally got a chance to meet with Governor John Evans, he told me, 'You people are politically insignificant.' That hit me right between the eyes.

"Looking back on it, he was probably just explaining political realties to me, but I vowed I was going to change that reality. So I started the Idaho Public Land Users Association, which soon went national and became the Blue Ribbon Coalition.

"We've become politically significant now because we're organized. We got Congress to pass a Recreational Trails Act that protected motorized recreation from environmentalist shutouts.

"But it's been an uphill battle. The federal agencies have become so riddled with green advocacy group members that we're having trouble protecting our rights."

Don Amador, a coalition representative, warned members of a speech by Mike Dombeck, chief of the US Forest Service, at the March, 1999, North American Wildlife and Natural Resources Conference. Dombeck announced that preserving fish and wildlife will supplant all other uses of the forest including timber, grazing, fishing, hunting, hiking, skiing, and other recreation uses. Roads are the culprit.[49]

Dick Cowardin, a former forest service employee and registered forester, said, "The Clinton administration is wrong to blame all of our fishery problems on roads. They should look at the explosive growth of the marine mammal population that eats millions of salmon each year and to overfishing by commercial fishing fleets. Closing forest roads to the American public is wrongminded and won't benefit anyone."

How can a government agency get away with this kind of abuse?

If top-level agency heads want you to suffer, you will suffer. More than 50 top agency appointees in the Clinton administration came straight from environmental groups. They want everyone except themselves off federal lands. They don't even have to pressure the administration. They *are* the administration.

But don't the rank-and-file federal employees take their ethics more seriously?

Not if their ethics are environmental ethics.

Grant-driven environmental groups such as Forest Service Employees for Environmental Ethics and Public Employees for Environmental Responsibility have members in federal agencies who would be delighted to run you off the land.

They're tucked away in every nook and cranny of the land managing agencies—a recreation planner on the Humboldt-Toiyabe National Forest, a zone botanist on the Gifford Pinchot National Forest, a forest archaeologist on the Los Padres National Forest, a social science coordinator in a regional office, a public affairs officer on the Colville National Forest. You get the idea.

And it's not just in the Forest Service or the Bureau of Land Management up north in logger land or out west in cowboy land or down east in New England.

It's everywhere.

Even in the rural Florida Keys, of all places.

That's where the National Oceanic and Atmospheric Administration gave office space and money to the Nature Conservancy to secretly ghost-write testimony to congressional committees for funding of the Florida Keys National Marine Sanctuary (managed by NOAA officials) and orchestrate a campaign to block a ballot measure that opposed the federal Sanctuary and its rules over all the Keys.

The Nature Conservancy (TNC) obtained a 1993 federal grant in the amount of $44,100 from the National Oceanographic and Atmospheric Administration (NOAA) ostensibly to support volunteer, outreach, and public affairs programs for the Florida Keys National Marine Sanctuary.

It's Requisition Number NC-ND2240-3-00305 dated February 11, 1993, if you want a copy of it through the Freedom of Information Act.

TNC employee Mary Enstrom received and spent the NOAA grant monies. She sent in her quarterly report telling what she did with the grant. Here's exactly what she wrote:

NOAA PERFORMANCE REPORT FOR QUARTER ENDING
SEPTEMBER 30, 1993

This report covers the period of July 1–September 30, 1993. It includes tasks described in the agreed upon work-plan, and other tasks outside of the work plan. The tasks below represent approximately 30% of my entire workload for the quarter:

1. Finalized pro-sanctuary ad in cooperation with Rob Fiengold of Marathon NOAA office.
2. Discussed public relations needs of the Sanctuary with Marci Roth, new organizer for the Center for Marine Conservation.
3. Drafted county Mayor Jack London's testimony to be given to U.S. Congressional Joint Hearing of the House Merchant Marine and Fisheries Committee and Committee on Natural Resources, concerning the crisis in Florida Bay and the importance of a healthy marine environment to the economy of the Florida Keys.
4. Drafted testimony of Scott Marr, President of the Keys Federation of Chambers of Commerce, to be given to Congressional oversight Committee. Testimony stressed the importance of a healthy marine environment to the Keys tourism industry.
5. Worked with Chris Fleisher, member of Tourist Development. council, in drafting testimony to Congressional Hearing.
6. Assisted Karl Lessard, commercial fisherman, with testimony to Congressional Hearing stressing the importance of healthy marine habitat to the future of the commercial fishing industry.
7. Identified "Local Economic Interests Panel," and assisted Charlene Daugherty, senior staff person for House Natural Resources Committee, organize panel.[51]

What did we just see NOAA and TNC do?

● ghost-wrote congressional testimony for a Florida mayor. The public didn't know. NOAA officials did.

● ghosted congressional testimony for a chamber of commerce president. The public didn't know. NOAA officials did.

● partially ghosted congressional testimony of a tourist council member. The public didn't know. NOAA officials did.

● influenced congressional testimony of a commercial fisherman. The public didn't know. NOAA officials did.

● influenced a committee staffer to stack the witness list of a congressional hearing. The public didn't know. NOAA officials did.

Stacking congressional witness lists is a time-honored committee pre-rogative. It is not a prerogative of executive branch agencies and private pressure groups. Zealous bureaucrats and grant-driven environmental groups have made it one.

Then we get to point 17 of the TNC report:

17. Developed and directed plan to counter opposition's push for a county-wide referendum against the establishment of the Sanctuary. Recruited local residents to speak out against referendum at two Board of County Commissioners hearings. Organized planning conference call with members of the Center for Marine Conservation, the Wilderness Society, and the Nature Conservancy to discuss plan. Plan was successful in blocking referendum (a 3-2 vote), and generated many positive articles and editorials using many of the messages discussed in plan.

Hidden influence. NOAA and its grant-driven environmentalists.

● NOAA and the Nature Conservancy interfered with the democratic process to prevent a vote that the federal government would likely lose.

● NOAA and the Nature Conservancy used public money to orchestrate the anti-democratic project with the Center for Marine Conservation (1997 income $8,182,412, assets $16,547,941) and the Wilderness Society (1997 income $15,386,978, assets $15,028,078).

● The Center for Marine Conservation has received cumulative EPA grants in the amount of $180,000.

● The head of the Wilderness Society at the time, George T. Frampton, was appointed a sub-cabinet officer in the Clinton Administration, and now heads the President's Council on Environmental Quality.

● The Nature Conservancy reported to the IRS a 1997 income of $421,353,191 and assets of $1,600,138,525. Yes, that's a *billion six.*

Agency lobbying to puff up their environmental programs and funding is nothing new. In 1995, Sen. Craig Thomas (R-WY), investigated what he called illegal lobbying by the Bureau of Land Management, whose employees spoke against a congressional rangeland reform plan and for Interior Secretary Bruce Babbitt's own reform measures.

Babbitt himself, while president of the League of Conservation Voters, revealed his mission for environmental issues, "We must identify our enemies and drive them into oblivion."[52]

With grant-driven environmental groups carrying the message.

And prescriptive foundations writing the message.

Rural cleansing. Dismantling industrial civilization piece by piece.

VILIFYING GOODS-PRODUCERS

The societal consequences of the iron triangle's success have yet to be measured. One impact, however, is getting some academic scrutiny: the vilification and moral exclusion of the resource class.

Rural goods producers, primarily loggers and miners, have been subjected to a campaign of vilification and moral exclusion similar to racism. Messages in the media, academia and official government reports make them perceive that their way of life is under attack by environmentalists in particular and the urban majority in general. Environmentalists file appeals or lawsuits that have sudden devastating effects on goods-producers. Government and media messages tell goods-producers they are "obsolete" as if goods were no longer necessary. Goods-producers live in a climate of occupational prejudice not unlike race prejudice.

We have run into what University of Washington Professor Robert Lee calls "the hidden dangers of moral persuasion, a kind of mind control the federal government is now practicing in an effort to change public attitudes about resource management and management of federal forests in the Pacific Northwest."[53a]

Dr. Lee came to this conclusion when he was invited to work with scientists in the administration's Forest Ecosystem Management Assessment Team (FEMAT) after the 1993 Timber Summit (*see* pp. 228-229). He found them to be making policy, not gathering information so that others could decide on proper policy. He objected. They told him to shut up and get with the program. No diversity of views allowed. Especially not views that respected the dignity of loggers, miners and ranchers.

He quit. And wrote a book about the ominous attitudes he saw.

"Using guilt, shame and ridicule to control people, and to reshape their values, holds terrifying political ramifications," Dr. Lee said. "FEMAT is a classic example of moral persuasion, using the same social control techniques used in China and North Korea. At times, these techniques have also been used by our own government and some U.S. companies. I don't want my mind rearranged by others."

So he wrote *Broken Trust, Broken Land — Freeing Ourselves From the War over the Environment*. In it he exposed the government's refusal to acknowledge the cultural upheaval it was causing.[53b]

Bob Lee was ostracized for his pains, a story predictable to most academicians. He is a fearless pioneer in stripping away the moral high ground from beneath those who practice moral exclusion.

But the exclusion and vilification goes on.

Miners are portrayed as costly, destructive, stupid social misfits in a federal-state document, the Environmental Impact Statement of the Rock

Creek Mine (ASARCO) proposal in Montana:

> Economic and social dependence on resource extraction indus-
> tries is widely regarded as an economic and social liability because it
> ties social well-being to declining economic sectors, locking residents
> into untransferable sets of skills (Baden and O'Brien 1994). Mining
> dependence decreases local social and economic capacity by hinder-
> ing local flexibility, capability, and diversity of social processes
> (Freudenburg 1992). The project would be expected to increase local
> labor costs, decrease average education levels, and weaken the sense
> of community (Swanson 1992c; Bloomquist and Killian 1988;
> Feudenburg 1992). Mining dependence increases community under-
> employment and decreases social adaptability (Krannich and Luloff
> 1991).[54a]

Mining workers are so outraged by this portrayal they don't know
where to begin to defend themselves. They have little chance in the media.

Richard Manning, a reporter who departed the Missoula, Montana,
Missoulian amidst accusations of environmental extremism, now writes
inflammatory rhetoric against miners. In his book, *One Round River: The
Curse of Gold and the Fight for the Big Blackfoo*t, he wrote of Phelps
Dodge and their failed proposal to mine near Lincoln, Montana:

> I haven't the slightest interest in providing balance to this story. I
> don't want to talk to them, because they are evil.[54b]

Intolerant and proud of it. That attitude is probably why Manning no
longer works for the Missoulian.

But Manning and an army like him write on.

Wilderness photographer Art Wolfe in *Backpacker* magazine wrote:

> I hate 'em. The whole damn logging industry should come down
> with a rare form of cancer. They're murdering. They've got a plan.
> They're not even wasting their time with the second growth. They've
> got that. They want to have all the old growth cut before anybody can
> stop 'em. They're ignorant, and they've got to learn a different way
> of life.[54c]

The media have a foundation-created Society of Environmental Journalists (1997 income $322,182, assets $120,568) for reporters to justify
their advocacy. There are even newspaper *editors* who sit on the boards
of major environmental groups.

But when it comes to resource-worker bashing, newspaper writers are particularly vicious in their portrayals.

During the Spotted Owl controversy, loggers were commonly portrayed in urban newspapers and editorial cartoons as being overweight, sloppily dressed, stupid, and as "being their industry"—cutting the last tree anywhere—rather than being employees who do not make policy.

Defenders of loggers were portrayed as hand puppets mouthing the industry's party line, as right wing extremists, or neo-Nazi brutes.

This type of offensive depiction of white supremacists as allies of the wise use movement was part of a foundation campaign to smear any who challenged the moral authority of environmentalism.

Pulitzer Prize-winning political cartoonist David Horsey may or may not have been aware of the organized smear tactic when he drew that cartoon—he did not respond to my repeated inquiries.

At one time or another, the wise use movement was depicted as being tied to nearly every "unacceptable flavor of the month"—Moonies, LaRouchies, Scientologists, neo-Nazis, militias, the Oklahoma City federal building bomber, and to arsons, assaults, rapes, death threats, and even murders, none of which mentioned the names of suspects or any arrests or convictions. If an enviro was the target, it must be wise use.

Simple accusation of guilt was enough to discredit goods producers and their defenders.

The media held a hanging and didn't even bother with a trial.

Timber workers were particularly vilified.

Such depictions are offensive to workers for at least three reasons. First is the image of workers as stupid sloppy people. Newspapers, which would not dream of depicting racial or ethnic minorities in demeaning ways, had little compunction depicting timber workers in such a manner.

The second reason for offense was the depiction of the workers as the industry. Workers do not decide which timber sales to harvest or how, yet workers were held responsible for the purported "sins" of the industry and thus for their own misery.[56]

The third reason is the trickery of the cartoon's premises: "there aren't enough trees left" (while showing *one* tree left) and "it's the owl's fault." There were plenty of trees left (if there weren't, what were the environmentalists trying to stop them from cutting?) and loggers well understood that the scarcity of trees was artificially created by environmentalist lawsuits, not by anything the spotted owl did.

The "century of overcutting" was a political slogan: loggers shook their heads at greens saving "old growth" that had been legally designated as America's timber supply during that century. The greens were simply trying to move the goalpost onto the next playing field. More bizarre, some of that "old growth" had grown into "forest cathedrals" only since the first wave of Pacific Northwest logging in the 1890s—it was actually second growth, but the environmentalist "experts" didn't know it.

If it looks old, don't cut it.

Richard Larson, associate editor of the Seattle Times, found himself attacked by environmentalists and fellow editors when he wrote a column about some of those inconvenient truths, particularly that the environmental movement had already stopped logging in all but a tiny remnant of federal lands where commercial timber harvest and replanting was still permitted. Larson was forced to shut up.[57]

Loggers felt the truth—and their lives—had been turned inside out by newspapers and their editorial cartoons.

Urban readers accepted such portrayals without thought or objection.

They did not know or care that vast commercial forests remain and have long been designated as America's timber supply.

They did not know or care that vast noncommercial forests have been permanently protected, never to be logged.

Loggers had been vilified into moral exclusion.

The urban newspaper portrayals matched urban reader prejudices. The urban newspapers knew their urban audience.

But their urban audience did not know what was behind their own urban prejudices.

Grant-driven environmental groups.

Prescriptive foundations.

Zealous bureaucrats.

They're destroying America's resource class.

They're destroying America's property owners.

No one sees.

No one cares.

SILENT SCANDAL FOOTNOTES

4a. Ronald Inglehart, *Modernization and Postmodernization: Cultural, Economic, and Political Change in 43 Societies*, Princeton University Press, Princeton, 1997.

4b. *The 1997 Development Report Card for the States* (book and CDROM), Corporation for Enterprise Development, 777 N. Capitol St., N.E., Suite 410, Washington, DC 20002.

4c. "Big gap between urban, rural in Washington," by David Postman, *Seattle Times*, Tuesday, March 3, 1998.

6a. "Dramatic Urban-Rural Prosperity Gap in Washington State Economy: Slump in natural-resource industries such as timber widen disparity with high-tech Seattle area," by Mark Jewell, Associated Press, *Los Angeles Times*, Sunday March 15, 1998, p. 4.

6b. "Locke Plan Aims to Bridge State's Urban-Rural Gap - Areas are Worlds Apart Financially," by Mark Jewell, A.P., *Seattle Times*, Sunday, February 15, 1998, p. B1.

7. "Dramatic Urban-Rural Prosperity Gap in Washington State Economy," *Los Angeles Times*.

11. Data tabulated by Paul F. Ehinger & Associates, Eugene, Oregon.

14a. Telephone interview, February 25, 1999.

14b. *Organic Administration Act* of June 4, 1897, 16 U.S.C. 437-475, 477-482, 551. Environmentalists dispute that this 1897 law correctly expressed the intent of the Act of March 3, 1891, that established the forest reserves, which were renamed "national forests" in 1907. For the legislative history of that 1891 Act, see: U.S. Congress, House, 50th Cong., 1st Sess., 1888, *Report No. 778*. The report addressed the original purposes of the forest reserves. "The bill provides '...that lands chiefly valuable for timber of commercial value, as sawed or hewed timber, shall be classified as timber land;' that the land shall not be sold, but the timber on the land in legal subdivisions of 40 acres shall be appraised and sold on sealed proposals to the highest bidder, and shall be removed from the land within five years from the date of sale, the timber so purchased to be deemed personal property for all purposes, including taxation."

15. On July 5, 1988, twenty-four Earth First!ers were arrested for blocking access to Okanogan National Forest Building for one day, in protest of timber sales said to affect lynx habitat. Arrested were: Bradd Mitchell Schulke of Seattle; David Fleak Potter of Seattle; John Craig Lilburn of Missoula, Montana; Michael Joseph Robinson of Santa Cruz, California; Lincoln Warren Kern of Seattle; Camalla Juanita

Moore of Seattle; Kirsten Lee Pourroy of Bellingham; Michael Phillip Peterson of Republic; George William Callies of Seattle; Karen Louise Coulter of Seattle; Tracy Lynne Katelman of Berkeley, California; Joanne Dittersdorf of Bellingham; Elizabeth Jane Fries of Bellingham; Thomas Grey of Bellingham; Peter Jay Galvin of Portland; Philip Randall Knight of Bozeman, Montana; David Eugene Helm of Ferndale; Kurt Stein Newman of Bayside, California; Lyn "Lee" Georges Dessaux of Santa Cruz, California; Todd Douglas Schulke of Seattle; Gregory Joseph Wingard of Kent; Steven Gary Paulson of Lenore, Idaho; Mitchell Alan Friedman of Bellingham; and Kimberly Dawn Reinking of Berkeley, California.

16. Paul F. Ehinger & Associates, 1998.

17a. Telephone interview, February 26, 1999.

17b. "Battered Communities: How Wealthy Private Foundation, Grant-Driven Environmental Groups, and Activist Federal Employees Combine to Systematically Cripple Rural Economies," Center for the Defense of Free Enterprise, Bellevue, Washington, June, 1998, p. 31.

17c. "Battered Communities," p. 30.

18. "Battered Communities," p. 31.

19a. 405 U.S. 538, 92 S.Ct. 1113.

19b. "Privatization: Toward More Effective Government," Report of the President's Commission on Privatization, David F. Linowes, Chairman, March, 1988, p. 242.

19c. All data on federal land ownership comes from *Public Land Statistics, 1996, Table 1.3, "Comparison of federally owned land with total acreage of States, fiscal year 1994,"* Government Printing Office, Washington, D.C., 1996. Available online at http://www.access.gpo.gov/blm/im-ages/1-3-96.pdf.

20a. Hawaii is the only state in the Union to have formerly been a constitutional monarchy that was illegally overthrown by U.S. military intervention, and had its own land tenure system in place. The relatively small amount of federal land in Hawaii today is either military base sites or purchases that were designated national parks such as Hawaii Volcanoes and Haleakala National Parks. To complicate matters, a Native Hawaiian movement is using old Hawaiian Kingdom law to cast clouds on modern titles because the chain of title was broken by some illegal act, such as the 1893 American overthrow of Queen Lili'uokalani's monarchy, asserting that modern titles are therefore invalid. A native title company is filing such reports at the Hawaii Bureau of Conveyances and preventing actual sales. Courts will have to resolve this issue. Who owns Hawaii could become a significant question in time.

20b. Land area from 1992 National Resource Inventory - Table 1 (USDA) URL: http://www.ngq.nrcs.usda.gov/NRI/tables/1992/table1.html. Includes federal trust land, tribal and TVA land areas.

21. Data on governments comes from *1992 Census of Governments, Volume 1, Number 1, Government Organization*, Bureau of the Census, Department of Commerce, Washington, D.C., 1996, p. 7.

22a. Telephone interview, May, 1998.

22b. IRS database, available online at http://www.nonprofits.org/loc.

23. W. Alton Jones Foundation brochure and statement in *Environmental Grantmaking Foundation 1996 Directory*, p. 303.

25. Freedom of Information Act response, File Code: 6270 (MBS #96-05-23), November 20, 1996, USDA Forest Service, Mountlake Terrace, Washington.

26. See footnote 15.

29. Organization data compiled from various sources, Encyclopedia of Associations, online from Dialog database; Foundation Center grant guides from multiple years.

30. *The Bullitt Foundation*, Environmental Grantmaking Foundations 1996 Directory, Environmental Data Research Institute, Rochester, New York, 1996, p. 81.

33a. "Heiress leads fight to save old forests," by Lynda V. Mapes, *Spokane Spokesman-Review*, Monday, August 23, 1993, p. A1.

33b. "Harriet Stimson Bullitt and Priscilla Bullitt Collins - The Bullitt Sisters: Has Life Among the Sheltered and Well-off Prepared Them for the Rough-and-Tumble Arena of Environmental Causes? by Theresa Morrow, *Seattle Times,* Sunday, November 11, 1990, (Pacific Magazine), p. 10.

33c. "Golden opportunity splits rural town - Chesaw, Washington, is divided over plans for a new mine," *The Spokane Spokesman-Review*, by Lynda V. Mapes, November 29, 1993, p. A1.

34. Note to Bonnie Lawrence, May 1998.

35a. "UM 'environmental' class spurs ethics debate," by Erin P. Billings, *The Independent Record*, Helena, Montana, Saturday, Oct. 12, 1996, p. A1. See Chapter 4 for the expanded story, p. 140*ff*.

35b. "Environmental Group Appeals for Change in U.S. Mining Laws," by Associated Press, *Rocky Mountain News,* Friday June 24, 1994, p. 22A.

35c. "Newmont to Take $33.8 Million Write-Off," by Kerri S. Smith, *Rocky Mountain News*, Saturday January 6, 1996, p. 47A.

36a. See website http://www.nwf.org/nwf/northeast/nfp/pgm_nfa1.html.

36b. Robert Shankland, *Steve Mather of the National Parks*, Alfred A. Knopf, New York, 1951.

37. Alan Gottlieb and Ron Arnold, *Trashing the Economy: How Runaway Environmentalism is Wrecking America*, Free Enterprise Press, Bellevue, Washington, 1994, second edition, p.362*ff.*

38. Transcript of EGA Fall Retreat, 1992, from tape, "Session 2: North American Forests: Coping With Multiple Use and Abuse."

41a. Compiled from Foundation Center records.

41b. "Governor Angus King says it's a historic moment for Maine, and he's right," editorial, *Ellsworth American*, Ellsworth, Maine, March 11, 1999.

42. Gina Brosig, "Long Term Implications of Conservation Easements," American Farm Bureau website http://www.fb.com/issues/analysis/easement.html., Feb. 25, 1998.

43a. Telephone interview March 11, 1999.

43b. EPA website http://www.epa.gov/envirofw/html/gics/gics_query.html.

45. Telephone interview, March 30, 1999.

47. Telephone interview, June 6, 1999.

48. Telephone interview, June 20, 1999.

49. "New Ethic for Forests Unveiled - U.S. Agency to Alter Goals for Public Lands," by Paul Rogers, *San Jose Mercury News*, Monday, March 29, 1999, p. 1A.

51. Published in "Feeding at the Trough," white paper by Center for the Defense of Free Enterprise, Bellevue, Washington, May 1995.

52. "Senate Confirms Babbitt Despite Questions About His Activism," by Martin Van Der Werf, *Arizona Republic*, Friday, January 22, 1993, p A1.

53a. "The Hidden Danger of Moral Persuasion: The Clinton Plan Laid Bare," interview with Dr. Robert Lee, *Evergreen*, June 1996, p. 46.

53b. Robert G. Lee, *Broken Trust Broken Land — Freeing Ourselves From the War over the Environment,* Book Partners, Wilsonville, Oregon, 1994.

54a. *Rock Creek Environmental Impact Statement, Chapter 4: Environmental Consequences*, p. 4-131. Written by Mark Kelly. The referenced studies were written by academicians and published in various academic journals.

54b. Richard Manning, *One Round River: The Curse of Gold and the Fight for the Big Blackfoot*, Henry Holt, 1998.

54c. Quoted in "Trouble in Timber Town: A Way of Life Is Torn Up By Its Roots," by Sandra Hines, *Columns*, December 1990, p. 10.

55. *A Response to "Forty Years of Spotted Owls? A Longitudinal Analysis of Logging Industry"* by Matthew S. Carroll, Charles W. McKetta, Keith A. Blatner, and Con Schallau. See also, Matthew S. Carroll, *Community and the Northwestern Logger: Continuities and Change in the Era of the Spotted Owl*, Harper-Collins, New York, 1995.

56. Political cartoons by Dave Horsey, *Seattle Post-Intelligencer*, and Brian Bassett, *Seattle Times*, all circa 1989-90.

57. "From timber towns, a cry for compassion," by Richard W. Larson, associate editor, *Seattle Times*, Sunday, October 6, 1991, p. A16.

PART TWO:

THE
BEWILDERING
ARRAYS

CHAPTER 2

PRESCRIPTIVE FOUNDATIONS

Many wealthy foundations have turned away from their original respon-sive position to become prescriptive, designing programs of their own and setting the political agenda. Since the late 1980s, the foundation community has become increasingly left-wing, activist, coordinated, bullying, and prescriptive. The Environmental Grantmakers Association has become a strategizing center that targets vast wealth against the resource class. Today a bewildering array of prescriptive foundations invisibly shapes the environmental movement, causing alarm among en-vironmentalists as well as those in the resource community.

PHILANTHROPIES THAT PROMOTE MISANTHROPY. They command immense capital, yet produce nothing. They finance uto-pian projects, yet destroy productive enterprises. They empower those who create only social change. They disable those who produce all our material goods. They preach social justice, yet wreck the resource class and minorities. They work against the individual. They promote big government. Their vast projects induce bizarre consequences such as anti-capitalist programs destroying small enterprises and concentrating wealth in big corporations. Their wealth is matched by their intellect, their cunning and their absolute ruthlessness.

That, to many, is a fair description of the environmental grantmaking community.

This growing stream of "big money" support has boosted the environmental movement's power in a time of declining grassroots contributions.

But it came at a cost. The Golden Rule applies: who has the gold rules.

Submission to money hasn't been all bad for environmentalism. In one of history's ironies, many new generation heirs of wealthy families are emerging as environmental true believers, now guiding foundations built on the profits of "evil polluters" to destroy the industries that made them rich. They may be less radical than some would like, but they're taking a severe toll on rural goods production and the resource class.

At least 2,500 grantmakers—foundations and corporations—fund the environmental movement, according to Environmental Data Research Institute (EDRI). The annual dollar amount can only be estimated.[66a]

The Foundation Center's *National Guide to Funding for the Environment and Animal Welfare* describes more than 1,200 grantmaking foundations and about 90 direct corporate giving programs, with 379 of them donating more than $356 million to the environmental movement in 1992. That's 379 foundations—less than 20 percent of the 2,500 known funders—whose $356 million must be a small fraction of the total.[66b]

The *Environmental Grantmaking Foundations 1997 Directory* profiled 740 foundations that collectively donated nearly $500 million to environmental organizations, somewhat less than a million per foundation.[66c]

The Boston Globe estimated a total of $4 billion a year. It is not likely that 2,500 grantmakers each donated an average of $1.6 million to green groups. Half that is probable. Government grants may bring it to $4 billion.[66d]

The 2,500 or so environmental grantmakers account for about 6 percent of all 45,000 foundations in America, which in turn make up only about 3 percent of all 1.5 million present non-profit organizations.

The total non-profit sector is important to consider, even though it is not all environment-related, because of the connections between organizations, as we shall see. The total non-profit sector accounts for 7.8 percent of all U.S. employment. Such economic power cannot be dismissed.[66e]

In fact, the total non-profit movement—NGOs, or Non-Governmental Organizations—annually spends more than $1 trillion in 22 countries studied by the Johns Hopkins Comparative Nonprofit Sector Project in its 1998 report, "The Emerging Sector Revisited." If viewed as a nation, it would rank eighth in economic power.[66f]

As of 1993, the United States had approximately 1.4 million tax-exempt organizations with operating expenditures of some $500 billion. That's half of all our hospitals, half of all our colleges and universities, almost all of our symphony orchestras, 60 percent of our social service agencies and most of our civic organizations.[66g]

The Foundation Center, a New York non-profit, reports about 45,000 grantmaking foundations contributed $19.46 billion in 1998, a 22 percent jump over the $15.98 billion reported for 1997. Stock market gains and a record number of new foundations—more than 50 each week—account for the increase.[67a] Although Internal Revenue Service records don't exactly correspond to Foundation Center estimates of how many foundations exist, they do reflect the same growth trend. In 1989, the IRS says, 37,000 private family foundations (those with single donors) filed the required 990 tax forms, compared with 54,500 in 1997, a growth rate of 47.3 percent. The value of private foundation assets grew 35 percent from $164.8 billion in 1990 to $222.5 billion in 1994, the last year for which there are figures.[67b]

BASICS OF NON-PROFIT ORGANIZATIONS

Non-profits are: (1) organizations; (2) that are not part of the governmental apparatus; (3) that do not distribute profits to their directors; (4) that are self-governing; and (5) that serve some public purpose that has been judged by the U.S. Congress (and in some cases state and local legislatures) to entitle them to full or partial exemption from many forms of taxation.

Categories of non-profit organizations:
1. *Charitable.* These include educational, religious, civic, health, and similar organizations.
2. *Social.* Fraternal orders and mutual benefit societies, but not night-clubs and similar self-interest groups.
3. *Trade associations.* Chambers of commerce, labor unions, industry associations, and the like.
4. *Political.* Propaganda groups, political party organizations, committees for legislative action.
The U.S. Tax Code includes government and municipal organizations, including administrative bodies such as road and water districts. However, economists include only nongovernmental organizations (NGOs) in the reports cited in this chapter.

Tax exempt. Certain non-profit organizations are exempt from taxation, though they may be taxed on income from businesses they conduct.
Tax deductible. Individual donations to qualified charitable non-profit organizations may be deducted from your personal federal income taxes. However, donations to political and certain other non-profit organizations are not tax deductible.

In the U.S., voluntary giving to non-profits amounted to more than $143.5 billion in 1997. Most of it went to civic causes such as fighting illiteracy, hunger, and homelessness, or for children's hospitals, and united funds. An unknown part went to agenda-driven social activism.[68a]

Federal grants to non-profits were approximately $130 billion in fiscal year 1996. How much federal money went to environmental groups has never been sorted out of the total. Two billion is likely.[68b]

A comparison of funding for left-leaning and right-leaning groups is revealing. Economics America, Inc., editors of *The Right Guide* and *The Left Guide*, found that "financial figures are still considerably less for the Right than their counterparts on the Left." Conservative and libertarian causes that protect private property and the resource class are far outstripped financially by those who act to harm them.[68c]

What this means to American society is impossible to understand without going inside the environmental grantmaking community and listening to their own words.

STAGNATION

By the mid-1980s the environmentalist victories of the early '70s were fossilized in federal regulatory programs. The Wilderness Act of 1964 was quietly administered by bureaucrats while hordes of unregulated hikers who paid no entry fee loved the wilderness to death. The Clean Air Act and Clean Water Act amendments submerged as pages of details in the *Code of Federal Regulations* that torpedoed little firms out of business and left Fortune 500 companies with fewer competitors. The Endangered Species Act grew within the U.S. Fish and Wildlife Service and the National Marine Fisheries Service, casting its pall of no-use over small private property owners across the nation. Interior Secretary James Watt, the eco-ogre of the Reagan administration, had resigned in humiliation over a tasteless and politically incorrect joke told at a luncheon.

By 1985, environmental groups had migrated to Washington, jettisoned their amateur naturalist leaders, sprouted lawyers and public relations consultants in top spots, and watched their grass roots rot. Even sympathetic journalist Mark Dowie argued in his book, *Losing Ground: American Environmentalism at the Close of the Twentieth Century*, that the nation's biggest environmental groups had lost touch with their grassroots constituencies. He quoted Bill Turnage, former director of the Wilderness Society, describing a major reason why: "If a foundation had a large interest in Alaska and a lot of money, you definitely had a large interest in Alaska."[68d]

BASICS OF FOUNDATIONS

A foundation is a modern innovation to provide for the **endowment of non-profit enterprises** and the **establishment of an association or corporation** to carry out its founder's plans.

Most foundations are set up as charitable trusts. The grantor conveys money or property by a deed of trust to a named trustee or trustees, to be disbursed as the instrument directs.

The **charitable trust** may or may not be incorporated. Most modern foundations are corporations. Technically, the foundation is the document of endowment or incorporation, but the term usually means the organization that administers the fund.

Both **public charities** and **private foundations** form part of the non-profit structure of the environmental movement.

Public charities are charitable organizations supported by members of the general public. They are allowed to operate programs to accomplish their tax-exempt purpose. Most environmental groups are classified by the IRS as public charities.

A private foundation is a charitable organization that is funded by one or a few persons rather than the general public. Although subject to stricter rules than a public charity, a private foundation is tax-exempt just like a public charity and may carry on the same activities. Often, a private foundation simply makes grants to public charities instead of operating its own programs.

Dowie grasped that non-profit organizations were increasingly turning to private foundations—and in the process allowing the foundations to set the political agenda. The money came rolling in, but the brash little volunteer-driven environmentalist David of the 1960s grew not into a great king after Earth Day, 1970, but turned into just another well-heeled special interest Goliath strutting around Capitol Hill.

Enviro lobbyists worried more about pay and perks than about the issues. Enviro staff worried more about fundraising than the issues. Enviro field organizers worried more about field trips than the issues.

The glamour was gone. So was the effectiveness.

Some of the money men noticed.

Chief among them was Donald K. Ross, director of the New York City-based Rockefeller Family Fund. Ross, born in 1944, was a hardcore activist who cut his policy teeth from 1974 as a young lawyer with the Ralph Nader-founded New York Public Interest Research Group (NYPIRG), and was soon elevated to executive director.

In 1979, after the near-disaster at Pennsylvania's Three Mile Island nuclear power plant, Ross organized two anti-nuclear rallies, one in Washington, D.C., that brought 65,000 protesters to the Mall (Ross said it was 125,000). Ross emphasized coalition-building for this rally, bringing in Friends of the Earth, the Association of Machinists and others to augment the usual leftovers from Vietnam war protests.

The other was the nation's largest anti-nuclear rally, nearly 200,000 people, at New York City's Battery Park landfill. Ross convinced stellar speakers to show up at both rallies, including Jane Fonda, Tom Hayden, Ralph Nader, Bella Abzug, and Barry Commoner, with singers including Bonnie Raitt and Pete Seeger. Both audiences chanted, "Hell no, we won't glow!" and "Two, four, six, eight, we don't want to radiate!"[70a]

Ross showed himself in one NYPIRG triumph after another to be a canny strategist and bold tactician.

He became director of the Rockefeller Family Fund (RFF) in January 1985 at the age of 40. It was a different world, a tight little island of Standard Oil wealth converted to an investment portfolio containing common stocks of oil and gas companies such as Amerada Hess and Unocal, mining companies including Asarco and Freeport-McMoRan, and timber firms including Weyerhaeuser and Boise Cascade.[70b]

The foundation had been established in 1967 by Martha, John, Laurance, Nelson, and David Rockefeller (the daughter-in-law and grandchildren of John D. Rockefeller). In its earliest years, the Fund was led by third-generation family members. Laurance was the real force; his clever deals—secretly buying up private land, donating it for national parks and then getting the visitor concession—had built RockResorts, the family's for-profit hospitality industry empire, into a thriving venture.

From 1970 onward, members of the next generation (referred to as "the cousins") comprised a majority of trustees and provided board leadership. In 1978, the first member of the fifth generation was elected to the board, and today half of the trustees are from the fifth generation.

They all remember how Grandpa (or Great-Grandpa or Great-Great-Grandpa) got rich. Old John D. had a simple method: Take over the competition. Eliminate those you can't take over. Combine forces and rule.

The board was entirely family members. It wasn't a huge foundation, granting only a million or two each year, but it got a lot of bang for the buck and it enjoyed an influence on other funders disproportionate to its size in the foundation world. It was one of only a handful of foundations that had figured out how to drive social change with intelligently targeted money. It regarded itself as a "catalyst" for non-profit groups, i.e., it generated areas of activism that weren't there before.

By funding startups and convincing other donors to join in, the Fund leveraged its relatively small assets and magnified its focused staff-work into big public impact. Imagination and creative grantmaking were the hallmarks. The person who had devised the Family Fund's strategy of leverage and focus was Robert W. Scrivner, who served as the Fund's director from 1972 until his death in 1984.

The Fund needed someone to carry on the strategy and perfect it.

Donald K. Ross was the man.

Ross wasted no time. He was particularly interested in "catalyzing" the environmental movement. The Council on Foundations—the lobbying, litigating and strategy arm of the foundation community (with 1,600 grantmakers that collectively hold $143.4 billion in assets and in 1997 gave away $7 billion)—steered Ross to its Environmental Grantmakers Affinity Group.

Within a few months Ross found himself talking to five other big-money foundation leaders in the affinity group when they discovered they would all be in Washington the next week. One of them said, let's all get together Saturday. They spent that Saturday talking about common interests and asking about each other's specific programs.[71]

When it was over, they felt it had been so useful they decided to do it again at least once a year. The next year nearly twenty people showed up and it became clear they were on to something.

In 1987 they decided they needed a secretariat and officially organized themselves as the Environmental Grantmakers Association with Don Ross as coordinator. It was not and is not incorporated. Strictly a voluntary gathering of donors. They exchanged grants lists and published a "directory" of foundation program interests. For a couple of years Jon Jensen of the Pew Scholars Program in Conservation housed the association in his University of Michigan offices, but it got too big and Don Ross brought it into the Rockefeller Family Fund's office. Today there are more than 200 EGA members, including a few corporate funders such as Arco Foundation and Chevron.

The Environmental Grantmakers Association has been characterized as "command central" of the environmental movement (there isn't really any such thing) and "the cartel of eco-money" (close enough, although a number of lesser eco-money power centers also influence events). EGA has indisputably been the most powerful shaping force on environmentalism in the past decade.

From EGA's official beginning in 1987 a small cluster of member foundations worked closely and set an interventionist tone. The core clique included the Rockefeller Family Fund (New York), Pew Charitable Trusts

---

ENVIRONMENTAL GRANTMAKERS ASSOCIATION MEMBERSHIP CATEGORIES

Membership in the EGA is open to all foundations and giving programs which act primarily as grantmakers, not as grantseekers, and whose philanthropic purposes include the protection of the natural environment.

1. Private Foundation or Charitable Trust
   Foundations whose giving is funded exclusively by income on an endowment. Files IRS Form 990-PF.
2. Community Foundation
   Funded in part or whole by endowment. Grantseeking limited, usually to enlarge endowment.
3. Corporate Foundation or Giving Program
   Funded by endowment or a percentage of corporate profits.
4. Public Foundation
   Publicly supported grantmaker funded primarily by endowment or single source of income. Files IRS Form 990.
5. Coordinative Organization
   Publicly supported organization whose primary purpose is to coordinate grantmakers. Generally supported by member dues.

(Philadelphia), W. Alton Jones Foundation (Charlottesville, Virginia), Bullitt Foundation (Seattle), Surdna Foundation (New York), Beldon Fund (Washington, D.C.), Schumann Foundation (New Jersey), the Joyce Foundation (Chicago), and the Cummings Foundation (New York), among others. These are quintessentially prescriptive foundations.

What exactly does it mean to be "prescriptive?" It has several levels.

The most superficial was identified by *Mother Jones*—a magazine published by the Foundation for National Progress, a non-profit organization receiving donations from foundations (1996 income $4.1 million)—which wrote, "by deciding which organizations get money, the grantmakers help the agenda of the environmental movement and influence the programs that activists carry out."[72]

This is *passive prescription*. It amounts to simply funding groups that are already doing what you like, and ignoring or blackballing the rest. It merely reinforces good behavior and extinguishes bad. You don't need to attach strings to your money because the recipients have done it for you. *Mother Jones* didn't get it quite right: You're not helping the agenda of the recipients, you're driving your own with selective grants.

But what happens if nobody is doing what you want done? What if the whole movement falls into stagnation?

Consider this exchange transcribed from a session of the 1992 Environmental Grantmakers Association annual conference:

Chuck Clusen (American Conservation Association): I think the [environmentalist] community as a whole is not very strategic. And I think we need to start rebuilding that. And figuring out how to not only get the most bang for the buck, but how to make it lasting bangs. And to do several things at once, and so on.

Anne Fitzgerald (Switzer Foundation): Do you detect, though, a resistance in the larger organizations to becoming grant driven?

Donald Ross (Rockefeller Family Fund): Yeah. I think a lot of them resist.

Chuck Clusen: A number of us have been involved in this, Anne. There's definitely a feeling on the part of the not-for-profit organizations that in cases of some of the campaigns that they resent funders, not just picking the issues, but also being directive in the sense of the kind of campaign, the strategy, the style, and so on. I guess, coming out of the advocacy world, and having spent most of my career doing it, I look at it as, if they're not going to do it on their own, thank God funders are forcing them to start doing it...The lobbying is not there in Washington. It's not being delivered. And, you know, I don't want to name names. I could name all the organizations that in many issues, you know, just how little they have on the Hill and how ineffectual it is in being connected to the grass roots and so forth.

Anne Fitzgerald: Do you think that's because the organizations have gotten so—certainly the major organizations—have gotten quite big and therefore bureaucratic?

Chuck Clusen: A lot of those organizations are bureaucratic. And when you compare it to the way, you know, a for-profit organization is run they don't by and large have the management. I mean there's not strategic decisions being made and then implemented. What you basically have, a lot of these organizations are a series of very bright, talented, self-initiating people who do their own thing, who resist any kind of supervision or resist any kind of coalition building or working cooperatively with others.

Hooper Brooks (Surdna Foundation): I think that basically the problem is most of these are not only bureaucracies, but they spend most of their time hitting their members for more money and sending them newsletters instead of getting out to the public. And I don't think you can neglect thinking about that. I do think we do have to get prescriptive.

Donald Ross: I think that there are things that could be done. I think funders have a major role to play. And I know there are resentments in the community towards funders doing that. And, too bad. We're players, they're players.

But I think we touched on a lot of problems, the internal problems within these big groups, the warring factions within them who are all trying to get resources, and there's too many groups and too few resources, and all that.

I think the fundamental effort that has to be made is a reorganization of the movement. I don't think it's realistic to think that groups like Sierra Club or NRDC are going to disappear and reform into something new. They'll stay, and they'll still send out those newsletters. I think we have to begin to look much more at a task force approach on major issues that is able to pool. And the funders can drive that.

And I think there isn't one of them, even the biggest, National Wildlife, or Audubon or Sierra Club, that has the capacity to wage full scale battles on major issues by themselves. They don't have the media, lobbying, grass roots organizing, Washington base, et cetera, litigation, all wrapped in one organization.

And so the trick, I think...where funders can play a real role is using the money to drive, to create, ad hoc efforts in many cases that will have a litigation component coming from one group, a lobbying component coming from another group, a grass roots organizing component coming from yet a third group with a structure that enables them to function well.[74]

That's quite an ambitious project, reorganizing a whole movement and turning it into a segmented, complex, coordinated, disciplined army of many units. It means continued support for the old organizations that won't go away, and vigorous recruitment or creation of new targeted groups. But Ross, who left the Family Fund in 1999, was right: funders can drive that.

The EGA has driven that. That is *aggressive prescription*.

There is one higher level: *absolute prescription*, pre-selecting grant recipients and accepting no uninvited applications, as we shall see.

Today there is an astounding multiplicity of little environmental groups growing up to cover every conceivable issue, plus coalitions with left-leaning movements of all sorts—peace groups, women's groups, labor

organizations, minority groups. Today the movement consists almost solely
of grant-driven activists—and many of them don't even know it.

A short surf almost anywhere on environmentalist websites will uncover examples. An easy one is the Environmental Defense Fund website
(home page at www.edf.org). Click on their Publications icon and scan
the Reports menu. Just pick the first thing on it: Biotechnology.

Click on that and it will take you to a report titled, *Biotechnology's
Bitter Harvest: Herbicide-Tolerant Crops and the Threat to Sustainable
Agriculture*. Its lead authors have Ph.D.s behind their names, but they
have environmental group employer names there too. The last credit reads,
"A Report of the Biotechnology Working Group."

What's the Biotechnology Working Group?

It's a task force. Just like Don Ross suggested.

Why does it exist?

Some leaders of foundations in the Environmental Grantmakers
Association want to shut down biotechnology research to save nature; others want to shut down biotechnology research because it might
solve real problems and hurt the credibility of alarmist projects like
the *Bitter Harvest* report; others want political control of it; others
want financial control of it. EDF leaders share some of these goals,
but are unwilling to commit more than a modest effort to them.

A perfect place for the task force approach.

Or the Working Group approach, to use a widely favored buzzword.

Click on the Biotechnology Working Group link and you find yourself on a page that tells you BWG "is composed of representatives of
public interest organizations and a state agricultural agency and citizen
activists who are presently working on biotechnology-related issues in
the environmental, agricultural, consumer, labor, and public health fields.
The purpose of the group is to strengthen the influence of the public interest community on the development of biotechnology by sharing informa-

IRS TAX CODE SECTIONS

Section 501(c)(3): Religious, educational, charitable, scientific organizations. If dominantly supported by the general public, files annual
report Form 990. If declared a private foundation by the IRS, files
Form 990-PF.

Section 509(a)(1): Proof of public support (from members of the general public). Required to avoid classification as a private foundation.

Section 501(c)(4): Educational and lobbying organizations. Contributions generally not deductible. Files Form 990.

tion, coordinating activities, and developing action strategies on specific issues." Getting to have a familiar ring, isn't it?

We find that the Biotechnology Working Group is "a project of the Tides Foundation, supported by foundation grants and in-kind contributions from its member groups."

The chart on the next page explains the complex structure behind the EDF Report.

THE STAR NEST

What is the Tides Foundation? It is one of the Environmental Grantmakers Association's most fascinating members because it is not a private foundation, but is a public charity. It has 501(c)(3) and 509(a)(1) IRS designations, which allow it to seek contributions and distribute them where desired—how to reorganize the environmental movement.

It's not a traditional foundation. It doesn't have an endowment. Instead, people and institutions that, for one reason or another, don't want to be publicly identified with a certain cause give money to Tides as *donor-advised fund*s, a little-known charitable giving vehicle that allows donors to recommend uses of their donations and also to remain anonymous (more about *that* later).

Tides becomes the "fiscal agent" (money funnel) of any group that donors wish to fund *or to create* to fit their agenda. Tides gives the recipient shelter under its tax exemption. Tides can train new leaders and equip their organizations to stand alone or simply run a temporary ad hoc operation to fill a short-term need. Thus, Tides has created a haven for donor-selected nongovernmental organizations that, for various reasons, would rather not obtain their own tax-exempt status from the Internal Revenue Service. In this manner Tides has nurtured literally hundreds of new groups to plague the resource class and rural communities.

The Tides Foundation was founded in 1976 by Drummond Pike, a left-wing activist in California, as a vehicle to promote social change and support new, controversial and even radical efforts.

The Tides Foundation originally supported three different but related programs: 1) **grants**: a) grantseeking, i.e., they obtained funds from large foundations, and b) grantmaking, i.e., they spent the money on other non-profit groups; 2) **projects**, i.e., they created or recruited existing, startup or temporary groups to fit any social engineering agenda with donor-advised funds; and 3) **management contracting**, i.e., they contracted with their own projects to provide them with financial, management and program assistance.

One stop shopping for all your left-wing needs.

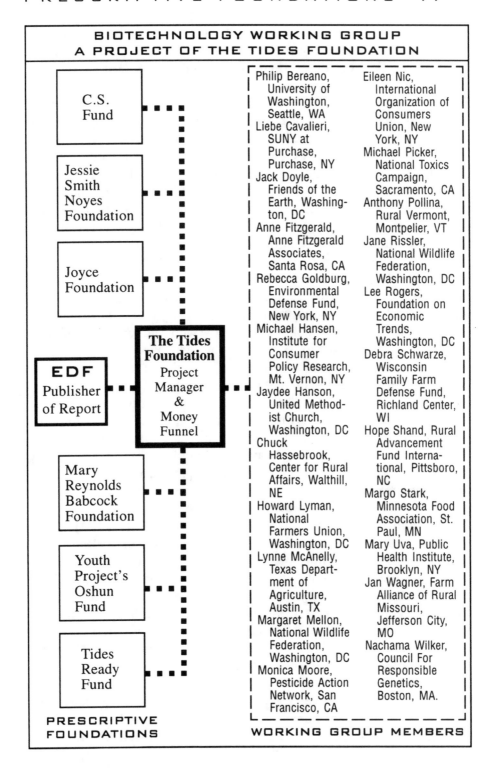

BIOTECHNOLOGY WORKING GROUP
A PROJECT OF THE TIDES FOUNDATION

C.S. Fund

Jessie Smith Noyes Foundation

Joyce Foundation

The Tides Foundation
Project Manager & Money Funnel

EDF
Publisher of Report

Mary Reynolds Babcock Foundation

Youth Project's Oshun Fund

Tides Ready Fund

PRESCRIPTIVE FOUNDATIONS

Philip Bereano, University of Washington, Seattle, WA
Liebe Cavalieri, SUNY at Purchase, Purchase, NY
Jack Doyle, Friends of the Earth, Washington, DC
Anne Fitzgerald, Anne Fitzgerald Associates, Santa Rosa, CA
Rebecca Goldburg, Environmental Defense Fund, New York, NY
Michael Hansen, Institute for Consumer Policy Research, Mt. Vernon, NY
Jaydee Hanson, United Methodist Church, Washington, DC
Chuck Hassebrook, Center for Rural Affairs, Walthill, NE
Howard Lyman, National Farmers Union, Washington, DC
Lynne McAnelly, Texas Department of Agriculture, Austin, TX
Margaret Mellon, National Wildlife Federation, Washington, DC
Monica Moore, Pesticide Action Network, San Francisco, CA

Eileen Nic, International Organization of Consumers Union, New York, NY
Michael Picker, National Toxics Campaign, Sacramento, CA
Anthony Pollina, Rural Vermont, Montpelier, VT
Jane Rissler, National Wildlife Federation, Washington, DC
Lee Rogers, Foundation on Economic Trends, Washington, DC
Debra Schwarze, Wisconsin Family Farm Defense Fund, Richland Center, WI
Hope Shand, Rural Advancement Fund International, Pittsboro, NC
Margo Stark, Minnesota Food Association, St. Paul, MN
Mary Uva, Public Health Institute, Brooklyn, NY
Jan Wagner, Farm Alliance of Rural Missouri, Jefferson City, MO
Nachama Wilker, Council For Responsible Genetics, Boston, MA.

WORKING GROUP MEMBERS

If an organization wanted to be a Tides Foundation project, essentially they turned over all of their administrative non-program activities to the Tides Foundation and paid the foundation 8% of their gross revenue. All organization employees were then employed by the Tides Foundation, provided with a benefit package and operated under the foundation's personnel policies. All governmental filings, tax reports, and annual reports were prepared and submitted by the Tides Foundation. All legal contracts were reviewed by TF lawyers prior to their being executed. All purchases greater than $250 had to be OKed by TF program representatives before purchase. Staff hirings/firings had to be reviewed by TF representatives. TF assigned an individual to the organization to assist with day-to-day non-programmatic operations. A fundraising plan was worked out and closely monitored. Sources of potential funding from other foundations were directed toward the program by TF representatives. If the project proved effective, the group might end up with its own articles of incorporation, moving to its own offices, with its own funding sources, legitimately doing the activism it had been groomed for. The public didn't know who paid for its grooming.[78a]

The San Francisco Bay Guardian reported, "Wealthy patrons give big chunks of money to Tides—and their names are kept confidential. The Tides donation is completely tax deductible. But the donor can discreetly designate an organization that he or she wants to see receive the money—and Tides will pass the donation along, minus a small administrative fee. Often, the recipient group doesn't know where the money really came from. And there's no way for the public to find out either. By the end of the 1980s Tides had significantly expanded another of its tasks: providing a tax shelter to small non-profits unable or unwilling to win tax-exempt status from the federal government."[78b]

Drummond Pike gained favor with John Peterson "Pete" Myers, director of the highly-focused W. Alton Jones Foundation. In 1992 Jones contributed to seven identifiable Tides donor-advised funds: $40,000 for the Student Environmental Action Coalition in Chapel Hill, North Carolina; $37,000 for Reducing Pesticide Risks Project; $30,000 for Least Cost Energy Analysis Project; $45,000 for the Nuclear Safety Campaign; $20,000 for the Project for Participatory Democracy; $15,000 to the Project for Particpatory Democracy for the Military Production Network; $20,000 for the Rural Alliance for Military Accountability.[78c]

Pike also gained favor with Rebecca Rimel, president of the giant Pew Charitable Trusts (over $15 million from Pew). In 1993 alone, Pew contributed to six identifiable Tides donor-advised funds: $600,000 to manage the Pew Global Stewardship Initiative "and related grantees;"

$275,000 for the Business Industrial Efficiency Initiative; $95,000 for the Environmental Working Group; $25,000 for the U.S. Network for Cairo 1994 (a temporary organization to boost the United Nations International Conference for Population and Development); $75,000 to publish a source book on the 1994 Cairo U.N. Conference; $2,872,000 for the Waste Reduction and Recycling Institute.[79a]

In the early '90s, Tides got donor-advised funds not only from Jones and Pew, but also from Columbia Foundation, the Foundation for Deep Ecology, the Richard and Rhoda Goldman Fund, the William and Flora Hewlett Foundation, the Homeland Foundation, the James Irvine Foundation, the Roberts Foundation, the Hoffman Foundation, the Charles Stewart Mott Foundation (General Motors money), the Nathan Cummings Foundation, the Ford Foundation, the Jessie Smith Noyes Foundation, and the Bullitt Foundation. By the end of 1996 the Tides Foundation had $55.3 million in assets, most of it supporting donor-advised funds.[79b]

Until 1996, the donor-advised fund projects were managed by the Tides Foundation. But to protect the Foundation from legal action that might be

---

THE DONOR-ADVISED FUND

A charitable giving vehicle which enables a donor to make an outright, irrevocable cash contribution through a simple letter of agreement. The recipient then acts as a steward of the contributed monies, and can use them to operate projects or invest them for both growth and income; if income is earned, it must be distributed annually. The donor may make periodic recommendations regarding distribution of the fund's income; as long as these recommendations are non-binding, the donor will receive an income tax deduction for the monies contributed.

BENEFITS

• The donor may stay actively involved, recommending different charities to receive distributions from the Donor Advised Fund each year.

• The donor enjoys administrative convenience.

• Giving to other charities may be done anonymously.

• Donor receives an immediate income tax deduction for the full value of the gift.

• Bypasses capital gains taxes on long-term appreciated securities.

• A Fund can be establish quickly and easily, with a minimum of paperwork.

taken against any of those groups that might get in trouble—and more
than a few harmed parties have considered lawsuits against environmentalists for ruining their lives—the Tides Center was spun off in April
1996, funded by a Tides Foundation grant of $9 million. A year later the
Tides Center's income was $38,813,246, and assets had grown to
$16,080,055. It has its own tax exemption and deductible status.

The legally separate Center now manages all "projects," except for
seven that were retained by the Foundation due to "imminent plans" by
each group to incorporate separately from Tides. The Center also operates its own philanthropy, providing grants to affiliated groups and related projects. At the turn of the century, the Center expected to be managing more than 260 projects in 28 states and five countries. More than
400 staff members will be spending $30 million annually on project man-
agement.

Yes, that's more than two-hundred-sixty "projects" Tides operates.

A truly bewildering array all by itself.

The spin-off of the Tides Center coincided with the move of the whole
Drummond Pike empire in mid-1996 to new facilities in the 55-acre
Letterman Hospital complex at the Presidio of San Francisco, a former
military base declared surplus by Congress and transferred to the Na-
tional Park Service as part of Golden Gate National Recreation Area (now
National Park).

The Tides Foundation topped the list of sixteen organizations with
their winning bid to lease the plum site, with its 1889-era hospital building and circa-1920s additions, nestled in a hollow just west of the Presidio's
Lombard Street gate. Presidio General Manager Bob Chandler said Tides
won because "they fit very well into the management plan's purposes for
a science-education center" and because of "their good track record and
financial capability to deliver." Others thought Drummond Pike's funders'
pull with the Clinton administration had something to do with it.

In 1996 Congress created the Presidio Trust, a federal corporation set
up as a public-private partnership, to manage most of the Presidio. President Clinton appointed six of the Trust's seven-member Board of Directors
in April 1997 (Interior Secretary Bruce Babbitt appointing the seventh),
with a mandate to become self-supporting within fifteen years.

The Tides Foundation, after performing a major rehab including expensive earthquake reinforcement, gave their new digs the pretentious
name, "Thoreau Center for Sustainability." It's touted as the most "environmentally correct" facility in the nation, featuring solar panels, tiles
made from recycled car windshields, double-glazed operable windows,

natural ventilation, energy-efficient light bulbs, toxic-free materials, cotton insulation (recyclable), and wood harvested by Native Americans.

The Thoreau Center is home to twelve non-profit organizations including the Tides Foundation, the Bicycle Coalition, Wilderness Society, Resourceful Women, the Transnational Resource and Action Center, the Ecological Literacy Project and the Institute for Global Communications.

Some Tides donor-advised fund groups, such as the Political Ecology Group, an aggressive in-your-face organization, are quite small. Others, such as the Transnational Resource and Action Center and its Corporate Watch program, are medium sized. Yet others, including the Pew Center for Civic Journalism and the Institute for Global Communications, are quite large.

As projects of the Tides Center these non-profit organizations are not required to file with the IRS any specifics about their own financial operations. They operate under the Tides Center's tax-exempt status. It's probable that some of the more than 250 Tides "projects" would not qualify for tax-exempt status for one reason or another.

Secrecy is one of the major advantages of Drummond Pike's leftist incubator and emporium. The Form 990s filed by Tides with the IRS are remarkably unrevealing. For example, information regarding exactly how each project is spending its money is not disclosed. So when Pew Charitable Trusts awards almost $13 million in grants in 1995 and 1996, Tides' Form 990 doesn't tell us what it's for.

However, Pew *does* have to reveal what it spends its money for, so a really determined researcher can plow through Pew's massive Form 990s for those years, match up contributions to Tides, and see what the stated purpose of each grant is.

There's a hitch, as usual. If the donor gives the grant "for general support," you haven't a clue what the recipient really used it for.

Then there's compensation: non-profits have to reveal on their Form 990s the compensation of their five highest-paid employees (Schedule A, Part I) and of the five highest-paid persons for professional services (Part II). Many of the people Tides names in these two sections are actually project directors for donor-advised fund programs. But Tides is not required to indicate which projects those people worked for.

However, it's possible with other help to figure out who some of them are. In 1992, Malka Kopell ($68,071) was the second highest paid "Tides employee" and was actually project director of Community Focus, a San Francisco activist group. In 1995, Ed Fouhy ($174,656) was actually executive director of the Washington, D.C.-based Pew Center for Civic Journalism, one of Tides's largest projects. Also in 1995, Pam Solo

($111,000) was actually executive director of the Social Venture Network, which represents some 450 "socially responsible" business owners, investors, and activists.

Drummond Pike himself took a salary of $77,083 in 1992, which was lower than his highest-paid project director, Mary Kelly ($85,900).

It's difficult to know what to believe in the Tides Form 990 reports, however, because the story shifts as time goes on. For example, in the 1992 Form 990 employee compensation section, China Brotsky ($51,000) was listed as Tides executive vice president. A 1996 biographical sketch, however, didn't mention her ever being an "Exec V Pres," as the Tides Form 990 stated. Here's the bio sketch version:

> China Brotsky, Director, Special Projects, Tides Foundation. China works as Director of Special Projects for the Tides Foundation and Tides Center. She joined Tides in 1990 as the Foundation's Chief Financial Officer. She has also served as Vice President for Operations at Tides. As Director of Special Projects, China managed the restoration and development of the Thoreau Center for Sustainability, in the Presidio National Park—home to Tides, TRAC and IGC. China Chairs the Advisory Boards of both IGC and TRAC. She also sits on the Board of Directors of the Greenpeace Fund and is a member of the Organizing Board of the Political Ecology Group.[82]

It doesn't tell us much about what jobs Tides employees really do, but it certainly shows us how extensively networked they are.

The anti-corporate star of the Tides empire is Joshua Karliner, Executive Director of Transnational Resource and Action Center and editorial coordinator of Corporate Watch. Karliner has taught global environmental politics at the University of San Francisco, served as Earth Summit Coordinator for Greenpeace International, and in the 1980s was founder and executive director of the Environmental Project on Central America. Quite a few Greenpeace connections in Tides.

It's not clear whether all this is perfectly legal.

It even annoys far-leftists, who feel that foundations are impeding leftward progress by imposing a less radical agenda, not enhancing it, as bizarre as that sounds to the average American rural dweller.

Nyah, nyah, my radical agenda's more radical than yours?

The very-left San Francisco Bay Guardian published a whole raft of anti-foundation articles in 1997, even one questioning whether Tides was following IRS rules properly.

Guardian writer Martin Espinoza asked Larry Wright, public affairs officer for the Northern California District of the IRS, about Tides and its 250-plus projects. Wright responded that it's unusual for a 501(c)(3) non-profit to have that many projects under its tax-exempt umbrella.

"Tax-exempt status is not transferable," Wright said. A non-profit holding the 501(c)(3), he added, has to prove that the activities of any and all of its sponsored projects satisfy the same stated tax-exempt purpose as that cited by the organization in filing with the IRS.

"In general when you have an organization that has established its own offices, its own directors, all of its activities have to be directly related," he said. "You can't just set up a clearinghouse; it can't pass along its tax-exempt status."[83a]

Maybe you can.

If you're the Tides Foundation. Or the Tides Center.

The puppy mill of the environmental movement.

COMPUTERS FOR SOCIAL CHANGE

The Tides Foundation's most successful project has been the creation of a worldwide computer network for left-wing activists, embodied in two organizations residing in the Thoreau Center: the Institute for Global Communications and the Association for Progressive Communication. The history of the Association for Progressive Communication (APC) began in 1984, when Ark Communications Institute, the Center for Innovative Diplomacy, Community Data Processing, and the Foundation for the Arts of Peace—all located in the San Francisco Bay Area—joined forces to create PeaceNet, the world's first computer network dedicated exclusively to serving leftist movements.[83b]

In 1987, PeaceNet became a project of the Tides Foundation, and the Institute for Global Communications (IGC) was formed to direct and support its activities through the usual contractual arrangement.

Parallel to this, with seed money from Apple Computer and the San Francisco Foundation, in 1982 the Farallones Institute created EcoNet to advance environmentalism. Farallones transferred EcoNet to the newly-formed Institute for Global Communications in 1987.

ConflictNet, "dedicated to serving nonviolent conflict resolution, dispute mediation and arbitration," according to its foundationese purpose statement, joined IGC in 1990. During the '90s came LaborNet and WomensNet—the five making up the IGC Networks.

The Institute for Global Communications began collaborating with a similar network in the United Kingdom, London-based GreenNet, in 1987 joining together seamlessly to demonstrate that transnational electronic communications could serve left-wing causes.

This transatlantic link was so successful that, with the support of the MacArthur, Ford and General Service foundations and the United Nations Development Program, by late 1989 IGC helped to establish five more networks, in Sweden (NordNet), Canada (Web), Brazil (AlterNex), Nicaragua (Nicarao) and Australia (Pegasus). In the spring of 1990, these seven organizations founded the Association for Progressive Communications (APC) to coordinate the operation and development of this emerging global network of networks.[84]

Today, APC has more than 25 member networks, and more than 40 "partners" not yet with full member capabilities, with more than 50,000 subscribers in over 100 countries.

APC provides: Internet access; training and support for users, trainers and facilitators; news and information services; communications consulting; online collaboration strategies and methodologies website development; public and private workspaces (mailing lists and newsgroups); customized information tools (databases and search engines). In countries without reliable communications infrastructure, APC uses links to low-tech sources and helps with improvements.

You can see why the Environmental Grantmakers Association loves the Tides Foundation and Tides Center.

R - E -A - C - H.

If you're a logger or a miner or a rancher or a farmer or a trapper or a resource worker or property owner of any kind, with APC and IGC, the enviros worldwide can be on your case before you know you have a case.

There are so many limbs and branches growing out of the Tides operations it's nearly impossible to track them all.

How so?

Tides projects have projects.

For example: Transnational Resource and Action Center (TRAC), that anti-capitalist, anti-corporate outfit, as we know, is a Tides project. Corporate Watch, an anti-corporate, anti-capitalist online web magazine, is a project of TRAC edited by TRAC's executive director.

For example: Corporate Watch is *also* a project of the Institute for Global Communications, which is a Tides project (see chart opposite).

For example: The Clearinghouse for Environmental Advocacy and Research (CLEAR), an opposition-research organization that finds and smears anyone who doesn't like what environmentalism does to them, is a project of the Environmental Working Group. The Environmental Working Group, an anti-pesticide, anti-industry, anti-resource-class task force supported by donor-advised funds, is a Tides project.

Projects within projects within projects.

TIDES TROUBLEMAKING TREE

DONOR FOUNDATION

TIDES CENTER

DONOR-ADVISED FUND

PROJECTS (FUNDERS)

INSTITUTE FOR GLOBAL COMMUNICATIONS	TRANSNATIONAL RESOURCE AND ACTION CENTER	ASSOCIATION FOR PROGRESSIVE COMMUNICATION (FORD, MACARTHUR)
Corporate Watch	SOCIAL VENTURE NETWORK	ENVIRONMENTAL WORKING GROUP (PEW, BULLITT, PACKARD, ETC.)
BIOTECHNOLOGY WORKING GROUP (C.S. FUND, NOYES, JOYCE, BABCOCK)	ECOLOGICAL SOCIETY PROJECT (FOUNDATION FOR DEEP ECOLOGY)	Clearinghouse for Environmental Advocacy and Research (Jones)
PEW CENTER FOR CIVIC JOURNALISM	PEW GLOBAL STEWARDSHIP INITIATIVE	RURAL ALLIANCE FOR MILITARY ACCOUNTABILITY (JONES)
PROJECT FOR PARTICIPATORY DEMOCRACY	DEFINING SUSTAINABLE COMMUNITIES PROJECT (IRVINE)	INSTITUTE FOR DEEP ECOLOGY (FOUNDATION FOR DEEP ECOLOGY)
BOULDER-WHITE CLOUDS COUNCIL (SIERRA CLUB, JONES, PEW)	CALIFORNIA CENTER FOR LEAD SAFE HOUSING (IRVINE)	FOREST ISLAND PROGRAM
CAMPAIGN FOR AN ENVIRONMENTAL ECONOMY (JONES)	BIODIVERSITY ACTION NETWORK (JONES)	AGRICULTURAL WETLANDS POLICY PROJECT
ENVIRONMENT AND DEMOCRACY CAMPAIGN IN CENTRAL EUROPE (MOTT)	FOREST TRUST (FORD)	REDUCING PESTICIDE RISKS (JONES)
THE MOVEMENT FOR ENVIRONMENTAL JUSTICE AND A SUSTAINABLE ECONOMY (CUMMINGS)	Network of Forest-Based Organizations (Ford)	MORE THAN 250 PROJECTS IN THE TIDES ORBIT
	WASTE REDUCTION AND RECYLLING INSTITUTE (PEW)	

EACH SOLID BOX = SEPARATE PROJECT
DASH-LINE BOX WITH ARROW = PROJECT OF PROJECT

TOUGH ACT

"Philanthropic foundations are sometimes criticized for having a social agenda," said the blonde Virginian to a University of Pennsylvania audience. "Well, you know what? They're right!"[86a]

That's Rebecca W. Rimel, unapologetic, ruthless, powerful, and noisy in public. She's president of Pew Charitable Trusts, fifth-largest U.S. foundation in terms of assets, with more than $4.7 billion, and third in grantmaking behind Ford and W.K. Kellogg. She sees to it that Pew's environmental grants rank only behind those of the John D. and Catherine T. MacArthur Foundation of Chicago and the Richard King Mellon Foundation of Pittsburgh.

Rimel's generosity keeps the Tides Foundation ferocious.

And a lot of other environmentalist operations, too.

There's just one hitch.

They do what she wants. Or else.

Sam Hitt, head of the Forest Guardians in Santa Fe, New Mexico, told High Country News in 1995, "When Pew steps in, it's like a death star in the solar system. They set up their own gravitational field and everyone begins to revolve around them. I've watched activists go through this dance of making themselves look fundable to Pew by altering their priorities to meet Pew's goals. I've had it with those guys."[86b]

Rimel is utterly unfazed by such grassroots criticism. Under her leadership, Pew has become a dynamic force in philanthropy. She has presided over what Council on Foundations head Dorothy Ridings calls "the most radical transformation of any charitable institution."[86c]

Beck, as her family calls her, got to her lofty perch by pure brains, talent and guts. Less than 20 years ago, she was an emergency room nurse in Charlottesville, Virginia, from a working-class family, no elite schools, no connections with the hot-shot academic institutions that supply most executives to the Golden Donors.

Rimel came to a quiet, closeted Pew in 1983 as director of the foundation's health program, selected by Tom Langfitt, an eminent neurosurgeon specializing in head injuries and one of the nine owners of stock in the Glenmede Trust Company, the controlling family entity of the Pew Charitable Trusts. Dr. Langfitt had first met her in 1979 at a conference and was astounded at an innovative paper she had written about brain injuries, unheard of in a person lacking a doctor's degree, whether Ph.D. or M.D.

Langfitt made sure Rimel got grants to continue her research. When he later became dissatisfied with Pew's health program, he invited Rimel to apply for the job, an act of faith. She got the job, learned fast and worked hard. By 1985, Rimel was Pew's vice president in charge of health and human services, conservation and religion. When Langfitt became Pew's president in February 1987, he purged the executive director, three of the four vice presidents (but not Rimel) and 13 of 15 program officers. Langfitt wanted to leverage Pew money like Robert Scrivner was leveraging the Rockefeller Family Fund's money. He clearly thought Rimel could do it: in 1988, she became Pew's executive director at age 37. A lot of insiders were angry at her rapid rise.

Urged on by Dr. Langfitt, Rebecca Rimel rebuilt Pew. She immediately hired a headhunter, former New York City deputy mayor Edward Hamilton, and told him, "I want candidates from nontraditional fields. If they have some foundation experience, OK, but they have to be real-world people." He found her six new program directors and eleven associates.

One of those directors came on board in 1990 and grew into the hidden menace of the resource class and property owners: Joshua S. Reichert, a man of remarkable background and connections and the real reason Pew's environmental program has been so successful. Rimel had the brains and the money and the ruthless will, but Reichert knew where the levers of power were.

Reichert holds a doctorate in social anthropology from Princeton (Laurance Rockefeller went there), with undergraduate work at the University of California at Davis. He spent time as an activist with the United Farm Workers, dealing with migrant laborers and Native American groups on farm labor conditions, bilingual education, and economic development.

He then went to the Inter-American Foundation, created by Congress as an agency of the United States, which provides assistance to grassroots organizations in Latin America. As a representative of the IAF, Reichert learned the bureaucrat trade and made many international connections that would propel him into the foundation world.

He caught the eye of the North Shore Unitarian Universalist Veatch Program, which hired him as executive director. The Veatch Program, established by a gift from congregation member Caroline Veatch in 1959, is a typical funder of "justice, equity, and compassion" projects with an extensive environmental component (1993 environmental grants, $2.1 million, 1994, $1.8 million). Barbara Dudley later served in the same job, and she went on to become head of Greenpeace in the United States. Dudley was an early participant in the Environmental Grantmakers Association.

Reichert then became executive vice president for conservation programs at Conservation International, a 1987 breakaway from The Nature Conservancy that made its own reputation "saving tropical rainforests" through debt-for-nature swaps. CI was created by Peter Seligmann, a former Nature Conservancy executive and ace fund-raiser. CI introduced Josh Reichert to everybody in Washington he didn't already know.

After producing marine conservation films, he moved on to the National Security Archive as interim director. The Archive is an odd hybrid, "an independent non-governmental research institute and library" located at the George Washington University in Washington, D.C. Don't let the academic setting fool you. It's a "progressive" front: the Archive collects and publishes declassified documents acquired through the Freedom of Information Act (FOIA), but mostly those that push a left-wing policy agenda. Its website looks like an anti-war, anti-nuclear, anti-conservative bumper sticker—and it's funded by the W. Alton Jones Foundation, which has only two purposes: environmentalism and anti-nuclear activism.

The Archive also looks like another one of those donor-advised funds: financial affairs are administered by The Fund for Peace, Inc, a New York-based tax-exempt corporation established in 1957 "to encourage research and public education on international affairs." The Archive's advisory board is chaired by Russell Hemenway, president of the National Committee for an Effective Congress, a "progressive" Democrat-oriented political action committee established by Eleanor Roosevelt and friends in 1948.

By the time Rimel's headhunter came looking for him, Joshua Reichert had a Ph.D., worked as a labor activist, had been a federal bureaucrat, served as an executive in a big-time environmental group, led a foundation, and directed a left-wing outfit with connections to a left-wing political action committee. He knew a lot of important people. A lot of important people knew him, which is what matters.

He was real-world enough for Rebecca Rimel.

Then came two real-world men who had learned their trade from Donald Ross: Thomas Wathen and John Gilroy, who came to Pew Charitable Trusts in Rimel's reconstruction.

With Rimel as their boss, Reichert, Wathen and Gilroy became the bully boys of environmental philanthropy.

Take this money. Do with it as we say. Make sure it works.

"We are very product-oriented," Reichert told the Boston Globe. "We need to demonstrate a return on these investments ... that is measurable."

Pew's 1995 $590,000 investment in the Alaska Conservation Foundation and the Alaska Coastal Rainforest Initiative could be measured easily: it killed two long-term timber contracts that the U.S government had begged for in the 1950s to stabilize a seasonal fishing-only economy.

An east-coast newspaper said of the return on this investment, "In

Alaska, environmentalists credit Reichert with devising the national strategy that helped bring an end to two subsidized logging contracts in the Tongass National Forest."[89]

Product-oriented.

Pew's biggest product is unemployment for the resource class.

Reichert told eco-writer Mark Dowie, "I don't want someone who knows the facts, or can articulate them persuasively; I want someone who wants to win and knows how."

He got it in Tom Wathen.

He helped arrange a $450,000 Pew investment in the Southwest Forest Alliance that strategized the sawmill shutdowns in Arizona that we saw in Chapter 1 (page 17). It was Pew behind the scenes; the lawsuit-wielding Southwest Center for Biological Diversity was part of the Southwest Forest Alliance. They won.

Precision Pine & Timber, Inc., closed its Snowflake, Arizona, planer mill in March 1995 because of court action that prevented harvesting timber in the Apache Sitgreaves National Forest southwest of Greer. At question was whether the Forest Service had performed a proper environmental review. The restraining order was granted by U.S. District Judge Paul Rosenblatt in a lawsuit brought by environmentalists Peter Galvin of New Mexico (interestingly enough, Galvin is another one of the Earth First!ers arrested in the site occupation of the Okanogan National Forest headquarters in 1988, mentioned on pages 25-26), the Greater Gila Biodiversity Project and the Southwest Center for Biological Diversity. In such lawsuits a bond is required to compensate the other side if a lawsuit fails. However, Judge Rosenblatt set the bond at only $1, saying the environmentalists were acting in the public interest and had limited resources.

Judge Rosenblatt had no idea who was funding his plaintiff. By 1998, some of the master strategists behind the attack on Southwest logging were sitting on a $4.7 billion endowment. (Full story begins p. 130.)

Ruthless. As the Boston Globe reported,

> Inside the downtown Philadelphia offices of the nation's fourth largest charity, Pew Charitable Trusts, Joshua Reichert plays a subtle game of kingmaker. As the man in charge of doling out the single largest block of money earmarked for environmental causes, Reichert's ideas have a way of becoming reality.
>
> When Reichert suggests two environmental groups should merge, they quickly meet to discuss the idea. When Reichert became frustrated that environmentalists are losing the public relations wars, Pew created a public relations firm to join the fray. If Reichert doesn't like the way a group is being run, he withholds its money.

Most importantly, Reichert consistently pushes environmentalists to be practical, even if that means bruising egos or accepting compromises that purists detest. Along the way, Pew has reshaped the debate on issues such as logging, air pollution and energy conservation— and made some enemies, too.

"They have been bullies.... They are arrogant," said Beth Daley, vice president of the National Center for Responsive Philanthropy in Washington, D.C., which monitors foundations.[90a]

The New Pew.

The old Pew was quite different, the philanthropy of Sun Oil Company baron Joseph Newton Pew Jr., a Republican Party boss who detested government regulation. The Pew Charitable Trusts is actually seven individual trusts established between 1948 and 1979 by the four sons and daughters of old Joe Pew.

Until 1948, the Pew family gave away money as a matter of conscience through personal donations. They went to hospitals, schools and cultural institutions in the Philadelphia area: to Presbyterian Church activities, to conservative organizations and publications. They gave money to the John Birch Society and other anti-communist organizations. They did it by writing checks to their favorite charities without planning, processing, evaluation or follow-up. It wasn't until 1977 that anybody managed the Pew donations at all, then Robert Smith, a bright young vice president of the oil company, did it.

Things have certainly changed since then.

Rimel's prescriptive stance jars with the passive giving practiced by the heirs of Sun Oil founder Joseph N. Pew. Aggressive prescription accurately describes Rimel's approach in pumping over $38.6 million in 1998 into causes that Pew himself would have loathed. She herself earned $330,470 in 1995. She sits on many boards, including the Council on Foundations, the foster parent of the Environmental Grantmakers Association.

The Philadelphia Inquirer quoted former program director Kevin Quigley as saying, "The donors would not only be rolling in their graves these days, they would be gyrating at very high speeds." To hell with donor intent.[90b]

Dead hands have no power. Rebecca Rimel does.

Her power comes from the $4.7 billion endowment money in Pew investment portfolios as of 1999. The trusts made $205 million in investment income in 1993 from timber stocks such as Weyerhaeuser ($16 million) and International Paper ($4.56 million), mining stocks such as Phelps

Dodge ($3.7 million), and oil stocks such as Atlantic Richfield ($6.1 million).[91]

Rimel's Pew insists on working the environmental movement through coalitions. The Philadelphia Inquirer wrote that Pew "has relentlessly pushed environmental groups to work together in alliances." Going it alone does not allow leveraging investments or finding models for replication. Characteristic Pew coalition grants include:

Community Farm Alliance, Frankfort, Kentucky. $130,000. "For the Southern Sustainable Agriculture Working Group, a 50-organization network in 13 southern states." The "community farm movement" joins organic farmers to urban and suburban consumers who put up money in advance for a year's worth of home-delivered groceries as produce comes in season, sharing the farmer's risk. The Alliance also helps organic farmers organize, pushes to legalize hemp growing for fiber, and advocates elimination of pesticides and chemical fertilizers.

Greater Yellowstone Coalition, Bozeman, Montana. $600,000. "For the Northern Rockies Ecosystem Protection Campaign to protect the forested wildlands and watersheds of the Northern Rocky Mountains." Foundationese for "anti-mining, anti-logging alliance."

The Minnesota Project, St. Paul, Minnesota. $70,000. "To support the Campaign for Sustainable Agriculture, which includes approximately 500 farming and environmental groups from around the country working to strengthen federal agriculture policies that enable more environmentally sound practices." Get out your foundationese dictionary, you can feel the anti-industry gremlins lurking in there everywhere.

B.C. Wild, Vancouver, British Columbia, Canada. $1,140,000. "To achieve protected status for a minimum 12 percent of British Columbia's threatened ancient forests and other wilderness areas." This anti-mining, anti-logging coalition includes the World Wildlife Fund Canada, Sierra Club of B.C., Canadian Parks and Wilderness Society, and Sierra Legal Defense Fund.

OPPONENTS

Among the first major problems that arose to thwart Pew's inexorable march to environmentalist victory was the wise use movement. This grassroots response to environmentalist destruction of the resource class and property owners was the most alarming thing that had ever happened to environmentalists.

In 1992, the Environmental Grantmakers Association addressed the problem at their annual retreat, held that year in Washington State's San

Juan Islands at the cushy Rosario Resort. In a session titled, "The Wise Use Movement: Threats and Opportunities," two foundation presenters told the tale.[92]

Debra Callahan, W. Alton Jones Foundation grassroots coordinator (she's now head of the League of Conservation Voters) explained:

> What we're finding is that wise use is really a local movement driven by primarily local concerns and not national issues. We tend— you know, when you think of Ron Arnold and you think of Wise Use, you know—you think of command and control, top-heavy, corporate funded front groups that are organizing local people to get involved, get out there and attack environmentalists.
>
> And that was the assumption I walked into this whole thing with. And, in fact, the more we dig into it, having put together a fifty— really constructed over a number of months—a fifty state, fairly comprehensive survey of what's going on with respect to wise use organizing activity, we have come to the conclusion that this is pretty much generally a grass roots movement, which is a problem, because it means there's no silver bullets.
>
> It means this is, is, you know, something that is going to have to be confronted in states and communities across the country in different ways depending on what the various local issues are that those wise use groups are dealing with and campaigning on.

Environmentalists have never admitted this guilty knowledge in public. It is too devastating. However, Callahan said as much, reproduced here from a verbatim transcription of the taped session:

> What people fundamentally believe about environmental protection is that, no it's not just jobs, and no it's not just environment, why can't we have both?
>
> The high ground here is capturing that message, ok? And in fact the wise use movement is trying to capture that message. What they're saying out there is "we are the real environmentalists. We are the stewards of the land. We're the farmers who have tilled the land and we know how to manage this land because we've done it here for generations. We're the miners and we're the ones who depend for our livelihood on this land. These guys live in glass towers in New York City. They're not environmentalists, they're elitists. They're part of the problem, and they're aligned with big government and they're out of touch. So we are the real environmentalists."

> And if that's the message that the wise use movement is able to capture, we are suddenly the equivalent of incumbents in this election year. We're really unpopular.

It is significant that the foundations were concerned about the wise use movement as a threat to their message and popularity, not to the environment.

Foundation leaders knew they were causing massive economic damage to rural communities, as confirmed by co-presenter Judy Donald of the Washington, D.C.-based Beldon Fund:

> There are, as Deb has made clear, ordinary people, grass roots organizations, who obviously feel their needs are being addressed by this movement. We have to have a strategy that also is addressing those concerns. And that *cannot* come from environmentalists. It can't come just from us. That's the—I think that's the dilemma here. People—it's not simply that they don't get it, it's that they do get it. They're losing their jobs.

The entire conference had centered around the word "transition" with a new meaning: rural cleansing, the replacement of resource jobs with service jobs. Foundation leaders knew it was class warfare, the elite class eliminating the resource class. Barbara Dudley, then of the Veatch Program, now of Greenpeace, stated this guilty knowledge bluntly:

> This is a class issue. There is no question about it. It is true that the environmental movement is, has been, an upper class, conservation, white movement. We have to face that fact. It's true. They're not wrong that we are rich and they are up against us. We are the enemy as long as we behave in that fashion.

Their solution: split the wise use movement apart with "wedge issues" and marginalize it with a smear campaign. This exchange between Judy Donald and Barbara Dudley illustrates:

Judy Donald (Beldon Fund): And I think if we pay for meetings where environmentalists get together to forge a strategy to counter wise use we may be going down the wrong track here. We have to be encouraging meetings where environmentalists and non-environmentalists, you know, and people who are losing their jobs talk about their real—both of their—concerns and together come up with a local solution.

And of course in the process the connections to the right wing have to be exposed, the connections to the extraction industry have to be exposed. I think we really should be thinking about all the ways in which we can bring those two communities together.

Barbara?

Barbara Dudley (Veatch Program): I just want to add that I think it's important not to just think about what we might fund to counteract this movement, but we need to think about what we shouldn't be funding. Because we have done a lot of funding of the family farm movement and let me tell you they are not fond of environmentalists. And deservedly so. There is a major environmental funder who is very big into sustainable agriculture whose quotation is now being spread throughout the family farm movement and it is: "I don't give a damn if we're left with only one farmer as long as he farms without chemicals."

And that, I can't tell you, from the work we've done with the family farm movement, how many times I have been embarrassed to be associated with environmentalists, and with environmental grantmakers and their projects. I don't know how many of you funded the *Beyond Beef* campaign, but that project has done more damage to any potential alliance between family farmers or ranchers or cattlemen and the environmental movement.

These upper class funders immediately got busy with projects designed to smear the wise use movement. Typical grants:

W. Alton Jones Foundation, Virginia, all in 1993:

Maine Audubon Society, Falmouth, Maine. $26,250. "The Grassroots Action Project, a project to promote coordination and organization efforts in the conservation community to counter anti-environmental efforts."

Missouri Coalition for the Environment Foundation, St. Louis, Missouri. $20,000. "'Exposing Unwise Abuse' in Missouri." Grassroots organizing against environmental backlash activities in the Ozark Mountains.

Piedmont Environmental Council, Warrenton, Pennsylvania. $25,000. "Property Rights Project."

Society for the Protection of New Hampshire Forests, Concord, New Hampshire. $26,250. "The Grassroots Action Project, a project to promote coordination and organization efforts in the conservation community to counter anti-environmental efforts.'

Vermont Natural Resources Council, Montpelier, Vermont.

$26,250. "The Grassroots Action Project, a project to promote coordination and organization efforts in the conservation community to counter anti-environmental efforts."

Western States Center, Portland, Oregon. $20,000. "To support WSC's efforts to research, assess and oppose anti-environmental activities and to promote support for environmentally sustainable economic policies."

Clearinghouse on Environmental Advocacy and Research, Washington, D.C. $145,000. "For the creation of a national information clearinghouse to collect and disseminate information on environmental backlash."

Jessie Noyes Smith Foundation, New York, in 1993:

Western States Center, Portland, Oregon. $15,000. "For research, public education and coalition building addressing Wise Use movement and need for sustainable development."

The 1997 Environmental Grantmaking Foundations Directory lists 16 foundations that specifically fund anti-Wise Use movement groups.

FUNDERS DONATING TO WISE USE OPPONENTS	
Alaska Conservation Foundation	Patagonia, Inc.
Beldon Fund	The Public Welfare Foundation
Bullitt Foundation	Rockefeller Family Fund
Educational Foundation of America	Town Creek Foundation
Flintridge Foundation	Universalist Unitarian Veatch
Foundation for Deep Ecology	Program at Shelter Rock
Maki Foundation	Winslow Foundation
McKenzie River Gathering Foundation	Margaret Cullinan Wray
The John Merck Fund	Charitable Lead Trust

"We must identify our enemies and drive them into oblivion."
Rural cleansing. Dismantling industrial civilization piece by piece.

Joshua Reichert has helped Pew create several environmental organizations, including a public relations firm which, according to the Philadelphia Inquirer, "played a key role in pressuring President Clinton to approve new air pollution rules" (see pages 210-215).[95a]

The public relations firm began very quietly in 1993 as Reichert circulated a proposal to other foundation leaders to join in funding a new venture he called "Environmental Strategies." Its foundationese mission statement was "to assist environmental organizations to conduct public education campaigns on priority national environmental issues."[95b]

What that really meant was to help environmentalists split the wise use movement with wedge issues and smear wise users as being anti-environment rather than being anti-environmentalist.

Most of the people who received Reichert's proposal had been at the 1992 Environmental Grantmakers Association retreat and agreed with Chuck Clusen's panel that no single Green Group had produced a full-spectrum power and pressure machine. Most agreed with Hooper Brooks that the foundations had to become prescriptive in order to force into existence the coalitions and alliances which could form that machine. The real job of the new public relations group would be to create synthetic coalitions. Reichert's concept paper for Environmental Strategies said:

> For considerable sums of money, public opinion can be molded, constituents mobilized, issues researched, and public officials button-holed, all in a symphonic arrangement. There are media spots, direct mail drops, phone banks, and old fashioned lobbying, tactics employed in specific target areas, all informed by opinion research. While business and industry has made extensive use of them, environmentalists have been slow to employ and, equally important, to coordinate these new political arts. As a result environmentalism has fallen behind in a political arms race that requires even higher levels of organized constituent involvement to influence officials and engender administrative or legislative action.[96]

Environmental Strategies was very quietly incorporated in Washington, D.C., on February 4, 1994. The incorporators were: Frances Beinecke, Natural Resources Defense Council; Donald K. Ross, Rockefeller Family Fund; Douglas Foy, Conservation Law Foundation; and Thomas Wathen, Pew Charitable Trusts (which gave $650,000 for startup through the Tides Foundation—another donor-advised fund).

Who are these symphonic arrangers?

If you've visited the Yale University campus, you know the name Beinecke seems to be everywhere, Beinceke Plaza, Beinecke Library. The NRDC's deputy director at the time, Frances Beinecke (Yale Class of '71), is the daughter of William S. Beinecke, a businessman who was the principal donor of the Beinecke Library. Frances is a trustee of the Yale Corporation, governing board of the university. She has since become the NRDC's executive director (1998). She co-founded the New York League of Conservation Voters (NYLCV) in 1989 with Paul Elston (her husband), Robert F. Kennedy Jr. and Larry Rockefeller, a lawyer with NRDC. When she helped incorporate Environmental Strategies, she was earning $88,718 a year at NRDC, with a $10,284 benefit package, a nice frill to the family fortune. She's rich and powerful and connected.

We know Don Ross well enough already.

But who's Douglas Foy? Aside from being the head of the Boston-based, foundation-nourished Conservation Law Foundation, he's a Princeton man (Class of '69) —the old school tie to Joshua Reichert. Foy received Princeton University's Woodrow Wilson Award in recognition of his achievements, which were cited as an example of Wilson's vision for "Princeton in the nation's service." He's very much the strategic thinker, as he showed himself in a lecture at his alma mater, stressing "that top-down regulation by government is an abject failure and that local involvement in environmental issues is essential since it fosters credibility and teaches what community means."[97]

Tom Wathen, last of the incorporators, had been an all-around Pew operative, Reichert's front man in the field cultivating the grass roots while Josh and Rebecca Rimel traipsed here and there, perhaps to the Amazon rain forest with Joseph N. Pew's grandson, J. Howard "Howdy" Pew II, an avid outdoorsman who visits environmental hot spots on grandpa's money.

Environmental Strategies received a good dose of start-up money ($125,000) from the W. Alton Jones Foundation, even though Jones didn't sign on as a named incorporator. The Pew/Rockefeller/Jones cluster pressured other foundations to fund their effort: Jessie Smith Noyes Foundation, Public Welfare Foundation, and the Florence and John Schumann Foundation, among others, joined in. Environmental Strategies started with $2 million but no leader.

By the summer of 1994, Reichert had interviewed scores of candidates for the top jobs at Environmental Strategies before finding the right team.

The original staff is indicative: it was a virtual Who's Who of Democratic Party politics. Philip E. Clapp, executive director, was a member of the national steering committee of Environmentalists for Clinton-Gore. Mike Casey, media relations director, came directly from the Democratic Congressional Campaign Committee. Staffer Arlie Schardt served as press secretary for Al Gore's unsuccessful presidential bid. Schardt runs his own outfit, Environmental Media Services. Hardball players all.

The media contracts were handled by Washington, D.C.-based Fenton Communications, long a favorite of the far left: During the 1980s, for example, Fenton Communications had contracts with the Christic Institute and the communist regimes of Angola and Nicaragua as a registered agent of a foreign government. Fenton Communications is best known for engineering the Alar scare that destroyed hundreds of family apple orchard businesses. David Fenton talked CBS's "60 Minutes" into reporting as fact an unproven claim by Beinecke's Natural Resources Defense Council that Alar, a root-applied chemical used to ripen apples, was a serious cancer risk to children. Horrified parents across the nation quit purchasing apples as a result of the report, which bankrupted whole communities of apple orchardists. In fact, the government was already phasing out Alar (which the NRDC knew) and not a single case of any disease at all was ever attributed to Alar. Shardt's Environmental Media Services shares office space with Fenton Communications.

That original name, Environmental Strategies, was not very cuddly. Two months after incorporating, on April 3, 1994, the incorporators changed it to Environmental Information Center and went public in November. Even that wasn't good enough, because it's now called "the National Environmental Trust."

From "Strategies" to "Trust" with "Information" in the middle.

The archetype of foundationese.

The PR outfit's first task was to combat the emerging wise use movement, then to create a new grassroots movement for environmentalists who had lost their authentic supporters.

The Environmental Information Center's original PR kit said it was "founded in November 1994 to combat environmental misinformation and help strengthen grassroots support for environmental protection." (No mention of the Environmental Strategies incarnation.)

Then the adequately grant-driven Environmental Information Center launched a series of "Strategy Sessions" in a dozen cities across the country to get things moving. The sessions were for local environmental group leaders only, no reporters invited. The programs went like this:[98]

After a hosted breakfast, EIC executive director Phil Clapp opened each session with a short pep talk about the goals of the meeting, how the Endangered Species Act debate was shaping up, and comments from a trusted (and already-funded) local leader.

Then came a session called "Coalition-Building" where everyone said who they were, who they'd been working with, and how they built a winning coalition in their area of specialization.

A "Message" session produced a handout ballot for everyone to vote on which messages they found to work best with fellow activists, general public, legislators, and media.

Just before lunch came the guts of the spontaneous grassroots campaign. The schedule said, "Discussion of successful techniques including targeting, canvassing, literature drops, petitions, press conferences and stunts, direct mail, phone banking, sign-on letters, constituent visits, paid ads attacking foes and defending friends, radio and TV actualities and PSAs, talk shows, newspaper op-eds, letters to the editor; and editorial board briefings, and opposition research and debunking, opinion polls."

In the Seattle session, organizers from the Pacific Northwest, Northern Rockies, and Alaska told attendees what they'd found did and didn't work in their campaigns.

After lunch, David Fenton of Fenton Communications told the group about the media, its role in politics, and how to use it better.

Fenton stressed, "Educating the media so as to educate the public," and gave examples from actual news reports. The Seattle session featured a Post-Intelligencer story he had planted on how logging kills salmon.

Fenton also emphasized "reaching different audiences on the Endangered Species Act such as religious, scientific, health, and children's constituencies. How we avoid creating sympathy for the other side."

John Hoyt of Pyramid Communications led a short panel discussion on what works to get on the radar screen of a member of Congress, followed by role playing on a visit to a reluctant congressman's office, using the technique of showing news media results to members and staff for maximum payoff.

Late in the day the group split into sections to discuss goals for the next 10 weeks, then worked backwards to set priorities, assess the people and resources needed, decide who does what, and write a timetable.

They ended the day trading phone, fax and e-mail information, then retired to cocktails for an hour of "informal discussion and networking."

At no time did anyone talk about doing anything directly on the ground in the environment.

Only a few invitees in the room had any idea of the magnitude of the campaign they had been invited into, and none knew who was paying for it.

As the EIC's Strategy Sessions rolled across the country, environmental groups by the dozen put their hands out for large grants to "reinvigorate the grassroots," an activity that hadn't previously interested them. They got the money. And did what they had been taught.

Media outlets subsequently reported a large and spontaneous growth of grassroots environmentalism. Why did the media cooperate?

Public Media Center:

$300,000 from Pew Charitable Trusts. "To design, coordinate and place series of issue and information bulletins in major newspapers to inform and educate policy makers, opinion leaders and American public about global stewardship issues."

Foundation for American Communications:

$75,000 from W. Alton Jones Foundation. "To train journalists to cover environmental issues in the context of major current events, and to put these issues into a local perspective."

Center for Investigative Reporting:

$100,000 from W. Alton Jones Foundation. "For reporting on current dynamics of national environmental organizing efforts."

$105,000 from Florence and John Schumann Foundation. "For research on environmental conflicts in the West."

Center for Media in the Public Interest:

$25,000 from Florence and John Schumann Foundation. "To train activists to effectively use advocacy media."

Society of Environmental Journalists:

$50,000 from W. Alton Jones Foundation. "To improve the quality and visibility of responsible reporting on key environmental policy issues."

World Media Foundation:

$250,000 from W. Alton Jones Foundation. "For a weekly environmental news and information program, LIVING ON EARTH."

Environmental Media Association:

$25,000 from Heinz Family Foundation. "Toward creating public service announcements (PSAs) on the environment."

Cartoonists & Writers Syndicate:

$100,000 from W. Alton Jones Foundation. "Ecotoons: A project to syndicate and publish collections of political cartoons with environmental themes."

And so forth.

OH, GOD!

Probably the most enchanting move of the Pew/Rockefeller/Jones cluster of foundations was the creation of the Evangelical Environmental Network. If you enjoy religion *a la mode*, you'll love this. The Evangelical Environmental Network (EEN) launched a multi-million dollar public relations campaign in January 1996 to convince the American people that the Endangered Species Act is the "Noah's Ark of our day."

The builders of that ark, Congress, were mostly Republicans in 1996, and they were considering the addition of property rights language to the Endangered Species Act, which meant that the government would have to pay when environmental regulations deprived property owners of the use of their property. The prospect of actually paying for what they took from property owners horrified environmentalists, who realized it would bankrupt the United States Treasury instead of the United States citizenry.

They had to get the message out that Congress wanted "to gut the Endangered Species Act."

They had to recruit the biggest voice around.

God.

Fenton Communications was as close as they could get.

According to the Washington Post, "The Environmental Information Center, a Washington-based organization funded by the Pew Charitable Trusts and other foundations, is underwriting the cost of ad production" for the EEN's Endangered Species Act campaign. Fenton did the rest.[101a]

EEN touted itself as a "mainstream coalition of evangelicals concerned about the environment."

The mainstream of what was not clear.

One of EEN's key leaders was Ron Sider, professor of theology at Eastern Baptist Seminary in Wynnewood, Pennsylvania, and president of Evangelicals for Social Action, which founded the network. Sider is one of the leaders of "Call to Renewal," a religious coalition established to counter the Christian Coalition. Sider had also been an outspoken critic of the GOP's "Contract with America," telling Christianity Today magazine... (Oh, yes, this might explain why the magazine took note:)

(Pew Charitable Trusts: $135,000 to **Christianity Today**, Carol Stream, Illinois. "To convene forum on population and consumption issues among leading evangelical theologians and analysts and to produce special issue of Christianity Today on global stewardship.")

...that the GOP plans to "slash $380 billion from programs for the poor" while giving "$245 billion in tax cuts to the rich and middle class"— a statement virtually indistinguishable from the White House line.

Which shouldn't be too surprising, since the Clinton administration was part of the project all along. Interior Secretary Bruce Babbitt for some reason had started giving speeches about his religious beliefs, about how he had been born a Catholic, left the Church, learned Hopi religious beliefs one summer, and "came to believe, deeply and irrevocably, that the land and all the plants and animals in the natural world are together a direct reflection of divinity, that creation is a plan of God."

Washington Post columnist Coleman McCarthy quoted Babbitt, and called it "a deeper, richer Catholicism."

"In late January, 1996," wrote McCarthy, Babbitt "invited to his office ten religious leaders who have been similarly awakened. They came to tell the secretary, and the country, about their group, the Evangelical Environmental Network."[101b]

Babbitt acted appropriately surprised.

The Evangelical Environmental Network was co-founded by Calvin DeWitt, president of the Christian Environmental Council and professor of environmental studies at the University of Wisconsin - Madison. In a January 31, 1996, EEN press release, DeWitt said: "People in their arrogance are destroying God's creation, yet Congress and special interests are trying to sink the Noah's Ark of our day—the Endangered Species Act. Few legislative issues ought to be as clear for Christians as this one. The Christian faith teaches respect for the works of God."[102]

Who says religion and politics don't mix?

Not to mention a little hypocrisy about special interests.

There is no chart representing the linkages in this Evangelical Environmental Network-Environmental Information Center-Fenton Communications-Pew Charitable Trusts-Rockefeller Family Fund-Natural Resources Defense Council-Environmental Law Foundation-Democratic Party-Christian Environmental Council-Bruce Babbitt-Department of the Interior-Al Gore-Evangelicals for Social Action-Washington Post-Christianity Today-And Who Knows What Else melange because once you got below the top few boxes it would just be an inky blob of lines.

And besides, it would be unseemly to have the top box labeled "GOD."

Tom Wathen left Pew in 1997 to become executive vice president of EIC, renamed "National Environmental Trust," and executive director Phil Clapp moved up to President. All the power players were in place.

THE WRATH OF PEW

One of the first coalitions to emerge from EIC's Strategy Sessions was the Endangered Species Coalition, an array of 230 large and small national, regional and local environmental groups. In 1993, Pew gave $300,000 to the National Audubon Society as fiscal agent for the coalition. W. Alton Jones Foundation gave $50,000. Audubon housed and paid the staff.

It didn't do a great job. Especially after the Republicans won Congress in 1994.

So the coalition hired former Indiana Democrat Congressman Jim Jontz in January 1995 to pull together some kind of winning campaign. He had a staff of seven and reported to a 12-member steering committee. Jontz's campaign was based on daily communication between staff in D.C. and activists around the country who used the information to put pressure on their congressional delegates.

Yes, that's lobbying, and yes, foundations can contribute money to non-profits that lobby as long as they follow specific rules.

Pew donated $75,000 to the coalition in March 1995, and promised to match that amount in November. Josh Reichert and Tom Wathen tried unsuccessfully to get other foundations to join Pew in continuing support for the flagging coalition.

Tom Wathen encouraged Jontz to submit a proposal adding a capital-intensive media campaign to his grassroots strategy. Wathen also suggested hiring the Environmental Information Center to direct the whole campaign.

Jontz was not happy with that, but tried to work with Phil Clapp to design a media and grassroots campaign with a $600,000 budget, and nearly $400,000 more in "maybe-money" from other foundations. Million bucks. Jontz and Clapp couldn't get along. The coalition steering committee voted in August to keep Jontz instead of hiring Clapp.

Wathen was annoyed. Reichert was annoyed. Pew pulled its $600,000 and the whole million disappeared.

Carl Pope, executive director of the Sierra Club, a member of the coalition, made a lot of calls to fix things up.

It didn't work. The next week, the steering committee changed its mind and put Clapp in charge. Within another week, Audubon unilaterally fired Jontz and the entire coalition staff of seven. High Country News reported, "Neither the steering committee nor any of the 230 groups they represented knew the firings were coming. According to Liz Raisbeck, director of government affairs for National Audubon in Washington, D.C., Audubon was in a financial crunch and could no longer fund the coalition."[103]

Sure.

W. ALTON JONES FOUNDATION

W. Alton "Pete" Jones's foundation didn't start out in 1944 the way it is now. Pete Jones was a hardheaded, straight-talking pioneer oilman. Born in 1891, he went from childhood on a bleak Missouri farmstead to head the Cities Service Company and own an estate in New York.

On January 3, 1962, Jones was killed in the crash of an airliner taking off from Idylwild airport. He left most of his money to his New York-based foundation "to promote the well-being and general good of mankind throughout the world." Too bad he wasn't a little more specific.

For much of its early history, under the direction of Jones's widow, the foundation gave primarily to museums, artists, and playwrights. In 1982 Occidental Petroleum bought out Cities Service Company and sent the value of the foundation's 1,774,621 shares through the roof. Suddenly it was one of the 100 richest charities in the United States.

Widow Nettie Marie Jones hired Charles H. W. Foster, former dean of the Yale School of Forestry, as director of the foundation, which moved to Charlottesville, Virginia in 1980. They still gave money for cultural programs, but took the pulse of the times and began concentrating on their "Secure Society Program" and "Sustainable Society Program" initiatives ("Society" has since been changed to "World").

When Nettie Marie Jones died in 1991, the second and third generations took over. Daughter Patricia Jane (Jones) Edgerton became president. Her husband, Milton Thomas Edgerton, is not a trustee, but their son, Dr. Bradford Wheatly Edgerton (a Los Angeles plastic surgeon), became Vice President and Trustee, and architect daughter Diane Edgerton Miller became Secretary (now Vice President). Bernard F. Curry, an older generation holdover (born 1918) and former bank vice president with Morgan Guaranty Trust, became Treasurer (now a trustee only).

The five remaining trustees included James S. Bennett, a CBS and Walt Disney television producer; William A. McDonough, a noted architect (he resigned, but we'll meet him again in a few pages); James R. Cameron; Scott McVay (executive director of the Geraldine R. Dodge Foundation); and another third generation son, William A. Edgerton, a Charlottesville architect who designed a residential community featured in the U.S. Department of Energy's website, "Center of Excellence for Sustainable Development" (he's now the Foundation's Treasurer).

On February 1, 1990, 40-year-old zoologist John Peterson "Pete" Myers was hired as director at a salary of $149,776, with $29,833 in benefits. Myers had been senior vice president for science and sanctuaries of the National Audubon Society in New York, and brought with him all of Audubon's connections. Myers remained on Audubon's board of directors for years, one of many interlocking directorates that will unfold.

Shortly after he took the Jones job, Myers, who got his Ph.D. in zoology at the University of California at Berkeley, told the Richmond News Leader, "There's a shift taking place in the foundation. We're figuring out what needs to be done and then trying to find an organization to do it. There's also a shift toward thematically grouped grants based on issues and toward larger, longer-term grants."[104]

Myers took Jones from responsive to prescriptive.

When Myers arrived, the Jones foundation had an endowment of $200 million, the 75th largest in America. At the end of 1998 its investments had grown to $413,750,908—modest only by comparison to the billions of Pew or the Ford Foundation. What Jones lacks in size it more than makes up for in focus, spending all $32 million of its 1998 grants on its twin obsessions, anti-nuclear activism and environmental activism. The money for cultural programs has virtually disappeared.

Jones has, in the past few years, emphasized book publication, supporting authors, publishers like Island Press, and promotional tours—virtually a self-publishing venture getting messages out to justify its approaches to dismantling industrial civilization.

Island Press, a division of the Center for Resource Economics (1996 assets $2,716,223), is environmentalism's premiere publishing house, funded since 1984 by MacArthur, Geraldine Rockefeller Dodge, Charles Inglehard, Richard King Mellon, Burlington Northern and others.

Island Press's 1997 book *Nature's Services: Societal Dependence on Natural Ecosystems* made a no-brainer point: "Free of charge, natural ecosystems provide a multitude of valuable services for people and the human economy." Gee, we didn't know that. Pew's Joshua Reichert wrote the introduction, so maybe his fellow Ph.D.s were just talking down to us.

In fact, Pew was behind the whole effort, which began after dinner one night at an Arizona meeting of the Pew Fellows in Conservation and the Environment. One brilliant soul, Gretchen Daily, a Stanford University professor of biological science, noted to her fellow Fellows that the failure to price natural events was a major hindrance to the formulation and implementation of policy. These policy-minded scientists needed a book on what every farmer knows: nature does stuff free that keeps us all alive. If they could put a price on that stuff, they could blame humans for hurting it in dollars and cents and drive policy against industrial civilization.

A number of Pew-supported scholars agreed to help write *Nature's Services*, and the first draft was presented at the next Pew Fellows annual meeting, in Purity Springs, New Hampshire, and refined into the product that got to the bookstores. It was paid for by the Packard Foundation, Pew Charitable Trusts, and W. Alton Jones Foundation. Daily was supported during the development of the book by the Winslow and Heinz foundations and by Peter and Helen Bing. Peter Bing, a wealthy Los Angeles M.D., is also a Stanford University trustee. The Bings have funded much of Daily's work.

Blurbs for *Nature's Services* say about the authors: "Their findings clearly demonstrate that these services—providing clean water, pollination, pest control, climate regulation, flood control, and fisheries, to mention only a few—are not only invaluable, they are irreplaceable. While insufficient information was available to calculate the economic value of all—or even most—ecosystem services, those which could be quantified measured, at a minimum, many trillions of dollars annually."[105]

Unlike most economists, this team only tallied the assets column and didn't subtract the liabilities to make a balance sheet. Evidently nature's disservices such as disease, food poisons, pests, earthquakes, volcanoes, floods, and severe weather don't count. Or, more likely, they blame it on human activity to further justify dismantling industrial civilization.

W. Alton Jones's most tasteless book effort to date was a self-serving platform for Pete Myers, a diatribe against man-made chemicals, bought and paid for by the Jones foundation and titled, *Our Stolen Future: Are We Threatening Our Fertility, Intelligence, and Survival?—A Scientific Detective Story.* It removed all doubt whether the foundation was promoting a little propaganda now and then.[106a]

In March 1996, foundation director John Peterson Myers joined with grandmotherly Theo Colborn (ensconced as a senior fellow at the foundation) and crusading Boston Globe journalist Dianne Dumanoski to write this disaster-of-the-month epic. As critic Ron Bailey noted in *Philanthropy*, "The book was underwritten by the foundation from conception to its splashy national promotion. Its conclusion, in brief, is that 'some man-made chemicals interfere with the body's own hormones.'"[106b]

Nobody asked why Vice President Al Gore wrote the book's foreword. They didn't need to. Gore is part of their network. More about *that* later. Gore wrote that studies have linked synthetic chemicals to a whole parade of horribles, including "low sperm counts, infertility, genital deformities, hormonally triggered human cancers such as those of the breast and prostate gland; neurological disorders in children, such as hyperactivity and deficits in attention; and developmental and reproductive problems in wildlife."

To promote the book, Jones funded Environmental Media Services (EMS), a PR firm headed by former Gore staffer Arlie Schardt, who we met briefly back on page 97. Before founding Environmental Media Services in 1993, Schardt served as national press secretary for Al Gore's 1987-88 presidential campaign, executive director of the Environmental Defense Fund, and covered politics and the civil rights movement for 8 years at *Time* magazine. He was also the news media editor at *Newsweek*, a writer at *Sports Illustrated*, associate director of the ACLU and editor of *Foundation News* magazine at the Council on Foundations. Notice how the Council on Foundations seems to be lurking in the background everywhere we go.

Schardt is currently chair of the Center for Citizen Initiatives (formerly the Center for US-USSR Initiatives), which operates environmental, urban agriculture and small business development programs in the former USSR.

And, oh, yes, Environmental Media Services is a Project of the Tides Center. What a surprise.

Shardt's EMS rolled out a major PR campaign that included a national book tour, an appearance on NBC's Today show by Theo Colborn, and multiple press conferences at the National Press Club in Washington. It was praised by everybody except a New York Times writer named Gina Kolata, who had the temerity to question the validity of the claims made in this mighty book. The Environmental Information Center bought a quarter-page ad on the Times's own editorial page to rip her a new bodily orifice. No dissent allowed. If you're rich enough.

Turns out Kolata was right.

As Ron Bailey wrote,

> Are these synthetic chemicals really causing hormonal harm?
>
> Many prominent scientists don't think so. "Implausible," asserted the director of the University of California Berkeley's National Institute of Environmental Health, Dr. Bruce Ames, in testimony before the U.S. Senate last year.
>
> John Giesy, Professor of Toxicology at Michigan State University and past president of the Society of Environmental Toxicology and Chemistry says, "Frankly, Colborn doesn't know very much. She reads the entire literature and picks and chooses things that support her preconceived views."
>
> Stephen Safe, a professor at Texas A&M University and a noted expert on environmental estrogens agrees: "If you look at the book carefully, it's a very unscientific presentation."[107]

Skepticism by the scientific community wasn't the worst the book got. The W. Alton Jones Foundation was about to get its foot caught in its own wringer: the urge to leverage one program with another backfired.

The Jones foundation funded researcher John MacLachlan at the Xavier/Tulane Center for Bioenvironmental Research in New Orleans. MacLachlan claimed to have discovered that very weak estrogen "mimics" such as toxaphene, endosulfan, and dieldrin became massively potent when combined. Combined manmade estrogens are synergistic! The prestigious scientific journal *Science* published MacLachlan's results in June, 1996, adding both an editorial and a popular report. Sensation!

Synthetic endocrine disrupters in combination hit the headlines. Myers was ecstatic. In an October 1996 speech to regional EPA pesticide inspectors, he said that MacLachlan's paper had a significant policy impact: "I believe that we are entering into a new era of scientific awareness about the health risks of pesticide use. And this new understanding has already led to a dramatic shift in the underpinnings of national food safety laws, most obviously the 1996 Food Safety Act."

Lynn Goldman, Assistant Administrator of the Environmental Protection Agency, bought it. You could just see her dreaming up all the new regulations.

But MacLachlan's findings couldn't be replicated, either by him or by other scientists. Every attempt to confirm synergism in synthetic estrogens came up empty. EPA's Goldman made excuses for MacLachlan, suggesting that the yeast cell line that they used to do the assay had been lost, or something.

After months of stalling, MacLachlan had to publish a complete retraction in *Science*. The editorial staff couldn't recall such a clearcut withdrawal.

Jones pretends nothing happened.

When you're that rich, the facts don't matter.

When you're that engrossed in messages, what do you need the real world for?

Jones is headquartered in downtown Charlottesville on High Street. The social tone of this smug Southern town is set by the ultrarich. As *Outside* magazine wrote of it, "You might get the idea that Charlottesville is the personal fiefdom of movie stars, billionaire polo players, and UVa's 18,011 college snots."[108a]

You can bump into Sissy Spacek or Jessica Lange at the grocery store or espresso stand. But probably not the Edgertons at their Timber Creek Farm. The job opportunities are limited if you're a newcomer, giving rise to a class of modem gypsies with a money umbilical to Washington, D.C., 110 miles north. The ambience nourishes the Jones foundation's belief that it knows how to run your life better than you do.

THE KETCHUP MAFIA AND FRIENDS

Mozambique-born Teresa Heinz (Teresa is pronounced "tah-RAY-zah") is a leading stockholder in the $10 billion H.J. Heinz Company, vice chairman of the 300,000-member Environmental Defense Fund, and as chairman of the Howard Heinz Endowment in Pittsburgh, Pennsylvania, gave out $8.2 million in environmental group grants in 1996. She funneled $447,923 to EDF in 1993 through her personal charity, the Heinz Family Foundation and donated $750,000 in 1997 from the Heinz Endowments.

Teresa Heinz, no longer the Audrey-Hepburnesque beauty of the '60s but still attractive as she enters her '60s (said one newspaper), has been deeply involved in environmental causes for decades. Very dedicated. Her Heinz Family Foundation's reports state the following: "Contributes only to pre-selected organizations; unsolicited applications not considered." Absolutely prescriptive.[108b]

Wren Winslow Wirth is the wife of Timothy E. Wirth, former Senator from Colorado, former Clinton administration State Department environmental official, now president of Ted Turner's United Nations Fund. He's the small potatoes of the family. Wren is president of the Winslow Foundation, assets $20,077,168 in 1996, annual grants a little under a million dollars a year, almost all to environmental groups.

Wren sat on the board of directors of the Environmental Defense Fund from 1983 to 1998, recruited by her close friend (since 1970) Teresa Heinz. Teresa is also treasurer of Wren's Winslow Foundation. The Winslow Foundation's reports say, "Grants are made to pre-selected organizations only." Absolutely prescriptive.[109a]

Francis W. Hatch is chairman of the Boston-based pharmaceutical-rich John Merck Fund, a former Republican candidate for governor of Massachusetts, and son-in-law of Serena Merck. He is the top funder of New England environmentalists, $1.4 million in 1993, $1.3 million in '94, $1.4 million in 1995, and similar grants thereafter. The John Merck Fund's reports state the following: "The Fund generally supports pre-selected organizations. It discourages the submission of unsolicited applications." Aggressively to absolutely prescriptive.[109b]

Socialite Teresa Heinz embodies the power and connections in the intricately networked foundation world. She virtually symbolizes the interlocking nature of environmental funders. "It is an extraordinarily incestuous world out there," said Robert Schaeffer, a Boston-based consultant who represents several groups that are heavily funded by foundations.[109c]

The Heinz Endowments, which are really two entities— the Howard Heinz Endowment, established in 1941, and the Vira I. Heinz Endowment, established in 1986—give large grants to people Teresa Heinz knows personally, such as environmentalist architect William McDonough, a family friend who once employed Heinz's son.

McDonough was also a trustee of the W. Alton Jones Foundation for years. McDonough also designed the new headquarters for the Environmental Defense Fund in 1985—and was still one of the five highest paid professional service providers in 1991 at $91,913. He also designed the corporate campus for Gap, Inc. (Gap's Donald and Doris Fisher give over $2 million a year to environmental groups through their Gap Foundation). He also designed the headquarters of the Heinz Family Offices in 1994. A 1997 Heinz Endowments grant for $50,000 went to the University of Virginia to support the Institute of Sustainable Design and to launch the Center for Sustainable Design and Civic Leadership, McDonough creations.

William McDonough is a Yale graduate and practicing architect, founder of William McDonough & Partners Architects and Planners, which moved from New York in 1994 to Charlottesville, Virginia. He moved because he was appointed Dean of the University of Virginia School of Architecture, and resigned as a W. Alton Jones Foundation trustee.

In 1996 the "Green Dean" won the first Presidential Award for Sustainable Development, the nation's highest environmental award, from President Bill Clinton. How did his name get to the Clinton administration? Teresa's chum Wren's husband Tim's chum Al Gore, maybe?

Extraordinarily incestuous.

McDonough has served as advisor to Businesses for Social Responsibility and the Social Venture Network, both projects of the Tides Center.

Extraordinarily incestuous.

Heinz herself is quite a veteran: in 1989, she helped stop a highway through the Amazon jungle, and in 1984 she and husband Senator John Heinz created a foundation that paid for causes such as a guide to socially responsible grocery shopping and a public relations firm that recruits Hollywood stars to support environmental efforts.

Following the 1991 death of Sen. Heinz in a freak helicopter-plane crash, Teresa Heinz turned the two endowments into aggressive supporters of the environment, mainly in Pennsylvania. In 1993, she made one of the biggest environmental gifts ever, $20 million for the H. John Heinz Center for Science, Economics and the Environment, a think-tank / research center. The idea was to bring environmental groups, industry, academia and government together to cope with environmental problems. If the track record of such mediatory efforts is any indication, industry will compromise away its ability to do business, piece by piece, year by year.

Teresa Heinz is now the wife of Sen. John Kerry.

She speaks foundationese fluently: The Boston Globe wrote in 1997, "If existing environmental groups can't do the job, foundations may set up new ones. This year, officials at the Heinz Endowments of Pittsburgh set up a $700,000 organization to scrutinize deregulation of the electric industry, complete with a 'grassroots' co-ordinator to whip up support among groups such as the elderly and organized labor."[110]

This is what the grant description in Heinz reports said: "Greater Harrisburg Foundation: $700,000 for support of the Pennsylvania Energy Project, Sustainable Systems Research and the Millennium Project, among others, in order to ensure a sustainable energy future for Pennsylvania."

No mention of deregulation. No mention of astroturf installation.

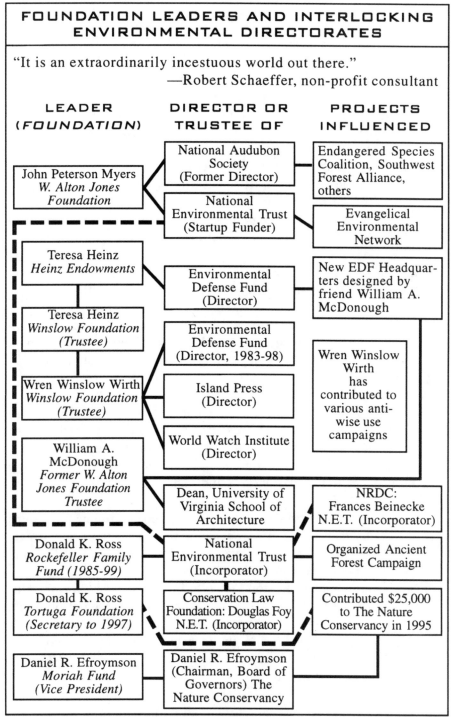

FOUNDATION LEADERS AND INTERLOCKING ENVIRONMENTAL DIRECTORATES

"It is an extraordinarily incestuous world out there."
—Robert Schaeffer, non-profit consultant

LEADER (FOUNDATION)	DIRECTOR OR TRUSTEE OF	PROJECTS INFLUENCED
John Peterson Myers *W. Alton Jones Foundation*	National Audubon Society (Former Director)	Endangered Species Coalition, Southwest Forest Alliance, others
	National Environmental Trust (Startup Funder)	Evangelical Environmental Network
Teresa Heinz *Heinz Endowments*	Environmental Defense Fund (Director)	New EDF Headquarters designed by friend William A. McDonough
Teresa Heinz *Winslow Foundation (Trustee)*	Environmental Defense Fund (Director, 1983-98)	Wren Winslow Wirth has contributed to various anti-wise use campaigns
Wren Winslow Wirth *Winslow Foundation (Trustee)*	Island Press (Director)	
	World Watch Institute (Director)	
William A. McDonough *Former W. Alton Jones Foundation Trustee*	Dean, University of Virginia School of Architecture	NRDC: Frances Beinecke N.E.T. (Incorporator)
Donald K. Ross *Rockefeller Family Fund (1985-99)*	National Environmental Trust (Incorporator)	Organized Ancient Forest Campaign
Donald K. Ross *Tortuga Foundation (Secretary to 1997)*	Conservation Law Foundation: Douglas Foy N.E.T. (Incorporator)	Contributed $25,000 to The Nature Conservancy in 1995
Daniel R. Efroymson *Moriah Fund (Vice President)*	Daniel R. Efroymson (Chairman, Board of Governors) The Nature Conservancy	

SMALL SAMPLE OF MASSIVELY INTERLOCKED ENVIRONMENTAL FUNDING LINKAGES.

Among the less visible Heinz grants that will one day haunt us is the 1996 $90,000 grant to Redefining Progress, a San Francisco non-profit, for a tax shift program to stop economic growth in favor of quality of life, a foundationese concept if ever there was one. Let them eat quality.

You can read the latest grants for yourself at http://www.heinz.org.

The Winslow Foundation's grants tend to follow the lead of the inner circle of the Environmental Grantmakers Association. Nothing very innovative, but deadly. Wren Wirth authorized $25,000 to the Alaska Conservation Foundation for "General support to groups working to protect Alaska's bioregional ecosystems," foundationese for shutting down the last pulp mill remaining in Alaska by choking off Ketchikan Pulp's timber supply.

Another Winslow $25,000 grant went to the Appalachian Mountain Club in Boston, "To aid in the coordination of a three-year New England regional response to the Property Rights/Me Firsters Movement (otherwise known as the Wise Use movement)." That bit of vilification was actually written by Winslow officials in their grant description.

"We are rich and they are up against us."

Francis W. Hatch is the reason why environmentalists in the Northern Forest Alliance are buying up chunks of Maine and trying to peddle them to the government instead of just pushing for nationalization in the form of gigantic new national parks, as originally envisioned (see pages 35-43).

Seeing the impact the wise use movement was having in rallying support for private property and the resource class, Hatch realized that the only way to achieve the goal was to stop the visible, controversial, confrontational tactics in favor of a gradual, incremental, forest-enveloping campaign spoken in foundationese—and a smear campaign against wise users.

As the Boston Globe said of Hatch, he "pressed environmental groups to gain clout by mobilizing grassroots support and not to underestimate the anti-environment 'wise use' movement, helping to make New England groups stronger than those elsewhere."[112]

Some groups, such as Restore: the North Woods, run by former Wilderness Society staffer Michael Kellett, didn't like the idea of wimping out, and didn't stay in the Northern Forest Alliance orbit. Kellett's anti-corporate ideology blinded him to the fact that the final result would be the same: private parties would no longer own the majority of New England, the government would.

Most environmental group leaders saw Hatch's point. They took his money and did what he said. Other foundations pushed them, too.

In addition to the anti-wise use astroturf "Grassroots Action Project" grants noted on pages 39 and 40, the John Merck Fund gave in 1995:

Conservation Fund, $60,000. "For two demonstrations of sustainable forestry and economic development of lands in northern New England."

Environmental Information Center, $60,000. "Two grants to support public education and media activities."

Natural Resources Council of Maine, $40,000. "To increase member involvement in environmental debates, and to build media coverage and public awareness of environmental issues."

The Tides Center, Environmental Media Services, $25,000. "For coverage of critical environmental issues."

Hatch spent a total of $704,500 in New England in 1995.

The Merck Family Fund, run by Francis W. Hatch III, spent $226,000 in New England in 1994.

GEEKS WITH BUCKS

Paul Brainerd is the epitome of the Microsoft Millionaire, even though he didn't come out of Microsoft. He started his millions not in the proverbial garage, but in a studio apartment below Seattle's Pike Place Market by creating PageMaker, software that turns a desktop computer into a miniature publishing house.

That was the beginning of Aldus Corporation, a pioneer of desktop publishing. Brainerd made about $120 million when he sold Aldus to Adobe Systems for $525 million in 1994. He took a year off in Alaska "to clear my head," and then turned from a computer magnate into a philanthropist and environmental activist. He used the proceeds from the deal to endow the $50 million Brainerd Foundation. Since then, the foundation has awarded about $6 million in grants to environmentalist group projects across the Northwest and Alaska.

Brainerd emphasizes his lifelong love of the outdoors, and his childhood in an Oregon timber town, with visits to his parents' summer cabin and long nature walks.

Brainerd's brand of prescriptive intrusion, like many other funders, has crossed international borders to impose his will on other nations. His funding has helped turn 11 million acres into non-resource areas in British Columbia, Canada, and, most recently, prompted a two-year moratorium on mining along Montana's Rocky Mountain Front.

Dozens of other rich Northwest nerds who have checked out of the computer world are beginning to think about what to do with their money, and Brainerd has made himself a model for them to follow.

"Certainly the potential is here in terms of wealth and brainpower," Brainerd told the Seattle Times. "The question is whether it can be harnessed and organized."[114]

Get in the harness, rich guys. Brainerd wants to take you for a ride.

Brainerd started a non-profit organization called Social Venture Partners in 1997 to inspire Microsoft Millionaires to give away their money and teach them how to do it with a strategy similar to venture capitalists, applying those principles in making its grants. Social Venture Partners's first round of grants totaled $300,000. Brainerd tells his peers about the quasi-erotic gratification of philanthropy ("It *feels* good") and is quoted by nearly every national publication that writes on the phenomenon of high-tech giving.

When he discovered that non-profit environmental groups often owned outdated computer technology, Brainerd partnered with the Bullitt Foundation to start ONE/Northwest. The organization has helped set up Web sites for environmental organizations and established more than 200 e-mail discussion lists, connecting activists around specific causes. It has also built an online database of more than 1,200 conservation organizations.

Brainerd is fiercely political. In a 1998 Seattle Times analysis, Brainerd ranked No. 25 of the state's top 50 political patrons of the 1990s, contributing nearly $130,000 from 1992 through 1996 to political candidates that environmental groups ranked as friends. He has also started a political-action committee called Conservation Strategies.

Intelligent. Thorough. Pitiless.

Brainerd occasionally hosts conclaves with environmentalists in his penthouse condominium above the Pike Place Market, where they can gaze at his art collection and admire the city's skyscrapers through the floor-to-ceiling windows while plotting strategy about how to eradicate the hydroelectric industry by removing dams in the name of saving salmon or how to take more land away from the resource class.

LORD TURNER AND LADY JANE

"How to become the biggest landowner in America and give money to radical environmental groups" could be the theme of Ted Turner and his Turner Foundation.

Ted Turner gives new meaning to the trite phrase, "mixed bag." His is one of the most astounding free enterprise success stories in history, with his self-made broadcast empire of CNN and his megabuck deal with Time-Warner. He has cut one of the most dashing figures in modern times with his outstanding sportsmanship, his colorful foot-in-mouth problems that earned him the monicker, Mouth from The South, and his bizarre marriage to anti-business activist, tycoon, and former actress, Jane Fonda. Although he has no college degree, he is widely read, particularly in history and the Bible. And he has given money to more radical environmental groups than just about anyone else in the foundation community.[115a]

Turner's is also the only major foundation I have tracked that has never given grants with strings attached—at least strings that I could detect.

In fact, one of Turner's grantees, New Mexico's Forest Guardians, sued the Forest Service over some bison that were ruled to belong to Ted Turner but the environmental group felt should belong to the government. The bison were part of a land deal between the federal government and Pennzoil Corp. nearly 20 years ago and were never formally transferred to the U.S. Forest Service. So when Turner bought Vermejo Park Ranch from Pennzoil in 1996 the Forest Service determined that the bison remained with the ranch. Forest Guardians wanted them back in the possession of the government and sued because they felt the Forest Service didn't fight hard enough.[115b]

It was quite a stink. Forest Guardians obviously felt no strings.

Turner has faithfully given Forest Guardians annual donations in substantial ($25,000 and $30,000) amounts.

It's hard to imagine a more "no strings attached" situation.

Turner Foundation is also run the least formally.

Founded in 1990, the Turner Foundation has only family trustees: Ted Turner (his full name is Robert Edward Turner III) and Jane Fonda (whom Turner married in 1991), plus Turner's five children: Jennie Turner Garlington, Laura Turner Seydel, Beau Turner, Rhett Turner, and Teddy Turner.[115c]

Executive Director Peter Bahouth was hired by Turner from Greenpeace USA at $43,750 a year (by 1997 it had crept up to $124,000).

The Turner Foundation makes all its money from dividends and sale of stock. It gives money to 450 to 500 grantees a year. Some goes to mainstreamers such as the National Audubon Society, but a large amount goes to radical outfits run by former Earth First!ers or—as the Boston Globe wrote—"Turner gives to upstart grassroots groups, such as anti-logging radical Tim Hermach."[115d]

Hermach is one of a small group of radicals who refused to accept money from the Rockefeller Family Fund-W. Alton Jones-Pew Charitable Trusts bunch because they were unwilling to dance on the end of big money strings. Turner enjoys giving money to the most radical of causes, which means he need attach no strings to get the performance he wants.

In selecting grantees, each Turner Foundation trustee is expected to have an understanding of the more than 4,700 applications received each year. Audubon magazine reported how the grant approval meetings actually proceed:

> "That's an amazing thing to watch," says executive director Bahouth. "The family members go through four huge ring binders of proposals. And they're as familiar with requests for $2,000 or $10,000 projects as they are with $200,000 proposals. Sometimes they'll argue for the former over the latter. And after being engaged in the issues brought to them by 4,700 proposals, they've got a very good idea of what's going on out there." (The National Audubon Society received more than $110,000 in grants from the foundation for 1998.)
>
> The energetic debates over how the Turner Foundation bestows its money can be a source of family squabbles—especially when funding votes go against the wishes of its paterfamilias.
>
> "I don't think Dad enjoys getting voted down on pet projects," says a grinning Beau Turner. "But he accepts it when it happens. And he knows, from the way we've voted, that we're involved in the issues. We're acting democratically as a family, considering choices for some pretty serious projects wisely."[116a]

Unfortunately for the resource class, some of those pretty serious projects are not very wise where people are concerned. Turner money has tipped the balance in many projects that put loggers, miners, ranchers and farmers into ruin.

Ted doesn't mind.

He's rich and he doesn't like loggers, miners, ranchers and farmers.

He has a hobby to keep his mind off those he hurts.

He collects land.

Ted Turner is currently the Number One private landowner in the United States, running a teeter-totter contest with Number Two, timber baron A. A. "Red" Emmerson of California's Sierra Pacific Industries, who is making land deals that will propel him to the Number One spot—for a while.

In Montana, Nebraska, New Mexico, Colorado, Georgia, Florida, South Carolina, and Argentina, Ted owns 1.35 million acres, more land than The Nature Conservancy, which owns or has conservation easements on 1.17 million acres in this country.[116b]

What does he do with this land?

He plays God.

Well, God with a cash register. A true neofeudal lord.

He restores nature. He's pulled out fences, forbidden pesticides, reintroduced native predators such as falcons and wolves, sold off the traditional ranch livestock—mostly cattle and domesticated sheep—that came with the property, replacing it with native bison and desert bighorn sheep. Fired most of the cowhands.[117a]

Turner says it's to restore the land to its pristine condition so people can come see it in the future and know what the wild west was really like.

But they'd better bring plenty of cash if they want to look.

Visitors who want to see what the wild west was really like will have to pay some wild prices. On Turner's ranches, there is elk hunting for nearly $10,000 a week during the season. Streams are open to fishing—for a price.

The ranch's lodge can accommodate up to 75 guests. Not free. Not cheap.

When Turner bought the 578,000-acre Vermejo Park Ranch in New Mexico for just under $80 million it made him owner of nearly 1.5 percent of the state. He already owned two other ranches in New Mexico, plus five in Montana and Nebraska.

As his hunting and lodging is not charitable, his venture into bison breeding is not just for looks or the ecology.

He started raising them on one of his Southern plantations. "I got three" of the animals, he said. "Then they had babies, and then I started dreaming about having 100. Then I said, 'OK, I'll get 1,000 of them.' And then, I started thinking about 10,000."

Russell Miller, general manager of Turner's ranches, said Turner sold about 900 bulls in 1995 for meat at prices of $750 to $1,500 and a handful of bulls to breeders for about $2,500 each.[117b]

And getting rid of all those exotic species like cattle and sheep so he can reintroduce native critters has an unspoken side, too.

The trees.

Turner logs them. Sells the logs. For money. To be cut up in a sawmill and made into *stuff*. For people to *use*. Like houses. And paper.

A lot of his environmentalist grantees won't believe that.

In fact, a story that keeps circulating tells how a group of devoted environmentalists who live in Southern Colorado sneaked across the state line and onto a timber baron's forested property where they took secret videos of these terrible people—loggers—cutting trees down. The environmentalists then showed the videos around to embarrass the bad timber baron for desecrating the land.

When the video got around to the timber baron, he scratched his head. He wasn't cutting any trees on his land—it was his personal getaway, not

TED TURNER
LAND OWNERSHIPS
THE YEAR ENDED 12/31/98

TURNER LAND: 1.37 million acres in 14 U.S. properties.
Plus 11,000 acres in Rio Negro and Neuquen provinces, Argentina
(Patagonia).

SOUTH CAROLINA:
1. 800 acres Saint Phillips Island, Beaufort County, South Carolina
coast. Rice plantation.

2. 5,000 acres Hope Plantation in Colleton County directly across
the Edisto River from Prospect Hill.

Turner granted conservation easements on both properties to the
Nature Conservancy.

FLORIDA:
3. 1984. 8,079.5 acres Avalon Plantation, Jefferson County near
Capp. $8 million payment to the estate of Mrs. Alexandra McKay,
the remarried widow of paint manufacturer Benjamin Moore.
Property manager: George Purvis.

4. 1998. 2,776-acre Magnolia Hills Plantation, Jefferson County.

MONTANA:
Russ Miller-manager of Turner Ranches, western properties.

5. May 1996. 32,093-acre Roe Ranch in Beaverhead County ranch
from Centennial Livestock. Several miles of the Red Rock River
meander through the property, just south of the Clark Canyon
Reservoir.

6. 44,000 acres. Snowcrest Ranch 17 miles south of Alder, Madison County, in the heart of Ruby Valley.

7. 107,000-acre Flying D Ranch in Gallatin County 30 miles west
of Bozeman. $20 million, or $187 an acre.

NEBRASKA:

8. 44,744 acres Milligan Ranch south of Rushville in northwest Sheridan County for $8.45 million. Bought from Milligan Farms and Ranches of Hooper, Neb, payment amounted to $188 an acre. That is well above market value, said Sheridan County Assessor Karen Palmer.

9. 1995. #1. 32,000 acre Spike Box Ranch in 1995. Cherry County.

10. 1996. #2. Coble family ranch, about 9,600 acres and offered to sell the remainder of their ranch this year (1997). Cherry County.

11. 1997. #3. 10,168 acres in the Sand Hills, southwest of Valentine. It is the second large property addition by Turner since he bought the Spike Box. The latest parcel sold for $2 million Cherry County records say.

NEW MEXICO:

12. 210,000-acre Ladder Ranch west of Truth or Consequences in Sierra County.

13. 360,000-acre Armendaris Ranch, located in Socorro County in southern New Mexico along the banks of the Rio Grande south of Socorro.

14. 1996. 578,000-acre Vermejo Park Ranch, Colfax County, State Highway 555 leads to gate and ends. Ranch straddles the New Mexico and Colorado border. Paid for by a company owned by Turner, Vermejo Park L.L.C. Price guessed between $70 - $90 million, informed speculation: about $100 million. David Vackar, manager. Elk hunting for $8,500 a week.

ARGENTINA:

15. Patagonia: Primavera, or Springtime, an 11,000-acre ranch that straddles the border of Rio Negro and Neuquen provinces, about 50 miles from a Patagonian resort town within 50 miles of the regional capital, San Carlos de Bariloche. $8 million ranch.

one of his commercial forests. And besides, the terrain didn't look familiar. Looked more like the neighbor's property, that Ted Turner fellow's.

The timber baron did a little checking. The story goes that he found loggers on Ted Turner's ranch cutting trees left and right.

Well, who can you believe these days?

How about Atlanta magazine? Right in Ted Turner's home town. They wrote:

> Turner Ranches is the largest commercial producer of bison in the country. The Flying D has 3,000 head. There are another 9,000 on other ranches. Even though the properties are laboratories for environmental management techniques, they are also a business, and they are run that way. Hunters pay $9,500 each for four-and-a-half-day guided elk hunts on several ranches. Timber is harvested. Bison are sent to market. The difference is that in Turner country sustainability is never sacrificed for short-term profits.[120a]

And PennzEnergy has announced plans to drill some 500 oil wells on Ted's Vermejo Park Ranch for a 3% royalty, estimated to be worth $81 million over 20 years. Oil is not just for short-term profit.

Turner has become notorious for not being beloved of his neighbors. On his Avalon Plantation in Florida, he appears to be a naughty man:

> Dressie Sloan, of the Jefferson County NAACP, has accused broadcasting executive Ted Turner of trying to get rid of his poor neighbors.
>
> She said Turner has not extended electric lines across his 8,100-acre plantation in the Panhandle to the homes of five black families who live by batteries and kerosene.
>
> "One word from Mr. Turner, and they'd have their lights," Sloan said. "He has the power and the money to do it, but he wants to squeeze them out."[120b]

Turner clearly doesn't like too many people. He told the annual meeting of the Society of Environmental Journalists in Chattanooga, Tennessee in 1998 that global public attitudes and actions toward the environment must go through a "natural revolution" if we are to survive on earth. Turner also challenged the Judeo-Christian view of a God separate from nature, the philosophy that man has "dominion over the earth" defined as the opposite of "stewardship," and the maxim: Be fruitful and multiply.

"We've done that, all too well," Turner said, referring to overpopulation on a global scale.[120c]

Turner, who has five children, suggested that families have only one child for the next century, so that the world's population could fall to just 2 billion people. "We could live in a kind of Garden of Eden. The majority of the world lives in hell, anyway."[121a]

Ask Dressie Sloan.

Turner probably has little idea of how much of a hell he has made out of the lives of the resource class and others.

We'll see more of Turner and his money in the next chapter.

Many foundations act aggressively or absolutely prescriptive.

Big ones, little ones.

Hundreds of them.

They are intricately networked.

They know each other. Their friends know each other.

They go to the same conferences.

They belong to the same associations.

They form the integral, inseparable, and indispensable tissue of the environmental movement. Environmentalism cannot be understood in any terms that do not incorporate and analyze prescriptive foundations.

Prescriptive foundations have a vision for your future.

Whether you like it or not.

And they have the money to make it happen.

"A lot of the environmental movement's message has been embedded in the society," said the Conservation Law Foundation's Doug Foy. "In many ways, we've won."[121b]

They have transmogrified the environmental movement from a grassroots citizen response into an institutionalized, calculated, strategized, orchestrated, computerized, elite-driven ideological instrument that is destroying property owners, the resource class, and industrial civilization piece by piece.

When confronted with this charge, they will speak foundationese.

SHORT SAMPLER OF FOUNDATIONS SHAPING AMERICAN ENVIRONMENTALISM

PEW CHARITABLE TRUSTS, Philadelphia. SOURCE OF WEALTH: Sun Oil (Sunoco). 1998 ASSETS: $4.7 billion. 1998 ENVIRONMENTAL GRANTS: $38.6 million. The most influential funder. Called "results-oriented" by friends and "a bunch of bullies" by critics. Creates new groups, demands personnel changes in recipients. Chief architect of forest preservation campaigns. Environmental boss Josh Reichert is overwhelming and canny. Expert at creating coalitions of cross-interest groups with money to small corps of trusted agents.

FORD FOUNDATION, New York. SOURCE OF WEALTH: Ford Motor Company. 1995 ASSETS: $7.5 billion. 1995 GRANTS: $17 million. Provided start-up money in 1970 for Natural Resources Defense Council. Global agenda minimizes its power over U.S. groups. However, gave $2.9 million in 1997 to promote "environmentally benign development" in the Northwest.

W. ALTON JONES FOUNDATION, Charlottesville, Virginia. SOURCE OF WEALTH: Citgo Oil. 1998 ASSETS: $413.7 million. 1998 GRANTS: $32 million. Donates solely to environmental and antinuclear groups. Pressing international banking system to adopt environmentalist agenda. Creates new groups and pressures old. Fights wise use movement with nationwide smear campaign.

JOHN D. AND CATHERINE T. MacARTHUR FOUNDATION, Chicago. SOURCE OF WEALTH: Insurance, real estate. 1995 ASSETS: $3.3 billion. 1995 GRANTS: $16.7 million. The MacArthurs owned vast Florida real estate, shopping centers, development companies and paper mills. Today, investment portfolio pays for activists in the Florida Keys, fights developers. Most grants go to international groups, to "genius" grants, to Chicago institutions, or education.

HEINZ ENDOWMENTS, Pittsburgh. SOURCE OF WEALTH: Food processing. 1995 ASSETS: $1.1 billion. 1996 GRANTS: $8.2 million. Teresa Heinz turned the two family endowments into aggressive funders of environmentalists, mainly in Pennsylvania. In 1993, gave $20 million for research center. Gives "genius" grants. Teresa Heinz is a major player in environmental politics and vice chair of the 300,000-member Environmental Defense Fund. Heinz Endowments gave $750,000 to EDF in 1997.

ROCKEFELLERS, New York City. SOURCE OF WEALTH: Standard Oil. 1994 ASSETS: $2.7 billion, among six foundations. 1996 GRANTS: More than $16.5 million, six foundations combined. Rockefeller Foundation, Rockefeller Brothers Fund, Rockefeller Family Fund, Winthrop Rockefeller Foundation, David Rockefeller Fund, and Rockefeller Financial Services, Philanthropy Department. Does not include donations of American Conservation Association, Jackson Hole Preserve, Inc., Colonial Williamsburg Foundation, and other Rockefeller philanthropies. Funds environmental movement worldwide. Donald Ross, former head of Rockefeller Family Fund, was long the power behind American environmentalism. Ross helped start Environmental Grantmakers Association. Lee

Wasserman replaced Ross in 1999. Wasserman, longtime environmentalist, was formerly a Pew consultant, director of Environmental Advocates in Albany (funded by Ross's Tortuga Foundation connection), an unsuccessful 1996 candidate for the New York House of Representatives, and director of the Environmental Planning Lobby in Albany.

BRAINERD FOUNDATION, Seattle. SOURCE OF WEALTH: Desktop publishing. 1996 ASSETS: $40 million. 1996 GRANTS: $1.4 million. Paul Brainerd, who virtually invented desktop publishing with Pagemaker software, sold his company in 1994. Foundation is dedicated to environmental activism and upgrading computer resources at environmental groups. A model for hundreds of "Microsoft Millionaires" who are deciding what to do with their money.

DAVID AND LUCILE PACKARD FOUNDATION, Los Altos, California. SOURCE OF WEALTH: Hewlett-Packard. 1996 ASSETS: $7.38 billion. 1996 GRANTS: $13 million. The 1996 death of David Packard, a pioneer of the computer revolution, nearly tripled value of foundation's stock. May become the top funder of environmentalists.

BULLITT FOUNDATION, Seattle. SOURCE OF WEALTH: Television stations. 1996 ASSETS: $100 million. 1998 GRANTS: $5.06 million. Death of Dorothy Bullitt in 1989 turned a little charity into a major player, boosting the value of the charity tenfold. Under Earth Day founder Denis Hayes, Bullitt backs a bank that loans money only to environmentalists' companies.

JOHN MERCK FUND, Boston. SOURCE OF WEALTH: Merck Pharmaceuticals. 1995 ASSETS: $102.7 million. 1994 GRANTS: $1.2 million. Led by Francis W. Hatch, former Republican candidate for governor—and son-in-law of Serena Merck—is top funder of New England environmentalists. Viewed as a liberal funder willing to back controversial issues and small groups. Pressed environmental groups to gain clout by mobilizing grassroots support and not to underestimate the wise use movement, helping to make New England groups stronger than those elsewhere.

WINSLOW FOUNDATION, Princeton, New Jersey. DONOR: Julia D. Winslow. 1994 ASSETS: $49.2 million. 1996 GRANTS: $2 million. President Wren Winslow Wirth was a long time board member of the Environmental Defense Fund, and is married to former Senator and Clinton subcabinet officer Timothy E. Wirth, now president of Ted Turner's United Nations Fund. Old friend Teresa Heinz is Treasurer. Winslow grants are influenced by the EDF agenda and by close friend, architect William A. McDonough, who was a trustee of the W. Alton Jones Foundation, whose director J. P. Myers was a board member of the National Audubon Society.

JESSIE B. COX CHARITABLE TRUST, Boston. SOURCE OF WEALTH: Wall Street Journal. 1993 ASSETS: $55 million. 1995 GRANTS: $1.1 million. After Jessie Cox's death in 1982, her children interpreted her broad will to include funding environmental protection. Has invested heavily in preserving forests of northern New England and urban groups such as Alternatives for Community and Environment in Roxbury. Like Merck Fund, Cox has urged grassroots activism to mask elitist reality. 1995 report underwritten by Cox, Merck and others said movement needs less confrontational approach.

PRESCRIPTIVE FOUNDATIONS FOOTNOTES

66a. Environmental Data Research Institute, *Environmental Grantmaking Foundations 1996 Directory*, 4th Edition, Edith C. Stein, publisher, Rochester, 1996, p *xv.*

66b. Margaret Mary Feczko, Ruth Kovacs, and Carlotta Mills, editors, *National Guide to Funding for the Environment and Animal Welfare*, The Foundation Center, New York, 1994, p. *vii.*

66c. Resources for Global Sustainability, *Environmental Grantmaking Foundations 1997 Directory*, 5th Edition, Rochester, 1997, p *xv.*

66d. "Environmental Donors Set Tone - Activists Affected by Quest for Funds," by Scott Allen, *Boston Globe,* Monday, October 20, 1997, p. A1.

66e. "Nonprofit groups gaining in power - Organizations creating big movement," David Briscoe, Associated Press, *Seattle Times,* Sunday, November 8, 1998, p. A11.

66f. Lester M. Salamon, et al., *The Emerging Sector Revisited*, Johns Hopkins University, 1998.

66g. Lester M. Salamon, *Holding the Center: America's Nonprofit Sector at a Crossroads*, available online at http://www.ncf.org/ncf/publications/reports/holding_the_center/hc_contents.html.

67a. "Grants Soar as Foundations Grow in Number and Worth," by Judith Havemann and William Branigin, *Washington Post*, Sunday, April 18, 1999, p. A2.

67b. Ann Kaplan, editor, *Giving USA 1998*, The American Association of Fund Raising Counsel, Inc. (AAFRC) Trust for Philanthropy, Washington DC., 1998.

68a. Citizens Against Government Waste, *Phony Philanthropy: How Government Grants are Subverting the Missions of Nonprofit Organizations*, by David E. Williams and Elizabeth L. Wright, November 17, 1998, Washington, D.C., p. 1.

68b. Alan Abramson and Lester Salamon, *The Nonprofit Sector and the Federal Budget: Update as of September 1997,* The Independent Sector, Washington D.C.

68c. "Organizations in The Right Guide," the editor, *The Right Guide*, Economics America, Inc., Ann Arbor, Michigan, 1998, p. *vi.*

68d. Mark Dowie, *Losing Ground: American Environmentalism at the Close of the Twentieth Century*, MIT Press, Cambridge, Massachusetts, 1995, p. 49.

70a. "The Protesters: 65,000 Protest Dependence on A-energy; 65,000 March on Capitol, Score Nuclear Dependence," by Paul W. Valentine, Karlyn Barker, and Thomas Morgan, *Washington Post*, Monday, May 7, 1979, p. A1. *See also*, "200,000 at nuclear protest," by Robin Herman, *New York Times*, Monday, September 24 1979, p. 1, sec. 2.

70b. Rockefeller Family Fund, Inc., Form 990-PF, Part II, 1985.

71. The story of the Environmental Grantmakers Association's beginnings came from a telephone interview with Pam Maurath, EGA staff, in December 1992.

72. "Oiling the works: How Chevron bought its way into environmentalism's power circle," by Eve Pell, *Mother Jones*, March-April 1991, p. 39

74. Transcript of E.G.A. Fall Retreat taped session, "Environmental Legislation: Opportunity for Impact and Change," October 3, 1992.

78a. "We can't afford a full office and staff. Where can we turn?" *Internet Nonprofit Center*. http://www.nonprofit-info.org/npofaq/03/14.html. A project of the Evergreen State Society, Seattle, Washington.

78b. "The New Power Brokers," by Eileen Ecklund, *San Francisco Bay Guardian*, October 8, 1997.

78c. W. Alton Jones Foundation, Form 990-PF, Part XV, 1993.

79a. *Grants for Environmental Protection and Animal Welfare*, 1994/1995, The Foundation Center, New York, 1995.

79b. Foundation Center records.

82. Tides website http://www.corpwatch.org/trac/about/about.html.

83a. "Tax Exempt Secrecy," by Martin Espinoza, *San Francisco Bay Guardian*, October 8, 1997. Available online at http://www.sfbg.com/News/32/02/Features/secret.html.

83b. "Computer Networks and the Emergence of Global Civil Society: The Case of the Association for Progressive Communications (APC)," by Howard H. Frederick. Paper presented at the annual conference of the Peace Studies Association, Boulder, CO, February 28, 1992.

84. Website of Institute for Global Communications, http://www.igc.org.

86a. "Shaking the Foundation - Pew's Rebecca Rimel has Big Money to Give and an Activist Agenda to Pursue," by Steve Goldstein, *Philadelphia Inquirer*, Sunday, March 8, 1998, A1.

86b. "Who knows best: grassroots or foundations?" by Mike Medberry, *High Country News*, October 16, 1995 (Vol. 27, No. 19).

86c. "Shaking the Foundation," *Philadelphia Inquirer.*

89. "The Greening of a Movement - Big Money is Bankrolling Select Environmental Causes," by Scott Allen, *Boston Globe*, Sunday, October 19, 1997, A1.

90a. "Teresa Heinz: Senator's wife uses influence, donations to effect change," by Scott Allen, *Boston Globe*, Sunday, October 19, 1997, p. A31.

90b. "Shaking the Foundation," *Philadelphia Inquirer.*

91. Pew Charitable Trusts, Form 990.

92. The session was based on two reports: 1) "The Wise Use Movement: Strategic Analysis and fifty state Review," by MacWilliams Cosgrove Snyder, Clearinghouse on Enviromental Advocacy and Research, Washington, D.C., September 1992, revised March 1993. *(Forbes* magazine called it "The Search and Destroy Strategy Guide.") and 2) "The wise use movement," released by Pete Myers and Debra Callahan, W. Alton Jones Foundation, Charlottesville, Virginia, February, 1992.

95a. "Shaking the Foundation," *Philadelphia Inquirer.*

95b. "Environmental Strategies: Concept Statement," by Joshua Reichert, Pew Charitable Trusts, Philadelphia, 1993, p. 3. Quoted in Dowie, "Losing Ground," p. 50.

96. "Environmental Strategies," Reichert, p. 6. Quoted in Dowie, p. 51.

97. Human Valuation of the Environment: A symposium in celebration of Princeton University's 250th Anniversary. "From Courtrooms to Town Hall: The Third Generation of Environmental Law." Available online at http://www.princeton.edu/~pei/News4.html.

98. Program of session, provided by an anonymous attendee.

101a. "Tending God's Garden - Evangelical Group Embraces Environment," by Bill Broadway, *The Washington Post*, February 17, 1996, p. C8.

101b. "The Noah Movement," by Colman McCarthy (editorial), *The Washington Post*, February 10, 1996, p. A23.

102. Evangelical Environmental Network press release, by Dr. Calvin B. DeWitt, Washington, D.C., January 31, 1996.

103. "Who knows best: grassroots or foundations?" by Mike Medberry, *High Country News*, October 16, 1995, (Vol. 27, No. 19).

104. "Out to Save the Earth - With $12 Million a Year," by Carlos Santos, *Richmond News Leader,* June 10, 1990, p. F-1.

105. *Nature's Services; Societal Dependence on Natural Ecosystems* by Gretchen C. Daily (Editor), introduction by Joshua S. Reichert, Island Press, Washington, D.C., 1997.

106a. Theo Colborn, Dianne Dumanoski, John Peterson Myers (Contributor) *Our Stolen Future : Are We Threatening Our Fertility, Intellgence, and Survival?-A Scientific Detective Story*, Plume (An imprint of New American Library), New York, 1997.

106b. "Leading the Charge: The W. Alton Jones Foundation's environmental scare tactics," by Ronald Bailey, *Philanthropy*, Vol. XII, No. 3, July/August, 1998, p. 16.

107. "Leading the Charge," *Philanthropy, 16.*

108a. "Charlottesville, Virginia," by Mike Steere, *Outside* magazine, July 1995.

108b. Foundation Center records.

109a. Foundation Center records.

109b. "Teresa Heinz," *Boston Globe.*

109c. "Environmental Donors Set Tone," *Boston Globe.*

110. "Environmental Donors Set Tone," *Boston Globe.*

112. "The Greening of a Movement," *Boston Globe.*

114. "Sowing the Seeds of Philanthropy," by Susan Byrnes, *Seattle Times,* Monday, February 15, 1999, p. A1.

115a. See biographies such as: *Riding A White Horse: Ted Turner's Goodwill Games and Other Crusades,* by Althea Carlson, Episcopal Press, 1998; *Ted Turner : It Ain't As Easy at Is Looks : A Biography* by Porter Bibb, Johnson Books, 1997; *Citizen Turner : The Wild Rise of an American Tycoon* by Robert and Gerald Jay Goldberg, Harcourt Brace Children's Books, 1995.

115b. "Transfer of buffalo invalid, Forest Service finds - Agency says NM owned by Ted Turner, by the Associated Press, *The Dallas Morning News,* Wednesday, January 20, 1999.

115c. 1997 Form 990-PF, Turner Foundation, Statement 7 and Statement 9.

115d. "Greening of a Movement," *Boston Globe.*

116a. "Welcome to Turner country," by Donovan Webster, *Audubon,* Friday, January 1, 1999.

116b. "On Ted Turner, Peggy Lee and a Certain Retired Bull," by James Warren, *Chicago Tribune,* Friday, January 15, 1999, *Tempo.*

117a. "Turner Conservation Work Spans Nation," by Julie Anderson, *Omaha World-Herald,* Sunday, December 27, 1998.

117b. "Buffalo roam in Turner's vast empire on range / Mogul owns 1.3 million acres for pastoral pursuits out West," by Geraldine Fabrikant, *New York Times,* published in *Houston Chronicle,* Friday, November 29, 1996.

120a. "Beau Turner," by Maryanne Vollers, *Atlanta Magazine,* August 1998.

120b. "Ted Turner Accused of Keeping His Neighbors in the Dark," by Associated Press, *Orlando Sentinel,* Monday, December 4, 1989, p. B3.

120c. "Ted Turner Calls for Environmental Revolution," by Jerome Simpson, *Environmental News Service,* Wednesday, 14 October 1998.

121a. "Ted Turner: 'At Time Warner, We're All Pissed Off,'" edited by Thane Peterson, *Business Week Online,* February 6, 1997.

121b. "Environmental Donors Set Tone," *Boston Globe.*

CHAPTER 3

GRANT-DRIVEN GREENS

A bewildering array of organizations call themselves environmentalists. The "greens" are a diverse, disparate and divergent lot. Some connect to the broader "progressive" movement of anti-corporate campaigns. Some limit themselves to foundation-driven rural cleansing plans, agreeing with the ideology, blind to the despotism, and feeling no strings. Others, especially the largest and wealthiest green groups, are controlled by a board of directors salted with foundation officers. Some radical groups are able to attract equally radical funders who give with no strings attached. All green groups operate on other peoples' money and those other people have agendas that harm the resource class.

THERE ARE ABOUT 12,000 ENVIRONMENTAL GROUPS in America. That's the estimate based on the Internal Revenue Service's *Publication 78, Cumulative List of Organizations.*

Most of them are grant-driven.

We've seen some of the machinery of grant driven greens. How green groups became grant driven to begin with: dissatisfaction of foundations with an environmental movement grown bureaucratic and detached. The foundations' determination to reorganize the movement. New emphasis on media, polling, and messages. Foundation-driven outreach to bring a wider constituency to the environmental debate, such as left-leaning advocates in the religious, scientific, and journalistic communities.

We have seen grumbles from environmentalists who resented being grant driven, and Don Ross's, "Too bad. They're players. We're players."

We will see that some green groups are all too eager to go along with foundations "not just picking the issues, but also being directive in the sense of the kind of campaign, the strategy, the style, and so on," in Chuck Clusen's words (p. 73)—as long as it comes with money and power.

THE COALITION MODEL

Today the dominant green group pattern is the coalition. The day of the stand-alone green group is waning, although the familiar institutional names like Greenpeace and the Sierra Club will stand indefinitely. It's how they're working that has changed and is still changing.

Foundations have forced green groups to work together, as we have seen. But how, exactly, do they work together? How are these coalitions formed, how do they choose leaders, how do they operate?

A classic example of the late 1990s coalition model can be found in the Southwest Forest Alliance, much like the Northern Forest Alliance we examined in Chapter 1 (pages 36-43). It is a confederation of more than fifty Southwest-based green groups, some of them well-known giants, some so small they don't even appear to be incorporated and have no entries in the IRS *Cumulative List of Organizations* (see the Southwest Forest Alliance member list opposite).

In the April 15, 1996 issue of High Country News, reporter Peter Aleshire described the Alliance's origins thus:

> They lobbied. They staged sit-ins. They crashed town hall meetings. They chained themselves to trees. They scrounged for pennies and sued every despoiler of public lands they could find.
>
> The guerrilla tactics of the Southwest's disparate environmental activists have worked. They have contributed to an enormous decrease in logging in the region's 11 national forests: Less than half the timber that fell there in 1990 falls today. And a blockbuster lawsuit last year [1995] forced the Forest Service to halt virtually all logging in the Southwest until federal biologists study its effects on the threatened Mexican spotted owl.

But the activists knew their victories were temporary. Without permanent protection, the last ponderosa pine and mixed conifer forests could still fall. They also realized that enduring change in forest management required public outcry to force the hands of reluctant politicians and Forest Service administrators. And to accomplish that they needed something they never have enough of — money.

So last year [1995] the leaders from 50 groups, including the Southwest Center for Biological Diversity, the Sierra Club, Audubon Society and the Forest Conservation Council, banded together under the name The Southwest Forest Alliance. They went after the big bucks, and they hit the jackpot.

The Pew Charitable Trusts has promised a two-year, $500,000 grant to the Alliance, if it can come up with a matching $425,000 — a sum it is well on its way to raising.[131a]

- Amigos Bravos Friends of the Wild Rivers
- Arizona Audubon Council
- Arizona League of Conservation Voters
- Audubon El Paso
- Audubon of Northern Arizona
- Audubon Prescott
- Border Ecology Project
- Carson Forest Watch
- Central NM Audubon
- Committee of Wilderness Supporters
- Earthlaw
- Forest Conservation Council
- Forest Trust
- Friends of the Gila River
- Friends of the Owls
- Huachuca Audubon
- Land and Water Fund of the Rockies
- Lifenet
- Maricopa Audubon
- National Audubon Society
- National Parks and Conservation Association
- New Mexico Environmental Law Center
- New Mexico Forest Partnership
- New Mexico Wilderness Study Committee
- Public Forestry Foundation
- Rio Grande Bioregional Project
- Rio Grande Restoration
- Sante Fe Forest Watch
- Sierra Club - El Paso
- Sierra Club - Grand Canyon Chapter
- Sierra Club - Prescott
- Sierra Club - Rincon
- Sierra Club - Rio Grande
- Sierra Club - So. NM Group
- Sierra Club - SW Regional Office
- Sierra Madre Project
- Sky Island Alliance
- Sonoran Bioregional Diversity Project
- Southern Rocky Mountain Service Corps
- Southwest Center for Biological Diversity
- Southwest Environmental Center
- Student Environmental Action Coalition
- Student Environment Center
- T&E Inc.
- The Sustainability Project
- The Wildlands Project
- White Mountain Conservation League
- Wildlife Damage Review
- Youth Ecology Corps
- Zuni Conservation Project
- Zuni Mountain Coalition

1999 SOUTHWEST FOREST ALLIANCE MEMBER GROUPS[131b]

That's so wonderful it sounds impossible.

It is.

The grant application says it went a little differently.[132a]

The cover sheet is a standard Pew item with the usual *Please attach a copy of this completed form to the front of your grant proposal.*

It reads:

TAX NAME OF ORGANIZATION: National Audubon Society, 700 Broadway, New York, N.Y. 10003-9510.

NAME OF PROGRAM TO BE FUNDED: The Desert Forests Campaign. [It will be renamed the Southwest Forest Alliance a year later.]

NAME AND TITLE OF HEAD OF PROGRAM: Mr. David Henderson, New Mexico State Director - National Audubon Society.

GRANT REQUEST: *(amount)* $225,000/yr. *(duration)* Two years. *(purpose)* To build a campaign that will lead to the permanent protection of the Southwest forest ecosystem through a series of legislative and administrative forest reserves and citizen sponsored forest managment plans.

Oddly, nowhere in the accompanying proposal can we find those 50 refreshingly diverse groups of the creation myth, only 11 rather lookalike usual suspects:

The Desert Forests Campaign is being organized by Arizona Audubon Council, Carson Forest Watch, Earthlaw, Forest Conservation Council, Forest Guardians, Forest Trust, Greater Gila Biodiversity Project, Maricopa Audubon, Sierra Club Plateau Group, Southwest Center for Biological Diversity, and Southwest Audubon. National Audubon Society will act as the Campaign's fiscal sponsor.[132b]

Audubon is in total control. Three of the eleven organizers were Audubons (Maricopa Audubon's president was Charles Babbitt, brother of Interior Secretary Bruce Babbitt). Three others are Santa Fe-based outfits that practically live in each others' hip pockets. No Hispanics. No Native Americans. Not even anyone born in New Mexico.

Where are those 50 legendary originators? The proposal promised to create a "Grassroots Support Network." It said, "Two grassroots activists will be hired to organize Northern New Mexico, Northern Arizona, and the Southern forests." Wait for the money.

The eleven-page Audubon proposal, dated October, 1994 and titled "The Desert Forests Campaign: Protecting the Bio-Economic Diversity of Southwest Forest Ecosystems," is divided into four sections:

I. **Background, Threats and Opportunities.**
II. **The Desert Forests Campaign.**
III. **Campaign Structure.**
IV. **Project Budget and Request to Pew Charitable Trusts.**

The *Background* paints an idyllic picture of a planetary Eden in Arizona and New Mexico, "sky islands" of high elevation mountain forests above the desert floor, lush and luxuriant vegetation, arroyos abounding in rare plant and animal species. It reads like a travel brochure.

Then come the *Threats:* if Audubon and friends don't stop the logging and mining and ranching, Southwestern forests will die. The worst threat is that, as a result of environmentalist successes, the baddies are stepping up the devastation.

Up to this point, it's all pretty much standard foundationese. Now it gets interesting. Here's Audubon's take on

Opportunities

It is readily apparent that this new level of threats is a response to successful, if less than systematic, environmental activism. The Forest Service has adopted our language, co-opted our concepts, and become more sophisticated in its management and justification. It is now time for the environmental movement to evolve as well. The next five years offer an excellent opportunity for the environmental community to come together in a systematic pro-active campaign to attain permanent forest protection through the legislation of a network of forest reserves and conservation biology based management plans.

Structurally, the Southwest is in an excellent position to attain this goal:

● An informal network of all the major forest activists already exists. We are remarkably unified in our vision and are well poised to organize a major campaign. In the last two years we have worked together on numerous lawsuits, petitions and appeals. Most recently, we worked together to produce a comprehensive critique of the Kaibab National Forest's proposed Forest Plan amendment.

● Because clearcutting has not been the predominant method of logging Southwest forests have not been converted to tree farms. Significant, unprotected roadless areas and forest areas still exist.

● Because Southwest forests are so diverse and support so many endemic species, they are uniquely suited to a biodiversity based forest campaign.

● The Southwest is unique in that virtually all its water originates on National Forest land. Clean, abundant water is far and away the

---

most valuable resource in this region and is in direct conflict with excessive logging and grazing.

● Ninety percent of Southwest forests are managed by U S Park or Forest Service. The rest is managed by three Native American Nations. With so few agencies involved, all with federal environmental mandates, strategizing and coordination will be made easier.

● The timber industry is a minor economic force in the Southwest. Its continued and inevitable decline will not cause the kind of upheavals evident in the Northwest.

● Tourism is the Southwest's largest industry. Arizona is the most popular destination birding area in the country. Permanently protecting our forests will increase and diversify the region's economy.

● The Southwest is one of the most urbanized regions in the country. Seventy-five percent of its population lives in Albuquerque, Tucson or Phoenix. The other twenty-five percent is largely concentrated in a handful of smaller cities. This population is recreationally oriented and can be reached very efficiently.

● Native American and traditional Hispanic cultures continue to thrive and are recognized as integrated parts of Southwestern culture. These communities and the values they represent are dependent upon healthy forest ecosystems....

● Finally, other regions such as the Southern Appalachians and Northern Rockies are organizing or proposing similar campaigns. These efforts will lend credibility to one another, creating a favorable climate for systematic regional and national forest protection.

We're not speaking foundationese anymore. This is War Room talk. Somehow it sounds less like Dave Henderson of Audubon's New Mexico outpost than Tom Wathen and Joshua Reichert of Pew Charitable Trusts. It is not what either Audubon or Pew would say in public.

"Clearcutting has not been the predominant method of logging Southwest forests." Southwest forests are still diverse and rich in species; there is still abundant clean water. In other words, the people who live there already do an excellent job of keeping Southwest forests healthy. Not for public consumption.

"Ninety percent of Southwest forests are managed by U S Park or Forest Service." They're subject to federal laws. Easy to get into court. Easy to lobby in Congress. Easy to influence through their network of federal employees who are members of allied environmental groups. Not for public consumption.

"The timber industry is a minor economic force in the Southwest,"

and its destruction *"will not cause the kind of upheavals evident in the Northwest."* A plain acknowledgement that environmentalists caused the Northwest's devastating unemployment, something Pew has spent a lot of money denying. And a strategic kissoff of timber workers as easy prey. Not for public consumption.

"The Southwest is one of the most urbanized regions in the country." A clear understanding of the urban-rural power gap and how to exploit it. Not for public consumption.

"Other regions such as the Southern Appalachians and Northern Rockies are organizing or proposing similar campaigns." Clear knowledge of the whole grant driven green network's plans. Not for public consumption.

The rest is similarly straight talk.

Section II, The Desert Forests Campaign itself, had two components: *Forest Proposals*, essentially What To Do, and *Biodiversity Advocacy*, essentially How To Do It.

The *Forest Proposals* centered around a multi-pronged strategy:

> Ecologically based forest management proposals will be developed for each ecosystem including every National Forest and Native American Nation which choose to participate. The proposals will form the core of the legislative and Forest Plan proposals. They will also be used for multi-species conservation plans, public education and administrative resistance.

The logic of this strategy is sheer intelligence; it will use the Endangered Species Act as a legal bludgeon and the media to legitimize their destruction of the resource class. The strategy of the *Biodiversity Advocacy* proposal, however, is sheer power.

> National Forest Management Act and Endangered Species Act petitions, appeals and litigation have provided the environmental movement its strongest tools. They have been used less than strategically, however, when focused on single species. Activists in the Southwest have petitioned for 32 endangered species and have thus far been very successful in strategically using these laws to obtain permanent ecosystem protection, create administrative legal tools, and create acute pressure points in need of immediate conservation resolution....
>
> Listed species will be used in strategic multi-species litigation and administrative appeals to protect critical forest stands and watersheds. Unlisted species will be subjects of Endangered Species Act

petitions. Multi-species, ecosystem based recovery plans and critical habitat petitions will be developed and incorporated as integral parts of the forest plan proposals.

Species are mere surrogates for a power move to control federal lands for the greens to use, excluding all others. There could be no straighter path to removing resource extraction from all federal land in the Southwest. The sophistication of the implementation plan is breathtaking:

Urban Mobilization and Media / Public Education

Because the Southwest populace is largely concentrated in less than a dozen urban centers, with 75% in Phoenix, Tucson and Albuquerque, it can be efficiently reached by a directed urban mobilization campaign. Mobilizing public support will be crucial to effectively reach the legislature and create widespread interest in forest reform.

In year one we will conduct strategic planning sessions with professional consultants to develop a compelling message best suited to the unique geographical and cultural conditions of the Southwest. We anticipate the first years design work to include:

1. An analysis of strengths, weaknesses, opportunities, and threats (SWOT), to determine (a) what successful / unsuccessful media messages Southwest forest activists have utilized; (b) how well we are packaging the meaning of our activism; (c) what our strengths and weaknesses as a movement are, (d) what resources are available within our coalition; (e) what resources need to be brought in from outside.

2. Polling and / or focus groups to gauge current public sentiment and knowledge, determine how well our message has gotten across, how well the industry and the anti-environmental movement's message has gotten across, and assess how much desert-dwelling urbanites know about Southwest forests and their plight; development of a compelling vision and messages targeted at specific audiences at specific times.

3. Design of an outreach program capable of transmitting and selling the vision and messages.

4. A public relations professional in Phoenix has agreed to work pro-bono to develop an initial vision, message and communications plan.

We expect to begin the outreach education campaign in earnest by year two. An urban canvass will begin operating in year two as part of the outreach program. New Mexico PIRG has expressed interest in contracting canvass work in New Mexico.

Grassroots Support Network

Developing an effective grassroots network is critical. Grassroots activists will be instrumental in developing and lobbying for local forest proposals. They will also file administrative appeals and provide on the ground knowledge to all facets of the campaign.

Grassroots activists will be teched-up and tied into an electronic network which includes computers, faxes, modems, a Desert Forest Conference on Econet, and a regular newsletter.

Good communication among activists is necessary to develop consistent positions, quick, effective response, and timely, accurate information flow.

Media, mapping, forestry and appeals workshops will be regularly organized in each of the three eco-regions to create activist groups where they are needed to support existing activists. A forestry specialist will also be available to aid in on ground analysis.

Two grassroots activists will be hired to organize Northern New Mexico, Northern Arizona, and the Southern forests.

Section III, the *Campaign Structure*, makes very clear who is going to farm those grassroots once they sprout: "The Campaign will be overseen by an 11 member board representing the campaign organizers."

And, "A Steering Committee of 5 people will act on behalf of the Board. The Steering Committee will ensure Campaign goals, strategies, and programs are implemented."

In other words, a tiny handful of people get to spend the money.

And what about that money?

There was a great deal more to this project than became publicly apparent.

As in the Northern Forest Alliance (pages 36-43), where funding was unclear because some went through a fiscal agent—The Appalachian Mountain Club—and some went directly to the participating groups, so the Southwest Forest Alliance had multiple funding avenues, the National Audubon Society as fiscal agent, and direct grants to the participating green groups. The Northern Forest and Southwest Forest campaigns obviously used the same model.

Section IV, Project Budget and Request to Pew Charitable Trusts, tells all:

The Desert Forest Campaign seeks $225,000 per year for two years from the Pew Charitable Trusts to implement The Desert Forest Campaign in Arizona and New Mexico.

The Campaign is a three year, $1,514,100 commitment by a network of grassroots and national environmental organizations. National Audubon Society will serve as the fiscal sponsor for the Campaign, with participating organizations receiving contracts from NAS to implement specific Campaign components. The following budget narrative provides an explanation of revenues and expenditures depicted on the budget form attached, and discussed year by year changes in the allocation of project funds as they are adjusted to meet the changing emphasis of the campaign as it evolves over a three year period.

Revenue

In year one, total project revenue is expected to be $496,545 with Pew Charitable Trusts contributing $225,000, or 45% of the total. Other foundations will contribute $226,145. Existing commitments to individual groups implementing portions of the Campaign include the Turner Foundatiom, for biodiversity advocacy, grassroots mapping, litigation and appeals ($50,000), the Harder Foundation for appeals and public education work ($10,000), the Sierra Club ($2,000) for mapping, the McCune Foundation ($15,000) for economic and cultural resource effects analysis of Conservation Plans, and the Ruth Brown Foundation ($5,000) for biodiversity advocacy. Other foundations being solicited by participating organizations for Campaign related work include the W. Alton Jones Foundation, the Ruth Mott Fund, Recreation Equipment Incorporated, the Santa Fe Community Foundation, the Surdna Foundation, the C. S. Fund, Foundation for Deep Ecology, [illegible] Foundation and Fund for Wild Nature, the Rockefeller Foundation, the Florence Schumann Foundation, the Nathan Cummings Foundation and the Tides Foundation.

Additional revenues are expected from business sponsors ($10,000), including the Business for Social Responsibility network in New Mexico, from individual members of participating organizations ($15,000), and direct funding of campaign costs and labor from participating organizations ($20,400).

After reading Chapter 2, you may harbor some doubts about who approached whom to originate this proposal. Dave Henderson may have indeed written it, but it certainly has the whiff of Environmental Grantmakers Association thinking about it.

National Audubon Society was clearly not reluctant to be placed in fiscal control of a 50-member, multi-million-dollar coalition: the prestige and bragging rights alone were worth the controversy Audubon doubtless anticipated.

Forest proposal coordination was contracted to the Forest Conservation Council. Biodivervsity advocacy, most of which has been litigation, was contracted to the Southwest Center for Biological Diversity and Earthlaw, a Denver-based public interest law firm.

It is clear that a great deal of foundation legwork had already been done before the proposal was presented to Pew. It is significant that this grant proposal names 17 Environmental Grantmakers Association funders on its face, but only 11 environmental groups.

Joshua Reichert approved the proposal in late 1994 for 1995 payment. The J.N. Pew Jr. Charitable Trust 1995 Grants list published the following entry:

National Audubon Society, Inc., New York, New York
For the Southwest Desert Forests Campaign. In support of the work of 48 environmental organizations to secure designated reserves within the national forests of Arizona and New Mexico (partial matching grant). $450,000 2 yrs.[139a]

The Campaign went to work, but soon ran into a public relations fiasco. When news of the Pew grant broke in late 1995, the commissioners of Rio Arriba County in northern New Mexico were furious. This sparsely settled county of mostly Hispanics and Apaches was in upheaval over a lawsuit filed by two Campaign members, Sam Hitt of Forest Guardians and John Talberth of the Forest Conservation Council. The suit, like those envisioned in the Campaign's proposal, was supposed to protect the threatened Mexican spotted owl, but had forced a halt to logging and restricted firewood gathering, even though owls had only been found in one remote area. It was the firewood that ignited first.[139b]

For hundreds of years, rural Hispanics have gathered firewood here. This is their land under the Treaty of Guadalupe Hidalgo, given to them in Spanish land grants as far back as the late 17th century.

It was bad enough when the Forest Service took control in the early 1900s.

Now they found that a green group lawsuit was keeping them from their firewood and their local logging—and that some new Campaign was planning to do the same to everybody in the Southwest.

In December, 1995, angry Hispanics joined timber and mining workers in Santa Fe, where they hanged and burned an effigy of Hitt and Talberth.

"Environmentalists haven't wanted to take the blame for their actions," said Max Cordova, leader of the 300 families of the Truchas Land Grant. "Until they recognize that, how can we deal with them?"

The conflict attracted national media, including the New York Times, Los Angeles Times, CBS, NBC and talk radio—but not the way Audubon and Pew planned it.

The stories pitted the poor families and their survival against white, urban environmentalists more concerned about a bird than about people. The L.A. Times wrote:

> Antonio DeVargas, who organized last week's demonstration and mock hanging, once led a campaign to scale back logging by a foreign-owned timber corporation that local people feared would denude the forests and leave local communities without a timber supply.
>
> But when the litigation over the owl threatened to put his homegrown logging operation, La Compania Ocho, out of business, said DeVargas, it was time to part company with the environmentalists.
>
> "It turns out they are no different from anyone else who has come in here," he said. "They just want to take control over our destiny."[140a]

DeVargas wrote a stinging three-page critique of the Campaign proposal, concluding:

> In short, the organizers will seek to suspend, through the legal system and media, all current economic activities of those who have subsisted on the land for generations. The forests will thus be preserved for posterity and incidentally, for those many monied interests who enjoy or profit from recreational usage, and who contribute to the Audubon Society.[140b]

But Pew's money and Audubon's managers said the Desert Forests Campaign had nothing to do with the lawsuit.

The Southwest Forest Alliance carried on its mission of rural cleansing.

THE MONTANA INITIATIVE WARS

Not all grant-driven greens are out to save wilderness, endangered species and open space. Changing the political process itself has become the focus of certain groups such as Washington, D.C.-based Americans for the Environment (AFE).

According to its innocuous-sounding website, AFE is "a non-profit organization dedicated to helping citizen activists use the political process to solve environmental problems, providing Americans concerned about the environment with the knowledge and skills needed to participate effectively in the electoral process."

That's foundationese for, "The aim is to change the law to disenfranchise as many for-profit corporations as possible, then use the changed electoral system to eradicate for-profit corporations completely."

Here we have the nexus between environmentalism and the broader "progressive" movement as described in the section on the Tides Center (p. 76ff). Extreme progressives such as Alliance for Democracy are operating a "Death Sentence" campaign to revoke corporate charters and put an end to corporations altogether. They have hundreds of allied groups. They are quite serious. They have petitioned states to revoke the corporate charters of Unocal, Stone Container, Philip Morris and other companies.[141]

Americans for the Environment is not quite as ambitious in its anti-corporate aspirations. They favor more incremental methods, such as ballot measures.

Using the Initiative and Referendum process, it's possible to drum up a ballot proposition campaign to change environmental laws in ways the legislature would never do. Propositions have the benefit of populist appeal: it is easy to make the public forget that corporations produce more than filthy pollution and filthy profits. When you command campaign skills like the Environmental Grantmakers Association and its beneficiaries do, it's no surprise that environmentalists have been able to win 62% of their ballot campaigns (59 out of 95 measures in several dozen different states in the period 1990-94). This is noteworthy since the overwhelming majority of ballot measures on all issues fail.

As most Americans would guess, it's illegal for a tax-exempt non-profit 501(c)(3) organization like Americans for the Environment to influence elections, so they confine themselves to teaching others how to do it—conferences, workshops, special projects and publications. To stay out of jail, AFE neither supports nor opposes candidates for public office, nor committees, entities, campaigns, or organizations working for the election or defeat of any candidate or party.

Others are organized under nonprofit laws for political action committees and can legally conduct and finance electoral campaigns. Foundations, as most Americans would never guess, can support such campaigns by carefully driving their grants through several large loopholes, mostly by funding "educational" activities closely tied to ballot

Type of Proposition	
[I] **Initiative**	An initiative is a measure placed on the ballot as the result of a popular effort, such as a petition drive among registered voters, for the purpose of proposing a new law, resolution, or constitutional amendment to be voted on by the electorate during an election.
[R] **Referendum**	A referendum may be placed on the ballot by a state legislature, or because of a constitutional requirement, or in some instances by citizen petition. The term referendum broadly refers to a measure on an election ballot that is subject to voters' approval or disapproval, allowing voters to approve or reject an act of legislature or amend the state constitution.
Status of Proposition	
Awaiting Approval	Title and language of measure have not been approved by state election officials.
Circulating	Petition signature drive in progress
Certified	Measure has been placed on the ballot by the state election board or secretary of state
Deadline	Last day to submit signed petitions to state election officials
Additional Terms	
Constitutional Amendment	A constitutional Amendment can be originated by the legislature and placed on the ballot. In some states the electorate may propose, through petition, an initiative to amend the constitution by ballot vote; the amendment must then be ratified by a requisite number of votes.
Bond Measure	State and local governments issue bonds to finance capital projects. In most states, the least expensive type of bond, general obligation bonds-pledging the full faith and credit of a government- need voter approval. Although G.O. bonds are financed by general funds, an issue of target specific revenues, such as property taxes, for repaying the bond. Revenue bonds, which must pledge a reliable source, such as user fees or other funds generated by the project, do not require voter approval.
Direct Initiative Amendment	Occurs when constitutional amendments proposed by the people are directly placed on the ballot and then submitted to the people for their approval or rejection.
Indirect Initiative Amendment	Occurs when constitutional amendment proposed by the people must first be submitted to the state legislature during a regular session.
Direct Initiative Statute	Statutes proposed by the people are directly placed on the ballot and then submitted to the people for their approval or rejection.
Indirect Initiative Statute	Statutes proposed by the people but must be submitted to the state legislature during a regular session
Popular Referendum	Occurs when the people have power to refer, through a petition, specific legislation that was enacted by the legislature.

—courtesy Americans for the Environment

measures—strategically timed polls, studies, surveys, voter registration campaigns, and such.

The Alliance for Justice, a Washington D.C. campaign reform organization, published a 1996 study titled *Seize the Initiative,* "a tool for nonprofit organizations on the legal do's and don'ts of 'seizing the initiative.'" They can do "education."[143a]

A section called "An Overview of the Law" offers strong advice:

"[T]he staying power of the coalition in 1996 were due, in part, to the clear understanding by 501(c)(3)s of permissible activities under the tax code and election law. Such an understanding should be the initial step in any initiative campaign."

Education is permissible. Although most environmentalist ballot measures deal with specific reforms such as banning hog farms (Colorado, 1998, won), or stopping the use of forestry herbicides (Oregon, 1998, lost), or some other rural cleansing particular, the big target of their coalition with other "progressives" is "campaign finance reform."[143b]

Campaign finance reform is based on the platitude, "money in politics is bad," which really means *your* money in politics is bad, *my* money in politics is good. Ellen Miller, executive director of the non-profit group, Public Campaign, said of campaign finance reform, "It is the reform that makes all other reforms possible."[143c]

Translation: "Kick your opponents off the playing field and it's easier to win the game."

Public Campaign, like Americans for the Environment, is a non-profit, non-partisan organization. It says it is "dedicated to sweeping reform that aims to dramatically reduce the role of special interest money in America's elections and the influence of big contributors in American politics."

One of Public Campaign's eight directors is John Moyers, executive director of the Florence and John Schumann Foundation, 1997 assets, $88,509,775. Grant-driven progressives.

Publications such as the *Funders' Handbook on Money in Politics,* published by the Ottinger Foundation, list dozens of campaign finance reform groups, including the Association of Community Organizations for Reform Now (ACORN) "Money and Politics Project;" Working Group on Electoral Democracy; Western States Center "Money in Western Politics Project;" U.S. Public Research Interest Group Education Fund - Americans Against Political Corruption; Eliminate Private Money; Missouri Alliance for Campaign Reform, and on and on.[143d]

What happened at Montana's ballot box in 1996 reads like a screwball comedy script for political Armageddon: a coalition of nonprofit organizations campaigned, qualified and won a state ballot initiative to outlaw for-profit corporations from contributing to state ballot initiative campaigns.

Their battle cry was, "Make Montana Safe From Out of State Big Money."

Two-thirds of their campaign was paid for by out of state big money.

But nobody knew that.

Their measure, Initiative-125, passed by a 52-48 percent margin.

I-125 banned all for-profit corporations from making either cash or in-kind contributions to ballot issue campaigns. It also extended that ban to the majority of nonprofits (for-profit corporations can use nonprofits as front groups). The only nonprofits that were allowed to make contributions were those that:

- Were organized for political purposes;
- Did not have any for-profit corporations as members;
- Received less than 5 percent of their income from for-profits; and
- Did not engage in business activities.

This new law posed some serious questions about the free speech rights of business owners. The Montana Chamber of Commerce and the Montana Mining Association sued in 1997. Both suits named Ed Argenbright, Montana's commissioner of political practices, as a defendant. Five left-wing organizations filed as defendant-intervenors.

After months of legal wrangling, U.S. District Court Judge Charles Lovell declared I-125 unconstitutional in late 1998. Argenbright and the five groups took the case to the Ninth U.S. Circuit Court of Appeals.[144a]

In the beginning, it all looked so local and grass-rooty and so—well, so *Montana*. No one suspected that Initiative-125 was hatched in Massachusetts, funded out of Washington D.C., Hollywood, Santa Barbara, and Atlanta, and shepherded through the appeals court by a Boston group that gets enormous grants from a New Jersey foundation.

The first anybody saw of the campaign was a University of Montana course notice in mid-1995. The Course Flow said there would be an Environmental Organizing Semester in Spring 1996. It said "weeks twelve through fifteen will focus on the planning and execution of a petition drive."[144b]

The syllabus announced that the professor who would teach the 12-credit Environmental Organizing Semester was one C. B. Pearson, who, according to his resume, was the former executive director of MontPIRG, the former executive director of Montana Common Cause, had been an assistant organizing director of the Fund for Public Interest Research back in Boston, Massachusetts, and was the former executive director of CalPIRG.[145a]

MontPIRG, incidentally, occupies an office on the University of Montana's campus.

The syllabus also announced guest lectures by Jonathan Motl, Helena attorney and head of Montana Common Cause, the group sponsoring the campaign finance reform initiative, I-125, and Lila Cleminshaw, a member of Montanans for Clean Water, sponsors of an anti-mining initiative, I-122.

The syllabus gave two important dates:

Thursday April 18, 1996

* Morning: Direct Democracy: The Initiative Process

Friday April 19, 1996

* Morning: On-going campaigns — Spring 1996; possibilities clean water and campaign finance issues.[145b]

Students on those dates did more than study. They went out and gathered many of the signatures needed to put both I-122 and I-125 on the ballot. According to state law, a public officer or employee may not use public time, equipment, personnel or funds for any campaign activity persuading or affecting a political decision. The University of Montana is a state-supported institution.

When questions arose about the ethics of this activity, attorney Motl said the 14 students enrolled in the course received instruction on the signature-gathering process during class time, but circulated the I-122 and I-125 petition on their own. Motl thought the students probably took votes among themselves on which petition they would circulate. He added that course expenses and its professor, C. B. Pearson, were entirely supported by private funds and thus nothing illegal transpired.[145c]

Private funds? That came as a surprise. Whose private funds?

Eric Williams of Environomics, a Montana-based consulting firm, began to snoop around.

Turns out that Motl was not just a guest speaker. He also served as "special consultant" to the Environmental Organizing Semester to "assist in the development and release of the investigative report and the petition portions of the course."[145d]

Then too, Williams discovered, a group called Montana Environmental Information Center had paid Pearson "a small consulting fee very early in the campaign just to help them plan the petition gathering stage."[145e]

Williams dug further. He found that in early June of 1996, C. B. Pearson sent a letter to a foundation requesting grants for the I-125 campaign. His cover letter to the Stern Family Fund, a $2.5 million foundation granting primarily to government and corporate accountability projects, said:

> I am the campaign manager for the petition drive to qualify Initiative 125, active with MontPIRG, their Foundation MontPIRF, Common Cause and the League of Women Voters, and will be the campaign manager for the fall campaign.
> We are in the process of completing a comprehensive study on the role of corporate money in the Montana Initiative process."[146]

Attached to Pearson's fundraising letter was *A Proposal To Get Corporate Money Out Of Montana's Initiative Process*. It was beginning to look a lot like the National Audubon Society proposal to Pew Charitable Trusts for the Southwest Forest Alliance.

Pearson's proposal revealed a far more convoluted plan than the public knew about:

> The coalition of supporters for I-125 are led by MontPIRG, Common Cause and the League of Women Voters. We expect to expand the coalition once we have qualified the initiative. Outreach has been completed to over 30 different organizations. Both the Montana Trial Lawyers Association and the Montana Lung Association have shown a strong commitment to joining in the effort but have not done so on paper yet. We fully expect the support of AARP and United We Stand. Other potential supporters include labor and senior citizen groups as well as environmental groups.
> The timing for proposing I-125 could not be better. Two important citizen initiatives which will draw large direct corporate contributions are moving to the 1996 ballot. Initiative 121, a minimum wage petition has recently made the ballot. The Montana Chamber of Commerce looks to be the main opponent. The other initiative is I-122, a clean water initiative targeted at mining companies, particularly cyanide heap-leach gold mines. Multi-national gold mining companies are the identified opponents. These two initiatives should demonstrate to the people of Montana the problem of unlimited direct corporate contributions as well as act as a good target for media hits and organizing public opinion for our reform. Both initiatives enjoy wide-spread public support in recent public opinion polls. The opponents to I-122

have made it clear that they will raise as much money as necessary to defeat the initiative and are using the fact that there is no limit on giving to ballot campaigns in their fundraising materials.

"We will focus on who the messenger is (most likely the League) and the message. We have had some luck at this point in cutting the message to our benefit."

The current list of opponents reads like a who's who among corporate bad guys. Opponents include the lobbyist for Western Environmental Trade Association, (WETA), the primary lobbying outfit for the timber and mining industry in the northwest and a main wise-use organizer, the lobbyist for the tobacco companies in Montana who is also the person running the campaign against the clean water initiative, and the executive director of the Chamber of Commerce.

No money has been allocated for polling and message development. There have been discussions with Celinda Lake [noted Democrat pollster] on possible polling options but nothing has been firmed up at this point. Celinda has talked about the possibility of tieing [sic] our polling questions to an existing poll to help save costs, etc.

We will focus on the seven major counties and their media outlets along with a county by county media and grassroots organizing strategy.[147a]

How similar all these proposals are when you get into them. The reliance on urban media for rural cleansing. The vilification of resource producers. The secret advance planning among colleagues. The hidden funding by prescriptive foundations. The use of popular organizations as fronts.

The I-125 campaign's use of the League of Women Voters was particularly egregious. The League received prominent media notice as a leading proponent of I-125, but the League didn't report spending a dime towards its passage. It was all talk and no financial contribution.[147b]

In fact, the League was paid to be a supporter. According to reports submitted to the IRS, MontPIRG paid $3,000 to the League of Women Voters for "Campaign Finance Reform/I-125" a month and a half before election day, but what happened to the money is unknown.[147c]

Another question about the proposal: why did Pearson emphasize those two other initiatives, I-121 and I-122? It was no accident. Americans for the Environment gave us the reason. In June of 1996, when this trio of campaigns was heating up in Montana, AFE published *The Populist I&R Movement: Direct Democracy in Action*. It said,

There is a fourth, indirect benefit which can accrue to ballot initiatives that arouse powerful public sentiments. When a particular proposal is contentious enough to actually bring out voters who would not otherwise come to the polls on election day (and environmental issues are sometimes of this type), there can be a spill-over effect on the other issues or candidates on the ballot ... Under the right conditions, environmentalists could enjoy a long-term electoral benefit by employing the same technique if they could devise a cohesive national ballot measure strategy, put more resources into obtaining expert guidance from campaign consultants, expand their use of focus groups and polling, and test (for instance through exit polls) whether or not environmental and animal welfare ballot measures can create a "surge vote" that can have an effect on voter turnout and the outcome of candidate races.[148a] (Parentheses in the original.)

Was anyone backstage coordinating these campaigns to create a "surge vote?"

Of course. The I-125 and I-122 campaigns paid MacWillams, Cosgrove, Snider, Smith & Robinson Consulting (MCSSR), of Takoma Park, Md., more than $78,000 to provide advertising, consulting, retainer and other services.[148b] Recall, it was MacWilliams Cosgrove Snider that did the 1992 anti-wise use "Search and Destroy Strategy Guide" (note, p. 126).

Lake Research, Inc., of Washington D.C. was paid a modest $2,000 by Montanans for Clean Water/For I-122 for "Professional Services," but nothing for the I-125 campaign.[148c]

The string-pulling hub was Ralph Nader's Boston-based Center for Public Interest Research (CFPIR), C. B. Pearson's old stomping grounds. *The Funders' Handbook* noted:

During 1996, CFPIR supported eight state projects through an integrated Campaign to Get Big Money Out of Politics. This campaign had two objectives: to advance the policy debate on money in politics, and to educate and unify the reform community."[148d]

So—there was an integrated campaign behind the Montana Initiative Wars, just like the Southwest Forest Alliance and the Northern Forest Alliance. Well, we should be expecting it by now.

When all the money supporting I-125 was counted by Montana's commissioner of political practices, six entities had paid the bulk of the total reported $114,980. They were:

- The Montana Public Interest Research Group, Missoula, Montana. $31,640.81.
- U.S. Public Interest Research Group, Washington, D.C. $35,000
- The 2030 Fund, Inc. a PIRG entity, Santa Barbara, California. $40,000.
- Common Cause, Helena, Montana. $5,296.82
- Hollywood Women's Action Fund, Hollywood, California. $1,000.00
- Individuals $1,945.00
- Reynolds, Motl & Sherwood (Motl's law firm) contributed $97.50 of in-kind services.

- The Montana Public Interest Research Foundation, Missoula, Mont., created a non-reported study, *Big Money and Montana's Ballot Campaigns,* that became a crucial campaign component, but was an "educational" product that did not have to be reported as a campaign contribution.

Raw funding score:
- 66 percent came from California and Washington D.C.
- 92 percent came from Public Interest Research Groups (PIRGs), both in-state and out of state sources.[149a]
- Only 2 percent came of individual Montanans.

The final irony came after Judge Lovell ruled I-125 unconstitutional. Attorney Jonathan Motl had the Boston-based National Voting Rights Institute file a notice of appeal on behalf of the defendant-intervenors. NVRI assumed full responsibility for handling the appellate phase of the case. Thus an out of state organization represented the citizens of Montana when I-125 moved to the Ninth Circuit Court of Appeals.[149b]

The National Voting Rights Institute gets a big percentage of its money from the Florence and John Schumann Foundation of Montclair, New Jersey. NVRI had a 1997 total revenue of more than $1.21 million, of which $812,113 came from the Schumann Foundation. $175,000 came from the Ford Foundation (New York City) and $65,000 from the Joyce Foundation (Chicago). All but $47,531 of NVRI's $1.21 million came from donations of $10,000 or larger, none of which were from Montana.[149c]

There's one more thing to be learned from the Montana Initiative Wars: Don't underestimate the power of the PIRGs. They may soon cram their "democracy" down the throat of an electoral system near you.

C. B. Pearson's old outfit, the Boston-based Fund for Public Interest Research, paid PIRG programs in Montana during 1996:

- Montana Membership Education and Services Project: $11,367
- Montana Public Education and Outreach Project: $11,281
- Montana Citizen Lobbying Project: $11,281[150a]

None of this showed up in the I-125 campaign reports, but it supported campaign related activities. The Fund also gave $31,200 to U.S. PIRG in 1996, which was the second-largest contributor to the I-125 effort.

Pearson really understands how these campaigns work: they always release a big study at a crucial point to steam up the public. The study, of course, has been thought out and agreed upon long in advance of the campaign; only the wording is left until the proper moment. In the I-125 campaign it was *Big Money and Montana's Ballot Campaigns*, co-authored by Pearson and Hilary Doyscher, a University of Montana Student. Others, including Jonathan Motl, were listed for special thanks.[150b]

The study was performed under the auspices of Montana Public Interest Research Foundation (MontPIRF), a 501(c)(3) sister organization to MontPIRG, which is a 501(c)(4) lobbying group. The study was paid for by grants from several foundations, notably the Turner Foundation in Atlanta.

In fact, a grant from Turner Foundation was used to create MontPIRF in the first place—a 1993 $10,000 contribution to the Montana Public Interest Research *Group*. MontPIRG never got the check. Instead, in 1994 that $10,000 went to the brand-new organization called the Montana Public Interest Research *Foundation*, IRS documents show.[150c]

In late January 1994 MontPIRF received the $10,000.[150d] The new organization's main product that year was a study titled "If Money Could Talk." That study was the big bomb in the passage of Montana's Initiative 118, an earlier and less stringent campaign finance reform measure.

In 1996 Turner gave MontPIRF another $10,000.[150e]

That year, MontPIRF's primary product was the *Big Money* study that touted I-125 as "the solution to this problem" of corporate contributions. *The 1996 Funders' Handbook on Money and Politics,* considered the most comprehensive guide on campaign finance reform organizations across the country, stated that MontPIRF's 1996 campaign finance reform "Project Budget" was $10,000.[150f]

In addition to the Turner money, MontPIRF received two grants from the U.S. Public Interest Research Group Education Fund (located at the same Washington, D.C. address as the U.S. Public Interest Research Group) between July 1 1995 and June 30 1997. The first grant was for $1,000, the second for $5,000.[150g]

OUTPOSTS

The "progressive" anti-corporate network overlaps the environmental movement in numerous layers. It is revealing to see how grant-driven some of these groups are. One we mentioned in passing a few pages back (p. 143) advertises itself thus:

> Western States Center is a unique regional organization of activists, community leaders and progressive elected officials in eight Western states: Alaska, Idaho, Montana, Nevada, Oregon, Utah, Washington and Wyoming.
>
> The Center was founded in 1987 to challenge the isolation felt by many western communities facing similar social, economic and environmental challenges, and to help stimulate creative and successful organizing efforts in the West. Our vision is a vigorous and informed grassroots democracy, supporting a new generation of public leaders and an agenda of social and economic justice and environmental protection.[151a]

For such an impassioned devotion to grassroots democracy, the Western States Center has a remarkably small membership fee income: Zero. Its 1996 income of $1,374,596 included $1,235,000 in foundation grants. No grassroots. Almost totally grant driven.[151b]

An analysis of the Center's 1996 expenditures shows that the bulk of its money went into personal pockets: $321,672 for staff wages, $45,999 to managers, $428,357 to consultants. Executive Director Dan Petegorsky got $46,000 in salary and $6,461 in benefits. It's a green welfare shelter for radical activists.

The Center's five 1996 programs and expenditures were:

● Community Leadership Training Program, $205,035;
● Western Progressive Leadership Network, $260,267;
● Western Voter Participation Project, $166,250;
● Money in Western Politics, $149,204.
● Wise Use Public Exposure Project, $139,824.[151c]

Each of these programs is an agenda item of a specific cluster of foundations. Grant information comparing two years of the Western States Center income illustrates the magnitude of prescriptive foundation funding and power over projects. The charts on the next two pages are filled with some familiar names—and others less known but no less ideologically controlling.

GRANTMAKER	1994	1995
Tides Foundation	$ 20,000	1,000
Tides Foundation/Pequod Fund	30,000	20,000
Tides Fndtn./Zuckerman Family Fund	0	15,000
A Territory Resource	45,725	11,015
Albert A. List Foundation	80,000	44,000
Carnegie Corporation of New York	25,000	0
Ottinger Foundation	10,000	0
Bullitt Foundation	70,000	80,000
Tides Fndtn. 777/Environmental Fund	20,000	$2,500
Jessie Smith Noyes Foundation	20,000	0
W.K. Kellogg Foundation	113,573	0
HKH Foundation	20,000	0
Schumann Foundation	106,259	130,000
Public Welfare Foundation	50,000	40,000
Angelina Fund	20,000	0
McKenzie River Gathering Foundation	1,500	0
Citizens Vote, Inc.	15,000	0
Beldon Fund	17,500	20,000
Oregon Community Foundation	7,500	0
Equity Foundation	500	0
Black United Fund	500	500
Fund of the Four Directions	10,000	10,041
W. Alton Jones Foundation	20,000	0
Funding Exchange	15,000	13,000
Alida R. Messinger	40,000	50,168
Surdna Foundation	30,000	35,000
U.S. West Foundation	5,000	5,000
Carpenter Foundation	1,500	0
Common Counsel	750	0
Kongsgaard-Goldman Foundation	10,000	0
Philanthropic Collaborative, Inc.	12,066	5,000
Margaret Reed Foundation	0	14,500
Christensen Family Foundation	0	1,000
Global Environmental Project	0	8,000
Tides Foundation/Alki Fund	0	5,000
Tides Foundation/Anonymous	0	1,000
Veatch Foundation	0	45,000
Bauman Foundation	0	15,000
Turner Foundation	0	20,000
Heart of America Fund	0	10,000
Ettinger Foundation	0	10,000
Harder Foundation	0	13,500
N.W. Fund for the Environment	0	12,500
Brainerd Foundation	0	3,000
New World Foundation	0	20,000
Peace Development Foundation	0	1,650
Washington Mutual Foundation	0	5,000
Environmental Support Center	0	2,110
True North Foundation	0	15,000
Arca Foundation	0	10,000
Institute for Adv. Journal.	0	1,000
Anonymous	15,000	0
Miscellaneous Foundation	0	1,102
TOTALS	$832,373	$746,586

Western States Center obviously took note of the Montana Inititiatve Wars. Their 1996 Form 990 says they gave these grants to Noncharitable Exempt Organizations:

- $5,000 Montana Alliance for Progressive Policy;
- $2,000 Montana Women's Vote;
- $5,000 Montanans for Clean Water.

Western States Center also appears to serve as a pass-through for considerable amounts of money on a routine basis. Their financial statement shows the following grants and contracts to others:

	1994	1995
Coalition for Livable Washington	10,000	0
Progressive Leadership Alliance	8,550	0
Voters Education	64,300	0
Montana AFL-CIO	13,000	0
Equality State Policy Center	13,381	17,100
Peace Development Fund	0	11,650
United Vision for Idaho	0	27,075
Utah Progressive Network Educ. Fund	0	19,000
Conservation Voters of Oregon	0	1,316
The Oregon Not In Our Town Project	0	600
Blue Mt. Work Group	0	19,000
Rural Organizing Project	0	1,473
Wyoming Grassroots Project	0	2,800
Miscellaneous	9	0
TOTALS	$109,240	$100,014

Anti-corporate or environmental activism, it's still about money and power.

CIRCUIT RIDERS

If the Montana Initiative Wars was all that was going on in Montana, mining would be in better condition. That wasn't all that was going on.

The Washington, D.C.-based Mineral Policy Center, founded in 1988, is a single-purpose stand-alone organization that understood the need for coalitions before foundation powermeisters made it fashionable.[153]

Part of the reason is that foundation powermeisters made up an important part of its board of directors from the beginning.

MPC's major contribution to the coalition cause has been the Circuit Rider program of outreach to identify or generate mining opposition in critical areas, provide technical assistance to local anti-mining groups and influence local government against mining.

That was something else that was going on in Montana.

While the circuit rider was visiting your green group, you were part of a de facto coalition.

The MPC circuit rider staff position was created in 1989 with a $149,000 grant from the Northwest Area Foundation. The concept was institutionalized with field offices opened later in Montana and Colorado.[154a]

The Mineral Policy Center fills an interesting single-issue niche in the movement. It spread its expertise around Montana (and the rest of the U.S.) in the years before the Montana Intitiative Wars, fighting individual mining operations with the following armory:

- Lobbying for laws that will make mining economically unfeasible—primarily by repeal of the 1872 Mining Act, elimination of the land patent system, demands for high hardrock mineral royalties, exorbitant reclamation bonding levels and other statutory obstructions.[154b]
- Filing lawsuits, usually with other groups such as the Sierra Club, in which MPC is a co-plaintiff against mines. Obtained power over mining companies through membership on court-mandated resolution committees.[154c]
- Organizing and training local opposition groups into effective anti-mining propaganda and action networks.[154d]
- Generating reports, photos, videos, studies and bad media for mines or proposed mines.[154e]
- Orchestrating appeals during the mine permitting process, usually with a local group in the lead position.[154f]
- Acting as nanny for anti-mining groups newly created by the Tides Foundation (e.g., Boulder-White Clouds Council in Idaho).
- Working with legal specialists on anti-mining lawsuits, e.g., Roger Flynn, a former Environmental Defense Fund lawyer who founded the for-profit "Western Mining Action Project" in 1994. WMAP's for-profit status makes it impossible to track funding, an intelligent tactic for total secrecy, yet foundations donate to it despite its for-profit status, particularly through National Audubon Society acting as fiscal agent.

The Mineral Policy Center's co-founders, former Sierra Club official, Philip M. Hocker, and Stewart L. Udall, Interior Secretary from 1961 to '69, had close ties to money—and an abiding intent to shut down the mining industry. Hocker resigned in 1997 to be replaced by Stephen D'Esposito, who previously ran the lobbying arm of Greenpeace USA for many years with an annual budget at times in the $30 million+ range and worked with Greenpeace International, a substantial international network.

MPC's original board of directors included several foundation officers: MPC director Deborah E. Tuck is also the executive director of the Ruth Mott Fund, an offshoot of the General Motors fortune of Charles Stewart Mott. MPC director John P. Powers is also a senior director of the Educational Foundation of America (the Prentice Hall textbook publishing fortune). Early funders also included Gilman Ordway, heir to the 3M fortune. Here again we see the pattern of privileged heirs acting to destroy the industries that gave them their elite status—or to protect their established interests from competitors by promoting onerous regulations that thwart newcomers and less well-capitalized rivals.

MPC's seed money came from a cluster of highly prescriptive private foundations including W. Alton Jones Foundation ($50,000); the American Conservation Association ($45,000), as Chuck Clusen mentioned on page 38, a Rockefeller Brothers Fund / Jackson Hole Preserve, Inc. instrumentality; and the Northwest Area Foundation ($149,000), a Minneapolis foundation with heavy environmentalist emphasis.[155a]

Stewart Udall once stated, "The most important piece of unfinished business on the nation's natural resource agenda is the complete replacement of the Mining Law. It permits, and indeed it encourages, uncontrolled despoilation of the public lands with irreparable damage to other resources. In far too many instances, there is no justifiable social or economic benefit from this destruction."[155b]

Udall, responsible for the national parks while Interior Secretary, and Laurance Rockefeller were connected through RockResorts, the Rockefeller holding company that owned numerous national park resort concessions: Jackson Lodge at Grand Teton National Park, condos near Haleakala National Park on Maui, Caneel Bay Resort at Virgin Islands National Park, and others.[155c]

The Rockefeller Brothers Fund sponsored a 1977 study titled The Unfinished Agenda which recommended repeal of the 1872 Mining Act. The Rockefeller motive for ending the 1872 Mining Act was entirely anticompetitive, in part to protect its Colorado Fuel and Iron Company (the end of the patent system would mean only established wealthy operators could afford to own or prospect for minerals) and in part to protect its national park concessions, which were created by first buying up scenic land, then donating it to the United States with the stipulation it be made a national park by Congress after backroom deals had been made to obtain the resort concessions.

A scan of 53 grants from 1989 to 1997 shows that MPC is backed by at least 23 private foundations that have collectively invested a minimum of $4,306,000 in support since 1989. The private foundations that fund MPC are primarily members of the Environmental Grantmakers Association that also fund MPC's allied groups.

MPC donors: American Conservation Association; Beldon II Fund; H. W. Buckner Charitable Residuary Trust; Bullitt Foundation; Compton Foundation; The Educational Foundation of America; General Service Foundation; W. Alton Jones Foundation; The Joyce Foundation; The J. M. Kaplan Fund; Richard King Mellon Foundation; Charles Stewart Mott Foundation; Ruth Mott Fund; The New-Land Foundation; Northwest Area Foundation; Jessie Smith Noyes Foundation; The Pew Charitable Trusts; Public Welfare Foundation; Rockefeller Family Fund; The Florence and John Schumann Foundation; Surdna Foundation; Town Creek Foundation; Weeden Foundation.

A few sample grants from 1995 to 1997:

Brainerd Foundation: $20,000 to support the Northwest Circuit Rider Program in its efforts to provide ongoing technical, organizing and outreach assistance to communities throughout the Northwest that are affected by hardrock mining [aimed at Montana in particular].

Brainerd Foundation: $3,000 Hardware and Technical Assistance Grant.

Bullitt Foundation: $30,000 in 1996, $25,000 in 1997.

Global Environment Project Institute: $20,000.

Ruth Mott Foundation: $50,000.

Patagonia: $5,000. "MPC works to raise public awareness about the impacts of the mining industry. Our grant supported the group's ongoing efforts to reform the 1872 Mining Law as well as its public awareness campaigns."

Pew Charitable Trusts: $70,000. To support environmental reform of federal hardrock mining policies through research and education, media outreach and support to local environmental groups.

Recreational Equipment Inc: $10,000. To help bring grassroots activists to Washington, D.C. to testify and participate in lobbying efforts to repeal the 1872 Mining Law.

Rockefeller Family Fund: $25,000. The second installment of a two-year grant totaling $60,000 for general support to bolster the Center's work to regulate mining, and to clean up and prevent environmental hazards.

True North Foundation: $25,000

Turner Foundation: $40,000 in 1995.

Wilburforce Foundation: $50,000 For general support.

Others now emulate the circuit rider idea.

W. Alton Jones Foundation in 1995 started a circuit riding project to help grantees who were behind the technology curve "learn about and make effective use of technology," and help "technologically savvy organizations make better use of their resources."[157a]

The main methods to accomplish these goals include providing hands-on technical assistance and one-on-one training from circuit riders, and providing funding for tools ranging from hardware and software, to classroom training, to Internet access.

W. Alton Jones says that its goals for circuit riding "do not encourage the use of gee-whiz technology for technology's sake, but the appropriate use of the right tool. Today, that tool is generally a computer connected to the Internet with any of a number of hardware accessories and software programs."

Jones hired its circuit rider with politics in mind. "We didn't want a pocket-protector computer geek. Instead, we looked for someone who understood politics and the political process. Someone who'd be as comfortable in the halls of Congress as in the innards of a software program."

Even after Jones hired their Circuit Rider, they didn't put him on the next plane out of town. "We plotted a strategy. We had limited time and we had to spend it wisely. Target group—65 advocates at over 50 organizations."

Jones picked a high-horsepower consultant to advise their circuit rider program: **tcn**, a member-owned communications technology cooperative founded in 1980 with the support of the Ford Foundation and the Carnegie Corporation. With its 4,500 nonprofit member organizations, tcn operates three programs: group purchasing, consulting and training/education.

TERMITES

Within the visible mounds of big coalitions and towering campaigns, termites burrow in the form of small, local and tightly focused anti-resource groups. They can devastate mining, logging, ranching, and farming by constant appeal writing, media releases, and hook-ups with other environmental groups that place one obstacle after another in the way of legitimate resource operations.

The Boulder-White Clouds Council, Inc., based in Ketchum, Idaho, is one such termite: small but intensive, formed in 1989 as a donor advised fund project of the Tides Center by environmentalist Pat Ford, who is not only president of BWCC, but is also the paid campaign director of Save Our Wild Salmon, vice president of the Idaho Conservation League, and a board member of the Greater Yellowstone Coalition.[157b]

Ford's Council works in one small area, the Boulder-White Clouds mountain region near Ketchum. By coincidence there is a mining region there too.

The Boulder-White Clouds Council office is quartered in a building co-owned by Thomas Hormel, an heir of the Spam money. Hormel is a director of the Global Environment Project Institute (GEPI), which also occupies the building and donates to the Boulder-White Clouds group. These quarters were arranged for BWCC by another slaughterhouse heir, J. Christopher Hormel, chairman of GEPI.

The building is full of friends' offices: Environmental Resource Center (which received $36,700 in 1996 from the Hormels' Global Environment Project Institute); the Idaho Conservation League; the Idaho Conservation League Public Lands Committee, the Snake River Alliance, and Southern Idaho Solid Waste.

So this little group isn't really so all alone.

The Boulder-White Clouds outfit gets its anti-mining money from a cluster of foundations, some more prescriptive than others: Borestone Mountain Poetry Awards Foundation, Brainerd Foundation, Bullitt Foundation, Global Environment Project Institute, Harder Foundation, Human-I-Tees Foundation, Lazar Foundation, Meyers Charitable Family Fund, Ruth Mott Fund, Patagonia, REI, and the Woodshouse Foundation.

BWCC makes life miserable for mining companies in the area, with considerable help from the Mineral Policy Center and from another termite, the Western Mining Action Project (mentioned p. 154), which is basically a one-man operation of attorney Roger Flynn, former (1994) staff member of the Environmental Defense Fund, who still shares space with EDF's Boulder, Colorado, office. Although WMAP is a for-profit venture that pays taxes, it still gets charitable grants. I could trace $160,000 in grants directly to WMAP through foundation records, $100,000 of which came from Educational Foundation of America (the Prentice-Hall publishing fortune) as a start-up grant in 1994, and $60,000 from the Bullitt Foundation in 3 separate grants, which went first to the National Audubon Society as fiscal agent and thence to WMAP.[158]

Flynn has also worked for the Colorado Mining Action Project and the Land and Water Fund of the Rockies.

All these little connections tend to get lost in analyses of the environmental movement, but they are far more numerous than the big well-known groups and coalitions. The little termite groups are perfectly adapted to fall in with any number of coalitions in the new style, swelling the ranks and adding their mite of credibility to that of others.

800-POUND GORILLAS

The Nature Conservancy is by far the richest environmental group in terms of assets and income stream, with 1997 total revenues of $421,353,191 and assets of $1,484,494,203.[159a]

TNC, as it likes to abbreviate itself, also has a squeaky clean reputation for being "science driven, non-confrontational and businesslike," in the words of Daniel R. Efroymson, former Chair of TNC's Board of Governors. It calls itself "Nature's real estate agent."

TNC operates the world's largest private nature preserve system, 1,340 preserves under Conservancy management consisting of 1,177,000 acres the Conservancy owns or has under conservation easement. TNC's membership stands at 900,000. It has protected 10.5 million acres in the U.S. since its incorporation in 1953.[159b]

Millions of people reading upscale magazines have seen TNC's wonderful print ad picturing an eagle soaring above a majestic landscape with the great cutline, "We have friends in high places."

Certainly such a popular and non-controversial organization can't be grant driven, can it?

Well, yes and no.

Yes, in the sense that in 1996 it received a whopping $203,886,056, or "60 percent of its annual revenue from grants awarded by foundations, businesses, and individuals."[159c]

1996 FOUNDATION GRANTS RECEIVED BY THE NATURE CONSERVANCY	
$1,159,765 Environmental Federation of America	$61,500 Compton Foundation
	$57,500 George Gund Foundation
$610,000 David and Lucille Packard Foundation	$54,000 Richard and Rhoda Goldman Fund
$575,000 John D. and Catherine T. MacArthur Foundation	$50,000 Heinz Family Foundation
	$35,000 General Service Foundation
$450,000 Mary Flagler Cary Charitable Trust	$25,525 Fanwood Foundation
$150,000 Wallace Alexander Gerbode Foundation	$15,000 Weeden Foundation
	$15,000 New-Land Foundation
$126,000 Charles Stewart Mott Foundation	$2,500 Morningstar Foundation
	$1,500 Tides Foundation
$93,000 San Francisco Foundation	$1,000 Hauser Foundation

No, in the sense that The Nature Conservancy itself *gives* so many grants "to partner organizations" and has so many foundation and corporate moguls on its Board of Governors that it constitutes a consolidated power center rivaling even the archetypal Environmental Grantmakers Association.

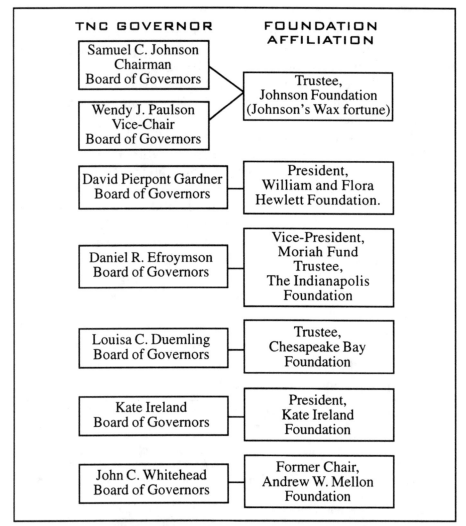

1999 INTERLOCKING NATURE CONSERVANCY - FOUNDATION AFFILIATIONS

It is difficult for the ordinary person to grasp the power, wealth , and connections controlled by the Nature Conservancy elite. The thirty-two members of TNC's Board of Governors, plus John Sawhill, President and Chief Executive Officer, include at least seven foundation officers (chart above) and at least nine corporate officers (opposite), current or former. Retired or former corporate and foundation officials do not entirely lose their influence, and in fact may gain through board positions such as the popular Nature Conservancy. The public policy influenced by this small group of people touches millions of lives every day, but few are aware.

TNC GOVERNOR	CORPORATE AFFILIATION
Carter Bales Board of Governors	Director, McKinsey & Company (International Consultants)
David C. Cole Board of Governors	Managing partner: Pan Pacific Ventures; Catalyst II. Director: Shiva Corporation; Daily Wellness Company. Former chairman, president and chief executive officer: Navisoft, Inc. Former president: AOL Internet Services; AOL New Enterprises.
Ian Cumming Board of Governors	Chairman, Leucadia National Corporation; Director, SkyWest Airlines.
I. Lamond Godwin Board of Governors	Chair and chief executive officer: Peachtree Asset Management Division of Smith Barney Inc. Managing director: Smith Barney Inc.
John W. Hanes, Jr., Board of Governors	Retired board of directors: Olin Corporation; Squibb Corporation. Former partner: Wertheim and Company.
Richard Heckert Board of Governors	Former Chairman, DuPont; former Chairman, National Association of Manufacturers
John Seidl Board of Governors	Former President, MAXXAM
John C. Whitehead Board of Governors	Chairman, AEA Investors; Former co-chair and senior partner: Goldman Sachs.
Ward W. Woods Board of Governors	Director: Bessemer Trust Company; Boise Cascade Corporation; Freeport-McMoRan, Inc.

1999 INTERLOCKING NATURE CONSERVANCY - CORPORATE AFFILIATIONS

John C. Sawhill, President and chief executive officer of The Nature Conservancy ($203,723 salary, 1998) is a walking influence center by himself. He is president emeritus of New York University, chair of the H. John Heinz, III, Center for Science, Economics, and the Environment, and chair of the Electric Power Research Institute Advisory Council. He is a member of the President's Council on Sustainable Development and the Commission on the Future of the Smithsonian Institution, a board member of Environment for the Americas, the Whitehead Institute for Biomedical Research, and the Center for Strategic and International Studies (CSIS). He is a former partner of McKinsey & Company, Inc.and a former U.S. Deputy Secretary of Energy.

Sawhill's unpaid position with the Heinz Center indicates that he's one of Teresa Heinz's favorite people. It was her $20 million grant that created the Center, recall. And she gives generously to TNC.

TNC has 274 employees and officers who are paid over $50,000 a year each. In 1996, TNC paid 50 firms or individuals over $50,000 for consulting, fundraising, legal counsel and other professional services. TNC paid out $15,792,253 in grants to partner organizations.

TNC is not only Nature's real estate agent, it's not doing bad as Nature's securities investor, either: in 1996 it received $26,886,460, or 8% of its total income, from capital gains on the sale of securities. TNC also got $12,235,056, or 4%, from dividends and interest on securities. What exactly all this securities trading has to do with saving nature is open to question, since TNC's investment portfolio is standard rich folks stuff with a lot of common and preferred stock in "capitalist, polluting, toxic, desecrating, bad-nasty corporations," mixed with mutual funds, bonds and U.S. government obligations totaling $434 million in 1996.

Then there's the real estate. TNC say it owns or has under conservation easement 1,177,000 acres in its private preserve system. Good. TNC also says it has protected 10.5 million acres in the United States. Good. If they own only 1.17 million of that 10.5 million, what happened to the other 9.3 million acres?

They sold a lot of it to the government.

Whoa.

The Nature Conservancy bought private land from private owners who thought it would remain in private hands and *sold it to the government?*

Yep.

Isn't that illegal?

Nope.

The government asks them to do it some of the time.

A letter from the Deputy Regional Director of the U.S. Fish and Wildlife Service (USFWS) to the Nature Conservancy dated August 30, 1985, reveals a long-standing government agreement for TNC to buy private land: "We are appreciative of The Nature Conservancy's continuing effort to assist the Service in the acquisition of lands for the Connecticut Coastal National Wildlife Refuge."[163a]

In this and numerous other letters, the government clearly agrees to pay TNC "in excess of the approved appraisal value."[163b]

Similar agreements for the federal government to buy TNC property at top-dollar prices exist all over the nation.[163c]

One federal officer who conducted such excess-cost purchases, Robert Miller, a chief of the realty division of the USFWS, was later hired by TNC at a high salary.

The Nature Conservancy is a conduit for the nationalization of private property. Nearly ten million acres so far.

Is it still going on?

According to the most recent figures available, in 1996 TNC received $37,853,205, or 11% of its total income, from sale of private land to federal, state, and local governments for use as parks, recreational areas, and nature preserves. Such land goes off the local tax rolls.

On top of that, The Nature Conservancy gets government grants and contracts worth millions each year. Green welfare. In 1996 they got $33,297,707, or 10% of their total income, from government contracts.

So Nature's real estate agent, which asks you to join up for 25, 35 or 50 bucks, was already in your taxpaying pockets to the tune of $71,150,912 in 1996.

TNC is a public charity, according to the IRS. Why doesn't TNC *give* the land to the government? What, and miss 37 million bucks?

Maybe TNC is a little greedy, and maybe not very "science driven," but those quiet land deals are more or less "non-confrontational and businesslike," as board member Efroymson claimed. Two out of three's not bad.

Then there's the case of the Moraine Nature Preserve in Indiana. It's also known as Gibbs v. The Nature Conservancy, Case H92-0371, Federal District Court for the State of Indiana, Northern District.

TNC helped create Indiana's Moraine Nature Preserve and wanted to enlarge it. They particularly wanted to enlarge it with the 135-acre farm of Professor Frederic A. Gibbs, M.D., now deceased. According to court papers, TNC also wanted to increase their income with Dr. Gibbs' entire estate.

Professor Frederic A. Gibbs, M.D. was a world famous neurologist. He and his wife, Erna, pioneered the field of electroencephalography (EEG) and in 1951 they received the coveted Lasker Award in Medicine for their work.

Their son, Dr. Erich Gibbs, said: "After my mother died of cancer in 1987, Dad's health declined sharply. He transferred responsibility for his affairs to my brother and me."

Both sons are also medical researchers.

"In his waning years, my father became legally blind, physically frail, and increasingly confused. By the time he was 84, he could not read, even with powerful magnification. As his Alzheimer's-like condition worsened, he became increasingly irascible, hating to be supervised. Caring for him became more and more difficult.

"Toward the end, the only place that he seemed reasonably at peace was on the Gibbs family farm in the northwest corner of Indiana, very close to Valparaiso. Here, with the help of dear friends, we carefully choreographed round-the-clock care so as to avoid fueling his paranoia about being supervised.

"During the summer of 1991, a neighbor accidentally wounded himself in the side with a shotgun and struggled to Fred's home. While the frantic caregivers called for emergency response and rendered first aid, this great physician, who had more than once in his career tended an injured person in circumstances of great personal risk, just wandered around the yard unconcerned, unable to grasp the significance of the situation.

"Things went as well as could be expected until The Nature Conservancy and local TNC supporters barged onto the scene.

"Behaving as friends and loved ones, this group offered to take Fred for outings and to participate in his care. In point of fact, they charged expensive lunches to his credit cards; secretly rifled through all the private papers in his home; took him to meet with attorneys; and turned him against his family.

"They wanted the Gibbs farm and Fred's estate, which they imagined to be worth millions, in order to expand their pet project, the Moraine Nature Preserve. This 'preserve' is hardly pristine. It is adjacent to what is perhaps the most notorious landfill in Indiana. And almost all of the land that has been acquired for the preserve has, like the Gibbs farm, been completely plowed and grazed during the past century.

"When the plot surfaced, TNC believed it had already acquired critical documents that would turn over Fred's estate and the farm to TNC upon his death. Supposedly he had carefully read, fully understood, and signed a new will that would leave virtually everything to TNC and nothing to his family.

"The Gibbs family, accompanied by legal counsel, met with TNC attorneys to explain that TNC had all its facts wrong—Fred had not been competent for years; had actively campaigned against TNC when he was vigorous, was not wealthy (having donated large sums to medical research); and had no control over his estate, which included only a partial interest in the family farm. We had what we perceived to be overwhelming medical and legal documentation, which included affidavits from scores of Fred's esteemed medical colleagues. This information was offered to the highest levels of TNC management. TNC's response was to ignore the evidence and accuse the family of having defrauded Fred and thereby TNC, as the beneficiary of Fred's estate.

"There was nothing the family could legally do to deny TNC and their supporters access to him. At one point, TNC supporters put Fred on a commercial jet, unaccompanied, so he could attend the annual meeting of one of the societies he had founded. He collapsed on arrival, disoriented, hallucinating and his heart unstable. He had to be hospitalized in a strange location. When he was sufficiently stable to fly in the company of a physician, he was transferred back to the Chicago area for further hospitalization, which included surgery.

"Shortly afterwards, TNC supporters sneaked Fred out of the nursing home where he was recuperating, and had him meet with one of the lawyers in their group. TNC and its supporters turned the last years of Fred's life into a torment. We will never forget him weeping in one of his more lucid moments and trying to ask our forgiveness for having fouled up in some way that he could not understand.

"After Fred passed away in 1992, the family sued TNC in Federal Court. From our point of view, the case was open and shut. We were convinced TNC would not have the audacity to go to court and risk a directed judgement. We were naive.

"The first few law firms that we retained withered under TNC pressure and abandoned us in the midst of critical proceedings. Fortunately we finally obtained extremely capable and courageous representation.

"At trial, TNC presented witnesses to testify that Fred read the newspaper every day and that he was actively involved in doing research. They even presented a nationally recognized medical ethicist, who testified that individuals can make rational decisions about the disposition of their estates, though they might be incapable of making rational decisions regarding their daily affairs.

"TNC might actually have won this case, were it not for the fact that the secretary for an attorney on the TNC side turned over the attorney's phone log to the Gibbs family. This phone log proved to be the missing link that tied everything together.

"When the messages were enlarged on huge posters for the jury to see, the effect was dramatic. There were messages stating that Fred could not be convinced to sign TNC's documents and asking the attorney what to do next. There was a message that Fred's Alaska State bonds were coming due and asking if the caller should get a safe deposit box in which to put the papers.

"It became so absurd that the jury began to laugh as the attorney repeatedly said during cross-examination that he could not recall the significance of his own messages, one message after another.

"On October 27, 1993, the jury found that undue influence had indeed been exercised over Dr. Frederic Gibbs. TNC was ordered to pay court costs and relinquish any claim on his estate.

"Without missing a beat, TNC attorneys filed a motion to set the jury verdict aside and asked for a retrial. When that was denied, TNC filed an appeal to the Seventh Circuit Court of Appeals. They lost the appeal."

The sad postscript to this horrifying story is that the Gibbs family could not recover its staggering half-million-dollars in legal fees and other trial-related costs and losses. In order to cover these expenses, the Gibbs farm was sold.[166a]

Another story of land grabbing:

In 1993 TNC tried to bully a German professor, Dr. Dieter Kuhn, into selling some land he owned in rural Illinois. Al Pyott, Illinois director of TNC, threatened Dr. Kuhn that if he did not cooperate in the creation of Cypress Creek National Wildlife Refuge, his land would be taken by force of condemnation through Pyott's influence with the U.S. Fish & Wildlife Service, which was listed in the local phone book *in the same entry* with TNC. Pyott wrote:

> The Nature Conservancy has, starting in 1987, made numerous efforts to contact you by letter, by phone, and through your agent, Mr. Clay, in an effort to discuss some basis for the acquisition of your property in Pulaski County.
>
> If your land is not acquired through voluntary negotiation, we will recommend its acquisition through condemnation.[166b]

TNC head John Sawhill had to write a letter of apology to Dr. Kuhn.[166c]
Sawhill may have been prompted to apologize by Congressman Glenn Poshard (D-IL), who told TNC that if they continued their campaign of threats and bullying land owners, he would withdraw support for future refuge acquisition funding.[166d]

Such clashes led to a 1994 General Accounting Office report titled, "Land Acquisitions Involving Nonprofit Conservation Organizations." It had been requested by Congress in the wake of a May 1992 Interior Department Inspector General Report on problems with these types of acquisitions, including undue benefits in financial gains.[167]

The GAO tried to determine the actual profits made by non-profit groups selling private land to the federal government, but could not. Two groups, the Trust for Public Land and the River Network, refused to provide Congress with their financial information "because of contractual obligations concerning confidentiality." Others used bookkeeping methods that made each transaction look like a loss (compared to an imaginary "market value" on land for which there was no market).

The Nature Conservancy was found to have sold one property to the Forest Service for over $1 million that had been donated to it. The profit on this parcel, after expenses, was calculated at $877,000.

Stung, The Nature Conservancy responded to this controversy by declaring that it would in the future donate lands to the government that had been donated to it, but said this would "pressure them into fund raising."

Overall, TNC said its bookkeeping methods showed it took a net loss on the private property it sold to the federal government. TNC did not calculate the loss to county and school district tax rolls as part of the social costs of its transactions.

Maybe TNC is not very "science driven" and "non-confrontational" when it comes to land and money, but they're certainly "businesslike," as board member Efroymson claimed. One out of three's not totally bad.

Okay, so TNC has its hand in the taxpayer's till and plays hardball in court and claims to have government bully boys backing up threats to condemn some property. But they wouldn't violate that "businesslike" ethic of theirs by playing dirty politics in lobbying, would they?

The following entry in TNC's internal Bioreserve Handbook describes the Norden Dam farmland irrigation proposal on the Niobrara River in Nebraska back in the early 1980s. The TNC description below was written in 1991 by John Flicker, then-vice president, to describe how TNC defeated the project:

We developed three theaters of action:
1. All "swing" Members of the House
In a typical water project vote, about 1/3 of the House will always vote no, about 1/3 will always vote yes, and about 1/3 are swing votes. Using a Sierra Club computer program, we applied several criteria, such as the 22 previous water project votes, to determine

who the swing members would be. It gave us a target audience of about 130 swing members.

2. The Nebraska Delegation

The House will tend to support the united local delegation. If the delegation is split, other members feel free to vote their conscience. We needed a split Nebraska delegation.

3. Nebraska State Government

Congress expects the Governor and the state legislature to strongly support a local water project. If they don't, Congress won't throw money at them that they don't want.

Each theater of action had strategy. The strategy started with theme. It positioned the issue as a taxpayer issue instead of an environmental issue. Several messengers were brought into the strategy to deliver the message to particular audiences:

— The Nebraska Tax Limit Coalition: Conservative anti-tax, anti-government organization.

— The Nebraska Water Conservation Council: New organization created to conduct door-to-door canvassing.

— Save the Niobrara Rivers Association: Local landowners group who serve as the plaintiff in the NEPA litigation in federal court.

The information, the players, and the money were the key factors in the campaign.

We had a personal relationship of trust with one member of each organization who controlled that organization. We then sent money to each organization to assist them in carrying out the strategy. No one but TNC knew the entire strategy.

In Nebraska, TNC was always behind the scenes. We never made public statements. Everything was done through surrogates who were credible in their own right.

Outside of Nebraska, TNC was more open. We designed a national campaign for each TNC state chapter to secure the swing congressional members in each state. Chapters agreed to take on local campaigns to assure votes from their states....

It took three years to implement the strategy. In the end, the Nebraska delegation split on the issue. A resolution in the Nebraska legislature supporting the project was blocked. The Governor withdrew support. The House of Representatives voted to withdraw all funding and to kill the project [in 1982].

More importantly, we did it in a way that did not alienate TNC in Nebraska. Since then, the Kiewit Foundation has given money to TNC, and the editor of Omaha World Herald has become chairman of the Nebraska Chapter.[168]

"Everything was done through surrogates." We will see that again and again in environmental group projects.

TNC must be delighted with this science driven, non-confrontational, businesslike deal.

That was a long time ago. Is TNC still doing this kind of lobbying? In fiscal year 1996, TNC spent $419,729 on lobbying. In 1997-98 TNC spent $993,396 on lobbying.

Perhaps The Nature Conservancy will open their current handbooks to public inspection so we can see what dirty tricks they might or might not be playing these days.[169a]

The Nebraska Chapter of The Nature Conservancy said in April 1999 that John Gottschalk, publisher (not editor) of the Omaha World Herald, was once on their board of directors. In April, 1999, Gottschalk denied ever being chairman of TNC's Nebraska Chapter. The Kiewit Foundation had no idea TNC was behind the killing of the Norden Dam project.

A substantive question arises about the 1,385 corporate associates and the large number of businesses that work with and donate money to The Nature Conservancy: Why?

Why corporations give to environmental groups, which, given their "progressive" colleagues, appear to do nothing but harm corporate interests, is a question addressed by two scholars in some depth.

Marvin Olasky, who teaches journalism history and media law and ethics at the University of Texas at Austin, pointedly noted that "love of mankind" (the dictionary definition of philanthrophy) plays a relatively small part in corporate grant making.

Professor Olasky wrote that personal, ideological and utilitarian reasons prevail:

> Contributions are made for one or more of three very practical reasons. First, corporate executives may direct funds to groups personally important to them, a choice often based on peer pressure or spousal involvement. Second, ideological considerations come into play because liberals and conservatives generally view the world in different ways. Third, public relations managers make calculated professional judgements as to which potentially critical groups need to be placated.[169b]

In other words, how can we get the most public relations bang for the buck and help a few groups that subscribe to our own beliefs (or those of our spouses)?

Of Professor Olasky's three, public relations approval clearly outweighs everything else in corporate giving to environmental groups.

Robert H. Nelson, a professor of environmental policy at the School of Public Affairs at the University of Maryland and a senior fellow at the Competitive Enterprise Institute, has a more machiavellian take on corporate giving to the environmental movement: It is a way for strong corporations to obtain government regulations so expensive they will price weaker competitors out of business. The result is a legal monopoly in a high-cost market.

Professor Nelson's way of stating it is more elegant: "Regulations behave as the private rights of the regulated." The result is the same.[170]

Bob Nelson first explained his theory to me while I was interviewing him in 1981 for a book I was working on. He was then a policy analyst at the Department of the Interior, working in the Office of Policy Analysis, which serves the Office of the Secretary.

I told him it was difficult for me to grasp that an industry would commit suicide by giving rope to its hangmen. He patiently explained that only the weakest part of an industry dies under heavy regulation, and those weaker firms don't contribute to environmental groups. The stronger survivors have bought a valuable service from environmentalists: lobbying by those who can occupy the moral high ground with strength sufficient to win against industry's vigorous pretense of defense.

The implications of Nelson's theory are disturbing. Is there collusion to influence public policy between corporate or trade association leaders and environmental group leaders that are not the strictly arm's-length relationships of adversaries?

Is the adversary process of lobbying environmental policy being compromised by "sweetheart deals" between the most powerful on both sides, corporations *and* environmental groups?

Serious questions for future public policy.

COMPREHENSIVE COALITIONS

Now back to the coalition model: The whole idea of reforming the environmental movement with a coalition strategy is to gather power.

Coalitions aimed at fundamental production points such as control of raw materials would obviously be most effective in the long run—no economy can operate without raw materials.

To date, the most comprehensive coalition to appear on the scene is the Wildlands Project. This coalition is the most radical in purpose: to "re-wild" America, that is, to gradually remove people and raw material production from the rural United States with no definitite stopping point. In their own words:

The Wildlands Project calls for reserves established to protect wild habitat, biodiversity, ecological integrity, ecological services, and evolutionary processes. In other words, vast interconnected areas of true wilderness and wild lands. We reject the notion that wilderness is merely remote, scenic terrain suitable for backpacking. Rather, we see wilderness as the home for unfettered life, free from human technological and industrial intervention.

Extensive roadless areas of native vegetation in various successional stages must be off-limits to human exploitation.

To function properly, nature needs vast landscapes without roads, dams, motorized vehicles, power lines, over-flights, or other artifacts of civilization, where evolutionary and ecological processes can continue. Such wildlands are absolutely essential to protect biodiversity.[171]

If that didn't sink in, read it again. Yes, it's written in foundationese, but it's low foundationese, not high foundationese. Low foundationese says a rural cleansing project is one that "must be off-limits to human exploitation," while high foundationese would say it's a "rural transition enhancement to enable more environmentally sound employment" or something similarly mush-mouthed.

The Wildlands Project has proposed to set aside at least half of North America for "the preservation of biological diversity." The resulting "wildland reserves" would contain:

● Cores, created from public lands such as national forests and parks, allowing for little, if any, human use;
● Buffers, created from private land adjoining the cores to provide additional protection;
● Corridors, a mix of public and private lands usually following along rivers and wildlife migration routes;

but would allow no cities, roads, homes, businesses, no aircraft over-flights, or natural resource extraction, i.e., an endlessly expanding area of America would be depopulated and de-developed.

A decade ago such proposals would not have been taken seriously.

In the late 1990s they had become part of Clinton administration policy through Al Gore (see pp. 234-246). We have seen the Clinton road moratorium. We have seen Clinton proposals to breach dams on the Columbia River. We have seen the bewildering array of Clinton manipulations in Chapter One. All moved the nation toward Wildlands Project goals.

We work in cooperation with independent grassroots organizations throughout the continent to develop proposals for each bioregion. The list is growing of groups that promote the vision of an ecologically sound North America, and we have included a list of many with whom we work to achieve our hopes and goals.

The Wildlands Project welcomes all groups and individuals interested in supporting these issues, and we look forward to working with these organizations.[172a]

The Wildlands Project is technically a coalition strategy project with a single lead organization: North American Wilderness Recovery, Inc. (1996 budget: $606,050), based in Tucson, Arizona. The organization is an outgrowth of a 1981 Earth First! idea called the North American Wilderness Recovery Project.[172b]

Funders of North American Wilderness Recovery include the Turner Foundation, which has donated $195,000 to its Tucson headquarters (1993: $25,000; 1995: $15,000; 1996: $35,000; 1997: $120,000); Patagonia; the Bullitt Foundation; the Lyndhurst Foundation and numerous other "golden donors."

North American Wilderness Recovery has been supported by foundation grants since before 1992, particularly by Doug Tompkins' Foundation for Deep Ecology, in annual amounts ranging from $50,000 in 1992 to $150,000 in 1996 and 1997. The Richard and Rhoda Goldman Fund gave $75,000 in 1996 and the Educational Foundation of America gave $50,000 in 1997.

In 1999 there were 23 "cooperating groups" or "colleagues" listed in Wildlands Project materials (see list opposite).

Each "cooperating group" has its own specific goals that reinforce the goals of the Wildlands Project. These groups are also grant-driven, with dominant funding from prescriptive foundations: Alliance for the Wild Rockies, MT (1996 budget: $305,099); California Wilderness Coalition, CA ($135,087); Northwest Ecosystem Alliance, WA ($246,632); Sky Island Alliance, AZ ($25,371); Coast Range Association, OR ($106,396); Forest Guardians, NM ($229,858); Northern Appalachian Restoration Project, NH ($119,993); Southern Rockies Ecosystem Project, CO ($46,712).

Wild Earth magazine, published in Richmond, Vermont, is a non-profit periodical. "The Wildlands Project is a separate non-profit organization that acts as a sister organization to Wild Earth. Wild Earth serves as the publishing voice for The Wildlands Project, and as an independent voice for the new conservation movement."

Alaska Wildlands
Brad Meiklejohn
Eagle River AK 99577

Yukon Wildlands
Juri Peepree
Whitehorse YUK Y1A 5T6

Yellowstone To Yukon
Bart Robinson
Canmore AB T1W 2V7

Northwest Ecosystem Alliance
Mitch Friedman / Tom Platt
Bellingham WA 98225

Siskiyou Project
Kelpie Wilson
Cave Junction OR 97523

LEGACY-The Landscape Connection
Curtice Jacoby
Arcata, CA 95518

Conception Coast Project
John Gallo
Santa Barbara CA 93101

California Wilderness Coalition
Rich Hunter
Davis CA 95616

Wild Utah Project
Jim Catlin
Salt Lake City UT 84111

Grand Canyon Wildlands Council
Kelly Burke
Flagstaff AZ 86002

Southern Rockies Ecosystem Project
Bill Martin / Marianne Moulton
Nederland CO 80466

Conservation Biology Institute
Reed F. Noss, Ph.D.
Corvallis OR 97330

Forest Guardians
John Talberth
Santa Fe NM 87505

Sky Island Alliance
Jack Humphrey
Albuquerque NM 87106

Hill Country Wild
Chris Wilhite / John Andrews
Austin TX 78713

Minnesota Ecosystems Recovery Project
Mike Biltonen
Red Wing MN 55066

Greater Laurentian Wildlands
Robert Long
South Burlington VT 05403

Appalachian Restoration Campaign
Than Hitt
Athens OH 45701

Southern Appalachian Biodiversity Project
Mary Ann Paine
Asheville NC 28802

Wildlaw
Ray Vaughan
Montgomery AL 36104

Southeast Wildlands Project
Linda Duever
Micanopy FL 32667-0949

Paseo Pantera Project - Wildlife Conservation Society
Jim Barborak
Gainsville FL 32609

Wildlands Mexico
Rurik List
Metepec 3 MX Mexico

1999 KEY WILDLANDS PROJECT COOPERATING GROUPS

The Wildlands Project is sufficiently institutionalized that literally hundreds of its projects may be circulating within administrative agencies at any given time. The resource class is simply swamped by the volume of issues they must confront.

FISCAL AGENTS

Even the most elite of the old-line conservation groups, the Wilderness Society, has adopted the coalition strategy wholeheartedly. The Wilderness Society's 1999 "Message from the Chairmen Christopher Elliman and Bert Fingerhut, emphasized the point:

> We realize that we cannot achieve our goals unless we work with other groups committed to protecting America's greatest places. The proliferation of local organizations has provided us with a growing number of dedicated allies. In addition, we are more active than ever in coalitions such as the Alaska Coalition, the Northern Forest Alliance, and the Utah Wilderness Coalition. During the past year we have even helped forge two new coalitions: the ForestWater Alliance and Americans for Our Heritage and Recreation.[174]

There is a reason: the Wilderness Society was the first fiscal agent of a grant-driven environmental campaign—the early 1990s' Ancient Forest campaign of the Pacific Northwest. The Wilderness Society was the first mainstream group to lend its power to foundation funders in order to reform the environmental movement on the coalition model. The Wilderness Society hardly had a choice. Things were not going well in the movement.

By the mid-1980s when Don Ross and Josh Reichert and Pete Myers, et al., decided to reorganize environmentalism, the Wilderness Society, the Natural Resources Defense Council, the Friends of the Earth, and Environmental Action—along with the Sierra Club, Greenpeace, the National Audubon Society, and virtually every other sizeable environmental group—had turned inward to their own constituencies.

They had busied themselves sending out direct mail appeals, developing sharp elbows getting to the television cameras, and hitting the phone banks to increase the donation level of high-dollar contributors. There was intense competition for a limited amount of money. The movement had fragmented and lost its grass roots.

Don Ross explained to his Environmental Grantmakers Association peers in 1992 the impact this inwardness had on issues:

About six EGA members, seven EGA members, pooled about a million dollars to wage a lobbying effort, a lobbying / media strategic effort on the Ancient Forest legislation this year [1992]. And the assumption going into that effort was that there was very strong grass roots activity in the Northwest, strong national lobbying in Washington, D.C., and that the problem was the issue wasn't an issue in most of the rest of the country, and the connections between the Washington lobbying and the Western enthusiasm was not present, and that this effort would fill that gap.

The great lesson was that our assumptions were wrong.

The major one was that the lobbying presence in Washington was pathetically weak. And what a lot of the effort went into was shoring up what we thought was our strong point, the Washington presence....

But there was a real vacuum. I think a lot of us have been blinded by their balance sheets.

You say this is a 20 million dollar group and this is a 30 million dollar group. They really aren't.

What they are, it seems to me, is, in that $20 million are 30 separate projects, perhaps, each one of which has two or three staff on it. And there's no ability on the part of most of those groups to mobilize their total organizations behind any issue.

So you look at a group that has a 30 million dollar budget that puts out direct mail talking about its commitment to the forest issue and then you look at its real internal commitment to that forest issue and it's one part-time lobbyist in Washington, maybe, who's doing three other issues in addition to that forest issue. And there's nothing else back there. And that's really what that lesson came out. It was a very depressing lesson. Because there was *real* money in that.[175]

The solution was the task force approach, to forge coalitions among groups that each possessed limited capabilities, but collectively could wield power effectively.

Their campaign-level intervention began in the autumn of 1990 at the Environmental Grantmakers' annual retreat, held that year in Estes Park, Colorado, when a group of funders including the Rockefeller Family Fund, Pew, W. Alton Jones, Surdna and Bullitt got to talking about the Pacific Northwest forest issue and agreed to meet again in a special strategy session a few months later at the Bullitt Foundation's Seattle bailiwick.

In 1990 the forest issue was a hit for environmentalists in the Northwest. The Northern Spotted Owl had become a celebrity bird for shutting down the timber economy under the Endangered Species Act.

In April of the year before, a small crew of Earth First!ers had trucked a big Douglas fir log around the country on a 19-city tour to raise national awareness of habitat as well as the owl.

In September of 1989, a National Audubon Society television feature broadcast on Ted Turner's TBS network, *Ancient Forests: Rage Over Trees*, notched up public awareness a little more.

An Ancient Forest Protection Bill was drafted and ready to run through Congress, sponsored by Indiana Democrat Jim Jontz.

At the Seattle strategy session the funders agreed on a program to project nationally the kind of energy and enthusiasm they saw in grassroots groups in the Northwest. They neglected to agree on the details. Don Ross explained to his foundation peers the next year:

> The Ancient Forest stuff was pooled within the Wilderness Society, actually acted as the fiscal agent. There was a three person board set up, with the Wilderness Society having one of the seats, to manage that money as a separate venture from the Wilderness Society—they were writing checks....
>
> It's complicated because there are three organizations [Americans for the Ancient Forests, the Ancient Forest Alliance, and the Western Ancient Forest Campaign] that are really involved in it that at various times have worked very closely together and at other times had a high degree of tension between them and not a great deal of communication. And partly we funders are responsible for it because at the very same time two separate groups of funders picked two separate horses on which to lavish large sums of money to run media campaigns. And despite great efforts to get them to work very closely together, it sometimes worked not as well as one would want.[176]

The two national campaign horses on which the two groups of funders lavished large sums of money were Fenton Communications and Chlopak, Leonard and Schecter, both media strategy firms of Washington, D.C.

David Fenton we have already met (pages 97*ff*).

Robert A. Chlopak is the former staff head of the Democratic Senate Campaign Committee, who brought deep experience with political campaigns to the ancient forest project. In addition, he had worked several years for Sawyer-Miller, a Washington, D.C.-based public relations, advertising, and media strategy firm, a strong credential.

The three groups they funded were:

● A grassroots group, the Western Ancient Forest Campaign (now known as the American Lands Alliance), which was controlled by a four-person board of directors made up of grass roots in California, Oregon and Washington. Its base of activity was Washington, D.C.

● Americans for the Ancient Forests, a synthetic group headed by Bob Chlopak. Billed itself as "the advertising arm" of the third group:

● The Ancient Forest Alliance, another synthetic group, this one a shell coalition of six other groups: 1) Americans for the Ancient Forests, 2) National Audubon Society, 3) Sierra Club, 4) Sierra Club Legal Defense Fund, 5) Western Ancient Forest Campaign, and 6) The Wilderness Society. Mostly a figurehead group to lend credence to Chlopak's political and media operation. The Alliance did send out a political action alert letter in March 1993 to a large mailing list (see pp. 222-223).[177]

The Environmental Grantmakers Association core foundations poured a huge amount of money into these three groups and their fiscal agent, The Wilderness Society:

Western Ancient Forest Campaign
   1991 $100,000 The Pew Charitable Trusts through Headwaters Community Association Ashland, OR
   1991 $25,000 Rockefeller Family Fund, Inc.
   1992 $132,500 The Bullitt Foundation
   1992 $20,000 Foundation for Deep Ecology
   1992 $25,000 HKH Foundation
   1993 $25,000 Richard and Rhoda Goldman Fund
   1993 $75,000 Surdna Foundation, Inc.
   1993 $200,000 The Pew Charitable Trusts
   1993 $65,000 The Bullitt Foundation
   1993 $15,000 Foundation for Deep Ecology
   1993 $25,000 Ruth Mott Fund
   1993 $100,000 W. Alton Jones Foundation, Inc.
   1994 $100,000 The Pew Charitable Trusts
   1994 $65,000 The Bullitt Foundation
   1996 $20,000 Foundation for Deep Ecology
   1996 $14,000 Turner Foundation, Inc.
   1997 $50,000 Rockefeller Brothers Fund

Americans for the Ancient Forests
   1992 $100,000 Surdna Foundation, Inc.
   1993 $150,000 W. Alton Jones Foundation, Inc.
   1993 $70,000 The Bullitt Foundation
   1993 $50,000 Surdna Foundation, Inc.

Ancient Forest Alliance

1992 $10,000 The Gap Foundation, through the Wilderness Society for California Ancient Forest Alliance.

The Wilderness Society as fiscal agent or directly for the project:

1992 W Alton Jones $250,000 to advance public understanding of ancient forests.

1992 W Alton Jones $100,000 For multi-constituency organizing and to disseminate educational information about public land management policies.

1992 W Alton Jones $75,000 To develop set of policy recommendations that can minimize job loss in communities in Pacific Northwest while maximizing environmental protection.

1992 W Alton Jones $50,200 To undertake nation review of public perceptions of environmental protection efforts.

1992 Ruth Mott $25,000 For national education campaign on ancient forests of Pacific Northwest.

1992 Town Creek Foundation $100,000 (unspecified).

1993 Bullitt Foundation $40,000 for Northwest Forests.

1993 Pew $200,000 to conduct national education campaign in support of ecosystem reserve for ancient coastal rainforests in Pacific Northwest.

1993 Pew $100,000 For analysis of employment impacts and economic benefits of preserving ancient rainforests in Pacific Northwest.

1993 Surdna $150,000 2-year grant. To compile in public document, specific of what must be done for ecosystem management of federal forests.

1993 Ford $300,000 Toward organizational shift toward environmental and development.

Donald Ross told his EGA peers that the Fenton and the Chlopak segments of the project received about $1 million each. Two million dollars to destroy the resource class in the Northwest. The media blitz they created was impressive, but not always what they wanted:

DONALD ROSS: Fenton uses this technique in a lot of his campaigns and it's pretty effective: He gathered together four or five activists, Jeff DeBonis of the Association of Forest Service Employees for Environmental Ethics, Andy Kerr, Michael Stewartt of LightHawk and the like, and scheduled intensive visits to major media centers, New

York City, Los Angeles, where they would spend two or three days with back-to-back meetings briefing editorial boards, news directors, feature writers. And there is no question that that effort produced a torrent of media, which involved everything from evening news, television stories on the forest to editorials to features in some of the newsmagazines and the like.

It was an effort that was loosely coordinated with the political work that was going on [Chlopak's segment], but *very* loosely coordinated.

And in some respects that revealed one of the problems of the effort: while it was successful in getting media, often times the media blitz was three months before any real political action was taking place and so by the time the political action was there and you wished it was on the evening news or you wished it was the editorial in the papers that people were picking up that day, it was stale news. It was Ancient News.[179]

They were finding out the hard way that they needed a better central control point and a better coalition model. Ross concluded:

There is no organization today that can wage any one of these national campaigns by itself. And given the experience on the forest issue and others, I'm somewhat pessimistic that a collection of national groups are going to be able to get together and divvy up the work in an effective way and manage a campaign.

What I keep thinking about now on these national efforts is that— and this would take a major role by large funders to help drive this— is that there's almost a modular kind of a campaign where you would take people from different groups and take different expertises together to assemble, so you'd end up with a task force of people from maybe five or six different groups that were under some central direction.

Part of the problem in the forest campaign is you had a lot of these elements including lots of these media folks, paid and free, but there was no central direction and no one was able to really say, okay, like a quarterback, you go this way, you go this way, you do this, you do that. There was never a control mechanism. So it became too chaotic.

There was the first explicit statement of the coalition model we saw at the beginning of this chapter in the Southwest Forest Alliance, with the

National Audubon Society as fiscal agent and Pew as control point for a large number of groups with their own constituencies and funders. This is the dominant model of environmentalism today.

And green groups have discovered how to create a grant-driven coalition on that model by building-in foundations from the ground up.

THE TAKU STRATEGY

Nothing could make this point better than an internal document written in 1998 by a cluster of environmental groups intent on stopping a mine in British Columbia, Canada. It is a long document, reproduced here without comment.[180]

TO SAVE THE TAKU RIVER
A Coordinated Campaign Strategy Outline
Prepared by:
Michael Magee
Sierra Defence Fund
(604) 685-5618
magee@sierralegal.org
In coordination with
Taku Wilderness Association
Nakina Centre for Aboriginal Life and Learning
Sierra Club of British Columbia
Environmental Mining Council of B.C.
BC Spaces for Nature
David Suzuki Foundation
Northwest Institute
The River League
American Rivers
Southeast Alaska Conservation Coalition
Walter & Duncan Gordon

THE CAMPAIGN NEED
The Taku wilderness is under threat of pending developments that impact on the lives and well being of the Taku River Tlingit First Nation (TRTFN) and the ecological integrity of one of North America's last remaining magnificent wilderness areas.

An aggressive, thoughtful and strategic campaign is urgently needed to stop the immediate threats to this area and to establish a plan for the longer term protection of its environmental values and of the people in the region.

In a serious effort to achieve these goals a coordinated strategy was organized in Vancouver in September of 1998 amongst key groups in the U.S. and Canada dedicated to preserving the Taku wilderness.

The groups who participated in this meeting and will continue to work on the project include:

Taku Wilderness Association
Nakina C. A. L. L. (Centre for Aboriginal Life and Learning)
Sierra Club of British Columbia
The River League
BC Spaces for Nature
Sierra Legal Defence Fund
Northwest Institute
Environmental Mining Council of British Columbia
American Rivers
Southeast Alaska Conservation Coalition

Groups who were not in attendance at the meeting but will play a role in a coordinated campaign include:

The David Suzuki Foundation
Earthjustice Legal Defense Fund

The purpose of this document is to:

● Provide a multi-organization, coordinated campaign outline that illustrates the specific goals, objectives, strategies, tactics, organizational structures, relationships and funding that will be required to win.

Background

The Taku River watershed is an 18,000 square kilometer (4.5 million acre) unroaded tract of land near the town of Atlin in northwestern British Columbia, Canada. This immense watershed, equivalent in size to the state of Massachusetts is the traditional homeland of the Taku River Tlingit and contains habitats representing 5 biogeoclimatic zones ranging from high plateaus to lush coastal temperate rainforests. It contains some of the richest wildlife habitat on the West Coast of North America and is home to grizzly bears, moose, caribou, black bear, mountain goat, salmon and many species of migrating birds. These species thrive here in large numbers due to the area's essentially untouched nature and the fact that it is only accessible by float plane, riverboat or by foot. This region is the highest producer of salmon on the Southeast shore of Alaska and Northwest British Columbia.

This spectacular area is now threatened by a proposal to construct a 160 km access road needed to re-open the Tulsequah Chief Mine located on the Tulsequah River just upstream from B.C.'s border with Southeast Alaska. The road is needed in order to transport ore to the shipping tidewaters of Skagway. Proponents, Redfern Resources Ltd., claimed that the Tulsequah Chief Mine will provide nine years of profitable mining activity. While this scenario has appeal for some factions, the mine would introduce massive quantities of Acid Mine Drainage to the watershed, endangering water quality and aquatic habitat for salmon and other wildlife. The proposed road also threatens the survival of a recovering woodland caribou population and threatens to disrupt grizzly bear habitat. The cumulative effects of this road would be increased hunting and poaching pressure, roadside developments, spur roads to new mining claims, and logging of the fragile boreal forest and globally endangered temperate rainforest. Wildlife experts both within and outside of government disagree with the proponent's claims that impact on wildlife in the Taku will be minor.

Current Status of Development

Redfern Resources is continuing to push ahead aggressively with their plans to establish the Tulsequah Chief Mine. There are several obstacles to this which include:

- A review by the International Joint Commission (IJC). The United States has requested that this issue be referred to the International Joint Commission for investigation as there are serious threats it will affect trans-boundary waterways. As this document is being written there has been no formal agreement from Canada referring it to the IJC, however, Canada has requested another meeting with the United States to review the agenda for eventual referral to IJC. The State Department has responded aggressively and is becoming increasingly educated with the Canadian Federal Government's delaying tactics, this in turn has served to delay some of the Special Use Permits (SUP) into December of 1998.
- Redfern Resources share prices are sinking and the company is increasingly unstable. This vulnerability is more evident when the financial assumptions of the Tulsequah Chief Mine proposal are examined more closely. Given the current economic conditions

there is high probability of exploiting this vulnerability and exposing the mine as financially non-viable.
● There continues to be the possibility that the Taku River Tlingit
First Nation (TRTFN) will challenge the provincial mine approval
process. Should this take place it would pose a serious threat to
the future development of the mine.

Campaign goals and objectives

1. Stop the Tulsequah Chief Mine.
2. To stop the mine in such a way that it ensures a developmental
moratorium on the Taku Watershed.
3. To ensure that a comprehensive Land Use Planning process is
completed that is agreeable and inclusive of the Taku River Tlingit
River First Nations (TRTFN).

Strategies

1. Stop the Tulsequah Chief Mine

The strategic objective in the early stages of this campaign will
be to stop the mine from proceeding in such a way that establishes a
moratorium on the area for further development. This will be achieved
through several tactical components including:

● A coordinated trans-boundary political effort focusing on the U.S.
Congress and key legislators within Alaska and Washington D.C.
Given the mine's potential negative impact on a highly profitable
Alaskan fishery and waterway it is highly probable that the U.S.
Congress can be leveraged to take further defensive actions
against such a threat.
● A comprehensive economic analysis of Redfern Resources. This
would include closer scrutiny of Redfern shareholder interests,
current mineral prices and the underlying financial calculations
they have used to substantiate the mine proposal. This data will
be critical in establishing within the financial community and
policymakers of the financial weaknesses of the Tulsequah Chief
Mine proposal and other similar initiatives that are being explored
in the Taku Watershed.
● Solidarity and support for the Taku River Tlingit First Nation
(TRTFN). The TRTFN have been considering taking further legal
and political action based on their aboriginal rights to oppose the
approval of the mine. The TRTFN must be given adequate capacity support and resources to defend any such actions should
they be taken.
● The International Joint Commission. While it would be the objec-

tive to stop the mine development long before any IJC reference is undertaken, the reference itself needs to be used to increase profile of the issue. Further pressure needs to be brought to focus on the Canadian External Affairs to make a final decision in referring this matter to the IJC. Most importantly, the process of moving the complaint to a formal investigation by the IJC must be used as a key media opportunity for heightened exposure on the Taku and to support the above noted initiatives.

2. Ensure a Development Moratorium

The Tulsequah Chief proposal has generated heated debate and attention in the local community, within the TRTFN, with the B.C. government and the U.S. One of the process issues that has been given the most attention is the weaknesses in the provincial approval process for the mine. This has underscored the significant need to develop a comprehensive land use plan that considers the socioeconomic future and ecological integrity of the Taku wilderness. To complete this a moratorium on development will need to be established. It is the objective of this campaign to stop the Tulsequah Chief Mine in a manner that provided ample financial and economic deterrence to future developments until a land use plan is agreed upon.

3. Ensure a Taku Land Use Plan

The success of establishing a comprehensible protected area in the Taku will depend largely on the longer term work and creditability of the Land Use Plan. Significant capacity support will have to be established for key groups including the TRTFN to complete work related to scientific, legal and social economic research.

For the purposes of this proposal, we will focus on the first two points. A planning committee will be established to work on the longer term details on requirements of a Land Use Plan. This will be the subject of a future proposal.

Campaign Structure

There will be several components to the campaign structure to ensure quick campaign development, decision-making and proper tactical assignments. The structure will be as follows:

- Taku Network: the Network will include all organizations and individuals who wish to support the campaign initiatives overall. This will be an information sharing Network with organizations receiving regular briefs and a being called upon for specific actions when necessary.
- The Taku Steering Committee: this will be the key groups with a more direct involvement and interest in the Taku campaign. The Steering Committee will assist in guiding overall priorities and

policy directions. The members of this committee will include:

Taku Wilderness Association
Nakina C. A. L. L. (Center for Aboriginal Life and Learning)
Sierra Club of British Columbia
The River League
BC Spaces for Nature
Sierra Legal Defence Fund
Northwest Institute
Environmental Mining Council of British Columbia
American Rivers
Southeast Alaska Conservation Coalition
The David Suzuki Foundation
Earthjustice Legal Defence Fund

● The Executive Committee: this committee will be a smaller group from the Steering Committee that will set the strategic direction of the campaign, make decisions on a regular basis and coordinate the activities of the key organizations. The Executive Committee members include:
Don Weir, Taku Wilderness Association
Alan Young, Environmental Mining Council of B.C.
Rick Careless, BC Spaces for Nature
Mike Magee, Sierra Legal Defence Fund

The campaign will have established several working groups to develop the critical strategic components. These working groups will be a combination of groups and individuals from the Network, assigned to groups depending on area of expertise. Each working group will have a lead organization.

Note: For the purposes of this proposal, working groups are assigned "global" budget estimates. Specific proposals for working groups would be submitted by the lead organization. These proposals may vary from the global estimates depending on the scope of the plan produced by the working group. The working groups include:
● COORDINATION (i.e. the Executive Committee):
This working group will largely be the work of the Executive Committee and a staff coordinator. Lead organization will be the Environmental Mining Council of British Columbia with support from the Sierra Legal Defence Fund. Budget estimate: $30,000 (CDN)
● TRANS-BOUNDARY STRATEGIES:
This working group will include BC Spaces for Nature, American Rivers, Southeast Alaska Conservation Coalition, Earthjustice Legal

Defence Fund, Sierra Legal Defence Fund, Taku Wilderness Association. Lead organizations will be BC Spaces for Nature and Taku Wilderness Association. Budget estimate: $40,000 (CDN)

● MEDIA AND COMMUNICATIONS:

This group will assist in cultivating major media stories, executing media strategies for specific initiatives, training and capacity support for key Network organizations. The group will include David Suzuki Foundation, Sierra Legal Defence Fund, The River League, Sierra Club of B.C., Earthjustice Legal Defence Fund. Lead organization will be Sierra Legal Defence Fund. Budget estimate: $30,000 (CDN)

● ECONOMICS:

This group will initiate a review of the underlying financial assumptions of the Tulsequah Chief Mine and the real costs and benefits of development in the Taku wilderness. The work will include an examination of Redfern Resources. The group will include BC Spaces for Nature, Taku Wilderness Association, Environmental Mining Council of BC. Lead organization will be the Environmental Mining Council of BC with support from BC Spaces for Nature. Budget estimate: $40,000 (CDN)

● COMMUNITY DEVELOPMENT AND LIAISON:

This group will focus on cultivating relationships and understanding in the local community. Work will include ongoing relationship building and support for the TRTFN and the Nakina CALL and communications with local industry and government officials. It may, from time to time, include capacity support for the TRTFN. The group will include the Taku Wilderness Association, Nakina CALL, The River League and The David Suzuki Foundation. Lead organizations will be the Taku Wilderness Association and the Nakina CALL. Budget estimate: $30,000 (CDN)

● RESEARCH:

This group will initiate the longer term planning and research that will be required for a proper land-use planning process. In the initial stages the group will identify the key socioeconomic, legal and scientific intelligence that will be required to accomplish such a plan. Working group members will include the Nakina CALL, Northwest Institute, Sierra Club of BC and The River League and the Taku Wilderness Association. Budget estimates will be developed as the necessary elements of the research are identified. It's expected this part of the overall strategy will be the subject of future funding proposals in later stages of the campaign.

Working Timelines:

For the purposes of this proposal the time lines are broken down into immediate and short-term modes. Medium and long term plans will be developed through the working groups and distilled through the Executive Committee for future presentation.

IMMEDIATE TERM: November 1998 through to January 1999 (three months). The goal in the short-term is to establish secure funding for the working groups and to initiate the strategy outlined in this document. Bridge funding will be necessary to hire a coordinator, provide an office and for capacity support to a few key groups such as the Taku Wilderness Association. This will be the work of the Executive Committee with lead initiative from Sierra Legal Defence Fund.

The working groups will have completed their medium and long-term campaign plans by the end of January 1999.

SHORT TERM: February 1999 through to June 1999 (six months).

By this point a coordinator will be well in place, funding secured (or at least identified). The Trans-Boundary Working Group should have well underway its tactical moves related to the International Joint Commission, Congress, and the Alaskan government. The Economics Working Group should have completed its initial review of the financial assumptions of the mine, the investor community, shareholder activity and other related economic factors. The Media Working Group should have significant work completed on cultivating major media stories on the Taku including CBC and CTV national news and the New York Times and Washington Post.

Draft
Taku Campaign Fundraising Strategy
December 1998

Note: All grant amounts in U.S. dollars except where noted. All project goal amounts in CDN dollars.

A. Coordination: EMCBC is lead organization
    Goal: $48-60,000
    First Priority
    Endswell Fund-$15,000 CDN committed
    EMCBC core-$10-15,000 CDN available
    Weeden Foundation-$15,000
    Lichen Foundation-$10,000 CDN

B. TRTFN Land Protection Plan (while not central to campaign, critical to ground First Nation and strengthen the community commitment to legal challenge of Redfern permit.)
    Goal: short-term $2,000 for consultant to work with TRTFN to develop proposal.

Long-term $200-300,000 over 2-3 year period to complete the plan.

Robert Schad Foundation - Bolton, Ontario

Hewlett Foundation

Packard Foundation

W. Alton Jones Foundation

Rockefeller Brothers Fund

Paul G. Allen Forest Trust??????

C. TRTFN Litigation and Community Liaison: SLDF is lead organization and fiscal agent for the TRTFN.

Goal: $180,000 of which $150,000 is the total estimated cost of Art Pape's representation of the TRT. $30,000 for Atlin community nurturing.

Litigation:

Brainerd Foundation - $20,000 March 1999 docket

Endswell Foundation-$10,000 CDN committed

W. and D. Gordon Foundation-$20,000 CDN

W. Alton Jones Foundation-$30-50,000

Lannan Foundation - $50,000/year. Possible two-year approach?

Wilburforce Foundation-$30,000

David Suzuki Foundation-30,000 CDN

Community Liaison:

Tides donor funds-$20,000

True North Foundation-$10,000

Turner Foundation $10,000???

D. Media and Communications

Lead group: SLDF

Goal: $30,000 for direct media work and training for TRTFN TR and other core actors.

Lichen Foundation-$10,000 CDN

Kongsgaard / Goldman Foundation-$10,000

Surdna-$20,000?

E. Community Support

Lead groups: Taku Wilderness Association (TWA) and Nakina CALL

Goal: $30,000

Foundation for Deep Ecology-$10,000-contact John Davis

W. & D. Gordon Foundation-$20,000

Kinney Watershed Foundation-$10,000 U.S. committed 12/98 to TWA

F. Transboundary Strategies

Lead groups: BC Spaces for Nature and TWA

Goal: $40,000 *does not include support for U.S. groups in

Southeast Alaska
W. & D. Gordon Foundation-$20,000 CDN
Weeden Foundation-$10,000
K/G Foundation $7,500
True North-$10,000
Lazar Foundation-$7,500
G. Economics/Corporate financing strategy
Lead groups: E.M.C.B.C. plus BC Spaces for Nature
Goal: $30,000
Foundation for Deep Ecology-$10,000
Tides Foundation-donor funds-$10,000
Lichen Foundation-$10,000

GLOBAL BUDGET

Note: lead organizations will submit funding proposals for specific components of the coordinated campaign. The budget figures presented here reflected the general needs that will be created by lead organizations taking on their respective work in coordination with other groups. These budget figures may alter once the working groups finalize their work plans in the immediate term. The global budget was derived to establish a coordinated pattern for submission of proposals to fund or from lead organizations.

COORDINATION	$30,000
TRANS-BOUNDARY	$40,000
ECONOMICS	$30,000
MEDIA AND COMMUNICATIONS	$40,000
COMMUNITY DEVELOPMENT AND LIAISON	$30,000
RESEARCH	future pending

TOTAL GLOBAL BUDGET (one-year) $170,000

Any questions?

GRANT-DRIVEN GREENS FOOTNOTES

131a. "Can Southwest activism and money coexist?," by Peter Aleshire, *High Country News*, April 15, 1996 (Vol. 28, No. 7).

131b. Southwest Forest Alliance website, http://www.swfa.org/member_groups.html.

132a. Cover letter, "The Desert Forests Campaign: Protecting the Bio-Economic Diversity of Southwest Forest Ecosystems," October 1994.

132b. "The Desert Forests Campaign: Protecting the Bio-Economic Diversity of Southwest Forest Ecosystems," October 1994, p. 10.

139a. Form 990-PF, Pew Charitable Trusts, 1995, Statement 9.

139b. "In New Mexico, an Order on Elusive Owl Leaves Residents Angry, and Cold," *New York Times*, p. 16, Sec. 1, Sunday November 26 1995.

140a. "Firewood Issue Fuels Battle in New Mexico Mountains Forests: Villagers say suit limiting access to key heating source puts wildlife protection ahead of human needs," by Frank Clifford, *Los Angeles Times*, Friday December 1, 1995, p. A1.

140b. "Summary and Critique of The Desert Forests Campaign Proposal," no date, provided by Antonio DeVargas.

141. "A Call to Citizens: Will Real Populists Please Stand Up." by Ronnie Dugger, *The Nation*, August 1995. See also websites such as "Revoke Stone Container's Corporate Charter!" (http://bcn.boulder.co.us/environment/earthfirst/LaSierra/Stonecol.htm); "The Case Against Unocal in One Page" (http://www.heed.net/doc1.html).

143a. Gregory L. Colvin and Lowell Finley, *Seize the Initiative*, The Alliance For Justice, Washington D.C., 1996, p. *iii*.

143b. Americans for the Environment website, http://www.afore.org/prop98/index.htm.

143c. Peter Montague, "Big-Picture Organizing, Part 6: Money in Politics," *Rachel's Environment & Health Weekly*, January 26, 1995.

143d. *Funders' Handbook on Money in Politics,* Ottinger Foundation, Amherst Mass. and CarEth Foundation, Amherst Mass. Feb. 22, 1996.

144a. "Political practices official fighting to reinstate ban on corporate contributions," by Erin P. Billings, *Missoulian*, December 23, 1998.

144b. "Environmental Organizing Semester: An Environmental Leadership Training Course," an attachment to the University of Montana Credit Course Proposal for Extension Teaching, July 26, 1995.

145a. C.B. Pearson, resume, supporting documentation for request of University of Montana approval of Environmental Organizing Semester, Missoula, Mont.

145b. Spring 1996 Syllabus, Environmental Organizing Semester, Green Corps and the University of Montana.

145c. "UM 'environmental' class spurs ethics debate," by Erin P. Billings, *The Independent Record*, Helena, Montana, Saturday, Oct. 12, 1996, p. 3A.

145d. "An Environmental Leadership Training Course, Introduction," Environmental Organizing Semester, Green Corps and the University of Montana.

145e. C.B. Pearson deposition, Montana Chamber of Commerce, et. al. v. Ed Argenbright, July 29, 1998, p. 64.

146. C.B. Pearson, letter to Michael Caudeil-Feagan, Stern Family Fund, Arlington, VA, June 7, 1996.

147a. "A Proposal To Get Corporate Money Out of Montana's Initiative Process," June 7, 1996.

147b. *Report of Receipts and Expenditures* to the Commissioner of Political Practices, Citizens for I-125, 1996.

147c. Montana Public Interest Research Group, IRS Form 990, 1996, Missoula, Mont.

148a. Roy Morgan and David Schauffler, "The Populist I&R Movement: Direct Democracy in Action," Americans for the Environment, Washington, D.C., June 1996.

148b. *Report of Receipts and Expenditures* to the Commissioner of Political Practices, Montanans for Clean Water, and Citizens for I-125, 1996.

148c. *Report of Receipts and Expenditures* to the Commissioner of Political Practices, Montanans for Clean Water, 1996.

148d. "Center for Public Interest Research, The State PIRGs' Campaign to Get Big Money Out of Politics," *Funders' Handbook on Money in Politics,* Ottinger Foundation, Amherst Mass., and CarEth Foundation, Amherst Mass. Feb. 22, 1996.

149a. *Report of Receipts and Expenditures* to the Commissioner of Political Practices, Citizens for I-125, 1996.

149b. "The Legal Challenge, Litigation Program of the Institute," National Voting Rights Institute web page, world.std.com/~nvri/, Boston, Mass., April 4, 1999.

149c. National Voting Rights Institute, 1995 IRS Form 990, Boston, Mass.

150a. Fund for Public Interest Research, IRS Form 990, 1996, Boston, Mass.

150b. C.B. Pearson and Hilary Doyscher, "Big Money and Montana's Ballot Campaigns: A Study of Contributions to Montana's Ballot Elections from 1982 to 1994," Montana Public Interest Research Foundation, Missoula, Mont., September 1996.

150c. Turner Foundation, Inc., 1993 IRS Form 990, Atlanta, Ga. and Turner Foundation, Inc., 1994 IRS Form 990, Atlanta, Ga.

150d. Turner Foundation, Inc., 1994 IRS Form 990, Atlanta, Ga.

150e. Turner Foundation, Inc., 1996 IRS Form 990, Atlanta, Ga.

150f. "Montana Public Interest Research Group," *Funders' Handbook on Money in Politics,* Ottinger Foundation, Amherst Mass. and CarEth Foundation, Amherst Mass. Dec. 5, 1996.

150g. U.S. Public Interest Research Group Education Fund, IRS Form 990, 1995 and 1996, Washington, D.C.

151a. Western States Center website. http://www.epn.org/westernstates/.

151b. Western States Center, 1996 Form 990, Part IV-A, lines 15 and 16.

151c. Form 990 for 1995 and Form 990 for 1996, plus website.

153. Mineral Policy Center website: http://www.mineralpolicy.org/.

154a. All foundation funding data for Mineral Policy Center is from Foundation Center records, Form 990 reports and IRS database.

154b. "Sides Dig in on Mine Law Debate," Wednesday, March 20, 1991, *The Christian Science Monitor.*

154c. "Reformers Make Claim on Private Mines' Yields," Thursday, March 11, 1993, *USA Today.*

154d. "New forces draw attention at mining conference - Environment, technology spotlighted in Albuquerque," Sunday, February 20, 1994, *The Denver Post.* See also *Mining Conservation Directory '94,* edited by Thomas J. Hilliard. January 1994, 143 pages: "This activist group directory serves as a guide to local action on mineral development threats. It lists more than 340 U.S. and international organizations working to prevent environmental destruction from mining."

154e. See MPC website.

154f. "Old Law Gives Miners the Gold, U.S. the Dross," Monday June 13, 1994, *Los Angeles Times.*

155a. All MPC foundation grants from Foundation Center records.

155b. This well-known quotation has appeared numerous places, and can be found on the MPC website, and in their periodical, *Clementine, The Journal of Responsible Mineral Development.*

155c. See my book with Alan Gottlieb, *Trashing the Economy,* pp. 116-121, for the Rockefeller in the national parks story.

153a. See the W. Alton Jones website, www.wajones.org.

153b. Boulder-White Clouds Council newsletter.

158. "Victor groups fight gold-mine land deal," Saturday, December 14, 1996, *The Denver Post.* See also, "Mine lawyers seek activists' records," Saturday, January 25, 1997, *The Denver Post.*

159a. Form 990, Part 1, 1997, The Nature Conservancy.

159b. All figures from Nature Conservancy website at http://www.tnc.org/welcome/about/about.htm.

159c. The Left Guide, 1998, p. 374.

163a. Deputy Regional Director, USFWS, to Dennis Wolkoff, TNC Eastern Regional Office, August 30, 1985.

163b. Philip Tabas, TNC Legal Counsel, Eastern Region, to Robert Miller, USFWS, Newton Corner, Massachusetts, November 7, 1986.

163c. *Getting Rich: The Environmental Movement's Income, Salary, Contributor, and Investment Patterns, with an Analysis of Land Trust Transfers of Private Land to Government Ownership*, Center for the Defense of Free Enterprise, Bellevue, Washington, 1994, pp. 26-32.

166a. Telephone interview with Dr. Erich Gibbs, April, 1999.

166b. Albert E. Pyott to Professor Dr. Dieter Kuhn, May 26, 1993.

166c. John C. Sawhill to Professor Dr. Dieter Kuhn, July 9, 1993.

166d. "Poshard draws line for environmental group," by Martia Ross, *Southern Illinoisian*, June, 1993.

167. Department of the Interior - Office of Inspector General Audit Report No. 92-1-833.

168. The Conservancy Bioreserve Handbook, Arlington, Virginia, 1991.

169a. Informants state that at least ten such manuals exist: Natural Heritage Program Operations Manual; Preserve Selection and Design Manual; Stewardship Manual; Trade Lands Operations Manual; Personnel Manual; Finance Manual; Development Manual; Operations Manual; Bioreserve Manual; Protection Manual. I am in possession of specific "bioreserve handbooks" for sites in California and the Great Lakes.

169b. Marvin Olasky, Patterns of Corporate Philanthropy, Capital Research Center, Washington, D.C., 1987, p. 1.

170. Telephone interview with Robert H. Nelson, May, 1999. See also his book, *Public Lands and Private Rights : The Failure of Scientific Management* (The Political Economy Forum), University Press of America, 1995.

171. "The Solution: Big Wilderness," The Wildlands Project website, http://www.twp.org.

172a. See Wildlands Project website.

172b. All financial data from Foundation Center records and IRS database.

174. The Wilderness Society website, http://wilderness.org/abouttws/annualreport97.htm.

175. Environmental Grantmakers Association 1992 Fall Retreat. *Workshop Session 23: Media Strategies for Environmental Protection.*

176. Environmental Grantmakers Association 1992 Fall Retreat. *Workshop Session 19: Environmental Legislation: Opportun ity for Impact and Change.*

177. Political alert letter dated March 3, 1996.

179. Remaining Donald Ross quotes from Environmental Grantmakers Association 1992 Fall Retreat. *Workshop Session 23: Media Strategies for Environmental Protection.*
180. Taku document obtained from governmental source on condition of anonymity.

PART THREE:
ECOLIGARCHY

CHAPTER 4

ZEALOUS BUREAUCRATS

An ecoligarchy of activist bureaucrats is working to create a new society in their own image. Many are former environmental organization executives who occupy top level positions within the federal government. Many are civil servants who belong to advocacy groups. Top bureaucrats dole out vast federal subsidies for green welfare. They operate programs that devastate natural resource production. They usurp powers claimed by Congress and the courts. They operate in secrecy and cover their acts with lies. They influence innumerable decisions that shape your future.

EVERYBODY WANTS TO RULE THE WORLD.
Bureaucrats get to do it.

No complex civilization can run without bureaucrats. The problem is not bureaucrats. The problem is bureaucratic abuse. Dangerous bureaucrats.

Which bureaucrats are most dangerous? Most aren't dangerous at all. By and large, the American bureaucrat, from lofty Cabinet officer to lowly civil service entrant, is honest and decent. As in every aspect of the human condition, however, there are always a few that bear watching.

Which ones? Fortune magazine said, "There isn't much challenge in identifying the obvious threats—headline-grabbing heads of giant Cabinet departments, such as Carol Browner of the Environmental Protection Agency and Bruce Babbitt of the Interior Department. The real trick is to anticipate threats from more obscure bureaucratic outposts. And only experts know where they lie in wait."[198a]

Identifying the threats to the resource class is relatively easy: they include all of the political appointees from environmental groups in the bureaucracy. During its tenure, the Clinton administration appointed more than 50 activists from advocacy groups (next two pages). All had ties to foundation money. All used facts generated by experts fed with agenda-driven government or foundation money. Some persecuted and prosecuted career experts who came up with inconvenient facts.[198b]

Complicating the problem is money—hidden taxpayer money flowing from government grants to those who support the administration's political agenda; private money flowing from wealthy foundations to activists who support the administration's political agenda.

The invisible threats to the resource class potentially include all members of environmental groups employed in the bureaucracy, particularly such grant-driven internal pressure groups as Public Employees for Environmental Responsibility and Forest Service Employees for Environmental Ethics. Such membership is kept secret as a matter of federal privacy policy, even though it materially affects the lives of the regulated.

THE MEAN GREEN

Vice President Al Gore is the most obvious of the obvious threats. He is the man who wrote the 1992 best-seller *Earth In The Balance*, a sour-eyed view of our "dysfunctional" society, surprisingly negative—and revealing—for a politician, son of a Senator, born to politics. In its pages, Gore openly expressed his environmental extremism.

Al Gore has close ties to key prescriptive foundations that share his views, particularly W. Alton Jones Foundation, as we shall see.

Every environmental issue Gore has promoted in the Clinton administration received highly orchestrated foundation-funded activist support.

We don't usually think of foundation money driving federal policy. In the world of Al Gore, it does. The external resources available to Gore give him unprecedented power.

Albert Arnold Gore is arguably the most powerful vice president in modern history. To this man President Clinton turned over large chunks of critical policy turf, not just the early much-hyped "reinventing government" project, but also areas of government that in-

SAMPLE OF FORMER ENVIRONMENTAL GROUP LEADERS IN THE CLINTON ADMINISTRATION		
NAME	**GREEN GROUP**	**ADMINISTRATIVE POSITION**
Robert Armstrong	Trust for Public Lands	Assistant Secretary of Interior, Land & Minerals Management
Kathleen Aterno	Clean Water Action	Former Deputy Assistant Administrator, EPA Office of Administration and Resource Management
Bruce Babbitt	League of Conservation Voters	Secretary of the Interior
Jim Baca	Wilderness Society	Former Director of the Bureau of Land Management, later Mayor, Albuquerque, New Mexico
Donald Barry	World Wildlife Fund	Counselor to the Assistant Secretary for Fish and Wildlife & Parks
Carol Browner	Citizen Action	EPA Administrator
David Doniger	Natural Resources Defense Council	Senior Counsel to EPA Assistant Secretary for Air and Radiation
J. Charles Fox	Friends of the Earth	Special Assistant (Reinvention), EPA Administrator Carol Browner
George T. Frampton	Wilderness Society	Assistant Secretary of the Interior for Fish and Wildlife & Parks; Chair, Council on Environmental Quality
David M. Gardiner	Sierra Club	Former Assistant EPA Administrator for Policy Planning and Evaluation
T. J. Glauthier	World Wildlife Fund	Associate OMB Director for Natural Resources, Energy and Science

SAMPLE OF FORMER ENVIRONMENTAL GROUP LEADERS IN THE CLINTON ADMINISTRATION

Douglas Hall	Nature Conservancy	Assistant Secretary of Commerce for Oceans and Atmosphere
Robert Hattoy	Sierra Club	Special Assistant to the Secretary of the Interior
Jean Nelson	Natural Resources Defense Council	EPA General Counsel
Mary D. Nichols	Tennessee Environmental Action Fund, Southern Environmental Law Center	Associate EPA Administrator for Air & Radiation
Rafe Pomerance	Friends of the Earth, World Resources Institute	Deputy Assistant Secretary of State for Environment, Health and Natural Resources.
Daniel Reicher	Natural Resources Defense Council	Deputy Chief of Staff and Environmental Counsel, Department of Energy
Alice Rivlin	Wilderness Society	Former Director of the Office of Management and Budget, former Federal Reserve Vice Chairman
Aileen "Ali" Webb	League of Conservation Voters	Former Director of Public Affairs, Department of Agriculture
Geoff Webb	Friends of the Earth	Former BLM Deputy Director for External Affairs
D. Reid Wilson	Sierra Club Political Action Committee	Director of Public Liaison Division, EPA Office of Communications, Education & Public Affairs
Brooks Yaeger	National Audubon Society, Sierra Club	Director, Office of Policy Analysis, Interior Department

trude into every aspect of your daily life: the environment, energy, technology, information systems, housing.[201a]

Clinton also assigned to him the social and economic development programs of the United Nations, giving him global issues such as climate change and population control.[201b]

The threat Gore presents was put succinctly by Bonner R. Cohen, editor of EPA Watch and a senior fellow at the Arlington, Virginia-based Lexington Institute:

> For Gore and his followers the object of the game is to put power in as few hands as possible and to ensure that those hands are either in Washington or in some United Nations body amenable to the vice president's influence. If they can't be co-opted by federal grants or political appointments, then state and local officials will be ignored.[201c]

Gore's contempt for those who disagree with him is well-known. Capitol Hill regulars who watched him as a senator during hearings recall his insolence. A favorite trick was to pose a question and let the witness start to answer, then begin whispering with a staffer. If witnesses paused so the senator could hear them, Gore instructed them to continue, then resumed his private conversation.

He wouldn't even give the witness the courtesy of pretending to listen.

Gore is severe in forwarding his environmental goals and ferocious in fighting his opponents outside of government. He put his power behind the campaign against the wise use movement, even to the point of planting negative stories in the media.

On February 24, 1994, ABC News Nightline with Ted Koppel ran a report titled, "Environmental Science For Sale." It was an investigation of the wise use movement, but with a surprise.

Koppel opened with a blunt revelation: He told viewers that Vice President Al Gore had given him the story, a highly unusual move in a medium that normally goes to extremes protecting sources.

Koppel explained that he and Gore had met by chance waiting for an airplane, and, over coffee, Gore urged him to investigate connections between the wise use movement and such elements as big industry, Lyndon LaRouche and the Unification Church of Rev. Sun Myung Moon—the exact smear campaign message recommended in the Environmental Grantmakers Association's 1992 annual meeting.

Where did Gore get this message? While Koppel explained to viewers that Gore's office had sent him a stack of documents, an image of the fanned-out papers filled the TV screen. In such graphics, the top document is always totally illegible to preserve anonymity.

However, peeking out from behind the first of Gore's documents was a letterhead reading "MacWilliams Cosgrove Snider"—authors of the anti-wise use "Search and Destroy Strategy Guide" commissioned by the Wilderness Society and funded by the W. Alton Jones Foundation.

Vice President Gore, Koppel told his viewers, was particularly concerned about Dr. Fred Singer of the Washington, D.C.-based Science and Environmental Policy Project, well known for debunking the ozone depletion and global warming scares.

Climate change dogma is one Gore won't allow to be challenged.

Laws have been passed against important industrial chemicals because computer models predict them to deplete ozone or cause global warming. Dr. Singer pointed out flaws in computer models, noting that realistic risk assessments rather than computerized guesswork or emotional scare tactics are needed for sound public policy.

Michael Oppenheimer of the Environmental Defense Fund told Koppel he was so worried about the wise use movement because, "If they can get the public to believe that ozone wasn't worth acting on, that they were led in the wrong direction by scientists, then there's no reason for the public to believe anything about any environmental issue."

What about Singer's Moonie ties and big industry money? When asked by Nightline, Dr. Singer acknowledged having accepted free office space and science conference travel expenses in the past from the Unification Church, as well as funding from large industries.

The Moon support lasted only a short time, but the industry funding continued. "Every environmental organization I know of gets funding from Exxon, Shell, Arco, Dow Chemical, and so on," said Singer.

"If it doesn't taint their science, it doesn't taint my science."

Koppel remarked, "In fairness, though, you should know that Fred Singer taught environmental sciences at the University of Virginia, that he was the deputy administrator of the Environmental Protection Agency during the Nixon Administration, and from 1987 to 1989 was chief scientist at the U.S. Department of Transportation. You can see where this is going. If you agree with Fred Singer's views on the environment, you point to his more impressive credentials. If you don't, it's Fred Singer and the Rev. Sun Myung Moon."

Koppel noted that Dr. Singer's predictions about the low atmospheric impact of the Kuwait oil fires was accurate and the environmentalists' forecast of doom was wrong.

At the end of the Nightline feature, Koppel said, "The measure of good science is neither the politics of the scientist nor the people with whom the scientist associates. It is the immersion of hypotheses into the acid of truth. That's the hard way to do it, but it's the only way that works.

"There is some irony in the fact that Vice President Gore—one of the most scientifically literate men to sit in the White House in this century—is resorting to political means to achieve what ultimately should be resolved on a purely scientific basis."[203a]

So it backfired. But, why ask the media to pick on Fred Singer?

Gore was pursuing a vendetta against Singer, and it was not going well. Gore needed a bigger hammer, and television is a bigger hammer.

It had started with an April, 1991, article on global warming by Fred Singer, Chauncey Starr and Roger Revelle, all prominent scientists, in the house magazine of Washington's Cosmos Club, which goes to about 3,000 members—not exactly the leading journal for Beltway policy wonks.

The authors of "What to do about Greenhouse Warming: Look Before You Leap" concluded: "We can sum up our conclusions in a simple message: The scientific base for greenhouse warming is too uncertain to justify drastic action at this time."[203b]

This mildly provocative article was selected for reprinting in a scientific volume on global warming, and advisory editor Justin Lancaster offered no objection to its inclusion—at first.

Then came two hitches: First, Roger Randall Revelle, geophysicist and oceanographer, honored as "the grandfather of the greenhouse effect," had been Al Gore's teacher at Harvard University as well as his mentor after graduation. Gore mentioned Revelle frequently in his book, *Earth in the Balance*. Revelle died of a heart attack at the age of 82 shortly after the Cosmos article appeared.[203c]

Second, the obscure Cosmos article became famous because it was quoted in a July 1992 New Republic opinion piece by Newsweek writer Gregg Easterbrook. Titled "Green Cassandras," it noted Al Gore's long association with Professor Revelle and cited the Cosmos article for its downplaying of global warming and any need for hasty political response.

Then Easterbrook's remarks got picked up in a nationally syndicated column by George F. Will, and other columnists quickly took up the chant. It was Big News.

Very Big News, because Al Gore was running for vice president at the time. The Cosmos article's message turned up in the televised 1992 vice presidential debates, challenging Gore's environmental credibility. The mere suggestion that Earth was not in the balance and that Candidate Gore had no idea what he or his scientific mentor were talking about could not be tolerated.

Gore personally telephoned Justin Lancaster, the editor of the forthcoming reprint—an oceanographer who had been a decade-long Revelle associate—to see whether the Cosmos article accurately reflected Prof. Revelle's views.[204]

Lancaster began a series of faxes to Gore staffers Katie McGinty and Anthony Socci on how to respond to the New Republic article. They talked about a written response to the Easterbrook article and the possibility of having Revelle's name removed from any further reprints of the Cosmos piece.

Lancaster prepared a letter for publication and faxed it to Gore's office with the cover note, "Is this close to what the Senator had in mind?"

Over a period of several months Lancaster made appeals by letter and telephone to Singer, to the editor of Cosmos, and to the editors of CRC Press, the firm that was reprinting the Cosmos article, demanding that Revelle's name be removed. Lancaster charged that it did not reflect Revelle's views and that Singer had taken advantage of Revelle at a time of ill health for the purpose of embarrassing Senator Gore. Gore staff member Anthony Socci wrote a similar demand to CRC Press.

On October 24, 1992, Fred Singer was dropped from the list of speakers at a Roger Revelle Memorial Symposium at Harvard.

Lancaster attended the Harvard symposium, where he distributed and later attempted to publish a statement claiming that "Roger Revelle was not an author" of the Cosmos article, that Dr. Singer "entered Revelle as a coauthor despite his objections," and that "subsequent to Revelle's death in 1991, Singer ambitiously distributed the article and has sought republication in a singular attempt to undermine the pro-Revelle stance of Senator Al Gore."

It was that final false claim that Fred Singer wouldn't take. He filed a libel suit against Lancaster, represented by the Center for Individual Rights, a public-interest legal group in Washington. Lancaster was supported in his defense by the Natural Resources Defense Council and the Environmental Defense Fund.

Singer's lawyers obtained documents and sworn statements from Lancaster. They began to stack up against Gore.

Among the discoveries was a letter from Dr. Revelle to Congressman Jim Bates written July 14, 1988, saying, "Most scientists familiar with the subject are not yet willing to bet that the climate this year is the result of 'greenhouse warming.' As you very well know climate is highly variable from year to year, and the causes of these variations are not at all well understood. My own personal belief is that we should wait for another ten or twenty years to really be convinced that the greenhouse effect is going to be important for human beings, in both positive and negative ways. From this belief I conclude that we should take whatever actions would be desirable whether or not the greenhouse effect materializes. A transition to nuclear power and development of publicly acceptable means for water and energy conservation are actions of this type."

Fred Singer's lawsuit was quietly turning into a disaster for Gore.

When the opportunity appeared, Gore sent a pile of foundation-funded anti-wise use documents to Ted Koppel at ABC News.

They went to veteran producer Tara Sonenshine. She wrote the story as if she were Gore himself. It was a hatchet job, plain and simple. It crucified, among others, University of Virginia Professor Patrick Michaels—who, like Fred Singer, challenged global warming computer models—for his funding from industry.

Sonenshine's segment was scheduled to air early in February, but Koppel didn't like its unfair tone and demanded changes. During an acrimonious staff meeting, Sonenshine departed. It's not clear whether she was fired or resigned.[205a]

It was also not clear at first that Sonenshine and Gore were so close.

Then the Washington Post reported that Sonenshine had been appointed special assistant to the president and deputy director for communications at the National Security Council.[205b]

Ten days later, "Environmental Science For Sale" was broadcast, much changed, a combination of clips from Sonenshine's work and a remake by respected ABC News producer Jay Weiss.

A few months later, Fred Singer reached an out of court settlement with Justin Lancaster. Lancaster issued a statement in which he "fully and unequivocally" retracted his claims against Fred Singer.

Message: Don't mess with Al Gore's beliefs or take the consequences.

Al Gore may not possess the charisma and grace of the classic American politician. To the general public, he is smart, but wooden and boring. He seems distant even when he's trying to connect. His remarks on the environment sound like some ancient Greek oracle.

But he knows how government works.

It works through an army of friends, inside government and out— foundations, activists, ex-staffers, and supporters—who will work and push and bully anyone necessary to turn beliefs into policy.

Al Gore has the best environmentalist network ever assembled. Bonner Cohen understands The Gore Green Network:

> Their mastery of the federal regulatory machinery is enabling the Gore brigades to put policies in place that have behind them the force of law. So insidious is the process that even Gore's severest critics don't realize how badly he is beating them. With each new regulation issued by a Gore loyalist, and with each new "research" grant approved by one of his lieutenants, America's social fabric undergoes a subtle but enduring change. The cumulative effect of the countless small steps his people are taking will bring about that "wrenching transformation of society" Gore postulated in his book, *Earth in the Balance*. Even if the political winds shift, sweeping Gore and his minions from power, they will leave behind them an edifice that was built to last. Undoing Gore's legacy will require an act of will worthy of Nietzsche.[206a]

This "cumulative effect of countless small steps" is known in Beltway parlance as Mission Creep.

As Pranay Gupte wrote in *Forbes*, "mission creep is to a government agency what new markets are to a business. It involves a gradual, sometimes authorized, sometimes not, broadening of a bureaucracy's original mission."[206b]

It is a way to concentrate money and power beyond what Congress originally approved when it funded an agency.

Playing mission creep is an old game in Washington. Rare is the little bureaucracy that does not grow up into a big bureaucracy, and such failures to expand are usually the result of an unskilled Empire Builder at the helm, or the honorable bureaucrat who administers policy instead of trying to make it.

The Gore Green Network can be sorted into three tiers, based on their degree of personal, bureaucratic, and political affinity:

1) The Mission Creeps. Personally loyal former staffers placed into key bureaucratic positions and non-profit pressure points.

2) Gore's Green Gang. Top policy circle who owe Gore their government positions, or support for their appointments, or their influence in the administration.

3) Gore's Green Galaxy. Politically resolute environmentalist friends with money, power, and tenacity. The Clinton administration made itself mission creep incarnate. Nobody ever played the game

THE MISSION CREEPS
(MOST INFLUENTIAL FORMER GORE STAFFERS)

GOVERNMENT

Carol M. Browner, Administrator, Environmental Protection Agency, ex-Citizen Action employee, Florida environmental regulation director. Husband Michael Podhorzer is lobbyist with Ralph Nader campaign reform organization, Citizens Fund. Gore Senate staff, transition team.

Kathleen McGinty, former Chair, President's Council on Environmental Quality, left to join husband Karl Hausker of Center for Strategic and International Studies on assignment in India. Gore Senate staff.

NON-PROFIT

Arlie Schardt, president, Environmental Media Services, Gore 1988 presidential campaign national press secretary, former executive director of Environmental Defense Fund.

Debra Callahan, director, League of Conservation Voters, Gore 1988 presidential campaign field director, former grassroots director, W. Alton Jones Foundation.

GORE'S GREEN GANG
(TOP POLICY CIRCLE)

Bill Richardson, Energy Secretary, ex-Ambassador to United Nations, former Representative from New Mexico.	**Bruce Babbitt,** Interior Secretary, ex-president, League of Conservation Voters, former governor of Arizona.	**George Frampton,** director, Council on Environmental Quality, former Wilderness Society president, ex-Interior official.	**Maurice F. Strong,** Founder, United Nations Environment Program, Canadian businessman, ex-government official. Gore NGO contact.
Timothy E. Wirth, Turner United Nations Foundation, ex-State Department environment official, former Colorado Senator.	**Jonathan Lash,** World Resources Institute, Co-chair of President's Commission on Sustainable Development.	**T. J. Glauthier,** Office of Management & Budget natural resources director, ex-World Wildlife Fund policy director.	**Gregory Simon,** Senior Domestic Policy Adviser, ex-staff of House Science, Space and Technology Committee.
Richard Holbrooke U.S. Ambassador to United Nations. Gore 1988 presidential campaign foreign policy adviser.	**James G. Speth,** Dean, Yale School of Forestry and Environmental Studies, former EPA director, ex-U.N. official.	**Rita Colwell,** Director, National Science Foundation, decides who gets environmental research grants. Gore selected her.	**Eileen Claussen,** Pew Center on Global Climate Change, ex-EPA official. Served with Wirth at State Department.

with greater skill than Al Gore. Gore's Green Galaxy contains a constellation of talented...

MISSION CREEPS

> **CAROL M. BROWNER**
> Born: Dec. 16, 1955, Miami, Florida
> Administrator, Environmental Protection Agency
> Appointed at Gore's specific request
> Education: University of Florida (undergraduate)
> University of Florida Law School
> Worked for Nader-founded Citizen Action
> Gore's Senate staff legislative director
> Secretary, Florida Department of Environmental Regulation
> Transition director for Vice President-elect Gore
> Husband: Michael Podhorzer, lobbyist for Citizens Fund

Carol M. Browner is the political animal *par excellence*. She's tough. She's aggressive. She's an ideologue with sufficient savvy to hide it. Early on she served as a staffer in the Florida House of Representatives, then legislative assistant to former Sen. Lawton Chiles. She met husband Michael Podhorzer while working for Citizen Action, a nationwide consumer, campaign reform, and environmental lobbying group founded by Ralph Nader in 1979. It claims 3 million members, an annual budget of $4.5 million (much of it from the usual prescriptive foundations), affiliates and chapters across 30 states, making it the largest consumer organization of its kind.[208a]

The EPA Bailiwick: Browner runs one of the creepiest of the mission creeps: from a modest beginning in 1970, the EPA has acquired nearly 20,000 employees and an annual budget of $7 billion. The numbers are a poor measure of EPA's power because 1) its regulations have the force of law, 2) the agency can jail people, 3) it can close factories, 4) it can override the judgments of local authorities, and 5) it subsidizes friendly scientists and environmental groups with government grants. A powerful instrument of rural cleansing.

EPA is perhaps the federal agency most susceptible to mission creep. It was created by President Richard Nixon in a reorganization order. Congress didn't authorize it or give it a mission or define its regulatory powers. It was stuck together from a mish-mash of existing federal programs. It took over what eventually grew into thirteen environmental statutes, each with its own constituencies.[208b]

EPA became the perfect instrument for a federal power grab, turning local issues—chemical spills, groundwater contamination, abandoned dump sites—into federal matters.

EPA administrators were not slow to see the possibilities. Douglas Costle in 1978 shifted the focus of the agency to protect not just the environment but also health—*your* health.

People care about the environment, but we're much more concerned about our health. Tell Americans about an alleged threat to our health and we break out in a sweat. If it's cancer, we panic. Costle launched the EPA on a cancer hunt, looking for carcinogens in foods and air and water. Cancerphobia expanded his agency's reach and wrung more money from Congress. Asbestos. Dioxin. PCBs. Alar. Sunlight.[209]

Creep, creep, creep. Through several administrators.

Then came Gore and Browner.

Browner put scads of mission creeps from environmental groups into top EPA jobs. A sample:

Kathleen Aterno, Clean Water Action: Deputy Assistant Administrator, EPA Office of Administration and Resource Management.

David Doniger, Natural Resources Defense Council: Senior Counsel to EPA Assistant Secretary for Air and Radiation.

J. Charles Fox, Friends of the Earth: Special Assistant (Reinvention) to EPA Administrator Carol Browner.

David M. Gardiner, Sierra Club: Assistant EPA Administrator for Policy Planning and Evaluation.

Jean Nelson, Natural Resources Defense Council: EPA General Counsel.

Mary D. Nichols, Tennessee Environmental Action Fund, Southern Environmental Law Center: Associate EPA Administrator for Air & Radiation.

D. Reid Wilson, Sierra Club Political Action Committee: Director of Public Liaison Division, EPA Office of Communications, Education & Public Affairs.

Browner's loyalty to Gore's centralizing vision can be illustrated by her victories in two key areas: racheting up regulations by decree and subverting local government decisions.

Regulations: EPA has gained a reputation for imposing many unnecessary costs on American industry, dismantling industrial civilization piece by piece—costs that do more to satisfy bureaucratic zeal than to clean the air or water. Browner gave EPA a lot of that reputation.

Her most spectacular victory came in 1997 over clean air regulations. The Clean Air Act requires the EPA to review standards for assorted pollutants at least every five years. These standards are legal definitions of what qualifies as healthy air. Once levels are set, the EPA wrangles with states, localities and industries over how they can be met. Compliance plans often stretch out over a number of years. Air quality has improved dramatically since passage of the Clean Air Act amendments of 1990. Cities that spent fortunes complying with clean air rules hoped—especially in areas that needed new jobs—that the standards would remain stable. They thought they had done the job. The EPA's own data showed that particulate levels had a huge drop over the previous decade. Most cities expected to be removed from the list of so-called nonattainment areas for ozone and particulate matter—smog and soot.[210a]

But the American Lung Association had sued the EPA in 1993, forcing the agency to review the existing standards regarding ground-level ozone and particulate matter. EPA examined 5,000 scientific studies, held public meetings and submitted its preliminary findings to a panel of outside scientists. On the basis of the data, the decision could go either way.

In November of 1996, Browner, following Gore's plan, set up a power play of breathtaking scope: she abruptly announced the most significant rewriting of federal air quality standards since the 1970s—the administration had already failed to get BTU taxes through Congress, and a secret 1994 White House memo proposed no fewer than 39 different taxes and fees on energy the administration could impose under existing statutes, without having to get congressional approval. This was the followup.[210b]

The new regulations would force scores of states and cities to do their State Implementation Plans (SIPs) all over, either finding new ways to cut pollution or facing sanctions, including the loss of federal highway money. It was a risky but bold way to begin phasing out the use of coal and other fossil fuels, as Gore had recommended in his book.

Why did Browner decide on such a massive and controversial rewrite? It was a strategic strike to defend bigger plans. Here's how it worked:

When the Republicans took over Congress following the 1994 midterm election, EPA found itself embroiled in a series of conflicts with the new GOP majority on Capitol Hill. In addition to pushing legislation aimed at reducing regulatory burdens on businesses and local governments, Republican lawmakers also sought to cut the budgets of wayward agencies.

With its long history of well-documented complaints from the regulated community, EPA was an inviting target. Browner handled the threat crudely at first, according to a report by the National Wilderness Institute:

On March 15, 1995, Dr. Rosemarie Russo, director of EPA's lab in Athens, Ga., received a phone call from EPA headquarters in Washington, DC. This was no ordinary phone call; it came from Acting Assistant Administrator Dr. Gary Foley. Foley asked Russo if anyone on her staff had good connections with any members of Congress.

Prompting the call was a vote in the House of Representatives scheduled for that afternoon on a bill sponsored by Rep. Clifford Stearns (R-Florida) which would cut EPA's budget. Foley explained that EPA employees were being asked to contact lawmakers and try to persuade them to vote against the bill. According to notes Russo made during the conversation, Foley said EPA employees should go about this "without getting into trouble."

Russo told Foley that the only person on her staff with such connections was microbiologist Dr. David L. Lewis who was friends with Rep. Charlie Norwood (R-Georgia). She asked if she should pass the request on to Lewis, and Foley answered affirmatively. According to Lewis's testimony, Russo was told by Foley that the instructions originated in the office of Administrator Browner.

For his part, Lewis flatly refused to contact Norwood, pointing out that having government employees lobby Congress from their offices and during government business hours was a clear violation of the Anti-Lobbying Act of 1940 which strictly prohibits executive branch employees from engaging in such activities. Russo agreed that the request was probably illegal.[211a]

Both Lewis and Russo accused EPA of wrongdoing and were subsequently harassed with false accusations by Browner's lieutenants, likely violating federal whistleblower protection laws. Both had to retain attorneys to defend themselves. After an extended legal action, EPA settled with Lewis, but reneged on their agreement. Russo is still fighting.

As it turns out, Stearns had proposed a bill to de-fund the National Endowment for the Arts (NEA), not EPA. So EPA headquarters had solicited an illegal act to lobby against something that didn't even exist.

That wasn't all. Nineteen EPA officials signed and published a letter protesting "egregious conduct" by EPA under Browner, ranging from creating backdated documents for filing with a federal court to punishing career scientists for the "wrong" answers in their research.[211b]

President Clinton mistrusted the Browner-Gore proposal. So Browner arranged to get help from the Pew-funded Environmental Information Center, which "played a key role in pressuring President Clinton to approve new air pollution rules," according to the Philadelphia Inquirer.[211c]

Browner also had a ready-made army of outside supporters to push for the new regulations—all funded by EPA grants.

American Lung Association. Between 1990 and 1994, the EPA gave the lung association's national office and its various state chapters more than $4 million. In 1995, the EPA gave the group close to $1 million more. The ALA sued the EPA almost every year, claiming the agency wasn't complying with the nation's clean air laws, which the EPA welcomed because each suit expanded the reach of the agency.[212a]

Natural Resources Defense Council. In 1995 alone, the council got more than $1 million from the EPA. NRDC has repeatedly sued the EPA, always charging that the EPA isn't doing enough to protect public health. Between 1993 and 1996, the agency paid more than $150,000 for the NRDC's legal costs. Several NRDC air pollution studies were funded in part by grants from the EPA.

World Resources Institute. $310,000 cumulative grants from EPA. $4,180,702 in total government funding, or 24 percent of its total $17,565,180 1995 revenue. WRI head Jonathan Lash is one of Al Gore's top policy circle insiders, well regarded for his loyal support of the Kyoto Protocol, lower automobile emissions through higher gas taxes, and as a supporter of Browner's new air regulations. Lash came to WRI in 1993 from the Environmental Law Center at the Vermont Law School where he directed the environmental law program. He was Vermont Secretary of Natural Resources and a senior staff attorney for the group mentioned above, the Natural Resources Defense Council.

New York University. $383,008 in 1996 over three years to Professor of Environmental Medicine George D. Thurston to study "acidic particulate matter." An activist advocate, Dr. Thurston organized dozens of scientists and health professionals at the Institute of Environmental Medicine at NYU School of Medicine, asserting that the current standards "are not sufficiently protective of public health. Tens of thousands of hospital visits and premature deaths could be prevented each year by more stringent air quality standards for these two pollutants [ozone and particulate matter]."[212b]

Harvard School of Public Health. $196,185 in 1996 over three years to Professor Joel Schwartz (a MacArthur Foundation "genius" grant recipient) to study "ultrafine particulate matter." Schwartz appeared as the main scientific witness at a May 1997 press conference held by the Natural Resources Defense Council at which he said the tiny specks in his study "have killed more people than AIDS" over the past five years. He vilified a meeting of scientists gathered to discuss the new regulations as "industry thugs" because they had accepted industry funding. Harvard's School of Public Health accepted $3 million in EPA grants in 1996.

SAMPLE OF EPA GRANTS TO ENVIRONMENTAL ORGANIZATIONS	
GREEN GROUP	**CUMULATIVE EPA GRANTS**
American Lung Association Washington, D.C. headquarters	$2,815,169 (1994) $300,000 (1997) $475,647 (1999)
American Association of Retired Persons (AARP) Senior Environmental Employment Program. Over 800 enrollees served EPA in clerical and technical positions, 40% in EPA offices.	$20,937,108
American Farmland Trust	$85,000
Appalachian Mountain Club	$5,000
Center for Environmental Law and Policy	$40,000
Center for Marine Conservation	$180,000
Citizens for a Better Environment	$148,987
Earth Share (Environmental Federation of America). Supports 44 other environmental groups.	$998,855
Environmental Defense Fund	$2,120,643 (1995-1999)
Green Mountain Institute for Environmental Democracy	$1,232,380
Lawyer's Committee for Civil Rights, Environmental Justice Community Outreach Project	$81,391
The Nature Conservancy	$2,529,483 (26 EPA grants between 1995 and 1997)
National Association of Physicians for the Environment	$350,000
North American Association for Environmental Education	$3,635,722

On cue, Carl Pope, executive director of the Sierra Club, said, "These standards mean fewer sick days for workers, lowered health care costs and more kids in school instead of the hospital."

Playing the children's health card always works, as Douglas Costle first realized. What member of Congress wants to face reelection hung with the stigma of holding out on sick kids?

Forbes magazine noted that attendees of Capitol Hill hearings snicker at Browner's constant references to her son, Zachary, when she testifies on environmental issues. But she never misses a chance to repeat the message. In her prepared testimony before Congress, Browner asked, "How do I put a dollar value on reductions in a child's lung function or the premature aging of lungs or increased susceptibility to respiratory infection?"

"If we can focus on protecting the children . . . we will be protecting the population at large, which is obviously our job," she told *Forbes*.[214a]

As Bonner Cohen asked: Who said that was her job?

Nobody, but that's what mission creep is all about.

Congress was furious that Browner didn't consult with them first before acting on this oppressive and costly new regulation.

In June, 1997, Rep. John D. Dingell (D-MI), then-ranking minority member of the House Commerce Committee, along with several prominent Democrats, threatened publicly to "go to war" with the White House over the standards.

By early July Browner painted Bill Clinton into a corner. The president had stayed out of the fracas as long as he could, but at the approach of his scheduled July 26 speech at a United Nations summit on the environment, European allies criticized him for being slow to agree to a timetable on reducing greenhouse gases blamed for global warming.

Then the grant-driven Environmental Information Center went to work—in an editorial campaign pooh-poohing the costs, ostensibly aimed at heavy industry, but in fact aimed at Clinton. "The U.S. Environmental Protection Agency (EPA) has proposed updates to the Clean Air Act that would cut soot and smog," wrote EIC's Thomas E. Natan. "Based on about 250 scientific studies, EPA believes that 15,000 premature deaths could be prevented. The agency estimates that health and social benefits would save an average of $17 for every $1 spent on pollution control."

Now Clinton was furious. But he couldn't say so.[214b]

By tinkering with the details, Bill Clinton found a way to save face and stalemate Congress. Particulate standards would be delayed for five years to allow completion of a nationwide monitoring network. Cities would then have at least another two years to devise a strategy for reducing air pollution. Leniency was promised to states participating in pollution programs.

On July 25, 1997, Bill Clinton came out in support of Carol Browner.

Clinton's decision was clearly seen as a tactical victory for Browner. Clinton administration officials even told the Washington Post of their resentment and said Clinton did not appreciate the public pressure.[215a]

It was a daring gamble for Browner and Al Gore, for it set them up to implement the global warming treaty without Senate ratification. The Kyoto Protocol and the new regulations both dealt with ozone and particulates— no coincidence. Now she didn't need to bother with Congress.

The goalpost had been moved onto the next playing field.

Until a federal appeals court struck the standards down in 1999 as an unconstitutional delegation of congressional law-making authority.[215b]

Subverting local governments: One of Browner's first actions after installing her environmentalist friends in EPA jobs was to set up the Office of Environmental Justice within EPA.

The environmental justice movement began in 1985 when Warren County, North Carolina, was selected for a polychlorinated biphenyl (PCB) landfill near poor, mostly minority communities. The decision sparked widespread protests, marches and more than 500 arrests, including District of Columbia Delegate Walter Fauntroy (chairman of the Congressional Black Caucus). They didn't stop the landfill, but they put "environmental racism" on the map and created the counterphrase "environmental justice."[215c]

Two environmental justice activists, Benjamin Chavis, Jr. (Commission for Racial Justice), and Robert D. Bullard (Clark Atlanta University), served on the Clinton transition team in the natural resources and environment cluster and assisted in preparing a briefing book for newly designated EPA Administrator Carol Browner.

Al Gore, of course, was the touchstone. In a December 1993 speech at the African American Church Summit in Washington D.C., he cited environmental discrimination as a national problem.

On February 11, 1994, President Clinton signed Executive Order 12898 on Federal Actions to Address Environmental Justice in Minority Populations and Low-Income Populations, ordering federal agencies to consider the health and environmental effects of their decisions on minority and low-income communities.[215d]

A White House report on EPA performance stated:

> The agency's future lies in promoting not only environmental safety, but environmental justice as well. Administrator Browner is acting to resolve both issues with major initiatives, and EPA's senior management must follow through on her proposals.[215e]

The mission creeps another creep. The Office of Environmental Justice enforces various laws and passes out taxpayer-funded grants for studying the effects of pollutants on poorer, mostly black, communities.

Sounds wonderful. It has a down side: federal agencies have a new tool for subverting state agencies and perpetuating rural poverty.

Example: In January 1997, Louisiana's Department of Environmental Quality approved a $700 million polyvinyl chloride plant to be built by Japanese-owned Shintech in the predominantly black southern Louisiana town of Convent, on a chemical plant-lined stretch of the Mississippi river dubbed "Cancer Alley" by environmental justice activists. Shintech would create 195 good-paying jobs in an area with 60% unemployment and low incomes.[216a]

On May 22, 1997, Tulane Environmental Law Clinic filed a petition on behalf of 19 groups opposing the Shintech project. The St. James Parish Chapter of the National Association for the Advancement of Colored People supported the project.

On September 10, 1997, Browner told Shintech no go. Blacks would suffer disproportionately from potentially cancer-causing emissions of the plant.[216b]

Louisiana Economic Development Director Kevin Reilly said, "It is demeaning and despicable for these people to play the race card." He said that poor people and blacks had little health risk and would have greatly improved quality of life from good jobs and access to health care.

In the April 1998 Journal of the Louisiana Medical Society, Vivien Chen and other researchers from the Louisiana State University Medical Center reported that the incidence of cancer in black women, white women and black men was below the national average in the river parishes. The cancer incidence for white men was equal to the national average, but no higher.[216c]

That's the incidence rate. The death rate of those who did get cancer, however, told a different story: black men and women in those parishes had above average mortality from cancer, as did white men. Only white women, who had a below average incidence of cancer, also had a cancer mortality rate below the national average.

Incidence rates may reflect toxicity.

Death rates may reflect poverty and no access to medical care.

Environmentalists only talked about the mortality rates, not the incidence rates.

Maybe Cancer Alley isn't cancer alley after all. It's Poverty Row.

After a bitter legal wrangle, in September 1998 Shintech scrapped the project.[217a]

Score: Browner 1, State of Louisiana, 0.

After this victory, an Environmental Justice conference was arranged in Louisiana so the National Environmental Justice Advisory Council (NEJAC), a federal advisory committee to the EPA, could visit "hot spots" in the region.

A local committee was assembled to arrange the tour.

Included on this planning committee were Carol Gaudin and Ernest Johnson, President of Louisiana NAACP, two African Americans who supported Shintech's project.

When Browner discovered they were on the committee, the two received telephone calls from EPA telling them they were no longer on the committee.[217b]

Rural cleansing, EPA style.

Now, what about Browner's husband, Michael Podhorzer?

He's a lobbyist for Citizen Action, according to newspaper accounts. Questions have arisen about possible conflicts of interest with two lawyers married to each other, one in government and another in a special interest group trying to influence government.

The Washington Post ran a 1994 feature on potential conflicts among married lawyers that mentioned Browner:

> William McLucas, head of the SEC's enforcement division, is engaged to Kaye Williams, a former SEC lawyer who last fall became assistant general counsel for the Securities Industry Association, the trade group representing firms regulated by the SEC. Williams says there's no problem: "We are both lawyers who have ethical obligations to keep client information privileged." Besides, she adds, she doesn't deal with enforcement issues.
>
> That's the same attitude taken by Environmental Protection Agency Administrator Carol Browner and her husband Michael Podhorzer, a lobbyist with the consumer group Citizens [sic] Action. Although the organization is involved in many environmental issues, Podhorzer says he handles only health issues.[217c]

As if EPA didn't handle health issues.

But there's more to this.

Website postings say Podhorzer is actually with Citizens Fund (1996 income: $3,609,576; Assets: $888,839), the 501(c)(3) arm of Citizen

Action. Citizens Fund provides research, training, organizing and networking support for the national issues campaigns of Citizen Action.[218a]

The twin organizations not only operate health campaigns, they're big in the campaign reform arena we examined in The Montana Initiative Wars.

.Here's what the Ottinger Foundation Handbook says:

> As a 501(c)(4) organization, Citizen Action lobbies for campaign finance reform through its Campaign for a Responsible Congress program. The Campaign organizes reform supporters at the district level in targeted states, uses Citizens Fund research to focus media attention on money in politics, and airs paid television spots on the issue in targeted markets.
>
> One of the most ambitious and far-reaching money-in-politics projects in the country, Citizen Fund's reform program works to build state-level coalitions for publicly-financed campaigns. Citizens Fund publishes reports on the connections between campaign contributions and public policy, and organizes in support of public financing of political campaigns in eleven targeted states.
>
> Citizens Fund research shows how campaign contributions buy special favor from legislators, enabling wealthy, corporate donors to profit at taxpayers' expense. For example, a study released by Citizens Fund in January detailed the potpourri of special favors which the proposed balanced budget amendment offered 1994 Republican campaign contributors.[218b]

So Citizens Fund does a lot of things besides health issues. What Citizens Fund doesn't do is tell you where it gets its money. As you may guess, it's mostly from the usual prescriptive suspects: W. Alton Jones Foundation, John Merck Fund, Beldon Fund, Joyce Foundation, Surdna Foundation, Turner Foundation, Schumann Foundation, Nathan Cummings Foundation, Ruth Mott Fund, Ford Foundation, and others.[218c]

A key example: While Browner headed EPA, her husband's group got money from W. Alton Jones Foundation "To inform public about health and environmental threats posed by pesticides and to promote protection and policy reform," $60,000 in 1995; "To build public support for implementing least toxic methods of pest control in and around school building and public spaces," $25,000 in 1996.

Who regulates pesticides? EPA. Who's sleeping with the Administrator? Michael Podhorzer, Citizens Fund, who handles only health issues.

Let's follow this another step: W. Alton Jones Foundation tells us its grants are by invitation only. Did they invite the Citizens Fund pesticide-related grants? The board members knew that their director, John Peterson Myers, was working on his pesticide-related book, *Our Stolen Future*. Funding the EPA Administrator's husbands' group certainly wouldn't hurt their chances of having her mentor Al Gore write the book's introduction (p. 106). Especially not after giving grants to Gore's buddy and 1988 presidential campaign press secretary, Arlie Schardt, to do the book's publicity through his Environmental Media Services, a project of the Tides Center, which won the contract to locate its headquarters in a national park run by a trust influenced by Interior Secretary Bruce Babbitt.

And Gore's 1988 presidential campaign field director, Debra Callahan, was given a nice job with W. Alton Jones Foundation as grassroots director. She went on to a nicer job in the spot Bruce Babbitt once occupied as president of the League of Conservation Voters before he was tapped for Interior Secretary. President Clinton spoke at the League's 1998 annual dinner, introduced by Deb Callahan.

If that's not "a potpourri of special favors," what is?

KATHLEEN ALANA McGINTY
Born: 1963, Philadelphia, Pennsylvania
Chair, Council on Environmental Quality, left office in 1998 to
    join husband on assignment in India
Appointed at Gore's specific request
Education: St. Joseph's University (B.S. in Chemistry, 1985)
Columbia University Law School (1988)
1-year American Chemical Society fellowship, Gore Senate staff
Permanently hired by Gore at Carol Browner's suggestion when
    fellowship expired; top environmental staffer
Member, U.S. delegation, U.N. Conference on Environment and
    Development in Rio de Janiero 1992
Husband: **Karl Hausker**, Ph.D., Adjunct Fellow of the Center for
    Strategic and International Studies; 1993-1995, deputy assis-
    tant administrator of EPA's Office of Policy, Planning, and
    Evaluation; 1987-1992, chief economist, Senate Committee
    on Energy and Natural Resources

Katie McGinty is one of 10 brothers and sisters who grew up in a Philadelphia city cop's household. At St. Hubert's Catholic High School for Girls she made the varsity basketball team and scored a free throw in their triumphant league championship game in 1981. Her undergraduate major was chemistry. During her three years studying law at Columbia University in New York, she also took courses in Columbia's graduate schools of biology and chemistry and worked 15 hours a week clerking for various New York law firms.[220a]

After winning a one-year fellowship to Senator Al Gore's staff in 1989, she proved herself by the usual long hours sustained by pizza and Chinese take-out, but more by her sharp insight and ambition. It was legislative staffer Carol Browner who recommended she be hired permanently as senior legislative assistant for energy and environmental policy.

The time on Gore's staff gave her impressive experience. She served as congressional staff coordinator for the Senate delegation to the United Nations Conference on Environment and Development held in June 1992 in Rio, as well as an official member of the U.S. Delegation to Negotiations on the Framework Convention on Climate Change and the Antarctic Protocol.[220b]

During the presidential campaign in 1992, McGinty served as liaison with environmental lobbyists, calling them to make sure that every negative remark President Bush made about then-governor Clinton's plans to clean up the air or water got the sharpest rejoinder and the most intelligent policy response.

She was only 29 when she was sworn in as the youngest officer of the Clinton White House.

Some scoffed.

Big mistake.

Fortune magazine got it right: "One of Washington's little secrets is that the young, anonymous aides who labor in the bowels of the White House are more influential in setting policy than any Cabinet officer. When it comes to the environment, that certainly is the case with Katie McGinty."[220c]

Katie McGinty was originally appointed as deputy assistant to the president and director of the newly created "White House Office on Environmental Policy."[220d]

On February 8, 1993, President Clinton said, "We are today changing the way government works, replacing the Council on Environmental Quality with a new office that will have broader influence and a more effective and focused mandate to coordinate environmental policy."[220e]

That little word "coordinate" conferred power on Katie McGinty beyond anyone's imagination.

Al Gore said, "In the last administration when the spotted owl controversy arose, there were five different positions taken by six different executive branch agencies. Now, there were a lot of reasons for that, but one reason surely was that the White House was not organized in a way that gave the President the opportunity to have a hands-on coordination of policy. This will change that."

It did.

In practical terms, it meant that Katie McGinty sat on White House teams with cabinet officers several ranks above her and ended up controlling—"coordinating"—good chunks of their departments.

No matter that Congress had "a lot of reasons" to set up those departments the way they were, in part to reflect the diversity of their constituencies and to keep too much power from being concentrated in too few hands.

Now the power was all in one place.

McGinty was running the administration's environmental policy from the beginning. Although she had only twelve full-time staffers and a handful of interns, she was Gore's trusted commander and she put his agenda in place. She was one of the few who could step into his office down the hall any time she wanted.

Timber Queen: She was immediately put in charge of the Pacific Northwest Timber Summit, planned for early April, 1993, in Portland, Oregon. The Summit conference was a Clinton campaign promise that Al Gore intended to keep.

The President announced the conference on ABC Kids Town Meeting in late February while responding to Elizabeth Bailey, a young girl whose logger father had been put out of work by environmentalists:

"First of all," said Clinton, "the problem has been made worse because the United States government has not come up with a solution. So that as you may know, the courts have stopped logging all over northern California and Washington and Oregon, including some places where people should be allowed to log. So I have committed myself to organize, along with Vice President Gore, a forest summit. And the Secretary of the Interior, Bruce Babbitt, in particular, is doing a lot of work on that now. We're trying to set up a forest summit out there to bring all the people together to try to come up with the best compromise that will permit us to save not just the spotted owl, but the other point I wanted to make is, the old-growth forest that remains, and still let people log."[221]

Now it was up to Katie McGinty to make it happen.

While the president reassured America that its forest policy would henceforth be based on science and not politics, McGinty convened an interagency group including the Departments of Agriculture, Interior, Labor, Commerce, Education, and EPA to craft a one-day conference.

Their assignment was to end the legal gridlock and save both jobs and the forest.

While the inside group worked on the invitation list, the format and other organizational details, Katie McGinty was also arranging the environmental movement's response and the post-conference decision-making team.

Shortly after President Clinton announced the timber summit, she was in contact with leaders of the Ancient Forest Alliance, discussing how to mobilize as much of the environmental movement as possible.

The Ancient Forest Alliance, recall, was the shell coalition of the biggest national green groups, brought together by core foundations in the Environmental Grantmakers Association (pp. 176-179).

By early March the Alliance had arranged the environmentalist position on the timber summit to McGinty's specifications: preliminary enthusiasm for the President's search for "the best compromise," tinged with skepticism sufficient to set up a post-conference drive for less goods and services from federal forests—rural cleansing.

On March 8 the Alliance sent out a direct mail appeal:

Dear Friend of the Environment,

The last remnants of our magnificent ancient forest ecosystems need your help—NOW! After years of overcutting, violations of the environmental laws, and political gridlock, the real battle is about to be joined. And the stakes are incredibly high!

For more than a decade, the Reagan and Bush Administrations, together with their allies in the timber industry, have waged an irresponsible and unprecedented campaign to liquidate ancient forests on public lands in the Pacific Northwest and California.

But President Clinton has promised change—and a Pacific Northwest Forest Summit to develop a solution that will protect biological diversity in the region's forests and promote economic diversity in its communities.

While specifics of the summit remain unclear, no single event will have a greater impact on the survival of our old-growth ecosystems.

Already, rich and powerful special interests have cranked up their lobbying machines to perpetuate the myth that jobs and environmental protection are incompatible. And they've aimed their assaults at the President, Members of Congress, and other policy-makers who can influence the summit and its outcome.

The timber barons would like nothing better than to continue business as usual—cutting the ancient forests until there is nothing left to cut.

The big companies started logging the virgin forests of New England in the 1800's and literally sawed their way across the country. In the process, they wiped out the "big trees" and left devastated regional economies in their wake.

Now they want to finish the job by logging this last fragment of our ancient forests in the Northwest. The timber industry isn't up against the ancient forests—it's up against the Pacific Ocean!

That's why it is imperative that President Clinton and your representatives in Congress hear from everyone who cares about biodiversity and the fate of our forests. They have to know that the American people support ancient forest protection.

We've enclosed "A Citizens' Resolution for America's Ancient Forests," which outlines four principles that are crucial to any ancient forest solution. It is imperative that President Clinton and Members of Congress adopt these principles.

They need to hear from you!

The ancient forests of the Pacific Northwest and California need your help. We are counting on you because of your longstanding commitment to ancient forest protection. Thank you for whatever you can do!

Sincerely,

Robert A. Chlopak	*Brock Evans*
Americans for the Ancient Forests	National Audubon Society
Carl Pope	*Vawter Parker*
Sierra Club	Sierra Club Legal Defense Fund
Jim Owens	*Michael A. Francis*
Western Ancient Forest Campaign	The Wilderness Society[223]

On March 27, the National Audubon Society issued an action alert that expanded on the "four principles" of the Resolution. They demanded that the solution must:

● Be based on sound science, not politics;

● Establish a forest reserve system which will ensure the survival of this endangered ecosystem and the plants and animals that depend on ancient forests for their survival;

● Provide specific direction to agencies responsible for managing the Pacific Northwest forests so that the poor forest management practices of the past are not repeated;

● Include the eastside forests of Washington and Oregon (east of the Cascade Range) and the northern Sierras of California;

● Provide for responsible long-term management of areas outside reserves;

● Offer re-investment in Northwestern communities, family assistance, and worker retraining programs;

● Examine the issue of raw log exports;

● NOT tamper with existing environmental laws or restrict citizen access to courts.

Planting these demands in advance was a masterful rural cleansing move that reflected Al Gore's agenda rather than Bill Clinton's, and it would ultimately generate conflict within the administration.

The direct mail piece itself was unremarkable propaganda: Typically, it made no acknowledgment that environmentalist lawsuits had created the Pacific Northwest timber crisis, as Clinton obliquely admitted to the girl during his ABC Kids Meeting—"the courts have stopped logging"—and blamed the suffering of loggers on their own overcutting, simply blanking out the realities of sustained yield and already-preserved lands in favor of the "nothing left to cut" mythology.

Katie McGinty's Ancient Forest Alliance contacts had funded many of those court actions:

By 1993 the **Sierra Club Legal Defense Fund** (1991 budget, $8.7 million) had received:

1991 **W. Alton Jones Foundation**: $200,000 "For Ancient Forest Litigation Project, to continue litigation encouraging sustainable management of national forests of Pacific Northwest."

1992 **W. Alton Jones Foundation**: $150,000 "To enforce land protection laws and protect ancient forests through litigation."

1992 **Ruth Mott Fund:** $30,000 "For general support of Pacific Northwest Ancient Forest Preservation Campaign."

1991 **Nathan Cummings Foundation:** $40,000 "To safeguard old-growth woodlands of Pacific Northwest and to cooperate with Canadians trying to protect ancient forests of British Columbia."

1992 **Nathan Cummings Foundation:** $40,000 "To safeguard old-growth woodlands of Pacific Northwest through variety of legal and educational strategies."

Plus many other "general support" grants that affected forests.

All six groups of the Ancient Forest Alliance were well funded in 1993 to promote the Gore / McGinty agenda for the timber summit:

Americans for the Ancient Forests 1993 grants:

W. Alton Jones Foundation: $150,000 For public education efforts for protection of ancient forests of Pacific Northwest.

Bullitt Foundation: $70,000 For Northwest Forests program. Grant made through Earthlife Canada Foundation.

Surdna Foundation: $150,000 To continue intensive, nationwide educational campaign on nation's stake in protecting remaining old growth forests of Pacific Northwest.

Western Ancient Forest Campaign 1993 grants:

W. Alton Jones Foundation: $100,000 For public education efforts toward protection of ancient forests of Pacific Northwest.

Ruth Mott Fund: $25,000 For grassroots advocacy on Northwest ancient forests.

Foundation for Deep Ecology: $15,000 For general support.

Bullitt Foundation: $65,000 For Northwest Forests program.

The Pew Charitable Trusts: $200,000 To coordinate public education activities of local conservation organizations in Pacific Northwest working on ancient forest preservation.

Surdna Foundation: $75,000 To continue partnership of local and national advocates for ancient forests in Washington, D.C., to intensify regional organizing in Northwest and to press for U.S. Forest Service budget reform.

The Wilderness Society 1993 grants:

Bullitt: $40,000 For Northwest Forests.

Pew: $200,000 To conduct national education campaign in support of ecosystem reserve for ancient coastal rainforests in Pacific Northwest.

Pew: $100,000 For analysis of employment impacts and economic benefits of preserving ancient rainforests in Pacific Northwest.

Surdna: $150,000 2-year grant. To compile in public document, specifics of what must be done for ecosystem management of federal forests.

National Audubon Society 1993 grants:

Bullitt: $80,000 For Northwest Forests program.

W. Alton Jones: $125,000 To monitor implementation of President Clinton's proposed forest plan for Pacific Northwest.

Sierra Club Legal Defense Fund 1993 grants:

Bullitt: $10,000 For Northwest Forests program.

This concentrated foundation influence on the Clinton Forest Summit was completely hidden. None of this was reported in the media. None of this was public knowledge.

The Non-Timber, Non-Summit Timber Summit: The timber summit, renamed the "Forest Conference" by the White House—"think forests, not timber," as one analyst put it—put Katie McGinty to one of her first tests of power in the administration.

No representatives of national groups were allowed on the agenda, only affected Northwest residents. The Ancient Forest Alliance and the timber-related Northwest Forestry Association reportedly disagreed over virtually every aspect of the session, from who should participate in it, to what issues should be on the table. However, the Alliance got Diana Draper of an Audubon chapter in Oregon and Vic Sher of the Sierra Club Legal Defense Fund's Seattle office seats at the table.[226]

What nobody knew was that McGinty had put together an elite team of loyal government scientists weeks earlier to "develop" a plan after the conference—a plan that was essentially decided upon in advance.

The public hype evolved into news conferences, vigils, and rallies with a carnival atmosphere in the days just before the event, with an environmentalist-sponsored concert of '60s-era rock performers one night, and a logger-sponsored country-western concert the next.

The Setup: At 10:30 a.m. on April 2, 1993, in Portland, Oregon's Convention Center, the real media circus began. The President and Vice President each made an opening statement. Around the table sat Agriculture Secretary Mike Espy, Interior Secretary Bruce Babbitt, Labor Secretary Robert Reich, Commerce Secretary Ron Brown, EPA Administrator Carol Browner, Deputy Director of the OMB Alice Rivlin, and Science and Technology Adviser Jack Gibbons.

In an eight-hour hearing, nearly fifty speakers told emotional stories about jobless workers and their distressed families, and environmentalists told how the forest was being destroyed.

The session resembled the "economic summit" Clinton held in Little Rock, Arkansas, before his inauguration—three separate roundtables with a succession of four- and five-person panels, each person making a brief statement, then the President leading a discussion of the issues of that roundtable.

Roundtable 1—Who Is Affected And How, focused on environmentalists and forest workers, with an assortment of locals including a fisherman, tribal leader, and an Archbishop.

Roundtable 2—Ecological and Economic Assessments: the White House called it "the expert panel" because it was mostly academicians, economists and biologists.

Roundtable 3: Where Do We Go From Here? was the most varied, with industry, environmentalists, bureaucrats, and others talking about ways to create jobs that use fewer trees. Rural cleansing dressed up.

Clinton clearly enjoyed directing the detailed policy discussion, a role well suited to his "I feel your pain" style. It was his show, and he capped it off with a closing statement that promised something for everyone, but no winner-take-all solution.

The media reported key messages:

Roundtable 1: Diana Draper, a lawyer and Audubon Society activist, said that the disappearance of some animal species was like the auto engine lights that signal impending breakdown. They are "the equivalent of all the lights coming on at once," she said.

Roundtable 2: "So little is left that environmentalists are not in a position to compromise that any further," said Andy Kerr of the Oregon Natural Resources Council. "The forest has been compromised all it can stand."[227a]

Roundtable 3: Bob Doppelt of Pacific Rivers Council warned that the declining forests were damaging spawning areas so badly that several species of fish could become endangered. And the impact of that, he implied, would make the battle over the spotted owl pale by comparison.

Katie McGinty had delivered the goods.

It took two months for the Forest Ecosystem Management Assessment Team (FEMAT) to come up with the Clinton plan.

Clinton had promised to solve the timber crisis "scientifically," to "integrate science into policy" with "ecosystem management" (actually "conservation biology," a much more ideological approach). Roughly, the idea is to look at all wildlife species in a given region, assess their habitat needs, determine how much habitat remains, then decide how much, if any, logging may occur.

The public did not realize the full implication of the conservation biology approach: human use of the earth comes last after everything else. People are just another species and are treated as objects.

Ecosystem management, on the other hand, does put people in the equation, integrating what is biologically possible with human expectations to decide where they intersect and how to manage the land.

"Integrating science into policy" has its own problems: scientists can be just as ideological as any other citizen. But they claim moral authority, and FEMAT scientists were in a position to impose their views as policy. If they decided people came last, then people came last.

The Sting: The FEMAT assessment team was a pre-arranged, pre-selected Katie McGinty Special. Led by biologist Jack Ward Thomas—a veteran of 27 years with the Forest Service, who would be appointed Chief seven months later—it was stacked with Gore loyalists with impressive scientific credentials who were accustomed to making ethical judgments and calling them science.[227b]

Thomas had been made team leader because he was one of the "Gang of Four" scientists who had published a noted study on old-growth forests that supported the conservation biology approach. The career paths of the other three scientists would likewise prosper with Gore and McGinty.

There was no question of FEMAT's scientific qualifications. There was no question they were inappropriately trained to make moral judgments. There was no question that they were out of touch with the people they would affect and insulated from the consequences of their actions.

The plan they were about to write was intended to become law.

University of Washington Professor Bob Lee, who had spoken on Roundtable 2 at the Forest Conference, was invited to advise on the FEMAT process. He was appalled at what he found.[228a]

The FEMAT team didn't bother to gather information so that others could decide on proper policy, said Lee, they had already made the policy themselves. Some of the FEMAT scientists suggested that gridlock couldn't be solved until the pluralist political system was short-circuited by putting "scientists" in political authority. Bob Lee didn't know about McGinty. He told them, "Science demands chronic doubt, not obedience to authority." They told him to shut up. He resigned and wrote a book about it, *Broken Trust, Broken Land.*

His conclusion:

> A few ecological "scientists" are succeeding in trapping people in a monopoly on "ecological morality." Massive social and economic disruption seems inevitable if scientifically justified plans are to be implemented. Human suffering is seen as regrettable, but necessary in order to protect nature.[228b]

When the FEMAT scientists got through making their moral judgments on Northwest forest species, the most timber they could find left to harvest was 1.2 billion board feet—about half of what the White House expected and one quarter of the Northwest's historic level. The Clinton Forest Plan was the ninth of their ten proposed alternatives, "Option Nine."

FEMAT's Option Nine imposed new forest reserves on commercial timberlands to protect endangered species, with only salvage logging allowed—recovery of damaged timber from storm blowdown, insects, disease and fire.

Option Nine also included $1.2 billion in worker relief over five years—money to retrain workers, which would permanently reduce the skilled timber labor force. Rural cleansing with rural welfare.[228c]

Now the administration had to sell the plan to Congress.

On Wednesday, June 23, Katie McGinty unveiled the forest plan to Speaker of the House Tom Foley (D-WA) in his second-floor capitol office, seeking support to turn the plan into law. Foley was furious with what he saw and told McGinty that lichen on old-growth trees in the rainy Northwest was getting more protection from the administration than people. McGinty came back empty-handed.[229a]

The conservation biology approach had met its first critic.

A week later Interior Secretary Bruce Babbitt tried to soothe Foley but got similarly blunt treatment. Foley said it was misleading to claim "that the administration had chosen an option that expanded or maximized the timber cut," he said. "In fact, the plan reduces timber operations by 80 percent from historic levels. It means huge job losses in communities; it comes close to meeting the goals of people who want to end timber operations."

It was clear that Congress would not support the president's "Forest Plan for a Sustainable Economy and Sustainable Environment" when he released it on July 1. Consequently, Clinton decided to implement his plan administratively and through the courts, avoiding the Congress and Foley. Clinton dropped parts of the plan that would require new legislation, and therefore Foley's cooperation.

The Clinton plan instantly became part of the gridlock.

Forest industry groups challenged FEMAT in court. On March 21, 1994, U.S. District Judge Thomas Penfield Jackson ruled that the scientists preparing the FEMAT report had violated the Federal Advisory Committee Act by failing to open its proceedings to the public and by selecting information from a limited circle of scientists. Jackson had no power to stop the president from using the report, but invited the plaintiffs to challenge the plan if it was adopted by the administration.[229b]

When the plan was adopted, the industry groups followed Judge Jackson's advice and challenged the plan. Their suit was consolidated in Judge William Dwyer's court with other lawsuits, and they did not prevail. The "big multinationals" lost again.[229c]

The agencies then imposed the FEMAT report as part of their normal forest management activities. And when they needed an excuse to stop a legitimate timber sale, there was always a friendly foundation to fund a lawsuit and always a friendly environmental group to file it.

But back in early August of 1993, the administration announced it would extend the FEMAT process to the national forests in eastern Oregon and eastern Washington, in what later became known as the Interior Columbia Basin Ecosystem Management Project. It would become another bureaucratic nightmare for rural resource people (p. 260).

At the same time, attention shifted to the salvage logging allowed by the Clinton plan. On August 16, the National Wildlife Federation called for no salvage logging in reserves.[230a]

On September 2, the Western Ancient Forest Campaign sent out an action appeal against Option 9 itself: "While the Administration has painted Option 9 as an innovative protection plan, it represents risky management at its worst. Unless activists generate a loud and strong response, the Administration will implement Option 9. The ancient forests of the Northwest deserve better."[230b]

Practically every forest-related environmental group in the nation did the same. The environmental movement stood solidly against the Clinton forest plan. Push the goalpost farther left.

McGinty's army was set to torpedo Bill Clinton's forest plan.

In December of 1993, Jack Ward Thomas was appointed Chief of the Forest Service, U.S. Department of Agriculture.

The next year was not a happy one for loggers. Between harvest reductions in the Northwest and various anti-logging lawsuits elsewhere, federal timber sales in 1994 were the smallest since 1955. Then record wildfires swept the West for the second summer running, destroying four million acres of timber and hundreds of homes and leaving dozens of forest fire fighters dead. The forest industry's long-ignored claims that the fuel buildup of downed timber was creating a forest health crisis suddenly commanded respect.

That fall, administration officials tried to defuse environmentalist criticism of the Forest Service's salvage program, renaming it the Western Forest Health Initiative and began shopping it around Capitol Hill. In November, Republicans swept Congress, placing key forestry committees in the hands of GOP timber-state lawmakers.

Now the salvage logging issue heated up. Bill Clinton the politician found that he could quiet the roar from the resource community by offering salvage timber sales. Congress wanted more timber and found they could get the administration to release it in salvage sales for forest health.

The foundations and grant-driven greens went into a panic. A successful salvage logging program worked out between the administration and Congress would set back rural cleansing for years, perhaps indefinitely. They had to mobilize to stop salvage logging. But how?

The Salvage Rider: On July 27, the White House signed the 1995 Emergency Supplemental and Rescissions Act which contained a rider to end the timber paralysis with salvage logging. To cut the endless chain of environmentalist lawsuits, the bill suspended the most onerous environmental laws for specified timber sales through 1996.[231a.]

Clinton had vetoed a similar measure earlier, but signed this one under pressure—his popularity ratings were sagging and he needed the other items in that budget bill.

After Clinton signed the bill he instructed the Departments of the Interior, of Agriculture, of Commerce and the Environmental Protection Agency to enter into a memorandum of agreement to speed up the timber release.

It was a declaration of war.

Al Gore, Katie McGinty, the foundations and the grant-driven greens were determined to block those salvage sales.

McGinty knew how.

Shortly after Bill Clinton signed the "Salvage Rider," as it was quickly dubbed, Katie McGinty summoned Forest Service officials to a meeting. It was supposedly routine, although it had never happened before. Forest Service Chief Jack Ward Thomas and Director of Timber Management Dave Hessel came to the Old Executive Office building with their boss, Jim Lyons, the Assistant Secretary of Agriculture for Natural Resources and Environment.[231b]

The meeting room was full of lawyers, including Peter Koppelman from the Justice Department—deputy assistant to Lois J. Schiffer, Assistant Attorney General for Environment and Natural Resources—who seemed to be presiding over the meeting along with Dinah Bear, general counsel of the Council on Environmental Quality. Katie McGinty sat at the conference table with several of her staff.

Thomas gave a detailed presentation on how he interpreted and intended to implement the law, based on intensive study of every line in the rider. The lawyers disagreed with Thomas on interpretation of the salvage rider. McGinty disregarded Thomas and his presentation.

When the meeting was over, both Lyons and Thomas realized that McGinty and her colleagues had no interest in their views whatsoever. They both thought she was putting the Forest Service under her thumb.

Their suspicions were soon confirmed: McGinty called another meeting the next week, this one in the office of the CEQ. Lyons and Thomas stayed away, although a number of agencies sent representatives. Hessel sat through the meeting, explaining how he was going to implement the salvage logging program, listening to instructions. He knew that his views were being politely ignored and felt his control over timber management slipping away.

The meetings with McGinty's staff became a weekly ritual.

She began a legal challenge of the salvage rider, demanding reinstatement for the environmental reviews specifically exempted by legislation.[232a]

Jack Ward Thomas didn't back down. He insisted that salvage logging was essential. He insisted that clearcutting was a proper management tool regardless what environmental groups said. He insisted on many other things Katie McGinty didn't want to hear. And he backed up Dave Hessel's salvage logging program.

Jim Lyons told Thomas to get rid of Dave Hessel. Thomas refused.

Katie McGinty, without explanation or discussion, ordered a series of Hessel-approved timber sales withdrawn. She used the weekly meetings to interfere in assessments, planning, and selection of alternatives in planning. Environmental groups were targeting specific timber sales and feeding McGinty the information. She obligingly shut down as many as possible and obstructed the rest.

McGinty was running the Forest Service.

Protest demonstrations popped up at one timber sale after another. The Sugarloaf sale in southern Oregon produced 219 arrests before it could be logged. The Roman Dunn sale, east of Eugene, Oregon, suffered more than $50,000 in eco-sabotage.[232b]

The Pacific Northwest had grown a radical grassroots network of small, highly localized groups, essentially one group per forested watershed. Most of them stood aloof from the foundation sphere—refusing to pull their punches for foundation bosses—but all had contacts with grant-driven trainers, organizers, media agents and supply sources. And those contacts had contacts with Katie McGinty.

In early September a federal judge released an injunction on 8.5 million board feet of arson-burned timber in Warner Creek, above Oakridge, Oregon.[232c]

Environmentalists had sued on the grounds that releasing the sale would encourage arson—although no suspect was ever identified, environmentalists insisted it was a logger.

Doug Heiken of the Oregon Natural Resource Council said, "Nonviolent civil disobedience will start when the logging starts in Warner Creek and not a moment sooner."

Thomas Creek Lumber & Logging of Lyons, Oregon, had until the next August to remove 520,000 board feet of timber it had paid for.

Siege Mentality: Heiken missed his guess. In November of 1995, radicals trenched and barricaded Forest Service Road 2408, the only route in Willamette National Forest leading to the Warner Creek sale. They built a drawbridge and allowed only other protesters into the forest. Federal law enforcement agents did nothing to remove them.[232d]

It was the beginning of a blockade that lasted 11 months. The protesters built a fort and dug 6-foot-deep trenches in the road. They camped there fall, winter, spring and summer. They got press all over America.[233a]

During 1996, eight timber sale protests cost at least $1,010,931 over budget for extra federal law enforcement. Federal law enforcement did nothing to remove the protesters from Warner Creek.[233b]

Peter Koppelman blamed the 104th Congress for "totally disrupting the peace." He said the salvage rider "has caused civil war in the forest." He was in contact with environmental groups and law enforcement.[233c]

In early August, Katie McGinty ordered the Forest Service to withdraw the Warner Creek timber sale.

In mid-August, Forest Service law enforcement officers went in on a Friday afternoon, bulldozed the protester's structures, chased away about a dozen protesters, and arrested five.[233d]

Three were later convicted of criminal trespass, but the judge declined to impose any sentence.[233e]

Jack Ward Thomas retired October 10, 1996.

The next July, Forest Service officials in Oregon met with a pro-timber citizen group, the Yellow Ribbon Coalition, to discuss problems loggers were having with vandalism on Forest Service jobs.

Darrell Kenops, supervisor of Willamette National Forest, and Bruce Gainer, the forest's chief law enforcement officer, met with coalition director Merrilee Peay and four members in the group's Springfield, Oregon, office. Newspapers had published Peay's editorials about the siege.[233f]

Peay's account of the meeting:

> After we discussed the vandalism, the conversation turned to Warner Creek and why law enforcement hadn't removed the environmentalists for eleven months.
> Bruce Gainer told us, "We have this all under control."
> I said, "Then how come the Warner Creek protest was allowed to go on so long?"
> Bruce Gainer said, "This went a lot deeper than you know."
> Kenops was silent.
> I said that we had heard that the order to not take down the protesters came from Katie McGinty's office.
> Bruce Gainer said, "You don't have to look any farther than that."
> Kenops just looked down at the table.[233g]

On June 14, 1999, Bruce Gainer said he had no recollection of any discussion of Warner Creek during this meeting.[233h]

Peay stands by her story.

The Democratic Process: On Thursday, February 12, 1998, Al Gore chanced upon Congressman Jim Turner (D-TX) at a freshman Democrat meeting. Turner buttonholed Gore and explained that high winds had swept through East Texas two days before, wreaking severe damage on their national forests.

Turner wrote Gore in a February 20 letter, "One issue that I would request your immediate assistance on is the need to move quickly to salvage and remove the timber from the national forests."

On March 10, Katie McGinty sent a five-page letter to the Forest Service giving her blessing to the salvage sale.

On March 11, Rep. Turner's office issued the following release:

> The U.S. Forest Service has been authorized to proceed immediately with salvage of the 270 million board feet of timber left on the ground by high wind storms that swept through East Texas last month, Congressman Jim Turner announced today.
>
> The environmental regulations standing in the way of the salvage were waived by the Council on Environmental Quality in Washington, D. C. Congressman Turner, who enlisted the assistance of Vice President Al Gore to obtain the waivers, said the decision represented a victory for "common sense over strict regulation."[234a]

In a short time, the salvaged timber from a Democratic Texas District was cut and on its way to the mill and the market—jobs and products.

It was the only salvage timber sale Katie McGinty ever approved.

She could afford it by 1998. President Clinton and Vice President Gore had been safely reelected. But back in 1996, they were in trouble because of such salvage sales. McGinty had helped them win reelection by finding a way to nullify the problem and win back enviro support.

Grabbing the Land: McGinty's idea was a bold stroke that skirted legality and defied Congress. Just prior to the 1996 election, Katie McGinty convinced President Clinton to make a surprise proclamation of 1.7 million acres of land in southern Utah as a national monument, the largest protective designation in almost 20 years. It caught everybody off guard, especially the Utah congressional delegation.[234b]

Environmentalists hailed the move and supported his reelection.

The area was known as the Grand Staircase-Escalante, named for two popular hiking destinations long proposed for protection by the **Southern Utah Wilderness Alliance** (SUWA)—1996 income: $1,507,595; assets: $1,433,915.

It created a huge stink: beneath the preserve's Kaiparowits Plateau lies what may be the nation's largest untapped energy reserve. It contains an estimated 62 billion tons of clean-burning, low-sulfur coal, 3 to 5 billion barrels of oil, and 2 to 4 trillion cubic feet of natural gas.

None of that is ever likely to be available.

The Southern Utah Wilderness Alliance has been trying to keep that wealth from ever being developed since it received its nonprofit IRS status in 1984. SUWA is a grant-driven green group funded by a familiar cluster of prescriptive foundations bent on rural cleansing in 5.7 million acres of the Southwest. SUWA's approach was to declare large areas off-limits to all roads, motorized travel and resource extraction under the Wilderness Act of 1964. Former Democratic Congressman Wayne Owens was chairman of the board for SUWA.

Sample grants to Southern Utah Wilderness Alliance:

1989 **Rockefeller Family Fund** $25,000 For efforts to preserve five million acres of southern Utah's Canyon Country as wilderness.

1990 **Rockefeller Family Fund** $25,000 For efforts to preserve five million acres of southern Utah's Canyon Country as wilderness.

1991 **Rockefeller Family Fund** $25,000 For campaign to preserve more than five million acres of Utah's Canyon Country and to create greater national awareness of battle for a unique wilderness.

1992 **Florence and John Schumann Foundation** $60,000 For traveling exhibit about public lands in Utah.

1993 **W. Alton Jones Foundation** $30,000 To use litigation to gain enforcement of environmental legislation and to oppose compensation suits that might have negative impact on environmental protection.

1996 **Pew Charitable Trusts** $100,000 To cultivate support from business community for wilderness preservation campaign.

National Monuments are an odd classification of land within the National Park Service: the president can unilaterally create them by proclamation under the obscure Antiquities Act of 1906, without congressional approval. The law was intended to protect archaeological sites such as cliff dwellings and other places of scientific interest, but many presidents have used the proclamation power to protect natural areas that Congress rejected as parks or wildernesses, so there has long been a political dimension to national monument designation. The new monument would be managed by the Bureau of Land Management.

How rural cleansing in the Utah canyonlands evolved from a prescriptive goal of wealthy foundations through grant-driven green groups into public policy is a study in secrecy, lies, Katie McGinty and Al Gore.

Secrets: In the summer of 1995, Southern Utah Wilderness Alliance issues director Ken Rait escorted Katie McGinty through the area that would become the new national monument. Gore and McGinty had adopted the 5-million-plus acre wilderness goals for the area that had been urged by SUWA and its prescriptive foundation funders.

A sense of urgency pervaded this visit: the Republicans now controlled Congress, and the Utah delegation was supporting a bill that proposed to designate 2.1 million acres as wilderness instead of the 5 million-plus acres the administration wanted.

McGinty was "on vacation" in and around the area for the better part of two weeks. A newspaper account said Rait used the visit as an opportunity to lobby McGinty for preservation and that she was struck by the beauty of the region. McGinty appears to have discussed the possibility of designating the area a national monument with SUWA officials, the Sierra Club, and other environmental groups—election year was coming up, and green groups were not happy with Clinton and the timber rider.[236]

At about the same time, Bruce Babbitt's Interior Department began to study the details of using a national monument to trump Congress. SUWA and other environmental groups had a direct line into Babbitt's office through his special assistant, Geoff Webb, who previously worked for Friends of the Earth and had spent considerable time in Utah for the environmental group working on nuclear waste storage and coal leasing issues. Webb had served as Bureau of Land Management Deputy Director for External Affairs during Jim Baca's abrasive nine-month tenure as BLM Director, and got assigned to Babbitt after Baca was fired in February of 1994 for antagonizing ranchers, loggers, miners, property owners and practically everyone else in the resource class.

The evidence that staff at Interior discussed the monument idea near the time McGinty toured Utah with Ken Rait is clear: In July of 1995, Interior Department Solicitor John Leshy assigned staff attorneys to evaluate the legalities of national monument designation, particularly the details of how to avoid the lengthy environmental review required by NEPA, the National Environmental Policy Act of 1969. Dave Watts and Robert Baum studied the issue and reported back on August 3, 1995:

> To the extent the Secretary proposes a national monument, NEPA applies. However, monuments proposed by the president do not require NEPA compliance because NEPA does not cover presidential actions. To the extent that the president directs that a proclamation be drafted and an area withdrawn as a monument, he may direct the Secretary of the Interior to be part of the president's staff and to

undertake and complete all the administrative support. This Interior work falls under the presidential umbrella.[237a]

Why would anyone in the Clinton administration want to know how to declare a national monument without environmental compliance? The only plausible answer is to avoid a public process and act in secrecy.

The proposal for a national monument in Utah thus originated with the Interior Department. Now the problem was how to create a paper trail to make it look like the idea came directly from the president.

The presidential umbrella they required, of course, was held by Katie McGinty. As election year began to heat up, she held a series of meetings with her staff on the Utah national monument plan.

The Paper Chase: On March 18, 1996, McGinty and her staff discussed creating a fake letter from the president to Bruce Babbitt. McGinty was in a hurry because she wanted to announce the new national monument in April, preferably as part of Earth Day celebrations. James Craig Crutchfield in the Office of Management and Budget drafted the letter and Linda Lance, CEQ Director for Land Management, edited it. Lance sent a cover e-mail with the letter to McGinty and six staffers, explaining:

> Attached is a letter to Babbit [*sic*] as we discussed yesterday that makes clear that the Utah monument action is one generated by the Executive Office of the President, not the agency.[237b]

Their phony letter began:

> Dear Secretary Babbitt,
> The President has asked that we contact you to request information within the expertise of your agency. As you know, the Congress currently is considering legislation that would remove significant portions of public lands in Utah from their current protection as wilderness study areas. Protection of these lands is one of the highest environmental priorities of the Clinton Administration.[237c]

Lance was not sure this was the best approach, and asked at the end of her cover e-mail, "Also, do we know whether the canyonlands and arches areas we're considering would be affected by the Utah wilderness bill."

McGinty told Lance this approach wouldn't work. Back to the drawing board. The next day Lance sent an e-mail to McGinty and four key staffers (reproduced here without editing or corrections):

> I completely agree that this can't be pitched as our answer to their utah bill. but i'm having trouble deciding where we go from

here. if we delink from utah but limit our request for info to utah, why? if we instead request info on all sites that might be covered by the antiquities act, we probably get much more than we're probably ready to act on, including some that might be more compelling than the utah parks? am i missing something or lacking in creativity? is there another utah hook? whatdya think?

I'm getting concerned that if we're going to do this we need to get this letter going tomorrow. almost everything else is pretty much ready to go to the president for decision, although some drafting of the formal documents like pres. memos still needs to be done.[238a]

The first fake letter didn't fly. The Justice Department wanted a broader presidential request to insure that Interior's administrative record would be sufficient to stand up in court if challenged, but Lance rejected the idea and wrote a new bogus letter, which she sent with the following e-mail:

Attached is a minimalist approach to the letter to Babbitt. Contrary to what justice may have suggested, I think it's important that he [the president] limit the inquiry to lands covered by the antiquities act, since that's the area in which he can act unilaterally. To make a broader request risks scaring people, and/or promising followup we can't deliver.

I realized the real remaining question is not so much what this letter says, but the political consequences of designating these lands as monuments when they're not threatened with losing wilderness status, and they're probably not the areas of the country most in need of this designation. Presidents have not used their monument designation authority in this way in the past—only for large dramatic parcels that are threatened. Do we risk a backlash from the bad guys if we do these—do they have the chance to suggest that this administration could use this authority all the time all over the country, and start to argue that the discretion is too broad?

I'd like to get your view, and political affairs, on this. Maybe I'm overreacting, but I think we need to consider that issue.[238b]

Lance's remarks were prescient, because once the monument was designated and the secrecy of its creation became known, Congress indeed argued that the president's national monument proclamation power was too broad, and the House passed a bill to rein it in.

McGinty had the timber rider to worry about and this Utah letter problem was depressing her. On March 25, she e-mailed her staff:

I'm increasingly of the view that we should just drop these Utah ideas. We do not really know how the enviros will react and I do think there is a danger of "abuse" of the withdraw/antiquities authorities especially because these lands are not really endangered.[238c]

The urgency of re-election overcame McGinty's serious doubts: she immediately agreed to let Linda Lance and another CEQ staffer, Tom Jensen, meet with Interior staff to iron things out. Only four days later she sent a memo to President Clinton recommending that he sign an attached letter to Babbitt (by this time it was the fourth draft).

There is no indication Clinton ever saw this memo.

Adding Escalante: The meeting of Lance and Jensen with Interior staff in the Secretary's conference room was productive. An e-mail reported:

> They discussed three new candidates for National Monument designation in Utah (Kiparowitz, Grand Gulch, and Escalante), each with pros and cons, and Interior agreed to review these options further. Interior/NPS complained that their park proposal was morphing into a Utah proposal, but Tom and Linda dismiss this complaint.[239]

The new areas were significant because they had long been advocated for protection by the Southern Utah Wilderness Alliance and its prescriptive foundation funders. However, the e-mail added:

> According to Linda Lance, the Parks Initiative is not currently on the President's schedule and no event is likely before the President's mid-April international trip. May/June is a more realistic timeframe. Interior may not be happy about this, but they created a false urgency by citing a pending Gingrich parks proposal. (It now appears that the only imminent Republican proposal is the Senate Omnibus lands bill, which is on hold because of Utah wilderness.)

Gold Mine Sweeper: The May/June date didn't materialize. Katie McGinty was deep in another controversy, this one involving Yellowstone National Park. In 1989, Crown Butte Mines, Inc. proposed to develop a Montana site known as the New World Mine near Yellowstone Park. Grant-driven green groups denounced the project as a threat to the Yellowstone ecosystem, even though the mine was two miles downstream from the nearest park boundary.

To prevent the mine's development, Superintendent of Yellowstone National Park Michael Finley had worked with fourteen environmental groups and invited the United Nations World Heritage Committee to investigate the threat posed to Yellowstone by the proposed Crown Butte mine.

The UN team recommended a huge buffer zone around the park and on December 5, 1995, placed Yellowstone on its list of sites "in danger" though even the Draft Environmental Impact Statement had not yet been completed.[240a]

Bruce Babbitt touted the designation as merely an attention-getting gesture to stop the mine, but Congress wondered how such administration moves affected U.S. sovereignty, particularly the power of congressional oversight. The House passed a bill to control such United Nations designations on United States property.[240b]

Katie McGinty went behind the scenes brokering a complex deal to stop the New World Mine, trying to get Crown Butte executives to agree to a land swap in return for its rights to an estimated $650 million in gold. The company would get federal land worth $65 million, but Crown Butte would agree to set aside $22.5 million to clean up water pollution problems at the mine site, almost all of which was private property not subject to the mining law.

The company had invested about $37 million in exploration, permits and engineering, but the foundation-funded Greater Yellowstone Coalition had kept the project on hold for six years.

And Bruce Babbitt kept complaining about the "antiquated" Mining Act of 1872 that allowed big corporations to claim federal land for only $5 an acre, never explaining all the later general mining laws that made such cheap land such an expensive investment.

McGinty was hoping for an agreement that could be announced during the president's vacation in August.

Back to the Fake Letters: The Utah project heated up again in mid-July, when it looked like the opportunity for a presidential "event" to announce the national monument would be coming soon. Tom Jensen wrote yet another draft of the fake Babbitt letter and sent it with the following e-mail to fellow CEQ staffer Peter G. Umhofer on July 23:

> Peter, I need your help.
> The following text needs to be transformed into a singed [sic] POTUS [President of the United States] letter ASAP. The letter does not need to be sent, it could be held in an appropriate office (Katie's? Todd Stern's?) but it must be prepared and signed ASAP.
> You should discuss the processing of the letter with Katie, given its sensitivity.[240c]

The rewrite of the fake letter was by this time merely a matter of changing tiny details for the paper trail. Jensen also supplied a cover letter for Katie McGinty to send to the POTUS recommending that he sign the attached Babbitt letter. McGinty was pleased with the result.

Three days later, Interior Solicitor John Leshy sent a memo to Charles Wilkinson, a University of Colorado professor enlisted to write the legal proclamation establishing the monument. It warned him any public release of information could prevent the monument from being formed.[241a]

Both Interior and CEQ had assurances that the White House would approve an announcement soon. Feeling the time pressure, McGinty e-mailed the following to CEQ staffer Todd Stern on July 29:

> The president will do the Utah event on Aug 17. However, we still need to get the letter signed ASAP. The reason: under the antiquities act, we need to build a credible record that will withstand legal challenge that: (1) the president asked the secy to look into these lands to see if they are of important scientific, cultural or historic value; (2) the secy undertook that review and presented the results to the president; (3) the president found the review compelling and therefore exercised his authority under the antiquities act. presidential actions under this act have always been challenged. they have never been struck down, however.
>
> So, letter needs to be signed ASAP so that secy has what looks like a credible amount of time to do his investigation of the matter. we have opened the letter with a sentence that gives us some more room by making clear that the president and babbitt had discussed this some time ago.[241b]

That August 17 date didn't work, but this time the Office of the President got the Babbitt letter and White House Chief of Staff Leon Panetta responded to it—but he knew nothing about it and needed to be briefed. Katie McGinty e-mailed Marcia Hale, staffer at the White House:

> Leon Panetta asked that I prepare talking points for you to use in making calls to certain western elected officials regarding the proposed Utah event.
>
> My notes indicate that Leon wanted you to call Governor Roy Romer, Governor Bob Miller, former Governor Mike Sullivan, former Governor Ted Schwinden, Senator Harry Reid, Senator Richard Bryan, and Representative Bill Richardson to test the waters and gather their reactions.
>
> The reactions to these calls, and other factors, will help determine whether the proposed action occur. If a final decision has been made on the event, and any public release of the information would probably foreclose the President's option to proceed.[241c]

Polling these Democrat politicals—none from Utah—and "other factors" (which included Southern Utah Wilderness Alliance, the Sierra Club, and select foundation funders) got positive responses.

POTUS Clinton signed the fake Babbitt letter on August 7, evidently no more aware of its deceptive history than Panetta had been.

Clinton's attention was on his vacation to Yellowstone National Park. McGinty had finished the negotiations with Crown Butte. On August 12 he announced to the nation—while the Republicans were nominating Bob Dole as their presidential candidate in San Diego—that his administration had just "saved" a national park with a land trade.

Clinton told the audience of dignitaries and celebrities including the late John Denver: "The agreement that has been reached with Crown Butte to terminate this project altogether proves that everyone can agree that Yellowstone is more precious than gold."

At the end of his speech, Clinton had Katie McGinty sign the agreement with Crown Butte executives to the applause of all.[242]

The day after the Yellowstone announcement, Clinton asked McGinty for information about the proposed Utah announcement "event."

On August 14, 1996, the day before the now-unnecessary Warner Creek protesters would be arrested, and three months before the presidential election, Katie McGinty wrote to President Clinton:

PURPOSE OF THE UTAH EVENT
The political purpose of the Utah event is to show distinctly your willingness to use the office of the President to protect the environment. In contrast to the Yellowstone ceremony, this would not be a "feel-good" event. You would not merely be rebuffing someone else's bad idea, you would be placing your own stamp, sending your own message. It is our considered assessment that an action of this type and scale would help to overcome the negative views toward the Administration created by the timber rider. Designation of the new monument would create a compelling reason for persons who are now disaffected to come around and enthusiastically support the Administration.

Establishment of the new monument will be popular nationally in the same way and for the same reasons that other actions to protect parks and public lands are popular. The nationwide editorial attacks on the Utah delegation's efforts to strip wilderness protection from these and other lands is a revealing recent test of public interest in Utah's wild lands. In addition, the new monument will have particular appeal in those areas that contribute most visitation to the parks and public lands of southern Utah, namely, coastal California, Oregon, and Washington, southern Nevada, the Front Range communities of Colorado, the Taos-Albuquerque corridor, and the Phoenix-Tucson area. This assessment squares with the positive reactions by Sen. Reid, Gov. Romer, and Rep. Richardson when asked their views on the proposal.

Opposition to the designation will come from some of the same parties who have generally opposed the Administration's natural resource and environmental policies and who, in candor, are unlikely to support the Administration under any circumstances. It would draw fire from interests who would characterize it as anti-mining, and heavy-handed Federal interference in the West. Gov. Miller's concern that Nevada's sagebrush rebels would not approve of the new monument is almost certainly correct, and echoes the concerns of other friends, but can be offset by the positive response in other constituencies.[243a]

Ken Rait of the Southern Utah Wilderness Alliance was in Washington while McGinty prepared this memo for Clinton. He says he knew nothing of it.

Lies: Three weeks later, in a time-honored ritual common to the Washington scene, the Utah monument plan was leaked to the press, in this case to Tom Kenworthy of the Washington Post. McGinty notified the White House and her staff on Friday, September 6:

We learned late today that the Washington Post is going to run a story this weekend reporting that the administration is considering a national monument designation. I understand that there are no quotes in the story, so it is based only on "the word about town." I have called several members of Congress to give them notice of this story and am working with political affairs to determine if there are Democratic candidates we should alert. We are neither confirming nor denying the story; just making sure that Democrats are not surprised.[243b]

Stunned disbelief was the immediate response by members of Utah's congressional delegation and Utah's Republican governor, Michael Leavitt. None had an inkling that the president was even thinking about establishing an almost 2,700-square-mile preserve in the red-rock wild lands of south-central Utah.[243c]

Environmentalists and the Washington Post knew all about it. Post reporter Tom Kenworthy sent the following e-mail to CEQ staffer Brian Johnson after writing the leaked story, asking for more leaks:

Brian: So when pressed by Mark Udall and Maggie Fox on the Utah monument at yesterday's private ceremony for [Arizona Representative] Mo [Udall], Clinton said: "You don't know when to take yes for an answer." Sounds to me like it's going forward. I also hear [Colorado Governor] Romer is pushing the president to announce it when he's in Colorado on Wednesday. Give me a heads up if its imminent—I can't write another story saying it's likely to happen, but it would be nice to know when it's going to happen for planning purposes—Tom Kenworthy.

ps—thanks for the packet.[244a]

Local governments in Utah went crazy with their congressional delegation, which scurried to find out what was going on, especially Representative Bill Orton, the only Democrat. He was sure this was going to cost him his seat in the coming election (it did). Nobody could learn anything.

Governor Leavitt got the story by fax on Sunday, the day after it appeared on page 3A of the Washington Post. On Monday he called Bruce Babbitt asking about the monument plan. "I don't know," said Babbitt. "Call the White House, that's their thing." Leavitt called the White House. At first they said it was a mistake, but said they'd get back to him.

It was Wednesday before a staffer returned his call. "Yes," was the message. "There's a serious proposal, but no decision."

Leavitt asked: "What's the timing?"

The staffer waffled. Bad sign. "It sounds like a policy decision's been made," Leavitt told the staffer. "I need to come to Washington to see Panetta, or the president."

While Leavitt was getting nothing from this staffer, Tom Kenworthy of the Washington Post e-mailed Brian Johnson of Katie McGinty's staff this short, cheerful message:

south rim of the grand canyon, sept 18—be there or be square[244b]

Leavitt got a White House appointment for the next Tuesday and flew to Washington the Sunday before. On Monday, Ken Rait of Southern Utah Wilderness Alliance told the governor that there would be an event at the Grand Canyon.[244c]

Rait later said he couldn't remember conveying the message.

The governor does remember.

The Tuesday White House meeting brought out Leon Panetta and Katie McGinty. For half an hour Leavitt, with state planner Brad Barber assisting, explained his own plan for the region, years in preparation, and begged them to hold off, saying that he needed to talk to the president.[244d]

The Deseret News published the following account of what happened next from an interview with Leavitt:

[Panetta] says "don't be too harsh on the president because there's still time for your input."

Panetta tells Leavitt, "You made a very compelling case," adding that Rep. Bill Orton, D-Utah, has also made a strong argument against the proposal.

"It is clear to me that Bill has put in some licks," Leavitt says.

"I said, 'If this is compelling, then the president of the United States needs to know that he is setting aside a part of my state that is equal in size to Rhode Island, Delaware and Washington, D.C., put together.'"

Leavitt is exaggerating but only by a few thousand acres. Panetta's eyes widen.

"He was very surprised," says Leavitt, who, with Panetta, pores over a map of the area, color-coded to show private, state and federal lands.

"What are these little blue squares?" wonders Panetta, pointing out the dozens of sections of state trust lands that would be claimed by the monument.

I said, "I need to talk to the president . . . and (Panetta) says, "Stay by the phone."[245a]

The president was off campaigning in Illinois and hard to reach. Leavitt stayed near the phone. At midnight in his hotel room, Leavitt gave up and turned in.

At 2:00 a.m. his phone rang.

"Governor, the president of the United States."

They talked for half an hour. Leavitt realized the monument would happen no matter what he did. So he offered to draft a memo recommending a commission of state and local government officials to set boundaries and to solve a number of management questions.

Clinton said, "Go ahead."

U.S. News and World Report reported that both Leon Panetta and senior presidential adviser George Stephanopolous expressed strong doubts to McGinty.

This could cost Orton his congressional seat, Panetta fumed, angry that his former House colleague and fellow Democrat had been kept out of the information loop by a "sneaky" McGinty. Panetta said he'd recommend that the president not go through with the plan. Stephanopoulos concurred. McGinty flared and threatened to quit, yelling that it was the right thing to do and too late to stop it now.[245b]

McGinty later said the story was not at all true. U.S. News stands by its story.

On September 18, Bill Clinton flew to the South Rim of the Grand Canyon and announced the creation of the Grand Staircase-Escalante National Monument to an audience of hundreds of environmentalists and celebrities including Robert Redford who knew where to be and when.

The administration had to honor decade-old mining leases to the Dutch firm Andalex Resources Inc., but said it had the authority to deny ancillary permits the firm would need to build roads on federal lands to get the mined coal out.

Utah Senator Orrin Hatch called it "the mother of all land-grabs."

The House Resources Committee began a congressional investigation of the secrecy and lies behind the new national monument. They asked for documents. They waited six months. Chairman Don Young obtained subpoena power and sent federal marshals to the White House at midnight to get the memos you have read in this account.[246a]

Katie McGinty handled all environmental issues much the same way. When she departed the CEQ in November 1998, her list of achievements was long.

The trail of human despair she left in rural America was longer.

BOUNTY HUNTER BUREAUCRATS

Let's say that you're an advocate for corporate reform. Let's say you pay two federal bureaucrats $350,000 each for whistleblowing on Mobil Oil Company for underpaying royalties. Then you must be the Washington, D.C.-based Project on Government Oversight, Inc. (POGO).

A nonprofit watchdog group, POGO awarded the money to Robert L. Berman, senior economist at the Interior Department's office of policy analysis, and Robert A. Speir, an Energy Department official, as part of a $45 million settlement against Mobil. POGO received $1.2 million from the settlement and split $700,000 between the two officials for their "public service."[246b]

Danielle Brian, POGO's executive director, began looking at royalty payments in 1994 and filed a lawsuit under the False Claims Act in 1997, charging oil companies were ripping off taxpayers by underpaying federal royalties in California by an amount that may have exceeded $250 million. Congressional investigators suspected that the payments by POGO may have been intended to influence regulations tightening royalty policies.

In a sworn deposition in August 1998, Brian said POGO did not pay whistleblowers and provided only moral, not financial, support. However, when it was learned in April 1999 that the two employees had been given the money in the fall of 1998, POGO issued a press release saying the cash had been given for their work as whistleblowers.

Berman and Speir had been trying to fix royalty abuse for more than a decade, POGO said. "We felt their role was equally as important as ours and that they should be rewarded for the courageous stands they took," said Beth Daley, POGO's spokeswoman.

The Justice Department launched a criminal investigation into the payments. POGO's Daley, as well as Berman and Speir, insists there was no wrongdoing involved.

Poe Leggette, a Washington lawyer who represents oil and gas producers, said, "These two employees were either working for the public or working for POGO. If they were working for the public, then it was clearly improper for POGO to pay them a so-called 'award.' If they were working for POGO, the Justice Department might be examining whether there was a bribe."[247a]

House Resources Committee Chairman Don Young (R-Alaska) wanted cash payments to federal whistleblowers stopped. "We have a duty to ensure that laws we enact are faithfully executed and that no federal employee is free to sell his services to the highest bidder," he said.

POGO's website states: "Our mission is to investigate, expose, and remedy abuses of power, mismanagement, and government subservience to special interests by the federal government."[247b]

POGO reported a 1997 income of $305,673 and assets of $110,592.

Sample Foundation grants to the Project on Government Oversight:
1992 **W. Alton Jones Foundation** $35,000 To monitor cleanup activities of Department of Defense and Department of Energy military contractors and to publicize abuses.
1993 **W. Alton Jones Foundation** $35,000 To monitor U.S. Departments of Energy and Defense on their implementation of environmental programs and use of environmental restoration funds.
1993 **The Scherman Foundation** $20,000 For general support.
1993 **Town Creek Foundation** $10,000 Purpose not specified.
1994 **Richard and Rhoda Goldman Fund** $20,000 For general support.
1994 **The Educational Foundation of America** $30,000 For program, Illegal Burning of Toxic and Hazardous Substances at Air Force Base Area 51 in Nevada.
1995 **The Scherman Foundation** $10,000 For general support.
1996 **The Scherman Foundation** $20,000 For continuing support, general support.

The POGO case also raises the question: when foundations write highly specific grants, are they legally responsible for the recipient's actions?

An important question for public policy

SERVING IDEOLOGY

Two environmental groups, Forest Service Employees for Environmental Ethics and Public Employees for Environmental Responsibility (PEER), consist of federal bureaucrats with the goal of changing federal policy from within to promote "biological diversity," which, as we shall see, has the inevitable consequence of placing human use of the earth, particularly federally owned earth, last after everything else.

Nobody elected them to do that.

Both groups were started by Jeff DeBonis, a former timber sale planner with the U.S. Forest Service. He left federal employment to form the Oregon-based Association of Forest Service Employees for Environmental Ethics (AFSEEE) in 1989. AFSEEE quickly became a whistleblower protection and media contact group similar to POGO. AFSEEE is heavily grant-driven (See funding history charts following two pages).

DeBonis departed AFSEEE to start Public Employees for Environmental Responsibility (PEER) in 1993, a new group doing the same thing with bureaucrats in the Bureau of Land Management, Bureau of Reclamation and other agencies. PEER's 1997 income was $569,449 with assets of $121,358.

Both groups received $100,000 startup grants from W. Alton Jones Foundation and major funding from the familiar cluster of usual suspects in the Environmental Grantmakers Association: Donald Ross's Rockefeller Family Fund, and other names we have seen many times, including Bullitt, Cummings, Pew, Surdna, Schumann, and Turner.

Both green groups promote rural cleansing and the eradication of the resource class.

AFSEEE dropped the "Association" after DeBonis left and is now known as Forest Service Employees for Environmental Ethics (FSEEE). Former Sierra Club Legal Defense Fund attorney Andy Stahl took over as executive director.

The Encyclopedia of Associations shows AFSEEE as a for-profit organization at its startup, but foundation funding came anyway, and the group received its IRS tax-exemption ruling in October 1995.

The group's literature says that it "Works to create a responsible value system for the Forest Service based on a land ethic which ensures ecologically and economically sustainable resource management. Seeks to revise and replace the Forest Service's present practice of

ASSOCIATION OF FOREST SERVICE EMPLOYEES FOR ENVIRONMENTAL ETHICS SAMPLE FUNDING HISTORY

YEAR	AMOUNT	FOUNDATION	PURPOSE OF GRANT
1990	$100,000	W. Alton Jones Foundation	**To** foster new, sustainable management vision among U.S. Forest Service workers
	$15,000	Rockefeller Family Fund	**For** seed money for new national organization, which challenges U.S. Forest Service to adopt resource management policy that will protect national forests
	$20,000	Nathan Cummings Foundation	**For** start-up costs for federation of professional foresters working for responsible national timber policy
	$10,000	Beldon Fund	**For** seed funding for new organization which promotes ecologically and economically sustainable policies within Forest Service
1991	$25,000	Rockefeller Family Fund	**For** organizing campaign among Forest Service employees to influence resource management policies, and to protect free speech rights of whistleblowers
	$20,000	Nathan Cummings Foundation	**For** government employees working towards more ecologically sensitive U.S. Forest Service
	$29,200	Columbia Foundation	**For** public education and outreach program that works to reform U.S. Forest Service so that it will preserve old growth forests on public lands and will adopt management practices that give priority to environmental preservation and sustainable forestry practices
1992	$100,000	W. Alton Jones Foundation	**For** general support
	$15,000	HKH Foundation	**Unspecified**
	$40,000	Nathan Cummings Foundation	**For** general operating support and **For** employees working to develop more ecologically sensitive U.S. Forest Service
	$25,000	Mary Reynolds Babcock Foundation	**For** chapter organizing and development in southeast U.S.
	$20,000	Ruth Mott Fund	**For** second-year program support
	$10,000	Town Creek Fndtn.	**Continuing** support
	$40,000	Bullitt Foundation	**To** expand work in Pacific Northwest
	$150,000	Pew Charitable Trusts	**To** encourage sustainable forestry within National Forests System by providing better support to agency personnel committed to forest protection and by establishing monitoring system to encourage good stewardship

YEAR	AMOUNT	FOUNDATION	PURPOSE OF GRANT
ASSOCIATION OF FOREST SERVICE EMPLOYEES FOR ENVIRONMENTAL ETHICS SAMPLE FUNDING HISTORY			

ASSOCIATION OF FOREST SERVICE EMPLOYEES FOR ENVIRONMENTAL ETHICS SAMPLE FUNDING HISTORY

YEAR	AMOUNT	FOUNDATION	PURPOSE OF GRANT
1993	$30,000	Mary Reynolds Babcock Foundation	**For** chapter organizing and monitoring teams in southeast U.S. to combine public education, chapter development and forest-monitoring teams to locate and publicize poorly managed sites, thus pressuring Forest Service to clean up sites and prevent further degradation
	$10,000	Town Creek Foundation	**Continuing** support
	$20,000	Turner Foundation	**Forest** projects
1994	$80,000	W. Alton Jones Foundation	**To** develop environmental impact assessment of U.S. Forest Service management practices on eastern slope of Cascade Mountains
	$50,000	Mary Reynolds Babcock Foundation	**For** Southeast organizing and monitoring project
	$45,000	Bullitt Foundation	**To** use expertise of U.S. Forest Service employees to draft legally and biologically defensible forest plan for Eastside forest and to evaluate current forest plans of each national forest in western Montana and Idaho
	$100,000	Educational Foundation of America	**For** Protecting Integrity and Ethics Program
	$15,000	Wallace Genetic Foundation	**Unspecified**
	$25,000	Turner Foundation	**Forest** projects
1995	$30,000	Compton Foundation	**For** Ecosystem Management Project
1996	$50,000	W. Alton Jones Foundation	**To** improve United States Forest Service environmental policies and to support employees who challenge unsustainable forest practices in Pacific Northwest
	$30,000	Bullitt Foundation	**For** Cedar Films to produce videos for forest managers and general public, that focus on Siuslaw National Forest
	$60,000	Pew Charitable Trusts	**For** matching grant for preparation of two conservation alternatives to official forest management plans
	$100,000	William & Flora Hewlett Foundation	**For** Conflict Resolution and Security Training Program, Green Grazing Program
	$60,000	Pew Charitable Trusts	**For** matching grant for preparation of two conservation alternatives to official forest management plans

encouraging overuse of public land by timber companies, mining firms, and cattle owners with a more ecological system of resource management. Acts as a support system for Forest Service employees who do not agree with the Service's present land management ethics."

Translation: FSEEE bureaucrats are subverting congressional policy to conform with their ideology of ending resource use of government lands, paid for by foundation money.

In early 1999, grant-driven FSEEE's director Andy Stahl discovered a method to send e-mail messages to 27,000 Forest Service employees, asking them to sign on to a letter urging President Clinton and Vice President Gore to shut down forest roads in rural America for environmental reasons. He got tremendous response from hundreds of low- and mid-level bureaucrats who signed his letter.

When rural industry defenders asked for the same e-mail privilege, Forest Service Chief Mike Dombeck changed policy and none of the more than forty pro-resource groups that asked for the same access got it.

Stahl gloated over his shut-out. "It's called democracy," he said. "Communication should be free and open."[251]

Evidently some communications are more free and open than others.

PEER says of itself: "Public Employees for Environmental Responsibility is a private, nonprofit organization that provides uniquely valuable services to government employees charged with safeguarding the nation's natural resources.

"Agency employees—scientists, land managers, law officers, and others—are on the cutting edge of natural resource protection. PEER believes they represent our nation's most effective line of defense against abuse of public lands, wildlife mismanagement and threats to human health.

"Rather than work on environmental issues from the outside, PEER works with and on behalf of these resource professionals to effect fundamental change in the way their agencies conduct the public's business. Above all, PEER promotes environmental ethics and government accountability."

PEER, like FSEEE, is heavily grant-driven (see chart on following page).

PEER also spends its time and foundation money smearing the wise use movement. One of its most bizarre campaigns was launched at a May 1995 news conference in Washington attempting to link wise use leaders with the bombing of the Oklahoma City Federal Building (!).

PEER's Jeff DeBonis hired a room in the National Press Building, sitting at the microphones with Jim Baca, the fired former BLM

PUBLIC EMPLOYEES FOR ENVIRONMENTAL RESPONSIBILITY SAMPLE FUNDING HISTORY

YEAR	AMOUNT	FOUNDATION	PURPOSE OF GRANT
1993	$100,000	W. Alton Jones Foundation	To analyze Bureau of Land Management's forest management practices and encourage reform.
	$40,000	Florence & John Schumann Foundation	To recruit, organize and support civil servants committed to upholding public trust through responsible management of nation's environment and natural resources
	$10,000	Compton Fndtn.	Unspecified
	$25,000	Bullitt Foundation	For program support
	$40,000	Educational Foundation of America	For environmental expose of Bureau of Land Management's Western Forest Management
1994	$20,000	Bullitt Foundation	For investigation and assessment of Bureau of Land Management's forestry management program based on information from agency's employees and on-site verifications
	$40,000	Surdna Foundation	For general support for new organization which empowers federal and state environmental employees to press for sound, science-based environmental and natural resource management
	$25,000	Turner Foundation	Unspecified
	$10,000	Compton Fndtn.	Unspecified
1995	$100,000	Florence & John Schumann Foundation	To support public employees committed to environmental quality and government accountability
	$15,000	Beldon II Fund	For general support
	$15,000	Richard & Rhoda Goldman Fund	For BLM Forestry Project, investigation into BLM's forestry practices
	$10,000	Foundation for Deep Ecology	For general support
	$25,000	Turner Foundation	Unspecified
	$50,000	Charles Stewart Mott Foundation	For support
1996	$100,000	Florence & John Schumann Fndtn.	To encourage environmental quality and government accountability
	$75,000	W. Alton Jones Foundation	To document incidents of violence and harassment against public employees of environmental agencies and pursue legal solutions
	$45,000	Jessie Smith Noyes Foundation	For project with Citizens Coal Council
	$10,000	Bullitt Foundation	For public lands forestry project
	$35,000	Turner Foundation	Unspecified

director, and David Helvarg, a Sierra Club writer whose book *The War Against the Greens* claimed the wise use movement was responsible for crimes against environmentalists, but neglected to mention any prosecutions or convictions. The PEER news conference was organized by David Fenton of Fenton Communications, who we met in Chapter Two.

At the news conference, DeBonis called for congressional hearings on violence by the wise use movement. The link to the Oklahoma City federal building bombing was a connect-the-dots exercise in which the Michigan Property Rights Association had monthly meetings that James Nichols, a militia supporter at that time being held as a material witness in the Oklahoma City bombing, had once attended.[253a]

Therefore, DeBonis implied, anything bad that happened to a federal employee was the fault of the wise use movement.

Fenton Communications had arranged for California Democrat Representative George Miller, ranking minority member of the House Resources Committee, to deliver a similar message and call for similar hearings, letting some time elapse in order to give the media story continuity and momentum.[253b]

Miller staged a news conference a week later (on the Capitol steps, for added drama) calling for congressional hearings "to assess risks to employees and the public."

Justice Department spokesman Jim Sweeney dismissed claims of wise use linkage as "speculation." The FBI found nothing.

Miller's hearings were never held for lack of evidence.

The "link" between the wise use movement and the Oklahoma City bombing, DeBonis and crew alleged, was the militias.

Baca admitted there was no proof of a link between militia groups, the wise-use movement, and anti-government violence, "other than that there's an atmosphere of militancy and a lot of common threads in their beliefs."

Baca asserted that the militia movement focuses on protecting citizens' rights to carry guns, while the wise-use movement is concerned with overturning environmental regulations that limit economic uses of private and public lands.

Such mischaracterizations were essential to the smear campaign.

But why were guns brought up?

The only reason that makes political sense is that the Clinton / Gore gun control agenda was going through Congress at the time. Activists and foundations wanted to do every thing they could to make guns and gun owners unpopular.

But what do foundations have to do with the gun control agenda?

FUNDING GUN CONTROL

The Washington Post reported in a 1999 story, "Some of the nation's leading private foundations and philanthropists such as billionaire George Soros are pouring millions of dollars into research and support in the battle to control gun violence."[254]

Soros's Open Society Institute was the first private group to directly help finance a lawsuit against a firearms manufacturer. It contributed $300,000 to plaintiffs in a successful Brooklyn, New York, case.

Elisa Barnes, a plaintiffs' attorney in the case, said Soros's contribution "made all the difference in the world" in winning the verdict, which held nine gunmakers liable for practices that allowed criminals to obtain guns.

Soros built his wealth on foreign currency exchange dealings. He established the Center on Crime, Communities and Culture in 1996 to fund crime prevention programs. It has since dispensed more than $13 million.

The 1999 Littleton, Colorado, high school massacre occurred just as representatives of thirty private foundations were at the Council on Foundations annual meeting in New Orleans discussing anti-gun efforts. Nancy Mahon, who directs Soros's New York-based Center on Crime, Communities and Culture, said the shootings made the funders "all the more determined to make a difference."

Increasingly, foundations are coordinating their anti-gun efforts as they do their environmental issues. Mahon's center helped organize the Funders Collaborative for Gun Violence Prevention, a consortium that raised $11 million in seed money. "The strategy is to show leadership from the philanthropies and say this is an important issue for our country," said Mahon.

The Funders Collaborative works to treat guns as any other consumer product and thus subject them to similar regulations and liability laws. The campaign is showing effects. Encouraged by successful lawsuits against the tobacco industry, numerous cities have adopted a similar strategy against gun manufacturers, trying to force the firearms industry to pay the costs of both accidental and criminal shootings.

Chicago's Joyce Foundation, a member of the Environmental Grantmakers Association, was the first to target guns as a "health" issue. It has handed out $13.2 million in 82 grants to 55 organizations working on gun issues since 1992. The foundation was endowed by heiress Beatrice Joyce Kean, who died in 1971. The Joyce family's wealth, like the Bullitt foundation's, originally came from the timber industry.

Joyce funds the Environmental Defense Fund, The Tides Foundation - Environmental Working Group (which works closely with FSEEE and PEER), and Sierra Club Legal Defense Fund, among many others.

"We need to see guns as a public health issue," said Deborah Leff, the foundation's former president who created its gun control program. "Nobody wants to see children being shot."

Playing the children's card always works.

SAMPLE JOYCE FOUNDATION ANTI-GUN GRANTS

1992 Childrens Defense Fund, DC, $10,000 For planning process to implement range of strategies against guns and violence.

1993 American Bar Association. Fund for Justice and Education, DC, $25,000 To organize national conference on guns and violence and to develop proposals for controlling firearm violence.

1993 Center for Teaching Peace, DC, $10,000 For Alternatives to Violence program in East Saint Louis, IL.

1993 Childrens Memorial Foundation, Chicago, IL, $58,865 To establish and hold first national conference of Handgun Epidemic Lowering Plan (HELP) network, group of public health professionals concerned about gun violence.

1993 Harvard University. School of Public Health, Cambridge, MA, $375,000 To establish Harvard Project on Guns, Violence and Public Health to reposition gun violence as public health issue and promote public discussion of strategies to reduce gun violence.

1994 Violence Policy Center, DC, $130,000 For general support of work on gun violence policy, analysis and education.

1995 Physicians for Social Responsibility, DC, $40,000 Toward launching national gun violence prevention program.

1995 National Opinion Research Center, Chicago, IL, $121,189 To conduct, analyze and disseminate results of nationwide survey of public attitudes on gun violence issues.

1995 NAACP Legal Defense and Educational Fund, NYC, NY, $25,000 To develop strategy for participation in effort to prevent gun violence/

1995 Michigan Trauma Coalition, East Lansing, MI, $414,858 For general support for Michigan Partnership to Prevent Gun Violence, effort to unite practitioners in medicine, law and public health to reduce gun violence.

1995 Foundation for National Progress, San Francisco, CA, $30,000 To expand coverage of gun violence in Mother Jones magazine.

1995 American College of Physicians, Philadelphia, PA, $91,807 To survey physicians and surgeons regarding experiences with and knowledge of gun violence issues and to disseminate findings among physicians and broader public.

1996 Violence Policy Center, DC, $200,000 To continue and expand research and public education activities focusing on gun violence as public health issue.

1996 Physicians for Social Responsibility, DC, $60,000 To expand Gun Violence Prevention Program, which enlists and trains physicians to help reframe gun violence as public health issue and to prevent gun injuries and deaths

1996 National Opinion Research Center (NORC), Chicago, IL, $145,237 To conduct and analyze national public opinion poll on gun policy issues.

1996 Minnesota Institute of Public Health, Anoka, MN, $158,700 To launch statewide initiative to reduce and prevent gun violence in Minnesota and to create state firearms injury reporting system.

1996 Johns Hopkins University. School of Hygiene and Public Health, Baltimore, MD, $620,000 For general support for Johns Hopkins Center for Gun Policy and Research.

1996 Harvard University, Cambridge, MA, $400,000 For continued support and expansion of Squash It campaign to prevent youth violence at School of Public Health in Boston.

1996 Community Media Workshop, Chicago, IL, $20,000 To inform journalists covering 1996 Democratic National Convention in Chicago about promising Chicago efforts on variety of urban issues, including school reform, welfare reform, employment, gun violence and the arts.

1996 Boston University. School of Public Health, Boston, MA, $300,000 To develop and maintain gun violence prevention World Wide Web site.

1996 American Academy of Pediatrics, Elk Grove Village, IL, $80,000 To train pediatricians from around country in skills that would enable them to return to their home districts and mobilize pediatricians there around firearms injury prevention counseling and advocacy.

1997 Public Policy Forum. Researching Community Issues Project, Milwaukee, WI, $114,895 To build public awareness of gun violence issues in Wisconsin and to build consensus among public and policymakers to treat firearms as consumer products.

1997 Physicians for Social Responsibility, DC, $150,000 For gun violence prevention program which enlists and trains physicians to help reframe gun violence as public health issue by acting as spokespersons with policymakers, media and their patients.

1997 National Opinion Research Center (NORC), Chicago, IL, $176,406 For annual national survey of public attitudes on gun policy issues.

1997 Medical College of Wisconsin. Department of Emergency Medicine , Milwaukee, WI, $361,551 To establish Midwest Firearm Information Center and to augment its current firearm injury reporting system by adding newly available federal data.

1997 Illinois Council Against Handgun Violence, Chicago, IL, $250,000 For On Target Coalition, network of organizations working to reduce gun violence in Illinois.

1997 Duke University. Office of Research Support, Durham, NC, $317,733
To conduct and oversee research to produce accurate estimate of annual
cost of gunshot wounds in United States.

1997 Childrens Memorial Foundation, Chicago, IL, $200,000 For Handgun
Epidemic Lowering Plan (HELP) Network, national network of health
organizations and others committed to preventing gun violence through
public health approach.

1997 American Medical Association, Chicago, IL, $80,000 To produce, dis-
tribute to physicians, publicize and evaluate effect of guidebook on health
aspects of firearms.

1997 Violence Policy Center, DC, $221,000 To develop and coordinate media
strategy for national effort to reduce gun violence.

All these grants played directly to bureaucratic and congressional gun
control initiatives, either through specific pressure group tactics or through
media pressure. Even the feisty and supposedly independent magazine *Mother
Jones*, a staunch foe of hidden financial influence, had its own financial influence from the Joyce Foundation.

You never know where foundation influence is going to lead.

And that's the problem with wealthy foundations, grant-driven greens,
and zealous bureaucrats: their intersections are invisible, unpredictable and
overwhelming.

RUBIK'S BUREAUCRACY

Foundation influence on bureaucrats is like a Rubik's Cube with all
the little cubes not only able to rotate, but also able to magically change
color so you can never solve the puzzle.

Just when you think you have one layer of bureaucracy figured out,
you don't.

A new layer pops up and you're back to cube one.

And that takes us full circle back to the nation's worst urban-rural
prosperity gap of Chapter One, Washington State's Columbia River Basin, and the people we met in its northeastern quadrant towns of Omak
and Republic and Colville.

The layers of foundation-influenced bureaucracy that rural people
have to live with are so thick in the Columbia River Basin that attempts to draw them on a map baffle even cartographers, who draw
maps for a living.

They have the Forest Service and Bureau of Land Management
with timber and grazing regulations. They have the Bureau of Reclamation with water and irrigation regulations. They have the U.S. Fish

and Wildlife Service with Endangered Species Act regulations. And they have the Al Gore / Katie McGinty nightmare, the Interior Columbia Basin Ecosystem Management Project, a replay of the FEMAT process that was promised back in 1993 at the Forest Conference in Portland, Oregon.

All this on top of state Growth Management Act regulations, State Environmental Protection Act (SEPA) regulations, and many others.

The people in Omak and Republic and Colville have a hard time keeping up with all that while trying to make a living.

Recall, the Columbia Basin is half of Washington State. The poor half. The morally excluded half.

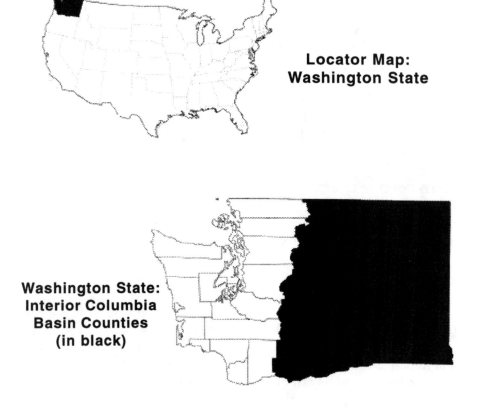

Locator Map:
Washington State

Washington State:
Interior Columbia
Basin Counties
(in black)

The State Employment Security Department can draw you an unemployment map so you can see at a glance the urban-rural prosperity gap. The populous urban Seattle-Tacoma metroplex counties—King, Pierce and Snohomish—have low unemployment numbers. Most Columbia River Basin counties don't.

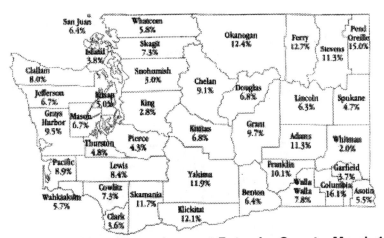

Washington State Unemployment Rates by County, March 1998
Washington State = 4.7% United States = 5.0% *Not seasonally adjusted*
—Source: State of Washington Employment Security Department, 1998

The state is 26.8% federally owned. The Forest Service manages most federal lands in the state.

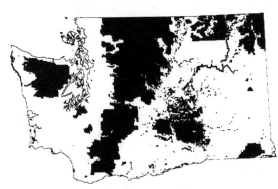

**COMPOSITE MAP:
ALL FEDERAL LANDS IN
WASHINGTON STATE
(IN BLACK)**

**NATIONAL FOREST
LANDS IN
WASHINGTON STATE
(IN BLACK)**

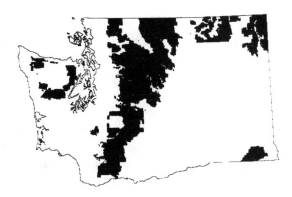

Then there's the Interior Columbia Basin Ecosystem Management Project. It's called ICBEMP for short. Locals pronounce that "Ick-Bump" or "Ice-Bump," depending on their mood. It is a monstrous 144 million-acre project covering parts of seven states, wrapped around nearly 75 million acres of federal land and 69 million acres of state, tribal, and private land.

—Based on ICBEMP, Upper Columbia River Basin DEIS, Vol 1., Ch. 5, p. 5.

I.C.B.E.M.P. OUTER BOUNDARY AND INNER WATERSHEDS
BLM and National Forest lands: 74,777,000 acres (52%); State and other Federal lands: 9,845,000 acres (6%); Tribal lands: 5,473,000 acres (4%); Private lands: 54,375,000 acres (38%); Totals: 144,480,000 acres (100%).

This grandiose planning area was demanded by the National Audubon Society in its March 23, 1993, action alert (p. 223) prior to the administration's Forest Conference. McGinty consulted with foundation leaders and green groups on the early concept. The lead national green group that shaped ICBEMP was the Wilderness Society, in concert with a regional lead group, Pacific Rivers Council, based in Eugene, Oregon.

It was the Pacific Rivers Council that promoted the watershed-based strategy you see reflected in the administration's map above. It is an administrative move to gain authority over rivers, touted as a "conservation strategy." This "strategy" was paid for by a number of **1993 grants** to Pacific Rivers: Pew Charitable Trusts $50,000; Surdna Foundation $30,000; W. Alton Jones Foundation $40,000; Bullitt Foundation $40,000; the James Irvine Foundation, $100,000; the William and Flora Hewlett Foundation $100,000; the Ford Foundation $100,000; the Ruth Mott Fund $15,000; **1994 grants**: Pew Charitable Trusts $150,000; Rockefeller Brothers Fund $60,000; and **1995 grants**: Northwest Area Foundation $348,000. Many more grants in the $10,000 to $20,000 range drove this strategy for capturing water and water rights away from the resource people of the Columbia Basin.

The Wilderness Society, as we have already seen (p. 177*ff*), was abundantly funded for "ancient forest" issues by the usual suspects, and acting as fiscal agent passing foundation money to smaller groups for specific projects. In addition, the Wilderness Society's Seattle office received $150,000 from the David and Lucille Packard Foundation "For Eastside Ecosystem Management Project in Interior Columbia River Basin" in 1995-96. The Washington, D.C. headquarters received $40,000 in 1996 from the Bullitt Foundation "To complete economic and ecological analysis of government's Interior Columbia Basin Ecosystem Management Project process, seek appropriate changes in final plan and train activists to monitor implementation of management plan that results." As ICBEMP developed, the Wilderness Society's tracks were clearly visible on the documents, as we shall see.

The administration had doubts about giving the power to shape ICBEMP to environmental groups—decision-making power, not merely advisory power—but really had no choice. The 1993 Forest Conference was intended to produce a plan that would break the gridlock of environmentalist lawsuits against timber sales, but only on the west side of the Cascade Mountains—in the "owl forests," as the White House called them.

Success for any plan that might come out of the conference required cooperation from environmental groups—particularly the Sierra Club Legal Defense Fund, the Wilderness Society, and the National Audubon Society, all plaintiffs or fiscal agents in key spotted owl lawsuits—to voluntarily release court injunctions they had won against a substantial number of timber sales. The administration had to offer them a quid pro quo. An Eastside plan for the interior forests was part of the price.

Al Gore and Katie McGinty had long embraced the conservation biology approach and dreamed of imposing it on the entire nation. They realized even a Democratic Congress was not likely to do that.

Conservation biology could be applied administratively in many places, but only in limited size. The Environmental Protection Agency, for example, was beginning to outline a number of "ecosystem demonstra-tion areas" in each of its ten regions, some of them, such as the San Francisco Bay/Delta Estuary Initiative, quite large.

But the interior of the Pacific Northwest offered real scope. The wa-tershed of the Columbia - Snake River system was immense. Powerful green groups and their foundation funders wanted an Eastside plan, and could be counted on to apply pressure for the most restrictive plan possible in the largest area possible.

Now the trick was to make it happen as quietly and effectively as possible, avoiding publicity and public outcry.

Easy: There would be no stand-alone executive order to establish the Eastside project. The order would be embedded in another document on another subject, like Congress does with amendments on an appropria-tions bill.

When the Clinton Forest Plan was released on July 1, 1993, it con-tained an "ICBEMP Rider."[262a]

Few noticed beyond the environmental groups and their foundation funders that helped put it there.

The Forest Plan contained two directives prompted by Katie McGinty: 1) "the Forest Service [is] to develop a scientifically sound and ecosys-tem-based strategy for management of eastside forests," and 2) the "strategy" should be based on a scientific study, the "Eastside Forest Ecosystem Health Assessment" completed just three months earlier by a team led by Forest Service scientist, Dr. Richard Everett.

The Forest Plan was signed by the president.

The "strategy" evolved into ICBEMP.

Everett had no advance notice that the White House would direct the agencies to base their strategy on his study. He never even met anyone from the White House. His study had been requested by Senator Mark Hatfield (R-Oregon) and Speaker of the House Tom Foley (D-Washing-ton) and ordered by the Agriculture Secretary and Forest Service in 1992. McGinty evidently regarded it as a windfall: it embodied the ecosystem management approach, it was fresh, and it sampled the appropriate area.

Late in 1993, Everett received notification that he had been ap-pointed science team leader for the Eastside Ecosystem Management Strategy, as it was known before it was renamed ICBEMP. Then Jack Ward Thomas was appointed Chief of the Forest Service.

When Thomas and Bureau of Land Management Director Jim Baca signed the charter of the Eastside Ecosystem Management Strategy on January 21, 1994, it said, "Thomas M. Quigley, Manager, Blue Moun-tains Natural Resources Institute, will be the Science Team Leader."[262b]

Quigley was an economist, not a natural resource specialist, and had never been a team leader. However, he and Thomas had been close colleagues for a long time. The boss gets to pick his (or her) team leaders.

Would ICBEMP have come out any differently had Everett done the job? Everett says he doesn't know, but, based on his earlier work, he would likely have used a smaller team than the 300 or more Quiqley hired, and would have spent less than the $40 million ICBEMP ultimately spent.

There might have been another consequence: it would have left land use decisions to the managers and political decision-makers. Also, the human impact of ICBEMP would have been much easier to see. As it was, the Draft Environmental Impact Statement of ICBEMP made it impossible to tell who got hurt and how much.

People like Charles McKetta of the University of Idaho, who tried to get the ICBEMP team to do a clear and clean socio-economic assessment, were excluded out of hand. The ICBEMP crew did everything in its power to obscure and confuse the question of who got hurt and how much.[263a]

Everett would not likely have done that. His loyalty is to science, not to Al Gore. He makes a crucial distinction between ecosystem management, which is what ICBEMP was supposed to do, and conservation biology, which is what ICBEMP actually did:

"Conservation biology," says Everett, "puts emphasis on biodiversity and its sustainability over time. It is concerned only with plant and animal habitat and does not consider human use of the land. Ecosystem management attempts to include the human population and its growth. Ecosystem management asks: What is biologically possible on the land? What are the human expectations of the land? And where is the intersection of those two?"[263b]

ICBEMP, unlike FEMAT, was not organized as a Federal Advisory Committee subject to open meeting laws. After learning from the successful court challenge to FEMAT, the administration chartered ICBEMP as a joint project of the Forest Service and BLM with agency line officers doing the work, thereby avoiding public scrutiny.

The people of Washington's northeastern tier of counties—Okanogan, Ferry, Stevens and Pend Oreille—present the Columbia Basin problem in microcosm.

Jackie Shiner of Republic, Washington—and chairman of the non-profit watchdog group, Upper Columbia Resource Council—says, "We've watched our lives turn into one day of anxiety after another since ICBEMP started. We've seen the aggressive nature of the Forest Service and the environmental groups that appear to be running it. The smaller rural communities have well-founded fears of being swallowed up by the federal government."[263c]

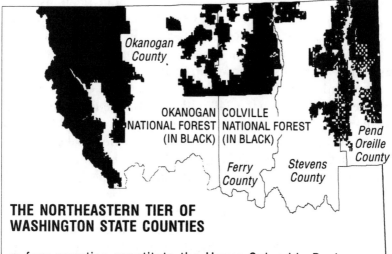

THE NORTHEASTERN TIER OF WASHINGTON STATE COUNTIES

- four counties constitute the Upper Columbia Basin
- two national forests of scattered lands divide at the Okanogan - Ferry county line
- checkerboard ownerships trap state and private land in federal forests

Bret Roberts, coordinator of the non-profit Ferry County Action League, says the Colville National Forest, which covers parts of Stevens, Pend Oreille, and Ferry counties (map above), is already imposing conservation biology on the ground, and has been since 1994, although no Environmental Impact Statement or Record of Decision has been approved.

Roberts notes the insider power of the Wilderness Society in drawing boundaries and making management decisions that the Forest Service appears to be adopting. The required Environmental Assessments for each of the smaller areas show Forest Service maps that copy Wilderness Society maps.[264a]

"It would appear that people in the executive branch of our government are allowing the Wilderness Society to exercise power in managing our national forests," said Roberts. "Not only is this wrong, but it also makes me ask myself, 'Have our government officials become pawns? Or are the environmental groups the pawns and they're just too stupid to see it?'"

"We kept seeing Wilderness Society maps at Forest Service public meetings. We kept seeing Wilderness Society land use recommendations becoming policy, especially about eliminating our roads. We had to object. So, in late 1998, 206 local people signed a petition to the District Ranger."[264b]

The petition requested: "Please send each petitioner Wilderness Society roadless area maps which were entered as part of the public record by the Forest Service at the Open House in Republic. How will their ideas be used and which environmental groups did the Forest Service work with in incorporating that data prior to the public input?"

The Forest Service never revealed the environmental group names.

All three Ferry County Commissioners requested that the Department of Agriculture's Inspector General, its top law enforcement officer, investigate the undue influence being exerted inside their national forest ranger districts by members of Forest Service Employees for Environmental Ethics (FSEEE) and Public Employees for Environmental Responsibility (PEER).

Commissioner Dennis Snook said, "The Inspector General declined to investigate in a letter to the commissioners. Before we made the letter public, PEER called us and angrily demanded to know why we had requested an investigation of insider access and undue influence of their members upon the Forest Service. Only we knew that the investigation had been requested."[265]

The irony of that phone call eluded the PEER officer.

The fact that such information leaked from the Agriculture Department's top cop to a private advocacy group speaks volumes.

What kind of insider access and undue influence had the Ferry County commissioners suspected?

The Forest Plan of the Colville National Forest has targets for producing goods and services. They've never been met.

They were supposed to offer 123.4 million board feet of timber for harvest. In 1997 they offered 59.1 million. Only 30.4 million board feet actually got harvested. They were supposed to pay the state $5 million. They paid $1.5 million.

Were these decisions influenced by Forest Service employees who were members of FSEEE or PEER?

A number of local Forest Service employees are well known members of FSEEE: Cindy Reichelt, Public Affairs Officer of Colville National Forest is FSEEE's Secretary/Treasurer, and her husband, Dennis Reichelt, Genetic Resources Specialist of Colville National Forest, is active with her.

Which FSEEE or PEER members have influence over resource decisions is something the government will neither investigate nor reveal.

The Wilderness Society and Pacific Rivers Council pressured for even lower national forest production targets. Al Gore and Katie McGinty made sure the Forest Service listened, and the numbers decline.

Al Gore and Katie McGinty were particularly intent upon destroying the mining industry, as we have seen in the Yellowstone and Grand Staircase-Escalante episodes. Around the time that ICBEMP was starting up, a confidential White House memo came to light showing the lengths to which they would go to stop any mine anywhere—even in Canada.[266a]

Dated May 14, 1993, only a month and a half after the big Forest Conference, Katie McGinty wrote to six cabinet-level officers about plans to stop the proposed $5 billion Windy Craggy copper mine in British Columbia's Tatshenshini River valley. She asserted that "both the President and Vice President have expressed great interest" in the Tatshenshini and convincing the British Columbia cabinet to ban mining there by offering to incorporate the region into a "protected zone" with "US lands such as glacier Bay National Park and the Tongass National Forest."

"The President," McGinty wrote, "would like to make an announcement on this with Prime Minister [Brian] Mulroney when he visits on June 1."

McGinty told the cabinet officers "to designate someone to attend a brief meeting on Monday, May 17, a 1:00 in room 360 at the Old Executive Office Building to develop a substantive and strategic plan of action. I would like to receive a draft of the plan by c.o.b. [close of business] Wednesday, May 19."

McGinty mentioned that "an interagency working group on Windy Craggy has been meeting since last year."

That working group was part of the transition team before Clinton's inauguration. In December of 1992, Al Gore had used a decision by the United Nations to designate Alaska's Glacier Bay National Park a World Heritage site as a platform to announce that he didn't want the Windy Craggy mine to go ahead. Canadian officials were not amused.[266b]

Thomas Cassidy, general counsel for American Rivers, the lead green group working on the Tatshenshini issue, proclaimed the mine dead. "Our view is that this new designation should end all consideration of the proposed Windy Craggy mine."

American Rivers at the time was being funded by W. Alton Jones Foundation, Pew Charitable Trusts, Bullitt Foundation, Surdna Foundation, Richard King Mellon Foundation, George Gund Foundation, American Conservation Association, and others among the usual suspects.

The iron triangle has a long reach.

The same anti-mining pattern was woven in the Columbia Basin.

Anne Novakovitch of Curlew, in Ferry County, points out that the Forest Service mapped a "habitat corridor" in its plans directly over the K-2 Mine operated by Echo Bay Mining Company.

"That creates an opening for environmental groups to come in and take the mining company to court for harming habitat," she said. "They're just trying to drive mining out of Ferry county, which has traditionally been a mining county."[267a]

The Endangered Species Act has become a weapon to destroy water rights and irrigated farms. In Okanogan County's Methow Valley, Peter Morrison saw the U.S. Fish and Wildlife Service suspend his water permits on six ditches watering about 1,000 acres of crops—ostensibly it was to save salmon, steelhead and bull trout listed for protection under the federal Endangered Species Act.[267b]

For the first time in nearly 100 growing seasons, the ditches were dry.

"I think it's terrible that they treat people this way," said Donald Johnson, mayor of Winthrop. "We are the taxpayers. It's our water. Our authority is just taken away. We have no rights. Our land will dry up."

No similar shutdowns were made on the Tolt and Green River watersheds that provide water for Seattle, although salmon use those rivers, too. Urban economies are sheltered from the Endangered Species Act. Rural economies are destroyed with the Endangered Species Act.

What if Seattle were required to remove all buildings and restore its original salmon streams such as Yesler Creek and Denny Creek that today are filled with skyscrapers and parking garages?

The Endangered Species Act has the power to do just that.

Alliances of environmental groups have pressured the U.S. Fish and Wildlife Service to list the Canadian lynx as an endangered species, and Pacific Rivers Council leads the push to list the bull trout and other fish species as threatened or endangered.

Mike Poulson of Connell, chair of the Washington Farm Bureau Natural Resource Committee, said "Environmental groups are just drawing lines on maps around places they want to kick people out of and then claiming it's lynx habitat or bull trout habitat. It's just another way to turn rural communities into ghettoes."[267c]

The same applies to every other species that environmental groups push to have listed as endangered: a tool for rural cleansing.

Bonnie Lawrence of Omak worries about zealous bureaucrats at the state level. She said, "Here in Okanogan County we have the Loomis Forest, a state common school trust lands property managed by our Department of Natural Resources (DNR). Logging and grazing income is earmarked for K-through-12 school construction. We had spent several years preparing a Loomis Landscape Plan that was supposed to resolve problems and manage the forest.

"Several environmental groups sued—under the Endangered Species Act on behalf of grizzly bears—to stop logging and roads in the Loomis. Our Commissioner of Public Lands, Jennifer Belcher—who was a Washington Nature Conservancy board member—entered an out-of-court settlement with them, which led to a campaign for the green groups to 'buy' 25,000 acres of the Loomis for fair market value. The claim was that the green groups would pay for the land and timber value and replace school funds.

"There went our management plan—ironically, it had been designed to improve lynx habitat. The settlement also squelched expert testimony that the Loomis doesn't even contain grizzly habitat. Yet, the DNR's agreement to file a grizzly management plan with the U.S. Fish and Wildlife Service for the Loomis Forest is part of the lawsuit settlement. If the Loomis is treated as grizzly habitat, it would complete the lockup.

"Everything about this deal has been cloaked in secrecy. Commissioner Belcher promoted the lowball price of $13 million, but a dozen school districts don't agree, and have come out against the sale. When the school districts requested a copy of the appraisal, their request was denied. Appraisal reviews came up with conflicting prices— $13 million, $17 million, $30 million. Anonymous donors gave money to the green groups to pay for the Loomis, something that would never be tolerated if a coalition of loggers wanted to buy it for sustained yield timber management.

"Then at a monthly Board of Natural Resources meeting, State Senator Bob Morton [R-7th District] revealed that there was another appraisal, valuing the Loomis at $27.46 million—done by the DNR staff in a secret 1998 meeting. Yet Commissioner Belcher would not acknowledge the fair market value judgment of her own staff.

"Documents provided to Sen. Morton showed a trail of internal staff e-mails planning how to deal with the backlash over the varying appraisals. The $27.46 million appraisal was kept secret within the DNR. Sen. Morton told Commissioner Belcher that withholding information from the Board made it appear there was fraud and that she should step down. Belcher denied any fraud, but would not make public the internal documents that had been provided to Sen. Morton, and he withheld them as well to give her the opportunity.

"The whole session was broadcast on the government cable channel. The newspapers did not even mention any of this controversy."[268]

State officials can behave just like federal officials when driven by the same ideology.

Resource Class Exit. What is happening in the Columbia Basin is happening on all the national forests in America.

Goods producers and property owners are being starved out.

Their communities are being colonized by urban elites who want them removed.

Their production is being pushed offshore, to "elsewhere," to other nations less able to manage resources.

Federal policy is effectively colonizing those other countries to make up for the prohibited domestic production, even as foundations and green groups pressure to shut down goods production worldwide.

The combined influence of prescriptive foundations, grant-driven environmental groups, and zealous bureaucrats has driven the people of the Columbia Basin and the rest of rural America to desperation and despair.

The iron trinagle has changed public opinion so that the urban majority does not care.

They are on the brink of total victory.

They have made biodiversity all-powerful.

The implications of this social change were stated plainly by former Forest Service Chief Jack Ward Thomas in an address to Resources for the Future in April, 1999:

> The overriding policy of the management of the national forests is the preservation of biodiversity. That policy or objective will be executed first. Then, if possible, maybe some production of goods and services.
>
> This situation has evolved as a direct result of the Endangered Species Act and the regulations issued by the Forest Service pursuant to the National Forest Management Act, which says the purpose of the ESA is "the preservation of ecosystems upon which threatened and endangered species depend." The clause in the regulation says preservation of "all native and desired nonnative vertebrates will be maintained in viable numbers well-distributed in the planning area." That regulation being more stringent even than the ESA.
>
> The period after the passage of ESA has seen an ever-increasing number of species of plants and animals considered "threatened" or "endangered." Usually significant numbers of these species are found in the national forests. Oddly, not because the situation is worse than before but because conditions are relatively better. Every such species requires special consideration from management.

With every such "listing" the Service gains a management partner with complete veto authority over proposed actions. Now, couple this with the requirement of the above-described clause in the Federal planning regulations and the consequences of a number of Federal court rulings, then consider the actions. It becomes crystal clear that biodiversity retention is the overriding mission or objective of the Forest Service.

Now that evolved set of circumstances bothers me. It bothers me a lot. It does not bother me so much as being a policy or a mission or objective; it does bother me that it has simply evolved out of a series of laws and pursuant regulations, court cases, and policy directions. It would be a simple matter to ratify that or reject it by Congress or the Administration. If that's determined to be the overriding objective, so be it. If the Congress disagrees it has the duty to clarify that situation or quit pounding the agency for carrying out that objective. Frankly, I don't think we are going to see any such clarification. That would take some nerve and I don't think that exists. I think it is far easier to mollify constituents on the extremes of the preservation-exploitation debate by leaving the Forest Service in the middle.

But I will say this to my friends in Congress and in the business of extracting and processing natural resources: If you expect anything other than a constant decline in the availability of goods and services from the national forests resulting from this de facto mission, you are dreaming about what was and not what will be.[270]

Former Chief Thomas did not expand his remarks to include a bothersome point: the Endangered Species Act also applies to private property.

Are we to expect the same "constant decline in the availability of goods and services" from that too?

Is the American Dream about what was and not what will be?

ZEALOUS BUREAUCRATS FOOTNOTES

198a. "Washington's Most Dangerous Bureaucrats, by Jeffrey H. Birnbaum," *Fortune*, September 29, 1997, on-line edition, http://www.pathfinder.com/fortune/1997/970929/dan.html.

198b. "Environmentalists Become Insiders in Administration," by Maura Dolan, *Oregonian*, Sunday, March 28, 1993, p. A21.

201a. "Wild 'N' Crazy Gore Quietly Expanding Power of his Office," by Kenneth T. Walsh, *Rocky Mountain News,* Sunday July 18, 1993, p. 4A.

201b. "The population and the wealth of nations," by Richard Grenier, *Washington Times*, Monday, September 12, 1994, p. A19.

201c. Telephone interview with Bonner Cohen, May, 1999.

203a. "Environmental Science For Sale," *ABC News Nightline*, Ted Koppel, Transcript No. 3329, February 24, 1994.

203b. "What to do about Greenhouse Warming: Look Before You Leap," by Fred Singer, Chauncey Starr and Roger Revelle, *Cosmos*, April 1991.

203c. Obituary: "Roger Revelle, Oceanographer and Population Expert; at 82," *Boston Globe*, Wednesday July 17, 1991, p. 27.

204. This section is based on: "'Global Warming' Libel Suit Reaches Settlement," news release by Center for Individual Rights, Washington, D.C., May 24, 1994; and "Singer's Global Warming Libel Suit Reaches Settlement," *Global Warming Network Online Today*, Alexandria, Virginia, May 27 and May 31, 1994.

205a. Telephone interview with Rogelio "Roger" Maduro, Leesburg, Virginia, February 25, 1994.

205b. "The Federal Page - In The Loop," *The Washington Post*, February 14, 1994, by Al Kamen, p. A13.

206a. Telephone interview with Bonner Cohen, May 1999.

206b. "Carol Browner, master of mission creep," by Pranay Gupte and Bonner R. Cohen, *Forbes*, October 20, 1997, p. 170. Online at http://www.forbes.com/forbes/97/1020/6009170a.htm.

208a. "Latest Cabinet Picks are Mostly Social Liberals - 3 Women Add Diversity to Team of Moderates," by Knight-Ridder Newspapers, *Atlanta Constitution*, Saturday December 12, 1992, p. A8.

208b. EPA History Office website, contains links to publications covering issues and administrative documents at http://www.epa.gov/history/.

209. Accounts of EPA cancer hunts may be found in: *Fear of Food: Environmentalist Scams, Media Mendacity, and the Law of Disparage-*

ment, by Andrea Arnold, Free Enterprise Press, Bellevue, Washington, 1990; and *The Asbestos Racket: An Environmental Parable*, by Michael Bennett, Free Enterprise Press, Bellevue, Washington, 1991.

210a. "EPA Tells 22 States to Curb Smog-Causing Pollution," Saturday October 11, 1997, *Los Angeles Times*. See also, "EPA Tells States to Clean Air - Or Else Federal Highway Funds Could Be Withheld, the Agency Said. PA. and N.J. Need Make Only Modest Improvements," Sunday, October 12, 1997, *Philadelphia Inquirer.*

210b. Secret memo, "Climate Change Action Plan," was later leaked.

211a. "The People v. Carol Browner: EPA on Trial," National Wilderness Institute, http://www.nwi.org/SpecialStudies/EPAReport/Overview.html.

211b. "Blowing the whistle on EPA's widespread abuse," letter signed by 19 EPA scientists, *Washington Times*, Wednesday, June 10, 1998.

212a. All EPA grant data from Grants Information Query Form at EPA website, http://www.epa.gov/envirofw/html/gics/gics_query.html.

212b. "A Bad Air Day Will industry lobbyists foul up the E.P.A's newly proposed regulations?" by David Corn, *The Nation*, March 24, 1997.

214a. "Carol Browner, master of mission creep," Forbes, October 20, 1997.

214b. "Clinton, Rubin reported 'distressed' over EPA's strict new air standards," *Washington Times*, Monday, June 30, 1997.

215a. "Clinton Backs EPA's Tougher Clean Air Rules," by Joby Warrick, John F. Harris, *Washington Post*, June 26, 1997, p. A01.

215b. "Air Quality Standards Rejected by Appeals Court Environment: EPA construed Clean Air Act too loosely in setting rules for smog and soot, judges say. Ruling is seen as setback for Clinton administration," by Robert L. Jackson, James Gerstenzang, *Los Angeles Times*, Saturday May 15, 1999, p. A1.

215c. "The Environmental Justice Movement: Continuing the Struggle for Civil Rights," (sub)TEX Volume 1, Issue #5 (February 1995). Online at http://www.utexas.edu/students/subtex/.web/volume1/issue5/Environmetal_Justice.shtml.

215d. Executive Order 12948 Amendment to Executive Order No. 12898, January 30, 1995.

215e. Environmental Protection Agency—Part 1: Accompanying Report of the National Performance Review, Office of the Vice President, Washington, DC September 1993.

216a. "Carol Browner, master of mission creep," *Forbes.*

216b. "The Shame of Shintech: A Political Game where everyone loses," by J. Michael Havelka, *WasteBiz*. Online at http://www.wastebiz.com/html/body_oct97f3.html.

216c. "Does Environmentalism Kill?" by Michael Gough, *EPA Watch*, March 10, 1999.

217a. "Judge refuses to halt Shintech bias claim hearing," *Baton Rouge Advocate*, Tuesday, September 1, 1998. See also, 217a. "Environmental justice test case averted by chemical company - Manufacturer will not build in poor, black community," *The Baltimore Sun,* Saturday, September 19, 1998.

217b. "The Environmental Justice Movement: Continuing the Struggle for Civil Rights," (sub)TEX.

217c. "Married With Conflicts Bill & Hill & Rod & Carla & the Problem of Capital Power Couples," by Owen Ullmann, Mike McNamee, *The Washington Post*, April 10, 1994, p. C1.

218a. See www.citizensfund.org.

218b. "Citizens Fund, Campaign Finance Reform Program," Ottinger Foundation Handbook, December 5, 1996.

218c. All cited grants in Foundation Center records.

220a. "Making the Team Takes Her to D.C. - Clinton Drafts a Philly Native to be His Special Assistant on the Environment and Energy," by John J. Fried, *Philadelphia Inquirer*, Sunday January 17, 1993, p. D1.

220b. "From Philadelphia to a Top U.S. Environmental Post," by Andrea Shalal-Esa, *Philadelphia Inquirer*, Thursday December 9, 1993, p. G5.

220c. "Washington's Most Dangerous Bureaucrats, by Jeffrey H. Birnbaum," *Fortune*, September 29, 1997, on-line edition, http://www.pathfinder.com/fortune/1997/970929/dan.html.

218d. "White House Office to Coordinate Environmental Policy - President Designs New Office to Streamline, Strengthen Policy - Focus on Environment and Economy, Global Issues," White House Office of the Press Secretary, February 8, 1993.

220e. "Statement by the President and Remarks by the Vice President on New Environmental Policy," White House release, February 8, 1993.

221. "Remarks by the President in ABC Kids Town Meeting," February 20, 1993, White House Library website.

223. Ancient Forest Alliance direct mail letter dated March 8, 1993.

226. "The Forest Summit - Learning How to Live With the Owl," by Kirk Johnson, *Seattle Times*, Sunday March 28, 1993, p. A15.

227a. "Clinton Calls on Cabinet to Craft Forest-Jobs Plan," by Paul Richter, *Los Angeles Times*, Saturday April 3, 1993, p. 1.

227b. For the full list of FEMAT team members, see file, "Ecosystem Management Assessment Working Group," White House Library website.

228a. Telephone interviews with Bob Lee, May, 1999.

228b. *Broken Trust, Broken Land: Freeing Ourselves From The War Over The Environment*, Robert G. Lee, Book Partners, Wilsonville, Oregon, 1994, p. 40.

228c. "Clinton Backs a $1 Billion Plan to Spare Trees and Aid Loggers," by Gwen Ifill, *New York Times*, July 1, 1993.

229. "Clinton vs. Foley - House speaker is furious at plan to protect Northwest forests," by Paul Koberstein, *High Country News*, July 26, 1993 (Vol. 25 No. 13).

229b. "Timber Firms Say Ruling Saps Clinton Plan," by Eric Pryne, *Seattle Times*, Tuesday March 22, 1994, p. B3.

229c. "Timber Industry Takes Loss in Court," *Seattle Times*, Friday July 1, 1994.

230a. E-mail transmission, "Stand Up for Ancient Forests," Written 7:54 am Aug 16, 1993 by nwfoga in cdp:en.alerts.

230b. E-mail transmission: "Topic: Ancient Forest Comments Needed Now," Written 7:18 am Sep 2, 1993 by wafcdc in cdp:biodiversity

231a. H.R. 1944, "Emergency Supplemental Appropriations for Additional Disaster Assistance, for Anti-terrorism Initiatives, for Assistance in the Recovery from the Tragedy that Occurred at Oklahoma City, etc."

231b. Telephone interviews with Dave Hessel, June, 1999.

232a. "Clinton to Seek Way to Override Logging Ruling," *Seattle Times,* Sunday, October 29, 1995.

232b. "Environmentalists Get Ready For Summer of Logging Protests," by Dana Tims, *Oregonian*, Monday, June 3, 1996, p. A1.

232c. "Judge Clears the Way for Salvage Logging; Opponents Vow Fight," by the Associated Press, *Seattle Post-Intelligencer*, Friday, September 8, 1995, p. B11.

232d. "Activists Barricade Forest Road," *Oregonian*, Friday, November 24, 1995.

233a. "Protesters Dig In to Save Old-Growth Forests Environment: From blocking a road to updating a Web page, activists rally to deter logging in Northwest," Jeff Barnard, by the Associated Press, *Los Angeles Times*, Monday, August 26, 1996, p. 5.

233b. FOIA letter from Forest Service Special Agent Thomas J. Lyons, dated October 9, 1996. File Code 6270-1 (96-122-R6).

233c. "The Last Frontier - The 'Salvage Rider' Isn't Saving Forests, It's Decimating Them," by Anne W. Semmes, Earth Action Network website.

233d. "Forest Service Agents Clear Out Protesters' Camp," by Bryan Denson, *Oregonian*, Saturday, August 17, 1996, p. B01.

233e. "Oregon Judge Opts Not to Sentence Trio in Warner Creek Protest," from correspondent and wire reports, *Oregonian*, Thursday, August 7, 1997, p. B10.

233f. "Eco-Protests are Treated Too Tenderly," by Merrilee Peay, *Oregonian*, Wednesday, August 7, 1996, p. B7.

233g. Telephone interview with Merrilee Peay, May, 1999.

233h. Telephone interview with Bruce Gainer, June 1999.

234a. Copies of the Jim Turner and Katie McGinty documents are available from Rep. Turner's office.

234b. "GOP Aims to Head Off Monument 'End Runs' - Murkowski bill would require studies - and congressional approval," by Lee Davidson, *Deseret News*, Monday, September 30, 1996.

236. "Even Wilderness Group Was in the Dark - Clinton aide pushed for monument despite strong doubts expressed by others," by Karl Cates, *Deseret News*, Thursday, January 16, 1997.

237a. White House e-mail files: August 3, 1995. To: Raynor [Robert] Baum. Re: Antiquities Act. Signed, Dave [Watts].

237b. White House e-mail file: Creation Time/Date: 19-MAR-1996 19:02:00.00. Creator: CN=Linda L. Lance/O=OVP. Subject: Letter to Babbit [sic] re monuments. To: McGinty, K; Glauthier, T; Jensen, T; Bear, D; Fidler, S; Crutchfield, J; Shuffield, A.

237c. White House e-mail file: attachment 3 Creation Time/Date: 19-MAR-1996 19:01:00.00. Subject: Parksltr.

238a. White House e-mail file: Creator: CN=Linda L. Lance. Creation Date/Time: 21-MAR-1996 18:36:00.00. Subject: Re: KM's comments on yesterday's monument letter. To: McGinty, K; :jensen, t, :bear, d; :crutchfield, j; :glauthier, t.

238b. White House e-mail file: Creator: CN=Linda L. Lance. Creation Date/Time: 22-Mar-1996 18:56:00.00. Subject: redraft of president's babbitt letter and question. To: Glauthier, T; McGinty, K; Jensen, T; Bear, D; Crutchfield, J; Beard, B.

238c. White House e-mail file: Creator: McGinty Creation Date/Time: 25-MAR-1996 13:21:00.00. Subject: Re: redraft of president's Babbitt letter and question To: T. J. Glauthier; Linda L. Lance; Jensen T.; Beard, D.; Crutchfield, J.; Beard, B.

239. White House e-mail file: Creator: James Craig Crutchfield (Crutchfield J) (OMB). Creation date/time: 3-Apr-1996 10:09:39.50. Subject: Parks Initiative update. To: T.J. Glauthier; Ron Cogswell; Bruce D. Beard; Marvis G. Olfus; Linda L. Lance; Thomas C. Jensen.

240a. "The Yellowstone Affair: Environmental Protection, International Treaties and National Sovereignty," by Jeremy Rabkin.

240b. "In The Loop - The Federal Page - Squashing the Muffin," by Al Kamen, *The Washington Post*, December 15, 1995, p. A23.

240c. White House e-mail file: Creator: Thomas C. Jensen (Jensen, T) (CEQ). Creation date/time: 23-Jul-1996 15:30:42.34. Subject: Potus letter re: Utah. To: Peter G. Umhofer CC: Kathleen A. McGinty.

241a. "Behind Closed Doors: The Abuse of Trust And Discretion In The Establishment Of The Grand Staircase-Escalante National Monument." Majority Staff Report, Subcommittee on National Parks & Public Lands, Committee on Resources, U.S. House of Representatives, One Hundred Fifth Congress, First Session, November 7, 1997, Washington, D.C.

241b. White House e-mail file: Creator: Kathleen A. McGinty (MCGINTY—K) (CEQ). Creation date/time: 29-JUL-1996 09:31:39.65. Subject: Utah letter. To: Todd Stern.

241c. White House document: August 5, 1996. Memorandum to Marcia Hale. From: Kathleen A. McGinty. Re: Utah Event Calls.

242. Remarks by the President in Announcing Agreement to Save National Park From Mine Development, Yellowstone National Park Wyoming 11:25 A.M. MDT, White House Library.

243a. White House memo. August 14, 1996. Memorandum to the President. From: Katie McGinty. Subject: Proposed Utah Monument Designation and Event.

243b. White House e-mail file: Executive Office of the President, September 6, 1996. To: Elisabeth Blaug, Thomas C. Jensen, Brian J. Johnson, From: Kathleen A. McGinty, Council on Environmental Quality. Subject: Wkly report graphs.

243c. "President Considers Carving National Monument Out of Utah Land," by Tom Kenworthy, *The Washington Post*, September 07, 1996, p. A3.

244a. White House e-mail file: Creation Time/Date: 10-Sep-1996 14:36:00.00 Creator: Kenworthy, Tom. Subject: utah, again. To: smtp: johnson.

244b. White House e-mail file: Creator: kenworthyt. Creation date/time: 11-SEP-1996 22:22:00.00. Subject: utah. To: johnson.

244c. "How Leavitt Tried to Stop Clinton's Escalante Plan, In Deseret News interview, governor tells about his 11th-hour efforts in D.C.," by Karl Cates, *Deseret News*, Thursday, January 16, 1997, A15.

244d. Telephone interview with Brad Barber, July, 1999.

245a. "How Leavitt Tried to Stop Clinton's Escalante Plan, In Deseret News interview, governor tells about his 11th-hour efforts in D.C.," *Deseret News*.

245b. "Topic: Coal-gate - Clinton's 'mother of all land-grabs' - On the sly, he created a huge preserve in Utah," by Michael Satchell, *U.S. News & Report*, January 20,1997.

246a. "Republicans Leave No Hearing Unheld In Seeking Culprit - White House official gets scolding for not telling who advised Clinton," by Lee Davidson, *Deseret News*, Friday, September 27, 1996.

246b. "Subpoena Authorization Approved For Inquiry Into Questionable $700,000 Payment To Two Federal Employees," news release by House Committee on Resources, Don Young, Chairman, June 9, 1999.

247a. "Payments to Interior, Energy staffers draw scrutiny," by Audrey Hudson and Jerry Seper, Washington Times, June 2, 1999.

247b. http:// www.pogo.org.

251. "Agency says thanks, but no thanks, after e-mail flood," *Deseret News*, Monday, April 5, 1999.

253a. "Militia Link Suspected in Acts Against Federal Land Workers - The FBI is Examining March Bombings of Forest Service in Nevada," by Heather Dewar, *Philadelphia Inquirer*, Tuesday May 9, 1995, p. A15.

253b. "Threats to U.S. Agents on Public Lands Detailed House Democrat Seeks Hearings on Violence, Condemns Rhetoric of Republican Colleagues," by Susan Schmidt, *Washington Post*, May 10, 1995, p. A20.

254. "Legal Assault on Firms Is Armed by Foundations," by David B. Ottaway, *Washington Post*, Wednesday, May 19, 1999; p. A1.

262a. Forest Plan for a Sustainable Economy and a Sustainable Environment, White House release, July 1, 1993.

262b. Project Charter, INTERIOR COLUMBIA RIVER BASIN ECOSYSTEM MANAGEMENT FRAMEWORK AND SCIENTIFIC ASSESSMENT and EASTSIDE OREGON AND WASHINGTON ENVIRONMENTAL IMPACT STATEMENT Signed January 21, 1994, Director, USDI Bureau of Land Management, Chief, USDA Forest Service. Online at http://www.icbemp.gov/news/charter.html.

263a. Prof. McKetta's studies include, "A Study of the Effects of Changing Federal Timber Policies on Rural Communities in Northcentral Idaho," by M. Henry Robison, Charles W. McKetta, and Steven S. Peterson, University of Idaho, Moscow, Idaho, February 1996.

263b. Telephone interview with Richard Everett, July 1, 1999.

263c. Telephone interview with Jackie Shiner, July, 1999.

264a. *Eastside Draft Environmental Impact Statement*, Volume 1, Chapter 2, p. 191. U.S.D.A. Forest Service. See also, *Lone-Deer Ecosystem Management Project Environmental Assessment.* USDA Forest Service Colville National Forest June 1999. Robert L. Vaught, Forest Supervisor. Fig. 3-11 "Conservation Groups Areas of Concern, Harvest Units in Proposed Action," "Conservation group areas of concern – as delineated by the Wilderness Society." Chapter 3, pps. 61-63.

264b. Telephone interview with Bret Roberts, July, 1999.

265. Telephone interview with Dennis Snook, July, 1999. Letter from Dallas L. Hayden, director, Program Investigation Division, U.S. Department of Agriculture, Office of Inspector General, dated October 8, 1998, to Dennis Snook, Chairman, Ferry County Board of Commissioners, stamped received by Ferry County Oct. 20. 1998. Hayden's letter misspelled Ferry County as "Perry County."

266a. White House Memo dated May 14, 1993, confidential to Secretaries Babbitt, Brown, and Espy, Administrator Browner, Counselor Wirth, and Lt. General Williams, cc. to Tony Lake and Leon Fuerte, from Katie McGinty.

266b. "Al Gore comes out swinging against proposed B.C. mine," by Mark Hume, *Vancouver Sun*, December 15, 1992, p. A1.

267a. Telephone interview with Anne Novakovitch, July, 1999.

267b. "Irrigation Curbs are a Rude Awakening in Methow Valley," by Lynda V. Mapes, *Seattle Times*, Sunday May 9, 1999, p. B1.

267c. Telephone interview with Mike Poulson, July, 1999.

268. Telephone interview with Bonnie Lawrence, July 1999.

270. Address to Resources for the Future, Jack Ward Thomas, April 30, 1999, Washington, D.C.

CHAPTER 5

CORPORATE TAKEOVER

Corporations are the next target of prescriptive foundations, grant-driven greens, and zealous bureaucrats. Their victory in decimating rural America's resource class by closing access to federal lands is nearly complete. Encouraged, the iron triangle is attempting to expand into all corporate activity, following their dream of bringing about a new "environmental age," which will replace the "industrial age," so that "extractive" industries vanish and "renewable" industries thrive. They devise vast government grants for zero-emission automobiles while choking off the natural resource supply needed to build those cars. They undermine corporate structures by placing "stakeholders" on an equal footing with "shareholders," blurring notions of ownership with concepts of control. But they have made a fatal error. They believe the thrust to narrow economic activity can be stopped at a point of their choosing. The true believers among them will never stop. The undue influence triangle is a runaway train that will one day crash with all of us aboard.

IT'S NOT EASY BEING GREEN IF YOU'RE CORPORATE.
No matter what corporations do, it's never green enough. They've tried everything. Conflict. Cooperation. Resistance. Innovation. Buyoffs. Public Relations. No model produces the desired results—public acceptance. Somebody always targets you.

CORPORATE GREEN

Gore's Green Galaxy contains a constellation of non-profit organizations that push businesses to "go green." "Go green" means stop extracting natural resources, retire the resource class, and go into high tech or service businesses, where greens can pretend that they don't need natural resource extraction (while their Internet messages use electricity equivalent to one pound of coal burned for every two megabytes transmitted).[280a]

The President's Council on Sustainable Development was convened by the Clinton administration to harness corporations to green group ideology by promoting high-minded goals that sounded wonderful but silently eliminated natural resource extraction as part of a proper society. Jonathan Lash, a Gore insider, was co-chair of the Council.[280b]

Lash is well networked with the "green business community," which consists of more non-profit grant-driven organizations than for-profit businesses, and most of the for-profit businesses are seeking federal grants.

The premier "green business" group is Boston-based CERES, Inc.— Center for Environmentally Responsible Economies (1997 income $1,033,578, assets $555,800). CERES was formed in 1989 with a grant from the Jessie Smith Noyes Foundation to promote the "Valdez Principles," now renamed the "CERES Principles." The "Valdez Principles" resulted from the disastrous 1989 Exxon Valdez oil spill in Alaska, which became the platform for the emergence of CERES.[280c]

The original CERES coalition consisted of fifteen green groups, several "socially responsible investors," the public pension funds of California and New York City, and some 200 Protestant denominations and Catholic orders. They used the strategy of shareholder resolutions to get their green business program on the corporate radar screen.

The ten "principles" are not enforceable, and cannot be used in litigation by environmental groups against corporations, but are more a credo, a green "This I Believe" statement for corporate bigwigs. In their current form, the ten principles are:

Protection of the Biosphere. We will reduce and make continual progress toward eliminating the release of any substance that may cause environmental damage to the air, water, or the earth or its inhabitants. We will safeguard all habitats affected by our operations and will protect open spaces and wilderness, while preserving biodiversity.

Sustainable Use of Natural Resources. We will make sustainable use of renewable natural resources, such as water, soils and forests. We will conserve non-renewable natural resources through efficient use and careful planning.

Reduction and Disposal of Wastes. We will reduce and where possible eliminate waste through source reduction and recycling. All waste will be handled and disposed of through safe and responsible methods.

Energy Conservation. We will conserve energy and improve the energy efficiency of our internal operations and of the goods and services we sell. We will make every effort to use environmentally safe and sustainable energy sources.

Risk Reduction. We will strive to minimize the environmental, health and safety risks to our employees and the communities in which we operate through safe technologies, facilities and operating procedures, and by being prepared for emergencies.

Safe Products and Services. We will reduce and where possible eliminate the use, manufacture or sale of products and services that cause environmental damage or health or safety hazards. We will inform our customers of the environmental impacts of our products or services and try to correct unsafe use.

Environmental Restoration. We will promptly and responsibly correct conditions we have caused that endanger health, safety or the environment. To the extent feasible, we will redress injuries we have caused to persons or damage we have caused to the environment and will restore the environment.

Informing the Public. We will inform in a timely manner everyone who may be affected by conditions caused by our company that might endanger health, safety or the environment. We will regularly seek advice and counsel through dialogue with persons in communities near our facilities. We will not take any action against employees for reporting dangerous incidents or conditions to management or to appropriate authorities.

Management Commitment. We will implement these Principles and sustain a process that ensures that the Board of Directors and Chief Executive Officer are fully informed about pertinent environmental issues and are fully responsible for environmental policy. In selecting our Board of Directors, we will consider demonstrated environmental commitment as a factor.

Audits and Reports. We will conduct an annual self-evaluation of our progress in implementing these Principles. We will support the timely creation of generally accepted environmental audit procedures. We will annually complete the CERES Report, which will be made available to the public.

Now if we could only get a few foundations, green groups, and zealous bureaucrats to be so forthcoming about their activities....

CERES currently has 54 investor, environmental, religious, labor and social justice groups in the coalition and boasts more than 40 corporate endorsers of their principles, including nine Fortune 500 companies.

Sun Oil was the first Fortune 500 company to endorse the CERES Principles—the Pew Charitable Trusts original shares of Sun Oil and Rebecca Rimel's gang may have had something to do with that. "Extraordinarily incestuous."

Sun got CERES in the door of other large companies such as Arizona Public Service, Bethlehem Steel, Catholic Healthcare West, General Motors, H.B. Fuller and Polaroid. Today, 46 companies and organizations have endorsed the CERES Principles.

CERES's foundation funders include the Beldon Fund, Beldon II, the Foundation for Deep Ecology, the Joyce Foundation (of anti-gun notoriety), Town Creek Foundation, New-Land Foundation, John D. and Catherine T. MacArthur Foundation, and the Charles Stewart Mott Foundation. Much of the Mott money came from General Motors, which is why CERES got in that door.

Stephen Viederman, president of the Jessie Smith Noyes Foundation is a member of the CERES board of directors, along with second-rank officials from the Natural Resources Defense Council, Sierra Club, Friends of the Earth, National Wildlife Federation, World Wildlife Fund, among others. Denis Hayes, president and CEO of the Bullitt Foundation, is honorary co-chair.

With a board like that, you can imagine what a business-friendly coalition CERES must be.

Other organizations pushing business to "go green" include the Virginia-based Global Environmental and Technology Foundation (1996 income: $6,760,832; Assets: $1,009,388). Hank Habicht, chief executive officer, and Tom Harvey, founder.[282]

GETF co-sponsored the January, 1999 National Town Meeting for a Sustainable America with the President's Council on Sustainable Development, a four-day conference that drew some 3,000 federal, state and local officials, corporate executives, air and water pollution experts, teachers and students to Detroit, Michigan. It gave Al Gore a platform for talking to voters about such issues as suburban sprawl, shrinking family farms, traffic congestion, the "rebirth of old factory sites" and the need to preserve rivers.

It also gave the administration a platform to announce plans to create a "center for global climate change and environmental forecasting" to better to better deal with "problems caused by carbon dioxide and fossil-fuel emissions." Transportation Secretary Rodney E. Slater also announced that communities will be allowed to borrow federal transportation experts to help plan projects, to design a "tool kit" of best practices for communities and to offer training sessions to local officials and citizens who want to learn how to seek federal funds for projects.[283s]

GETF also helped arrange a January 1999 session for Virginia's Environmental Business Council (EBC), a quasi-governmental organization established in 1998 to promote the state's 2,600 environmental businesses. The EBC was the work product of Virginia state agencies and the White House Council on Environmental Quality, which jointly drew up its plans— one of the last projects approved by Katie McGinty before she departed. CEQ gave the new organization links to 24 Federal programs that directly support the development of new environmental technologies. Companies attending the January 21 meeting were briefed by federal officials on the most effective means of accessing the business opportunities offered by these federal programs.[283b]

GETF is funded by the Ohrstrom Foundation.

The for-profit segment of the "green business" community is heavily dependent on government grants and contracts for its existence. Your tax dollars at work.

Other organizations influential in the "green business" community include Sustainable Business.com, an online-only project of The EnviroLink Network (1996 income: $179,302; assets: $38,571), a Pittsburgh-based non-profit green group operating on the Internet. Sustainable Business.com president Rona Fried, Ph.D., has become an authentic Guru of Green Business with a vastly informative website and frequent cogent commentary. Fried's writings offer probably the clearest view into the mindstyle of Gore's Green Galaxy. Here are excerpts from one of her more pointed articles:

> Steel, often thought of as the symbol of the Industrial Revolution, now carries a recycling symbol. More than half the steel produced today is made from scrap. Paper mills are moving from the forest to the cities, as they hone in on the source of abundant feedstocks - scrap paper. In New Jersey, a state with little forest cover or iron ore, 13 paper mills run only on waste paper and eight steel mills manufacture steel largely from scrap. Why is this? Natural resources are increasingly scarce and thus more expensive; waste is plentiful and increasingly, abundant.

The blueprint for how business is conducted is shifting from Industrial Age operating assumptions of "take, make and throw away" to fit the situation society faces today. It makes sense to use scarce natural resources sparingly, and keep them circulating in the system. Society, in its instinctual desire to survive, is tightening the screws on companies that refuse to play by the new rules. The authors of Interface Inc.'s 1997 Sustainability Report say, "We believe institutions that continuously violate these [natural] principles will suffer economically. The walls of the funnel will continue to impose themselves in the form of environmentally concerned customers, stricter legislation, higher costs and fees for resources and waste, and tougher competition from companies who anticipate the narrowing limits and adjust accordingly."

Companies, these days, find more freedom through adaptation and reinvention than by retaining the status quo, an indication that a profound transformation is underway. Leaders from many disciplines believe we are witnessing and participating in a societal transition on a scale comparable to the Agricultural and Industrial Revolutions - the Environmental Revolution....

A 1997 survey of Canadian and American executives conducted by the Society of Management Accountants of Canada asked business leaders why their company considered sustainable business practices important. The most important reason given, after compliance with legal requirements, was "because it's the right thing to do."

In our global economy, many corporations post revenues and assets higher than the gross national product of many countries. Business is a more powerful institution than government. As global consciousness and social values come to the forefront, the private sector is increasingly called upon to go beyond compliance and participate in fundamental ways as leaders of society. The Industrial Age view that business' sole function is to produce products, services, and profit is less and less acceptable to society.

Carl Frankel sees it this way: "A handful of powerful forward-thinking decision-makers and policy-formers can really make a difference. We are battling for the hearts and minds of 50 people. That's why people like Ray Anderson of Interface are really important."[284]

It is remarkable how isolated from resource producers these people are. It is as if there were no real people out there providing food, clothing, shelter and all other material goods. These savvy business leaders virtually ignore the need for natural resource extraction in their eagerness to tout the virtues of closing all the loops. Most astonishing, these highly intelligent people can talk about "the walls of the funnel narrowing" only in the context that they, the early adaptors, will beat out the laggards. They never ask where the narrowing stops.

They do not ask because they believe they are in a favored position.

They are not.

They have no idea that the iron triangle exists. They are captives of a juggernaut, not captains of a dream machine.

The movement they ride has a final destination beyond their imagination, and zero extraction of natural resources has inevitable consequences.

That stark reality is a step beyond Gore's "advanced" thinking.

The inhabitants of Gore's Green Galaxy cannot see that the moral imperative driving their own adopted movement will not allow the narrowing to stop just because their business is green:

You Can Never Be Green Enough.

Environmentalism is a moral crusade. Moral crusades generate true believers, not accommodating neighbors.

In a moral crusade, positions can only harden.

You Can Never Be Green Enough.

For every neighbor who says, "Maybe this is green enough," there will always be a true believer who says, "No, this is not green enough."

Such greener-than-thou combats generate a never-ending spiral of allegations: "compromise," "capitulation," "sellout," "betrayal," "opponent," "enemy," "target."

The demands will increase.

The walls of the green business funnel will intersect.

As they are already intersecting for rural America's loggers, miners, oil and gas explorers, ranchers, farmers—all resource producers.

QUIRKS

The narrowing funnel walls often take bizarre twists. Consider one of the best-known cases of a corporate giant trying to be green: McDonald's and the styrofoam hamburger box.

In the late 1980s, many environmental groups voiced opposition to non-biodegradable packaging, particularly plastics such as styrofoam. McDonald's restaurants liked the styrofoam fold-over "clamshell" sandwich package because of its light weight and insulating properties that kept a burger just right for the consumer.

It was a time when stringent new regulations were poised to shut down one-third of the nation's landfills and local legislation was being proposed to ban many plastic packaging products.

McDonald's opposed such measures, but was not deaf to pressure groups. It had recently stopped cooking its french fries in beef tallow because of green group outcry. The company was looking to improve its image as environmentally and nutritionally conscious at the lowest possible real cost.[286a]

Shelby Yastrow, McDonald's senior vice president, said that the firm's marketing studies indicated neither a loss of market share nor a potential market gain as a result of environmental issues. McDonald's had little economic incentive to dump the styrofoam clamshell.

It came as a surprise, then, when on August 1, 1990, after intense negotiations, the McDonald's Corporation and the Environmental Defense Fund (EDF) jointly announced that the styrofoam clamshell would be replaced by coated paper wrapping.

Further, the unlikely couple agreed to a six-month joint task force to identify ways of dealing with the hundreds of millions of pounds of trash the fast food company generated each year.

EDF would get no money. The task force was set to look at possible solutions, including redesign of packaging and shipping materials to do more with less, and the potential for composting that might turn waste french fries into potting soil.

McDonald's also pledged to annually purchase $100 million of products made with recycled materials to build and equip its restaurants.

The company subsequently established a recycling program of its own called McRecycle USA.

EDF President Fred Krupp said, "We are determined to see McDonald's make fundamental changes in the way it operates. It's time to turn the golden arches green."

Because of their joint effort, McDonald's and EDF won the President's Environmental and Conservation Challenge Award.

Why did McDonald's allow EDF to tell it how to run its business?

The real reason is that Fred Krupp hijacked a national campaign against McDonald's organized by the grassroots Citizens Clearinghouse on Hazardous Waste. Now known as the Center for Health, Environment and Justice, the feisty group was founded in 1981 by Lois Gibbs, leader of the campaign at Love Canal.[286b]

The Citizens Clearinghouse on Hazardous Waste, despite its popular reputation of running on a shoestring budget, had enough foundation backing to give McDonald's a severe case of public relations heartburn.

They got money from: W. Alton Jones Foundation, the Bullitt Foundation, Mary Reynolds Babcock Foundation, Ford Foundation, the John Merck Fund, the Moriah Fund, Charles Stewart Mott Foundation, Jessie

Smith Noyes Foundation, George Gund Foundation, the Florence and John Schumann Foundation, Town Creek Foundation, the Public Welfare Foundation and others.

Krupp barged in and offered McDonald's a deal with his much bigger and richer organization (grant-driven by some of the same foundations) in return for less than the Hazardous Waste bunch wanted.

Krupp gained a victory which the EDF has since highlighted prominently in its fundraising.

However, part of the deal was that McDonald's could not use the settlement in its marketing or advertising.

But it wasn't green enough. Ralph Nader said of the proposed joint study, "By concentrating on 'waste management' rather than offering to end the production of waste, McDonald's ignores the human health dangers posed by hazardous chemical emissions produced as McDonald's unneeded plastic and styrofoam packaging is manufactured. Grassroots environmental groups are not convinced that McDonald's is serious about creating a better environment."

Mark Dowie, author of *Losing Ground*, said the EDF-McDonald's arrangement was an example of "high-level capitulations" that "unfortunately allow companies such as McDonalds to look a lot greener than they are. The corporate exploitation of 'win/win' compromising has been relentless, with company after company competing through paid and free media to out-green one another. Such activity on the corporate food chain is both predictable and understandable. But environmental complicity, and its own public relations-driven tendency to turn compromise into false triumph, illustrates the impending moral bankruptcy of many mainstream organizations."[287]

Something nobody mentioned: Teresa Heinz—a major stockholder of H.J. Heinz Company—sat on EDF's board.

H.J. Heinz was a major supplier of products to McDonald's.

That could be a powerful motive to rescue McDonald's from a bruising grassroots campaign and polish its environmental image.

Is that what really happened?

Nobody asked, so we don't know.

With this classic case open to so many interpretations, what is the public to make of corporations cooperating with green groups?

● It's insincere corporations "greenwashing" only for public relations purposes.

● It's opportunistic environmental groups trying to 1) show the public how reasonable they are; and 2) show their members how powerful they are.

● It's a genuine effort to reach an accommodation between businesses and environmentalists rather than remaining stuck in conflict.
● It's a hidden agenda of one elite protecting another elite.

PRIVATE TIMBERLANDS

The public got over losing the McDonald's styrofoam burger box with minor trauma. The firm's reputation as an environmentally responsible business has survived despite the true believers' attempts to tarnish it.

But the private timberlands of America present a more serious problem. With the end of goods production on federal forests in sight, the private timberlands of America will be our only source of domestic forest products. If that too is eliminated, the public will not get over it so easily.

It is reasonable to ask whether even the most prescriptive foundation or grant-driven green group would use their bureaucrat allies to cut off such a vital part of the nation's economic production as private forests.

Conn Nugent of the Nathan Cummings Foundation provided some insight into that question when he described the mission of the environmental movement to the 1992 Environmental Grantmakers Association annual meeting: "The current use of the earth by humans is unsustainable. And the damage is done through billions of microeconomic behaviors. And stopping, modifying or transforming those behaviors at any place along the economic spectrum from the raw material to the land fill, through the law or through culture, is what we do in this business."

The funnel walls are now narrowing on private timberlands.

Why? At that same 1992 meeting, Ted Nordeau of the Consultative Group on Biological Diversity—a consortium of grantmakers that promotes biodiversity projects—voiced a view widely held by environmentalists: "Species don't know the difference where the property lines are. And if we're thinking about horrors, if we're thinking about ecosystems, if we're thinking about sustainability of ecosystems biodiversity, some kind of melding of the private and public forest interests has to be brought together."

Pressure to reduce or stop private forest production comes from the usual iron triangle sources:

● green group lawsuits using the Endangered Species Act, which has jurisdiction over private property as well as federal lands;
● foundation grants promoting the end of timber harvest on private lands—e.g., the Tides Center has a donor-advised fund project called Wood Reduction Clearinghouse to protect natural forests by reducing human wood consumption;

● federal and state regulations that reduce or eliminate private timber harvests, e.g., California's Forest Practices Act.

To these we add the movement for "environmentally preferable purchasing," one of Conn Nugent's "cultural" means of "stopping, modifying or transforming" our "unsustainable" behaviors: the concept of buying products or services that result from practices judged to be environmentally sound.

The "environmentally preferable purchasing" movement ranges from

● organic crops grown in soils on which no pesticides have been applied for three years, to

● claims of "recycled content" and "biodegradability," to

● energy-efficient home appliances and safe cleaners, to

● "cruelty-free" products not tested on animals or that contain no animal products, to

● questions of minimizing transportation to and from the workplace and substituting electronic communications for paper.

And many other items.

Compliance with "environmentally preferable" standards may be guaranteed by the producer or certified by a third party.

The problem with self-guaranteed compliance is credibility. Will the purchasing public believe the claims of the producer?

The problem with third-party certification programs is the opportunity for illegal undue influence on markets. If a certification program links producers to retail outlets or end users, it could be seen as price fixing or restraining trade in non-certified products. The Green Seal standard-setting organization has been publicized by Bruce Babbitt's Department of the Interior on a special website:

> The U.S. Department of the Interior is committed to the concept of environmentally preferable purchasing of products and services. The Department has identified "Green Seal," an independent, non-profit standard-setting organization, as potentially useful to prospective vendors and Department employees alike in defining environmentally preferable objectives.
>
> Accordingly, we are making Green Seal standards available to Department employees and other users of this website. The U.S. Department of the Interior does not specifically endorse Green Seal or any other standard-setting organization nor does it specifically require or endorse these standards. As other standard-setting organizations become known to the Department, links to these organizations will be added to this website.[289]

Note the cautious wording used to avoid anti-trust lawsuits—necessary because market- or end user-linked certification programs fall into a questionable restraint-of-trade area by their very nature. If you lock sellers out of a market because they don't agree with your version of "green," you could find yourself explaining that to the Federal Trade Commission.

Forest products have now moved into this arena.

Two major types of private-land sustainable forestry programs now compete for acceptance:

● an industry-based "Sustainable Forestry Initiative" operated by the American Forest and Paper Association (AFPA), and

● a certification accrediting program operated by the Forest Stewardship Council (FSC).

The AFPA program applies only to producers: the only members are timberland owners who wish to practice sustainable forestry according to standards approved by the association's board of directors. It is not a certification program and has no links to markets or end users.

The Sustainable Forestry Initiative requires companies to adhere to five principles (each with detailed standards):

● Sustainable forestry
● Responsible practices
● Forest health and productivity
● Protecting special sites
● Continuous improvement.

Compliance is monitored by an Expert Review Panel. In addition, a Voluntary Verification system allows third-party audits. Industry firms seem to prefer Certified Public Accountant auditors with no interest in the outcome. Fifteen firms have been thrown out of AFPA for non-compliance.

The FSC program, which only accredits certifiers, and does no certification itself, applies to timberland owners, mill owners, wholesalers, retailers, and a mix of green and social justice groups, including a church. Forest Stewardship Council members include:

● green groups: American Lands Alliance (formerly Western Ancient Forest Campaign); Environmental Defense Fund; Forest Trust; Friends of the Earth, GreenPeace; National Wildlife Federation; Natural Resources Defense Council; Rainforest Action Network; Sierra Club; Wilderness Society; World Resources Institute; World Wildlife Fund;

● retail lumber outlets: Home Depot; Big Creek Lumber Company; Northland Forest Products;

● timberland and mill owners: Collins Companies; Big Creek Lumber Company; Columbia Forest Products; Art Harwood of Harwood Lumber;

- a certifier: Scientific Certification Systems;
- and Native American tribal organizations;

among others.

In order to be FSC certified, a company must:

  - Meet all applicable laws
  - Have legally established rights to harvest
  - Respect indigenous rights
  - Maintain community well-being
  - Conserve economic resources
  - Protect biological diversity
  - Have a written management plan
  - Engage in regular monitoring
  - Maintain high conservation value forests
  - Manage plantations to alleviate pressures on natural forests.

An FSC website stated: "Wood products coming from FSC endorsed forest operations can carry the FSC label. Because the products carry the FSC label, environmentally and socially conscious consumers will be able to distinguish among different products and can choose to support well managed forests. Consumers, through their purchasing decisions can encourage producers to manage their forest in an environmentally and socially responsible manner. Producers, distributors and retailers can be rewarded with increased market share and/or a premium price for their efforts."[291]

FSC certification requires tracking the chain-of-custody of the wood to prevent contamination with non-certified wood in order to carry the FSC label.

Supporters of both systems mistrust the other.

FSC supporters say the AFPA program needlessly takes too many trees out of private forests. Too much production.

AFPA supporters say the FSC program needlessly leaves too many trees in private forests. Too little production.

FSC supporters say that the industry has such a bad reputation that its own program can never win public acceptance, which will only invite further government intrusion into the management of private timberlands.

AFPA supporters say that FSC impinges so heavily on owner decision-making ability that it is as bad as government intrusion, and that its environmentalist members are separately pushing for harsh regulation of private timberlands anyway.

Each denies the others' claims.

The AFPA standards are applied by owners of 55 million acres, while FSC certifiers cover 4.5 million acres in the U.S., 31 million worldwide.

The AFPA program covers U.S. producers of 90% of pulp and paper and 50% of solid wood, while the FSC covers no pulp and paper and less than 1% of solid wood.

The Forest Stewardship Council is worth examining because it is built upon an organizational model that can affect any industry.

The FSC, founded in 1993 in Ontario, Canada, was started with a 1992 seed money grant of $100,000 from the MacArthur Foundation "To establish international organization to monitor certification practices regarding sustainable harvesting of forest products."

The impetus came from the 1992 "Earth Summit" in Rio de Janiero, Brazil, where participating nations agreed that "one of the most important roles consumers could play in protecting the planet was to make better decisions about the products they buy."[292a]

Agenda 21, the summit's blueprint for an environmentally sustainable future, encouraged governments to expand "environmental labeling to assist consumers to make informed choices."[292b]

The MacArthur Foundation and the Rockefeller Brothers Fund were the "thought leaders" of the global certification campaign.

A number of environmental groups, including FSC's current green group members, got together with foundation executives around the summit to talk about it. FSC was the result.

The MacArthur Foundation gave another $25,000 to FSC in 1993, at a location in Richmond, Vermont, and another $350,000 in 1996 to FSC at its current headquarters in Oaxaca, Mexico.

In addition, Surdna Foundation gave FSC $100,000 in 1997 at its Vermont office.

Publicly accessible IRS master files show no listing for the Forest Stewardship Council, so income and asset data are not available.[292c]

It is difficult to track the money going to the Forest Stewardship Council from foundation records because numerous fiscal agents have received funds on behalf of the FSC:

● the Moriah Fund (Daniel Efroymson) gave $45,000 for FSC to Jonathan Lash's **World Resources Institute** in 1996;

● the Rockefeller Brothers Fund gave $150,000 for FSC to the **New England Environmental Policy Center** and $200,000 for FSC to the **New England Natural Resources Center**, both in 1997;

● the Pew Charitable Trusts gave $200,000 for FSC to the **New England Environmental Policy Center** in 1997;

● the Ford Foundation gave $330,000 for FSC to the **New England Environmental Policy Center** in 1998.

Connections. Perhaps more significant than its funding sources, the Forest Stewardship Council is part of a larger foundation-driven campaign built on the coalition model we examined in Chapter Three (pp. 130*ff*).

The most closely related organization in the coalition is Certified Forest Products Council, based in Beaverton, Oregon. Launched in 1997, CFPC is a trade association promoting certified forest products.

CFPC is technically not linked to FSC—no interlocking directorates—but it was created by the same people in the same foundations that created FSC, and, as we shall see, participates in programs coordinated with FSC by organizations we have already met.

In 1995, the MacArthur Foundation and the Rockefeller Brothers Fund, along with others, decided to further promote forest product certification, and gave grants to a consulting group, Environmental Advantage (EA) of New York, to design a market mechanism that would drive certification in the U.S. market—something like a recruiting arm for FSC.

They held meetings with various industry people from Home Depot, The Gap, Anderson Corporation, Starbucks Corporation, and others, also attended by the Natural Resources Defense Council, World Resources Institute, World Wildlife Fund, and others, to discuss creation of a "buyer's group" based on a European model being operated in the United Kingdom by the Worldwide Fund for Nature, parent organization of the U.S.-based World Wildlife Fund. That is, an environmental group would operate the new trade association.

The businesses in the discussion bluntly told the foundation people, "If you want to create such an organization in the U.S., it will not be run by an environmental group. It will be a stand-alone entity run by business for business. If not, we're not interested."

Amounts paid to Environmental Advantage for this certification study: MacArthur Foundation: $225,000 in 1995, two grants in 1996, one $375,000, another, $40,000. Rockefeller Brothers Fund: $35,000 in 1997. Wallace Global Fund, $45,000 in 1997.

After two years of discussion, they incorporated the Forest Products Buyer's Group in January of 1997. The group contracted with a New York headhunter to conduct an executive search, which resulted in the hiring of David Ford as president. Ford came from the timber industry, and was probably the only experienced timber association executive in the United States who supported third-party certification.

He had the right background: he'd worked for the Washington, D.C.-based National Forest Products Association before it reorganized to become the American Forest and Paper Association, and later worked for the Beaverton, Oregon-based Independent Forest Products Association, which represents smaller independent timber companies.

Ford says, "I saw certification as a tool that would allow us to create the kind of public credibility that we needed to be able to go back and operate on public lands. The conflict model didn't work. Based on my experience in D.C., we had lost the war. Our social license to practice forestry—granted through Congress and the administration—was revoked. We needed a vehicle that would re-create a level of trust and understanding that would allow us to move forward. Certification was it."[294a]

Ford came on board and got things moving. In September, 1997, the Good Wood Alliance merged with the Forest Products Buyers Group to form the Certified Forest Products Council.

The Good Wood Alliance, founded by Scott Landis, author of two noted woodworking books, had been a group of small wood-using businesses that wanted environmentally friendly raw materials for their products, mostly furniture, cabinets, and artisan goods. Originally named Woodworkers Alliance for Rainforest Protection (WARP), the Good Wood Alliance published a quarterly journal, Understory, funded for most of its seven years by W. Alton Jones Foundation. Understory was kept and is the journal of Certified Forest Products Council. Good Wood was noted for its online directory of certified wood producers.[294b]

The Good Wood Alliance gained acclaim with its wood objects and sculpture for the exhibition Conservation By Design, held in 1993 at the Museum of Art, Rhode Island School of Design, and which completed a tour of American galleries. Designers and artists from North America, Europe and Australia participated.

David Ford and his new organization applied for and received grants from the Compton Foundation ($50,000 in 1997), Ford Foundation ($200,000 2-year grant in 1998), Pew Charitable Trusts ($200,000 2-year grant in 1998), and others. 1997 income was $471,076, assets $223,838. Ford says he was not pressured by the foundations in any way.

The Certified Forest Products Council has prospered under Ford's direction. Ford does not work with timberland owners or sawmills, but comes at certification from two perspectives: recruiting sellers of wood products and consumers of wood products. He contacts firms of any type to see if they have environmental policies of their own and whether they would be interested in certified products for new construction and remodeling, then seeks suppliers for those interested.

CFPC received a 1998 award of excellence in advertising from Architectural Record magazine.

There have been a few lumps: Those dreams that "producers, distributors and retailers can be rewarded with increased market share and/or a premium price for their efforts" are proving elusive.

In a 1999 column in Understory, CFPC board member Paul Fuge wrote, "The lure of a price premium for certified wood products was promoted by forest certifiers and accepted as gospel by many hopeful retailers in the mid-1990s. Several consumer surveys lent support to the popular assumption that a pool of eager consumers would be willing to vote for good forestry with their wallets, and a 10 percent premium for certified wood products was widely anticipated. With all due respect to those pioneering surveys, I believe they were fundamentally flawed by a reliance on consumer opinions rather than actions."[295a]

Fuge's message was that the price premium is not there. People are not very willing to pay more for green products at the checkstand.

"It's not price premium, it's market share," says David Ford.

That remains to be seen. Part of this hope seems to be pegged on big retailers like Home Depot selling only certified forest products. That could be legally tricky.

David Ford is well aware of the anti-trust implications of certification: "The first thing I did here was go out and hire legal counsel to draft an anti-trust policy statement. Every time we have a meeting we have anti-trust counsel present. I am going to extremes to avoid any anti-trust problems."

Frank Gladics of Independent Forest Products Association—Ford left IFPA for CFPC and set up offices right across the hall from his old employer—says the real motive of the few timber owners who have agreed to certification is peace with environmental groups that were putting them out of business.

Gladics is skeptical. "I don't see any change in behavior of the environmental groups in the Forest Stewardship Council. I know that Wade Mosby of Collins Pine talks about becoming a local hero and poster child for environmental businesses, with free publicity and all of that. But the polarization is still there."[295b]

Ford says, "I think the real problem is that some of the companies don't like us having direct dialog with some of their customers about these issues."

Many wonder about the relationship of CFPC with the Forest Stewardship Council and its big environmentalist component.

Ford says, "We don't have a relationship with FSC. We're an independent non-profit group. We evaluate many certification schemes. Right now we say FSC's is the best choice. But we have no relationship."

His organization's funders don't seem to know that.

A 1997 grant description of the Wallace Global Fund reads:

Americans for the Environment (AE) - $50,000

Support for the *Sustainable Forestry Public Education Campaign*, an integrated communications effort headed by the public relations firm of MacWilliams, Cosgrove, Snider, Smith and Robinson. The Campaign coordinates the efforts of the Certified Forest Products Council (CFPC), Forest Stewardship Council (FSC), and several environmental NGOs to brand the FSC as the preeminent independent, third-party certifier of forest products, and to design strategic media plans for the FSC and the CFPC to further the common goal of sustainable forestry.[296]

Wait a minute.

Who's running this show?

Why is this money going to Americans for the Environment?

You will recall from Chapter Three (pp. 140*ff*) that Americans for the Environment describes itself as "a non-profit organization dedicated to helping citizen activists use the political process to solve environmental problems, providing Americans concerned about the environment with the knowledge and skills needed to participate effectively in the electoral process."

What exactly are we going to vote for about certification? Are we going to face ballot initiatives banning the sale of non-certified products from private forests?

And why MacWilliams, Cosgrove, Snider, Smith and Robinson? Most people describe them as a "media strategy" firm. They do focus groups, consultations and message design—to rearrange your mind, as Bob Lee might put it.

MacWilliams, Cosgrove, Snider is also the firm that produced the anti-wise use "Search and Destroy Strategy Guide," which recommended that funders do a smear campaign and drive wedges between wise use groups as the best way to deal with those who oppose environmentalists.

What are they going to recommend to funders about private timberland owners who do not agree with certification?

The Wallace Global Fund also gave 1997 sustainable forestry grants to New England Environmental Policy Center, Forest Stewardship Council-International, and World Resources Institute.

The "extraordinarily incestuous" tag certainly fits the certification movement (see diagram opposite for a partial view of the connections).

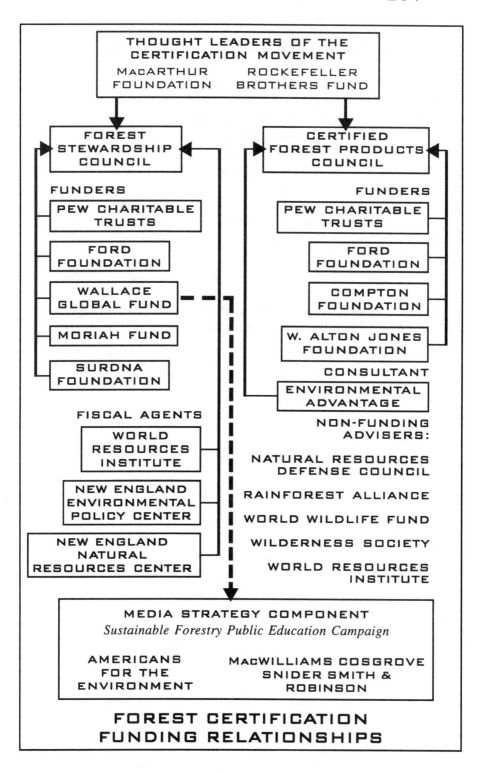

THOUGHT LEADERS OF THE
CERTIFICATION MOVEMENT
MACARTHUR   ROCKEFELLER
FOUNDATION   BROTHERS FUND

FOREST
STEWARDSHIP
COUNCIL

CERTIFIED
FOREST PRODUCTS
COUNCIL

FUNDERS

PEW CHARITABLE
TRUSTS

FORD
FOUNDATION

WALLACE
GLOBAL FUND

MORIAH FUND

SURDNA
FOUNDATION

FISCAL AGENTS

WORLD
RESOURCES
INSTITUTE

NEW ENGLAND
ENVIRONMENTAL
POLICY CENTER

NEW ENGLAND
NATURAL
RESOURCES CENTER

FUNDERS

PEW CHARITABLE
TRUSTS

FORD
FOUNDATION

COMPTON
FOUNDATION

W. ALTON JONES
FOUNDATION

CONSULTANT

ENVIRONMENTAL
ADVANTAGE

NON-FUNDING
ADVISERS:

NATURAL RESOURCES
DEFENSE COUNCIL

RAINFOREST ALLIANCE

WORLD WILDLIFE FUND

WILDERNESS SOCIETY

WORLD RESOURCES
INSTITUTE

MEDIA STRATEGY COMPONENT
Sustainable Forestry Public Education Campaign

AMERICANS
FOR THE
ENVIRONMENT

MACWILLIAMS COSGROVE
SNIDER SMITH &
ROBINSON

FOREST CERTIFICATION
FUNDING RELATIONSHIPS

There is no doubt of David Ford's sincerity in wanting to step out of the conflict of the past three decades and bring people together to find solutions.

He knew nothing about the Wallace grant to Americans for the Environment. The MacWilliams Cosgrove Snider Smith & Robinson group did some consulting for CFPC on strategy, but Ford and his board of directors were not happy with the results and hired their own public relations consultant. CFPC subsequently used MCSSR from time to time on highly specific and limited issues, such as critiquing print ads before placing them in magazines.

There is some doubt whether the extraordinarily incestuous connections in the certification movement will end the conflict or simply carry it underground where undue influence cannot be seen.

That is a question which, in its broadest form, faces all corporations today.

Is some coalition of prescriptive foundations, grant-driven greens and zealous bureaucrats influencing the future in ways you cannot see?

CORPORATE TAKEOVER FOOTNOTES

280a. Mark P. Mills and Peter W. Huber, "The Internet Begins With Coal," Greening Earth Society, Washington, D.C., June 1999.

280b. White House Office of the Press Secretary: Monday, June 14,1993, "On Earth Summit Anniversary President Creates Council on Sustainable Development For Economic Growth, Job Creation, Environmental Protection," Washington, D.C.

280c. www.ceres.org.

282. www.getf.org.

283a. "New Transportation Dept. Center to Study Environmental Issues," by Stephen Barr, *Washington Post*, May 2, 1999, p. A6.

283b. "Environmental Business Council Slates Statewide Meeting to Plan Export and Industry Growth Initiatives," GETF news release, January 21, 1999, Annandale, Virginia.

284. "The State of Environment & Business," by Rona Fried, Ph.D., www.sustainablebusiness.com.

286. "The Greening of McDonald's; Fast-Food Giant to Study Ways to Reduce Its Garbage," by Martha M. Hamilton, *Washington Post,* August 2, 1990, p. C11.

286b.http://www.essential.org/cchw/cchwinf.html.

287. "Covering The Earth With 'Green PR'" by Joel Bleifuss, *PR Watch*, Volume 2, Number 1, First Quarter 1995.

289. www.doi.gov/oepc/gseal.html.

291. www.web.net/fscca/

292a. "Informed Consumers Can Protect the Planet," by Rodrigo Prudencio, *Christian Science Monitor*, Wednesday, July 10, 1996, p. 19.

292b. www.unesco.org/general/eng/programmes/science/programme/environ/agenda21/

292c. IRS master files at www.irs.ustreas.gov/plain/tax_stats/soi/ex_imf.html produce no result for the entry Forest Stewardship Council.

294a. Most of this section, including the account of the organizing procedure for CFPC, is based on a telephone interview with David Ford, July, 1999.

294b. http://www.web.apc.org/goodwood/menu.html.

295a. "Whither Green Premiums?" by Paul Fuge, *Understory, the publication of the Certified Forest Products Council.* Winter 1999, Volume 9, No. 1. Online at http://www.greendesign.net/understory/winter99/index.html.

295b. Telephone interview with Frank Gladics, July, 1999.

295. www.wgf.org/grants97_env.html.

FUTURES

Envision living without electricity. No petroleum. Roads with no traffic. Factories crumbling ruins. Corporations extinct, swept away in public outcry. No new metal production because mines have been outlawed. No lumber because logging is forbidden. No ranching or fishing because no one is allowed to harm animals. The vegetables that make up the human diet are grown by hand labor without mechanical power and without beasts of burden. Technology is a fading memory. Collectives and philosopher-kings rule bio-regions everywhere. Shrinking human populations are surrounded by expanding wilderness. Disease visits often and none can control it. Industrial civilization is dead. Humanity has gone back to nature.

IF YOU'VE READ THIS FAR, NOT SO IMPOSSIBLE. Overdrawn, yes. To underline the point:

Environmentalism has consequences.

How overdrawn is this appalling image?

We have seen in these pages arrogant, secretive and deceitful foundations, grant-driven green groups, and powerful government officials unduly influencing your future behind closed doors. We have seen corporate entanglements.

How will this affect you?

If the things you have read in this book are true—and I invite you to test every sentence—is the above paragraph out of the question?

At the farthest extreme, are we to take seriously the words of David M. Graber, a research biologist with the National Park Service, in his prominently featured *Los Angeles Times* book review of Bill McKibben's *The End of Nature:*

> I, for one, cannot wish upon either my children or the rest of Earth's biota a tame planet, be it monstrous or—however unlikely—benign. McKibben is a bio-centrist, and so am I. We are not interested in the utility of a particular species or free-flowing river, or ecosystem, to mankind. They have intrinsic value, more value—to me—than another human body, or a billion of them....
>
> It is cosmically unlikely that the developed world will choose to end its orgy of fossil-energy consumption, and the Third World its suicidal consumption of landscape. Until such time as Homo sapiens should decide to rejoin nature, some of us can only hope for the right virus to come along."[302a]

Tom Clancy made a best-seller of such human extinction sentiments: *Rainbow Six*, a novel in which a wealthy and ecologically-enlightened pharmaceutical mogul contrives, with a few powerful allies, the murder of every last human being, courtesy of "the right virus"—genetically enhanced, undetectably packaged, and ingeniously distributed by our drug tycoon. Everyone is to die except for a few thousand carefully chosen environmentalists saved to watch the re-wilding of the planet from a specially built multi-million dollar secret base.[302b]

But that's just entertainment, isn't it?

Of course.

And Clancy wrote *Rainbow Six* because outrageous statements like Graber's have struck a potentially lucrative spark with the public, didn't he?—the real-crime fame of *The Unabomber Manifesto*, eco-prophetic books like anarchist John Zerzan's *Future Primitive*, the formation of groups with crazy names such as the Voluntary Human Extinction Movement, *ad nauseam*—well, didn't he?

There's no danger there, is there?

Respected scholars wonder. And have wondered for some time.

Back in 1982, social analyst Robert Nisbet wrote,

> It is entirely possible that when the history of the twentieth century is finally written, the single most important social movement of the period will be judged to be environmentalism. Beginning early in the century as an effort by a few far-seeing individuals in America to

bring about the prudent use of natural resources in the interest of extending economic growth as far into the future as possible, the environmentalist cause has become today almost a mass movement, its present objective little less than the transformation of government, economy, and society in the interest of what can only be properly called the liberation of nature from human exploitation. Environmentalism is now well on its way to becoming the third great wave of the redemptive struggle in Western history, the first being Christianity, the second modern socialism. In its way, the dream of a perfect physical environment has all the revolutionary potential that lay both in the Christian vision of mankind redeemed by Christ and in the socialist, chiefly Marxian, prophecy of mankind free from social injustice."[303]

One may reasonably wonder whether "the liberation of nature from human exploitation" might in real life look like a Tom Clancy novel.

If you see enviromania all around you, are you concerned? Do you see it in nature shows on educational television, in wildlife features on cable channels such as Discovery and A&E, in Saturday morning kiddie cartoons such as *Captain Planet*, in Disney films such as *Pocahontas*? Do you see it in Al Gore's book, *Earth in the Balance,* where he wrote that the goal of preserving the environment will be the fundamental organizing principle of society in the coming century? Do you see it in federal laws and administrative initiatives?

George Reisman, Professor of Economics at Pepperdine University's Graziadio School of Business and Management in Los Angeles, sees it:

> The environmental movement openly declares its hostility to the Industrial Revolution, which masses of unthinking people take to mean opposition merely to black smoke belching from factory chimneys. It should be clear ... that the fact is that even if environmentalism does not succeed in removing modern technology from the world, it can easily succeed in recreating pre-1750 conditions for the masses of people in the presently advanced countries, merely through throttling further rapid progress in agriculture and mining. The environmental movement is often characterized as elitist. It is elitist. Economically, it is a latter-day movement of feudal aristocrats, seeking the existence of a privileged class able to pocket the benefits of the economic progress that has taken place up to now, while denying those benefits to the broad mass of the public. It is a movement of monopolists, typified by the mentality of homeowners of the type who, having gotten

'theirs,' seek to stop all further development of land in their area. It is the movement of neofeudal mentalities who desire a world of broad open spaces for themselves, spaces that are essentially own-erless, and who care nothing for the plight of crowded, starving masses, who are to be denied the benefit of access to those open spaces, which are to be closed to all development. Essentially it is the old story of the feudal lords who are to have vast forests set aside for their enjoyment, while the serfs dare not remove a log for their fires or kill an animal for their meal.[304]

If the things you have read in this book are true, environmentalism *is* throttling rapid progress, not only in agriculture and mining, but also in every other sector of material goods production, including energy and transportation—goods that keep you alive.

If the things you have read in this book are true, there *are* neofeudal lords setting aside huge chunks of America for themselves and their elites while working to deny the benefits of progress to the public.

If the things you have read in this book are true, the environmental movement is in the process of dismantling industrial civilization piece by piece.

As we have seen, the structure of the environmental movement is not so simple as we thought.

It should be clear now that it consists of an iron triangle of
● wealthy foundations,
● grant-driven environmental groups, and
● zealous bureaucrats
welded together in an undemocratic, elitist political coalition that con-trols our future far more than the public believes, and perhaps even *could* believe.

This handful of people with charitable tax-exemptions influence public policy to destroy the lives of hundreds of thousands of goods producers.

They act behind a veil of secrecy.

They lie about their actions.

They were not elected.

They are totally unaccountable.

What is to be done?

EPILOGUE FOOTNOTES

302a. David A. Graber, "Mother Nature as a Hothouse Flower," *Los Angeles Times Book Reviews*, Sunday, October 22, 1989, pp. 1-9.

302b. Tom Clancy, *Rainbow Six*, G. P. Putnam's Sons, New York, 1998.

303. Robert A. Nisbet, *Prejudices: A Philosophical Dictionary*, Harvard University Press, Cambridge, 1982, p. 101.

304. George Reisman, *Capitalism : A Treatise on Economics,* Jameson Books, 1996, p. 316.

BIBLIOGRAPHY

Books

Alan Abramson and Lester Salamon, *The Nonprofit Sector and the Federal Budget: Update as of September 1997,* The Independent Sector, Washington D.C.

Andrea Arnold, *Fear of Food: Environmentalist Scams, Media Mendacity, and the Law of Disparagement*, Free Enterprise Press, Bellevue, Washington, 1990.

Ron Arnold, *At the Eye of the Storm: James Watt and the Environmentalists*, Regnery Gateway, Chicago, 1982.

Ron Arnold, *Ecology Wars: Environmentalism As If People Mattered*, Free Enterprise Press, Bellevue, Washington, 1987.

Ron Arnold and Alan Gottlieb, *Trashing the Economy: How Runaway Environmentalism is Wrecking America,Second Edition,* Free Enterprise Press, Bellevue, Washington, 1994.

Ron Arnold, *EcoTerror: The Violent Agenda to Save Nature - The World of the Unabomber,* Free Enterprise Press, Bellevue, Washington, 1997.

Michael Bennett, *The Asbestos Racket: An Environmental Parable*, Free Enterprise Press, Bellevue, Washington, 1991.

Porter Bibb, *Ted Turner : It Ain't As Easy at It Looks : A Biography,* Johnson Books, 1997.

Althea Carlson, *Riding A White Horse: Ted Turner's Goodwill Games and Other Crusades,* Episcopal Press, 1998.

Matthew S. Carroll, *Community and the Northwestern Logger: Continuities and Change in the Era of the Spotted Owl*, Harper-Collins, New York, 1995.

Alexander Cockburn and Ken Silverstein, *Washington Babylon*, Verso, New York, 1996.

Theo Colborn, Dianne Dumanoski, John Peterson Myers (Contributor) *Our Stolen Future : Are We Threatening Our Fertility, Intellgence, and Survival?-A Scientific Detective Stor*y, Plume (An imprint of New American Library), New York, 1997.

Gregory L. Colvin and Lowell Finley, *Seize the Initiative*, The Alliance For Justice, Washington D.C., 1996.

Gretchen C. Daily (editor), *Nature's Services; Societal Dependence on Natural Ecosystems,* introduction by Joshua S. Reichert, Island Press, Washington, D.C., 1997.

Mark Dowie, *Losing Ground: American Environmentalism at the Close of the Twentieth Century,* MIT Press, Cambridge, Massachusetts, 1995.

Economics America, Inc., *The Right Guide,* Ann Arbor, Michigan, 1998.

Environmental Grantmaking Foundations 1996 Directory, Environmental Data Research Institute, Rochester, New York, 1996.

Margaret Mary Feczko, Ruth Kovacs, and Carlotta Mills, editors, *National Guide to Funding for the Environment and Animal Welfare,* The Foundation Center, New York, 1994.

The Foundation Center, *Grants for Environmental Protection and Animal Welfare, 1991-1992,* New York, 1992.

The Foundation Center; *National Guide to Funding for the Environment & Animal Welfare,* New York, 1992.

Robert and Gerald Jay Goldberg, *Citizen Turner : The Wild Rise of an American Tycoon,* Harcourt Brace Children's Books, 1995.

Alan Gottlieb, editor, *The Wise Use Agenda,* Free Enterprise Press, Belleuve, Washington 1988.

David Helvarg, *The War Against the Greens,* Sierra Club, San Francisco, 1994.

Ronald Inglehart, *Modernization and Postmodernization: Cultural, Economic, and Political Change in 43 Societies,* Princeton University Press, Princeton, 1997.

W. Alton Jones Foundation, "The wise use movement," by John Peterson Meyers and Debra Callahan, Charlottesville, Virginia, February 6, 1992.

Ann Kaplan, editor, *Giving USA 1998,* The American Association of Fund Raising Counsel, Inc. (AAFRC) Trust for Philanthropy, Washington DC., 1998.

Robert G. Lee, *Broken Trust Broken Land — Freeing Ourselves From the War over the Environment,* BookPartners, Wilsonville, Oregon, 1994.

MacWilliams Cosgrove Snider, "The wise use movement: Strategic Analysis and Fifty State Review," Clearinghouse on Environmental Advocacy and Research, Washington, D.C., March 1993.

Richard Manning, *One Round River: The Curse of Gold and the Fight for the Big Blackfoot,* Henry Holt, 1998.

Robert H. Nelson, *Public Lands and Private Rights : The Failure of Scientific Management* (The Political Economy Forum), University Press of America, 1995.

Marvin Olasky, *Patterns of Corporate Philanthropy: Public Affairs Giving and the Forbes 100*, Capital Research Center, Washington, D.C., 1987.

M. Henry Robison, Charles W. McKetta, and Steven S. Peterson, "A Study of the Effects of Changing Federal Timber Policies on Rural Communities in Northcentral Idaho," University of Idaho, Moscow, Idaho, February 1996.

Lester M. Salamon, et al., *The Emerging Sector Revisited*, Johns Hopkins University, 1998.

Robert Shankland, *Steve Mather of the National Parks*, Alfred A. Knopf, New York, 1951.

Articles and Studies

Matthew S. Carroll, Charles W. McKetta, Keith A. Blatner, and Con Schallau.*A Response to "Forty Years of Spotted Owls? A Longitudinal Analysis of Logging Industry."*

Center for the Defense of Free Enterprise, "Battered Communities: How Wealthy Private Foundation, Grant-Driven Environmental Groups, and Activist Federal Employees Combine to Systematically Cripple Rural Economies," Bellevue, Washington, June, 1998, p. 29.

Center for the Defense of Free Enterprise, *Getting Rich: The Environmental Movement's Income, Salary, Contributor, and Investment Patterns, with an Analysis of Land Trust Transfers of Private Land to Government Ownership*, Bellevue, Washington, 1994.

Citizens Against Government Waste, *Phony Philanthropy: How Government grants are Subverting the Missions of Nonprofit Organizations*, by David E. Williams and Elizabeth L. Wright, November 17, 1998, Washington, D.C.

Corporation for Enterprise Development, *The 1997 Development Report Card for the States* (book and CDROM), 777 N. Capitol St., N.E., Suite 410, Washington, DC 20002.

Ronnie Dugger, "A Call to Citizens: Will Real Populists Please Stand Up," *The Nation*, August 1995.

Environmental Grantmakers Association, 1992 Fall Retreat. *Workshop Session 23: Media Strategies for Environmental Protection.*

Douglas Foy, "From Courtrooms to Town Hall: The Third Generation of Environmental Law,"paper prsented at Human Valuation of the Environment: A symposium in celebration of Princeton University's 250th Anniversary.

Howard H. Frederick, "Computer Networks and the Emergence of Global Civil Society: The Case of the Association for Progressive Communications (APC)," paper presented at the annual conference of the Peace Studies Association, Boulder, CO, February 28, 1992.

Pranay Gupte and Bonner R. Cohen, "Carol Browner, master of mission creep," *Forbes*, October 20, 1997.

David Helvarg, "Anti-enviros are getting uglier: the war on Greens," *The Nation*, Nov 28, 1994 v259 n18.

David Helvarg, "The anti-enviro connection (paramilitary groups and anti-environmentalists)," *The Nation*, May 22, 1995 v260 n20.

Thomas J. Hilliard, editor, *Mining Conservation Directory '94,* January 1994.

Sandra Hines, "Trouble in Timber Town: A Way of Life Is Torn Up By Its Roots," *Columns* (University of Washington magazine), December 1990.

Bob Lee, "The Hidden Danger of Moral Persuasion: The Clinton Plan Laid Bare," interview with Dr. Robert Lee, *Evergreen*, June 1996

Peter Montague, "Big-Picture Organizing, Part 6: Money in Politics," *Rachel's Environment & Health Weekly*, January 26, 1995.

National Audubon Society, grant proposal to Pew Charitable Trusts, "The Desert Forests Campaign: Protecting the Bio-Economic Diversity of Southwest Forest Ecosystems," October 1994.

Ottinger Foundation, *Funders' Handbook on Money in Politics,* Amherst Mass., with CarEth Foundation, Amherst Mass., Feb. 22, 1996.

C.B. Pearson and Hilary Doyscher, "Big Money and Montana's Ballot Campaigns: A Study of Contributions to Montana's Ballot Elections from 1982 to 1994," Montana Public Interest Research Foundation, Missoula, Mont., September 1996.

Eve Pell, "Oiling the works: How Chevron bought its way into environmentalism's power circle," *Mother Jones*, March-April 1991.

Sierra Defence Fund, To Save the Taku River," A Coordinated Campaign Strategy Outline, Prepared by: Michael Magee, Vancouver, British Columbia, Canada, 1998.

Ken Silverstein and Alexander Cockburn, "The Collapse of the Mainstream Greens," *CounterPunch*, Vol 1, No. 17, October 1, 1994.

Fred Singer, Chauncey Starr and Roger Revelle, "What to do about Greenhouse Warming: Look Before You Leap," *Cosmos*, April 1991.

Leslie Spencer, "Fighting Back," *Forbes*, July 19, 1993.

Donovan Webster, "Welcome to Turner country," *Audubon*, Friday, January 1, 1999.

Government Reports and Documents

Department of Commerce, *1992 Census of Governments, Volume 1, Number 1, Government Organization*, Bureau of the Census, Washington, D.C., 1996.

Environmental Protection Agency—Part 1: Accompanying Report of the National Performance Review, Office of the Vice President, Washington, D.C., September 1993.

"Privatization: Toward More Effective Government," Report of the President's Commission on Privatization, David F. Linowes, Chairman, March, 1988.

Project Charter, Interior Columbia River Basin Ecosystem Management Framework and Scientific Assessment and Eastside Oregon and Washington Environmental Impact Statement, Signed January 21, 1994, Director, USDI Bureau of Land Management, Chief, USDA Forest Service.

Public Land Statistics, 1996, Table 1.3, "Comparison of federally owned land with total acreage of States, fiscal year 1994," Government Printing Office, Washington, D.C., 1996.

U.S. House of Representatives, "Behind Closed Doors: The Abuse of Trust And Discretion In The Establishment Of The Grand Staircase-Escalante National Monument." Majority Staff Report, Subcommittee on National Parks & Public Lands, Committee on Resources, One Hundred Fifth Congress, First Session, November 7, 1997, Washington, D.C.

White House, Executive Order 12948 Amendment to Executive Order No. 12898, January 30, 1995.

White House, Forest Plan for a Sustainable Economy and a Sustainable Environment, July 1, 1993.

INDEX

Nightline (ABC News), 201-203
Niobrara River, 167
Nisbet, Robert, 302-303
Nixon administration, 208
Noranda Inc., 35
Nordeau, Ted, 288
Norden Dam Project, 167-169
North American Wilderness Recovery, Inc., 172
Northern Forest Alliance, 35, 37, 41-43, 112, 137, 148, 174
Northern Forest Lands Council, 36
Northern Forest Land Study, 36
North Shore Unitarian Universalist Veatch Program, 87, 93
Northwest Ecosystem Alliance, 25, 27, 172-173
Norwood, Charlie (Congressman), 211
Novakovitch, Anne, 266-267
Jessie Smith Noyes Foundation, 79, 97, 280, 287
Nugent, Conn, 288-289

Occidental Petroleum, 103
Ohrstrom Foundation, 283
Okanogan County (Washington), 6, 263-264, 267
Okanogan County Citizens Coalition (OC3), 34
Okanogan Highlands Alliance, 27, 34
Okanogan National Forest, 11, 14, 26, 89
Olasky, Marvin, 169
Omaha World Herald, 168-169
Omak (Washington), 258, 267
Omak Wood Products, 11, 14
Open Society Institute, 254
    Center on Crime, Communities and culture, 254
Oppenheimer, Michael, 202
"Option Nine," 228*ff*
Oregon Natural Resource Council, 232
Orton, Bill (Congressman), 245
Ottinger Foundation, 218
Our Stolen Future, 106, 219
Outside magazine, 108
over-regulation, 7

Owens, Jim, 223
Owens, Wayne (Congressman), 235

Pacific Rivers Council, 227, 260
David and Lucille Packard Foundation, 123
PageMaker, 34, 113
Panetta, Leon, 241-242, 244-245
Parker, Vawter, 223
Patagonia, Inc., 156, 158, 172
PeaceNet, 83
Pearson, C. B., 144, 149
Peay, Merrilee, 233
Pend Oreille County (Washington), 6, 263
Perschel, Bob, 42
Peterson, John (Representative) 43
Peterson, Mike, 14-15, 25, *59n*
Pew Center for Civic Journalism, 81
Pew Charitable Trusts, 35, 39, 41, 71, 78, 86*ff*, 96, 101, 122, 131*ff*, 175, 282, 294
    grants, 134, 156, 248-249, 261, 292
Pew Fellows in Conservation and the Environment, 105
Pew, Joseph N., Jr., 90
Pew Scholars Program in Counservation, 71
Phelps Dodge, 34, 90-91
Philanthropy, 106
Phildelphia Inquirer, 90
Pike, Drummond, 76, 78, 80
Gifford Pinchot National Forest, 50
Podhorzer, Michael, 208, 217-219
Polaroid Corporation, 282
Pope, Carl, 103, 214, 223
Poshard, Glenn (Congressman), 166
Poulson, Mike, 267
Precision Pine & Timber, Inc., 89
Predator Project, 25, 28
prescriptiveness,
    absolute, 73-74, 109
    aggressive, 73, 109
    passive, 72
President's Commission on Sustainable Development, 280, 282
President's Commission on Privatization, 19
Presidio of San Francisco, 80

Unification Church, 201-202
United Nations Conference on Environment and Development, 220
United Nations Development Program, 84, 201
United Nations World Heritage Committee, 239-240, 266
U.S. Census Bureau, 22
U.S. Department of Agriculture, 43
Inspector General, 265
U.S. Department of Commerce, 44
U.S. Department of the Interior, 198, 289
Office of Policy Analysis, 170
Office of Surface Mining, 44
Minerals Management Service, 44
U.S. Department of Justice, 238, 253
U.S. Department of Transportation, 202
U.S. Fish and Wildlife Service, 163, 166, 257-258, 267
land area managed by, 20, 44, 68
U.S. News & World Report, 245
University of Idaho, 263
University of Maryland, 170
University of Montana, 144-147
University of Virginia, 202
Upper Columbia Resource Council, 34, 263
urban-rural prosperity gap, 4-7, 35
Utah Wilderness Coalition, 174

Vaagen Brothers Lumber Company, 10
Vaagen, Duane, 10-11, 14-15, 23
Valdez Principles, 280
Veyhl, Erich, 37
Viederman, Stephen, 282
vilification of resource producers, 53
Virgin Islands National Park, 119
Virginia's Environmental Business Council, 283
Voight, Bob, 37
Voluntary Human Extinction Movement, 302

Wall, Gale, 25
Wallace Global Fund, 296-297

Warner Creek timber sale, 232-233
Washington Farm Bureau Natural Resources Committee, 267
Washington Post, 101, 205, 243-244, 254
Washington Wilderness Coalition, 29
Wasserman, Lee, 122-123
Wathen, Thomas, 88-89, 96-97, 102-103, 134
Watt, James, 68
Watts, Dave, 236
Webb, Geoffrey, 200, 236
Weeden Foundation, 40
Weiss, Jay, 205
Western Ancient Forest Campaign, 176, 223, 225, 230
Western Environmental Trade Association, 147
Western Mining Action Project, 154, 158
Western States Center, 95, 151-153
grants received, *chart*, 152
grants to others, *chart*, 153
wetlands regulations, 8
Weyerhaeuser Company, 70, 90
White House,
Office on Environmental Policy, 220
"Western Forest Health Initiative," 230
Wild Earth magazine, 172
Wild Horses and Burros Protection Act of 1971, 46
Wilderness Act of 1964, 68
Wilderness Society, 37, 42, 52, 68, 81, 112, 223
grants received, 178, 225
as fiscal agent, 174*ff*
role in ICBEMP, 260-265
Wildlands Project, 170*ff*
key cooperating groups, *chart*, 173
Wilkinson, Charles, 241
Will, George F., 203
Willamette National Forest, 233
Williams, Eric, 145-146
Windy Craggy mine, 266
Winslow Foundation, 109, 112, 123
Wirth, Timothy E., 109, 207

THE TRILOGY

If you found **UNDUE INFLUENCE** compelling, you'll want to understand the environmental movement in total depth—which means you'll want to own the *entire* Ron Arnold *EXPOSING ENVIRONMENTALISM* trilogy that tells it all:

TRASHING THE ECONOMY: How Runaway Environmentalism is Wrecking America, by Ron Arnold and Alan Gottlieb 670 pages, revised edition, paperback, $19.95. Profiles of sixty leading environmental groups, who they are, where they came from, who gives them money and what they do with it!

EcoTerror: The Violent Agenda to Save Nature - The World of the Unabomber by Ron Arnold 336 pages, paperback, $16.95. Probes the dark side of environmentalism, lists hundreds of crimes committed to "save nature," names the convicted, tells who's *not* a criminal, and explores the reasons behind environmentalist violence.

Buy the first two and we'll send a copy of the third in the trilogy— **UNDUE INFLUENCE**—absolutely free! Great for gift giving!